# Getting Away With Murder

## CRIMINAL CLERICS IN LATE MEDIEVAL ENGLAND

Peter Johnstone

Kendall Hunt
publishing company

Kendall Hunt
publishing company

www.kendallhunt.com
*Send all inquiries to:*
4050 Westmark Drive
Dubuque, IA 52004-1840



ISBN 978-1-4652-9168-4



Printed in the United States of America

# Contents

Introduction

**Chapter 1**
Establishing the Clerical Plea: Privilege or Benefit? ........ 1

**Chapter 2**
The Church, Churchmen and the Benefit of Clergy in England ........ 31

**Chapter 3**
Dissention, Discord and Double Jeopardy ........ 59

**Chapter 4**
The Prostitution of Oaths, Self-Slaughter and Judgments of Blood ........ 77

**Chapter 5**
Custody Pending Trial, Immuration and Clerics as 'Jailbirds' ........ 109

**Chapter 6**
Sanctuary, Abjuration and Exile ........ 133

**Chapter 7**
Outlaws and Gang Members ........ 179

**Chapter 8**
From Tonsure to Reading, From Demands to Requests ........ 207

**Chapter 9**
Untenable Legal Dilemmas:
The Bishop and The Monk ........................................ 249

**Chapter 10**
Immunity for All ........................................ 269

Bibliography ........................................ 295

Index ........................................ 327

# Introduction

This book is about special privileges that were available to clergymen who committed a felony in England during the Middle Ages. One of these extraordinary provisions, benefit of clergy, started life when Roman emperor Constantine converted to Christianity. Soon afterwards he apparently decided that priests should be protected from the ordinary criminal law and be judged exclusively by other clergymen. Benefit of clergy came to England and remained largely unaltered for many centuries. During the Middle Ages this situation changed dramatically so that by the third quarter of the fourteenth century the special privilege had not been removed it was laicized. Henceforth claiming to be a priest to avoid hanging became available to any Englishman who could read. Benefit of clergy (also referred to as *privilegium fori*) was not the only excuse allowed at law during this time. Any man could run from a crime scene and if he reached a church claim sanctuary for forty days. After this period of time he had to stand trial or admit his guilt before the coroner and exile the realm for the reminder of his life. Another option was to fail to appear at court and be sentenced to life as an 'outlaw'. In theory at canon law a cleric was not permitted to claim sanctuary, he was not permitted to admit his guilt before a coroner and he was not permitted to exile the realm. The simple explanation was that these options were all secular provisions and since a cleric should only be judged by another cleric he should not be using privileges available to laymen. What actually happened was that England's clerics committed a broad range of felonies and then used (and abused) whichever legal option best suited their circumstances; so they behaved much like any other criminal and manipulated gaps in the law to avoid accountability. The difficulty this created was that much of medieval society had the expectation that clerics would behave in a godlier manner. When they failed the justification for being treated differently evaporated.

There has been little commentary on benefit of clergy and less still that discusses this plea in conjunction with clerical use of sanctuary, abjuration and outlawry. Of benefit of clergy the general opinion has been that it was a legal oddity and a farce. Helmholz[1] deals with the topic in describing the laws applicable in England at the time. He makes the pertinent comment that *privilegium fori* has never enjoyed good press with English historians.[2] His valuable commentary includes reference to Gabel's work[3] before ending on the note that, "In the end, however, benefit of clergy remains hard to admire'.[4] Powicke[5] unpicks the relationship of the clergy in English society as they existed under two rules of law and he explores the role and function of the Church in attempting to mold the clergy into a compliant, educated and responsible workforce informed in its actions by papal decretals that (sought to) reign supreme over secular legislation and practices. The issue of benefit of clergy is commented upon within the context of clerical privileges generally and more specifically to sketch a picture of the complexity of the organization of the Church and its multiplicity of roles; protector of souls, guardian of morals and major landowner throughout Europe. A few commentators introduce *privilegium* as a sidebar conversation, generally as part of a larger exposition of the Church in society throughout the Middle Ages,[6] or, as in the case of Cross, as a legal fiction, 'that queer old exemption, benefit of clergy'.[7]

---

[1] Helmholz R.H. *The Oxford History of the Laws of England* Vol. I. Supra. Further material on the canon law is covered in greater detail in Helmholz, R.H. *Canon Law and the Law of England,* London, Hambledon Press, 1987 esp. Chap. 7 'Crime, Compurgation and the Courts of the Medieval Church'

[2] Helmholz, Vol. I. Supra. pp. 511–514. p. 511

[3] Gabel. L. *Benefit of Clergy in England in the Later Middle Ages,* New York, Octagon Press, 1969 (reprinted)

[4] Helmholz. Vol. I. Supra. p. 13 and Jones, W.R., The Two Laws in England: The Later Middle Ages, *The Journal of Church and State,* Vol. 1. Issue. 1. (1969) pp. 111–131

[5] Powicke, M., *The Thirteenth Century* 1216–1307, Oxford, Clarendon Press 1953

[6] Logan, F. D., *A History of the Church in the Middle Ages,* London, Routledge, 2002 is one of many quality publications that gives coverage of the role and function of the Church throughout the period of study. He also deals with the challenging question of when do the Middle Ages end? He suggests 1492. p.351

[7] Cross, A.L. The English Criminal Law and Benefit of Clergy during the Eighteenth and Nineteenth Centuries, *American Historical Review,* Vol. 22. No. 3. (Apr. 1917), pp. 544–565. p. 565

A number of legal scholars of previous centuries such as Blackstone and Maitland[8] devote at least one chapter to *privilegium clericus* principally as an ideal that grew from its Roman origins and culminated in the great row of the 12th century between Henry II and Becket.[9] Disparaging views of the clerical benefit were expressed by Andrews in 1909, 'Obviously any such test would be quite impossible now, even if the age had not outgrown so ridiculous a statute'.[10] Poole[11] is of the view that benefit of clergy is one of a range of options that provided an alternative to outlawry. Cheney's authoritative article deals with the issue of the punishment of felonious clerks.[12] Brundage[13] joins the later twentieth century *privilegium* discussion in his chapter *Canon Law and Private Life* where he takes into account the efforts by churchmen and canonists, over time, to exert authority over numerous felonies outside of the limited scope of moral crimes. John Aberth's *Criminal Churchmen in the Age of Edward III The Case of Bishop Thomas de Lisle* in 1993[14] is an in-depth (and

[8] Maitland, F.W., Henry II and the Criminous Clerks, *The English Historical Review*, Vol. 7. No. 26 (Apr., 1892), pp. 224–234

[9] Also: White, E.J., Benefit of Clergy, *The American Law Review*, Vol. 46. 1912. pp. 78–94, , Ogle, A., *The Canon Law in Medieval England: An Examination of William Lyndwood's "Provinciale" in reply to the late Professor F.W. Maitland*, London, John Murray, 1912

[10] Andrews, W. *Old Church Life*, London, Andrews & Co, 1909. p. 14. Alexander, J.W., The Becket Controversy in Recent Historiography, *Journal of British Studies*, Vol. 9, No. 2 (May. 1970), pp. 1–26

[11] Poole, A.L., 'Outlawry as a Punishment of Criminous Clerks' in Edwards, J.G., Galbraith, V.H., and Jacob, E.F., (eds) *Historical Essays in Honour of James Tait*, Manchester, Manchester University Press, 1933. pp. 239–246. p. 245

[12] Cheney, C.R., 'The Punishment of Felonous Clerks', *The English Historical Review*, Vol. 51. No. 202, (Apr., 1936), pp. 215–236 and Cheney, C.R., *The English Church and its Laws 12th-14th Centuries*, London, Variorum Reprints, 1982. Cheney was fortunately still alive to oversee the work and make any corrections as needed. It is noted that 'felonous' and 'felonious' are commonly employed

[13] Brundage, J., *Medieval Canon Law*, London, Longman, 1997

[14] Aberth, J., *Criminal Churchmen in the Age of Edward III. The Case of Bishop Thomas de Lisle*, University Park, PA, Pennsylvania State University Press, 1993. Also: Bates, J.C., 'Edward Leche-A Recidivist Criminous Clerk', *Nottingham Mediaeval Studies*, Vol. 30. (1986) pp. 97–100 and Firth, C.B., Benefit of Clergy in the Time of Edward IV, *The English Historical Review*, Vol. 32, No. 126 (Apr., 1917), pp. 175–191 and Baker, J.H., Benefit of Clergy in England and its Secularization 1450–1550, in *Ins Wasser geworfen und Ozeane durchquert: Festschrift főr Knut Wolfgang Nőin*, Kőln, Bőhlau, 2003

fascinating) study of a felonious bishop who perpetrated a wide range of assaults on people and property during the fourteenth century. I rely heavily on his work in the chapter 9. McHardy's[15] chapter considers the mechanisms in place for the Church courts to deal with criminous clerks, specifically the bishops' registers; the work draws extensively upon the materials provided by the Canterbury and York Society and the Lincoln Record Society. The result is a comparative exposition that builds upon Gabel's and provides a rich resource particularly in respect of canonical procedures, the use of bishop's prisons and the Christian courts trial. She concludes that the clash between the competing twelfth century criminal jurisdictions is surprising as 'both powers wanted a decrease in violence and a rise in respect for legality'.[16]

The leading authority on benefit of clergy remains Leona Gabel's work of the 1920s. She elevated the topic from relative obscurity and registered it as an important area for research. Her book follows the origins of the privilege, procedure in the lay courts and explanation of the term clericus and a conclusion that draws together the range of crimes and offences subject to *privilegium*. She also provides a brief discussion about church reform and secular legislative moves to restrict the use of clergy. Attempts to contextualize the growth and use of clergy are limited to the final chapter where she suggests that the benefit had 'far-reaching social significance'.[17] In her conclusion the direction that clericus might take is introduced; the idea that criminal society 'at large' would take up the clergy option and that even the courts Christian may have been complicit in encouraging criminality amongst the clergy (and increasingly the laity) due to the almost certainty of purgation is posited. Gabel believes that clerical criminality was incentivized by the ease with which clerks could absolve themselves and this led

---

[15] McHardy, A.K., Church Courts and Criminous Clerks in the Later Middle Ages in *Medieval Ecclesiastical Studies in Honour of Dorothy M. Owen,* Woodbridge, Suffolk, Boydell Press, 1995. pp. 165–183

[16] McHardy. Supra. p. 182

[17] Gabel. Supra. p. 116

to a sense of 'evil' that grew out of the privilege. She proposes that the introduction of the Reading Test was further evidence of the demonization of benefit of clergy; considerations that do not 'lessen the magnitude of the evil inherent in so lax a system as that which benefit of clergy flourished...'.[18]

What Gabel achieves is considerable. Her work remains the leading authority (in English) on the subject of benefit of clergy. She does not explore the important relationship between clergy and sanctuary or abjuration or outlawry; all of which were used by clerics alongside claiming their clergy. And she does not explore the impact of clergy from a societal perspective. Her work does not lay the foundations for an explanation of the absorption of clergy into mainstream English middle age life nor how juries and the judiciary became complicit in accepting the recitation of one psalm as proof of literacy. Overall Gabel formulates the opinion held by the majority of commentators to date; benefit of clergy was of negative value, it was an evil that was simply 'bad'.[19]

In the main I must disagree. Canonical privileges did not operate in isolation across medieval England they operated as part of it. The Church, in all its manifestations, was an integral part of the medieval world and its representatives, inferior and superior, oscillated between ecumenical and secular allegiances in order that they survived, flourished, succeeded, and contributed to the development of disparate groups of people into a complicated society. The absorption of benefit of clergy into mainstream legal practice was a product of increased literati, urbanization, the growth of consumerism and a rejection by the laity, jurors and justices, of increasing sanguinary laws. Accepting and applying benefit of clergy was a natural outgrowth of a system that (albeit much criticized) worked. In fact it worked so well that it travelled to the colonies of America despite the rejection of established European religion and canon law held

[18] Gabel. Supra. p. 120

[19] Gabel. Supra. p. 126

by the early colonists.[20] When around 1350[21] a literacy test overtook tonsure and clerical garb as the measure for establishing legitimacy to claim benefit of clergy it was *de facto* extended to all who could read. The plea was now available for use (and abuse) by the general population; all ranks of men, women and even children.[22]

In this book I suggest that benefit of clergy should not be dismissed as some anachronistic relic of an emperor's conversion to Christianity. In my view it was a fundamental part of the fabric of canon law that provided a mechanism for ensuring anyone associated with the Church was provided some measure of protection from secular princes seeking to own the physical and intellectual wealth of the Church. And it protected parish priests from a citizenry who wanted a guaranteed passage to heaven but did not want the providers of that promise to have special treatment when they demonstrated their own frailties and humanism.[23] In the end the clergy not only acquiesced to laicization they openly worked with lay defendants to protect them[24] and to create possibilities for greater use of the clergy plea. Secular clergy in particular also fought for the retention of church asylum for the laity, and they worked to ensure that the coroner adhered to the applicable laws in determining mode and compliance with abjuration laws.

The use and abuse of benefit of clergy is an important example of the lessening of the impact of canon law in England. It is a clear

---

[20] See: Johnstone, P., *Benefit of Clergy in Colonial Virginia and Massachusetts*, Dubuque, IA, Kendall Hunt, 2015

[21] (1350) 25 Edw. III, st.3. c. 4

[22] Comments, The Regression of Ecclesiastical Jurisdiction, *The Yale Law Journal*, Vol. 32, No. 6 (Apr., 1923), pp. 594–602. p. 595. N. 8 re a boy of twelve years in 1302 and a woman in 1348

[23] 1345 Year Book 19. Edw. III (Rolls Series) 176 cited in *The Yale Law Review, Supra.* p. 596. N. 9

[24] Evidence of assisting the laity in the reading test are plentiful in Gabel, Supra. pp. 54–55, 64–74, 76–78, 124, 125, 126, also see: Comments, *The Yale Law Review*, Supra, p. 595. N. 8 re a vicar who taught a felon to read during his imprisonment was arraigned for felony but acquitted

example of two legal systems, canon and common law, merging with secular becoming the dominant. The mechanism for this was in part fought out over the twelfth and thirteenth centuries by William of Normandy and then Henry II and Becket. Clear lines of demarcation were established by Innocent III, but with time they became malleable; not exclusively or even principally through legislative provisions[25] but through the practice, adaptation and integration of low level clerics in and amongst the society they served. Throughout the thirteenth and fourteenth centuries the numbers of the lower ranks of secular clergy grew considerably and the vast majority of these men were unbeneficed. It is not surprising that in the face of a life of meager existence many of them resorted to crime at the same time remaining associated with the Church.[26] This is in part why clericus changed over time; why it prospered in the face of clear examples of abuse and why it grew to be standard procedure in all felony trials in the courts secular.[27]

In this book I explore the origins and development of clericus and its use and abuse in England during the Middle Ages. Much

---

[25] There are numerous specific provisions that demonstrate the division of ecclesiastical and secular legislation but equally there are many examples of the courts, Christian and temporal applying both canon and common law especially in matters over dispute of title and landownership. C.f. Comments, *The Yale Law Review,* Supra. pp. 600–601, and Helmholz, R.H., Conflicts Between Religious and Secular Law: Common Themes In The English Experience, 1250–1640, *Cardozo Law Review,* Vol. 12, (1990–1991), pp. 707–728 and Helmholz, R.H., 'Scandulum in the Medieval Canon Law in the English Ecclesiastical Courts', *Zeitschrift der Savigny-Stiftung f r Abteil;ung, Rechtsgeschichte. Kanonisteische* Vol. 96, No. 127 (2010), pp. 258–274

[26] Boureau, A., 'Privilege in Medieval Societies from the Twelfth to the Fourteenth Century, or: How the exception proves the rule' in Linehan, P., and Nelson, J.L., (eds) *The Medieval World,* London, Routledge, 2001

[27] The secularization of benefit of clergy is evident in legislation that made certain offences non-clergyable such as: (1496) 12. Hen. VII, c.7. Petty treason, (1512) 4. Hen. VIII, c. 2. Murder in churches or highways and (1531) 23. Hen. VIII, c. 15, sec. 13, wilful murder, except to clerks in orders (note the distinction 'in orders') and the formal requirement for compurgation in 1576, 18. Eliz. C.7. sec. 2,3. Extension of the privilege to peers in 1547, 1 Edw. VI. C. 12. Sec. 14, to women in 1692, 3 W. & M. c.9. sec. 5,6 and the reading test was fully abolished in 1705, 5 Anne, c.6, sec. 6

of the contents focus on the period between the twelfth century (commencing with the Becket debacle) and the subsequent amelioration of clergy into secular trials by the end of the third quarter of the fourteenth century. The object is not to revisit what Gabel has covered or to re-trace where the compromises were worked out between the canon law and common law. It is to set benefit of clergy into the position it warrants in the discussion of life, society and law of the later Middle Ages. It is also my intention that benefit of clergy is explained as one of a number of privileges operated jointly by the medieval English Church and temporal authorities alongside sanctuary and the related secular provisions for outlawry and abjuration. Much has been written about sanctuary, outlawry and abjuration but very little has been said about these topics alongside, and in the context of, benefit of clergy.

This book is deliberately descriptive. It investigates and evaluates examples of use and abuse of benefit of clergy, sanctuary, abjuration and outlawry (The Excusory Quartet). It covers a complicated period of history one that (inevitably) created lacunae and options for criminals of all color, Christian and secular, to flout the law. With numerous examples to draw upon this book exposes a gray zone of legality in which courts Christian and secular competed for authority. It is the time when English bishops were required by law to construct prisons to house priests (clear evidence itself of the number of clergymen criminals) and the students of Oxford University, clerics by definition, pushed the limits of tolerance canon and temporal as they engaged in murder and mayhem. By the close of the thirteenth century it is clear that secularization will (must) happen; quite when is not obvious yet. Lax secular rule during the first twenty years of the fourteenth century did nothing to abate the opportunistic criminal and the monarchy closed with confusion and increasing levels of criminality across the realm. Benefit of clergy was in widespread use, especially by the lower orders and those on the extreme periphery of clerical designation. A reading test was becoming commonly employed in place of tonsure and it is clear that benefit of clergy was no longer as exclusive as it once had been. Secularization had begun; urbanization, massive depletion of the population and large increases in unbeneficed clergy during the next century would complete the transition. The thirteenth century tested the status of benefit of clergy, the fourteenth century witnessed its transformation.

Many statutes and court cases are cited throughout this book and it may help the reader in understanding the material if they have an overview of the primary sources referred to and a brief explanation of some of the terms used to explain the courts. This is followed by a commentary about the chapter contents. I have written this book with the intention that a chapter can be read individually or read in its entirety from the beginning. I would respectfully suggest that all readers familiarize themselves with the contents of chapter I as this sets the scene for all later discussion.

Since 1887 the Selden Society has been responsible for translating in the region of 8500 legal documents. Some of that data is the basis for this book. The large number of benefit of clergy cases used are drawn from Selden's Select Ecclesiastical Cases, Rolls of the Eyres, Select Cases from the Coroners' Rolls, the Calendar of Patent Rolls, Calendar of Close Rolls, Assize Rolls, Rolls of Gaol Delivery and *Coram Rege* Rolls (KB) Select Cases in the Court of the King's Bench. Bishops Registers are also a source of cases and the publications of Record Societies (Canterbury and York). Other sources include: *Leges Henrici Primi, The Constitutions of Clarendon,* Gratian's *Decretum,* Blackstone's *Commentaries on the Laws of England,* Pollock and Maitland's *The History of the English Law Before the Time of Edward I,* and *Statutes of the Realm.*

## Chapter I. Establishing the Clerical Plea: Privilege or Benefit

This chapter deals with the history of the clericus plea from its origins at Roman law and its submersion into Anglo-Saxon England up until the time of the Norman invasion of 1066. The discussion then moves to an explanation of the structure and form of the Church in England and an overview of the ranks of the clergy. Benefices and pluralism were a significant problem in the Middle Ages and may well have stimulated criminality amongst the lower orders. An explanation of these terms and the impact of them is provided. The idea that the clerics plea was an integral part of life throughout the Middle Ages is introduced in this chapter. Other members of the 'Excusory Quartet' are explained and brought into the discussion. This chapter lays the foundation for an evaluation of the Becket debacle and includes a few cases which illuminate the actions of felonious clergymen that are discussed in detail in following chapters.

## Chapter 2. The Church, Churchmen and the Benefit of Clergy in England

This chapter expands upon the material introduced in the first chapter and explores the implications of the legislative actions taken by William I that impacted England's clerics. Following this relevant chapters of *Leges Henrici Primi* are examined and evaluated against the backdrop of increasing tension between Rome and England and the canon and (developing) Common Law interface. Examples of the attempts by England's monarchy to periodically assert authority over the Church are introduced and discussed. The chapter concludes with an overview of the Church courts and with the recognition that canonical purgation was viewed as an escape from justice by lay society; the bishops Consistory Courts were often little more than a showpiece that always seemed to exempt clerics of blatant criminality and herald them as innocent.

## Chapter 3. Dissention, Discord and Double Jeopardy.

The main thrust of the chapter is to understand the implications of the disagreement between Henry II and Becket and the intentions of *Clarendon*. A number of cases from throughout Henry's reign are introduced to demonstrate the outrageous abuse of law that the clericus plea facilitated in practice. These examples span the *Constitutions of Clarendon* 1164 until the end of Henry II's reign in 1189. The source for these are *English Lawsuits from William I to Richard I Vol. 107 (I and II) Selden Society*. There are also examples of where Henry had attempted to bring the two systems of law together and the strong rebukes he received from the prelates of England. (Case 449 is of particular note). It is not possible to discuss benefit of clergy without referencing the position taken by Becket and his view of Double Jeopardy. The revulsion for his murder compounded this interpretation and effectively stalled the progression of laicization the clergy plea. The incisive actions of Innocent III in 1215 forcefully reiterated the ability of the Church to influence secular law and in doing so he paved the way for the divisions between Civil and Common Law that exist today. The 4th Lateran Council also ended the high point of influence the Church would have over the secular law in England but a clear division between the two (competing systems) had not yet been achieved.

The volume and magnitude of criminality committed by every rank of England's churchmen was a significant factor in establishing the eventual dominance of secular law. The following chapters comprise a broad range of examples that testify to the excessive use and abuse of all the mitigatory pleas by churchmen and confirm that secularization was appropriate and justified.

# Chapter 4. The Prostitution of Oaths, Self-Slaughter and Judgments of Blood

Primary sources consist of: the Roll and Writ File of the Berkshire Eyre of 1248,[28] the Three Rolls of the Kings Court in the Reign of Richard I, Rolls of the Justices in Eyre for Lincolnshire (1218–1219),

[28] Eyre rolls are the records of the hearings before the kings justices held within each county (except the palatines of Chester and Durham who had their own system) for the years 1194–1348. Criminal offences are recorded as crown pleas. The court records were kept on rolls of parchment. Each roll is made up of lengths of parchment stitched together, known as membranes. Given, J.B., *Society and Homicide in Thirteenth-Century England*, Stanford, Stanford University Press, 1977. p. 83. This excellent work draws upon the study of the Eyre rolls of Bedford, Bristol, Kent, Norfolk, Oxford, Warwick and London between 1202 and 1276 and provides information about 2,434 victims of violent crime and 3,492 suspects

Select Cases from the Ecclesiastical Courts of the Province of Canterbury, c. 1200–1301, The Earliest Northampton Assize Roll A.D. 1202 and 1203 and Gaol Delivery Rolls.[29]

Traditionally the Eyre was the curia, the king's court, and was attended by the monarch. This became less the case during the 13th century and the Eyre became the court of professional judges and local magistrates which in turn became the Assize Court of the circuit judge. The term justices can be confusing. It should be used to describe magistrates only but is commonly used to describe the appointed adjudicator of a legal tribunal. From 1234 onwards the Common Pleas sat at Westminster and in theory dealt with civil matters whereas the *coram rege* (King's Bench) heard criminal cases. Records of the Westminster Court and those of the counties, Eyre courts, appear as Rolls of Justices of Common Pleas, Rolls of Curia Regis and Rolls of the County Eyre (e.g. Shropshire). At the Assize of Clarendon, 1166, Henry II established the assize courts consisting of itinerant justices, consequently the term Assize Roll and Eyre Roll may both appear in citations.[30] Between the years 1323–1421 when the travelling king's judges sat in the counties, one of their tasks was to clear the gaols of all outstanding cases. These records are referred to as Gaol Delivery Rolls.[31] By the thirteenth century the Justice in

---

[29] The Gaol Delivery Session relates to prisoners awaiting trial who were all tried at one time before the Eyre. From 1279 onwards the GDR or GD sessions are a separate entry in the Eyre Rolls

[30] Generally referencing of cases is highly varied, some authors cite KB 27 and then a page. This refers to the referencing system at the National Archives, Kew, London. KB 27 contains all known records from 1200–1702 of Common Pleas and KB (In 1702 the records were split)

[31] The easiest method for locating a case is to search (manually) under the county and date. Turner, R.V., The Origins of Common Pleas and King's Bench, *The American Journal of Legal History*, Vol. 21. No. 3, (Jul, 1977), pp. 238–254. Individual Eyres and Select Cases in the Court of the King's Bench have been published in Latin and some also English through the Selden Society http://heinonline.org/HeinDocs/Selden_Society.pdf The 61 volumes of the *Calendar of Close Rolls* are available for viewing on site at the National Archives, Kew and electronically by subscription. http://www.british-history.ac.uk/subscribe.aspx?i=closerolls For KB 27 http://www.nationalarchives.gov.uk/

Eyre had virtual exclusive jurisdiction over all matters involving a sentence of loss of life or limb which *de facto* meant all homicides. The justices were assisted in their deliberations by a jury of local citizens. Clerics could not be compelled to serve on secular juries as in the eyes of the law they held the same status as women, children and monks; they did not exist.[32] Jury members once sworn-in were presented with a list of questions known as 'articles of the eyre' which they were required to answer, *veredictum*. These articles comprised of questions about reported crimes that had taken place in the smaller divisions of territory within the county; hundreds (Wapentakes) and boroughs. This distinction is important because the Rolls submitted back to Westminster by the justices reflected the crimes that had taken place in the individual boroughs across the country. At this time the Rolls[33] rarely reveal the occupations of the victims or defendants. By default any defendant entering the clergy plea held the occupation of cleric. By the end of the 14th century when the Reading Test has supplanted tonsure the true occupation of clericus defendants started to appear.

The period covered in chapter 4 is the thirteenth century. A time when the legal landscape of England was changing dramatically

---

search/search_results.aspx?Page=1&QueryText=KB+27&SelectedDatabases=BOOKSHOP%7cRESEARCHGUIDES%7cWEBSITE Additionally some cases are cited as *Cal. Pat. Rolls* meaning the *Calendar of Patent Rolls*, digitizing these rolls (1216–1452) was undertaken by Boynton, G.R. of Iowa University and are available at http://www.uiowa.edu/~acadtech/patentrolls/ Year books run from 1270–1535 and comprise of English cases, legal opinions and facts. Some have been reproduced by The Selden Society, Supra. Pipe Rolls (of the Exchequer) are the records of accounts from every county and occasionally hold information related to criminous clerks. They exist for the period 1130–1832 and are housed with the National Archives, Kew, London. Information about the Pipe Rolls is available from the Pipe Roll Society, http://www.piperollsociety.co.uk/page5.htm

[32] At canon law clerics were forbidden per 4th Lateran Council. For a discussion of the situation with regard to clerics serving on juries see: Pattenden, M., The Exclusion of the Clergy from Criminal Trial Juries: An Historical Perspective, *Ecclesiastical Law Journal*, Vol. 5, No. 24 (Jan., 1999) pp. 151–163

[33] The Eyre Rolls are lodged within the Public Record Office at the National Archives, Kew, Surrey, England http://www.nationalarchives.gov.uk/

and all criminals, clerics and laymen, took the gaps between laws to profit. As the magnitude of criminality increased reliance upon any legal excuse from the 'Excusory Quartet' is evident. It is during this period that clarifications of the clergy plea are played out. Is the secular tribunal responsible for hearing a clergy plea before a trial has taken place or should guilt be determined and then a plea entered? This unclear and malleable situation was itself in part the genesis of the eventual acceptance of a Reading Test rather than accepting clerical status on the basis of tonsure. It is in this chapter that we learn of the exploits of the students at Oxford University. They were a murderous bunch at times, fortunately for them they were considered members of the Church for the duration of their studies. Abuse of the clericus plea, fleeing to sanctuary, abjuration and outlawry are frequent events.

## Chapter 5. Custody Pending Trial, Immuration and Clerics as 'Jailbirds'

Roving gangs of criminals had become a real issue towards the end of the thirteenth century. Once a suspect was identified getting them to appear in court was a major problem too. If detained pending trial agreeing upon the appropriate custodial location and who was responsible for the suspect was in a state of flux. The country was at war and men returning home from service abroad were unemployed; many resorted to crime and vagrancy as means to survive. Within England's broken community the local clergyman was a source of comfort and sanctuary; little wonder he sometimes received stolen goods or harbored a fleeing felon or even participated in the occasional criminal enterprise.

At a higher level clashes between the laws spiritual and temporal were a common feature of the period. Archbishops of Canterbury, Pecham and Winchelsey, were particularly vocal in their criticism of the the crown and what they viewed as the encroachment of the secular law into the business of the Church. The judiciary were grappling with the application of the clergy plea and who held the right to establish the veracity of claims; the result was that fluid interpretations of the law were prevalent. In one instance a brutal attack on a civilian by two clerics was deemed to be a simple trespass (and not eligible for a benefit of clergy plea). The temporal justices retained jurisdiction and imposed a heavy fine on the criminous clerics.

The issue of vacant sees was also a battleground between the monarch and England's prelates. During Edward I's reign it has been estimated that a vacant bishopric produced £60,000 of revenue for the crown. This was also one of the last occasions when Trial by Battle was utilized (and by clerics). Two monks were in dispute with a lord over the ownership of a manor. They hired a champion to defend their claim. Battle was held in London in 1287. The monks champion was killed and the brothers had to forfeit their claim to the property. Shortly after this one of the most daring and provocative crimes of the Middle Ages was perpetrated in London. The criminals were all clergymen and the victim was the king. In 1303 cleric Richard Pudlicott and a gang of monks stole the crown jewels. The king responded by arresting all the monks from Westminster Abbey. He reluctantly released them after hostile protestations by the Church that the men were entitled to their clergy. In the end the only person prosecuted (and hanged) was Pudlicott. His attempts to claim benefit of the clergy were ignored, by crown and prelate.

If evidence was needed that monks and priests were engaged in crimes then the requirement that all bishops construct prisons for clergymen was certainly persuasive. These buildings were often attached to the bishop's palace. The diocese would also hire public houses, castles and regular jails (gaols) to hold their miscreants. One such establishment was the Bird Cage Public House in Thame, Oxfordshire.

Prison breaks were frequent given the lack of genuine security. Some clerics fled the realm others lived the remainder of their lives as outlaws, a few were forgiven by their king and re-instated back into the parish of their crimes. By the close of the thirteenth century use of the Excusory Quartet by all ranks of the English Church was established practice.

## 6. Sanctuary, Abjuration and Exile

Primary source material includes a number of references to and discussion of Statutes of the Realm, Select Cases from the Coroner's Rolls AD 1265–1413, The Northamptonshire Coroners Rolls 1323, Select Cases in the Court of the King's Bench Under Edward I, Select Cases in the Court of the King's Bench Under Edward III, The London Eyre of 1244 and of 1276, The Calendar of Close Rolls, 1286 and 1299, Proceedings of the Eyre of Oxfordshire 1285, The Staffordshire Assize Roll 1271–1272, The Calendar of Patent Rolls Under Edward III 1364–1367, The Episcopal Registers of Bishop Godfrey Giffard and The Register of William Giffard, Lord Archbishop of York.

This chapter provides evidence that benefit of clergy was not a plea in isolation but one of four excuses (options) utilized interchangeably by criminal clergymen. The difference between clericus and the others is that whereas clericus was meant to be exclusive to clergymen sanctuary, abjuration and exile were all unavailable to them; these three were secular law provisions and therefore offended the principle of clerics being judged exclusively by other clerics. Canon law forbade clergymen from claiming sanctuary, abjuration and exile. Suffice to say this was of little consequence to most criminal clergymen. What is perhaps more surprising is that in more than one instance bishops were actively involved in the secular processes and facilitated the sanctuary, the abjuration and exile. And on occasions they even pled the crown for a pardon in order that an exiled cleric could return to England and resume his role as priest.

In this chapter the history and legality of sanctuaries and some of the more curious and flagrant abuses of church asylum, abjuration and exile are explored. For example: In 1279 a fugitive had managed to reach the grounds of a church and claim the forty-day cooling-down period provided by sanctuary. A group of men acting under the direction of the sheriff of Bristol forcibly dragged the sanctuarian from the Church and beheaded him. This was now a sacrilegious crime as the sanctity of the Church had been offended. The bishop took over the matter of dealing with the men responsible for the beheading. He ordered that they exhume the body (and head) and bury them in consecrated ground. The five were then to walk barefoot from the burial site to another village church every market day for five weeks. Upon arrival they would be flogged by priests (specially appointed to inflict the punishment). This case is of interest for a number of reasons: it exemplifies the duality of the bishop in society; he was a prelate and also as secular lord who often sat as judge temporal and spiritual. It is also of note that the bishop viewed spiritual law as trumping secular (in reality this was more indicative of two laws that had considerable overlap) and the matter of priests flogging laymen, albeit they had been banned for 64 years from being involved in punishments that drew blood, was never discussed.

Within the cases cited in this chapter are a number of examples of the granting of pardons. Pardons were the exclusive right of the crown and could be granted to remove exile status or outlawry. They were in some respects a form of currency as a pardon could be purchased. Clearly all ranks of the clergy were in the business of buying pardons because the cost was set at law and varied depending upon rank: £1000 for an archbishop, £200 for a regular clergyman. Acceptance of the authority to permit clerics to abjure was confirmed by Edward II when he promulgated legislation that confirmed a cleric could not be compelled to abjure but the option was available to him. In a show of respect for church he held that exiled clerics returning to England without a pardon could not be executed on sight (summary beheading), temporal criminals could. Witches, heretics, and those tempted to practice necromancy, remained banned from claiming sanctuary.

# Chapter 7. Outlaws and Gang Members

In the early fourteenth century special tribunals were established for the purpose of dealing with the backlog of outstanding criminal trials and the problem of outlaw gangs. Claiming a person as an outlaw was a sentence imposed by the temporal court. It could also be assumed (self-inflicted) by an individual criminal who fled the scene of a felony and remained a fugitive for life. Outlawry like exile was negotiable and was rescindable (in-lawed) by the crown upon payment of a fine and/or a pledge to participate in military service. The earliest case of ecclesiastic outlawry was 1163. Following this in 1248 a clergyman was found guilty of murder, *in absentia* (which did not exist at Common Law but was applied anyway). The cleric was 'exacted and outlawed'. By the fourteenth century outlawry amongst churchmen was quite popular and particularly attractive to professional criminal clerics such as gang members. At times churchmen contracted with a criminal gang to supply 'services'. This was most common when a bishop or abbot had a dispute with another cleric or secular lord over ownership of property. The Coteral gang were available for work of this nature. One of their first dealings with churchman took place when they were contracted by the canons of Lichfield cathedral to evict the vicar of Bakewell. They were paid £20 for the job. For the reminder of the career of this gang they always had (participating) gang members who were also serving churchmen. On March 20, 1331 the entire Coteral gang were declared outlaws. Membership included six canons, one dean of chapter, one cathedral registrar, a clerk of chancery, a canon of Lincoln and bishop elect, and a parson (who received a pardon for murder). Within three years they were back in business. James Coteral had secured a royal pardon and was now employed by the crown to track down and apprehend another gang of churchmen from Leicestershire.

The Foleville gang operated around the same time as the Coterals. The gang members comprised of an assortment of criminals including the leader Eustace and his brothers Robert, Richard and Walter. By August 1326 the gang members had managed to have themselves declared as outlaws. This was in large part due to them kidnapping and murdering a baron of the exchequer. By 1332 they worked alongside the Coterals to kidnap a judge of the King's Bench. He was held ransom in the sum of 1,300 marks. Only one principal ever appeared in court for this crime. Over the course of his lifetime Eustace Folevlle committed five murders, his brothers were accessories. All four were principals to kidnapping, extortion, theft and robbery. Throughout the entire duration of his criminal career Richard Foleville was an ordained priest. It was to his own parish church he took sanctuary and where he died a bloody death attempting to kill his pursuers.

The damage inflicted upon the reputation of the Church by gangs such as the Coterals and Folevilles was immense. Those that were working towards the removal of special privileges for the clergy had gained a significant edge thanks to these criminals. Within thirty years the legal playing field had been levelled; all men could pretend to be churchmen.

## Chapter 8. From Tonsure to Reading, From Demands to Requests

The primary source material utilized in this chapter (and chapter 9) comes from the registers of William Melton (five volumes), the Eyre of London 1321 (one volume) and the Eyre of Northamptonshire 1329–1330 (two volumes). The paucity of printed work on the topic of benefit of clergy is apparent again when exploring the criminal career of the Bishop of Ely, Thomas De Lisle. (Chapter 9). The sole monograph is Aberth's *Criminal Churchmen in the Age of Edward III: The Case of Bishop Thomas De Lisle* and consequently I rely largely on this valuable contribution.

The Northamptonshire Eyre was established in large part due to the king's concern over high levels of criminality across the country, in particular the surge in criminal gangs. It is from this record we learn of the gruesome burning to death in an oven of John fitz John and that the female principal was accompanied by a Carmelite friar. Apparently even benefit of clergy might not have saved this man and he opted for a life of outlawry. At the same Eyre we hear of felonious clerics who turn approvers (informant) and supplied the crown with evidence against accomplices that ensured they would hang. In return the clerics were released. Quite how this can be excused by the Church is beyond imagination given Becket's martyrdom and the subsequent papal ban on clerics being involved in bloodletting in 1215. Anyway the actions of these approver clerics were followed again at the same Eyre, this time the criminal cleric was also the receiver of the stolen goods that he then turned approver for.[34]

By the end of the thirteenth century the nation was in turmoil. England was at war with Scotland, Wales and France. The king needed money to finance his military campaigns and all levels of society were pressed into paying additional taxes. Crime was bound to increase and the use of any available excuse to avoid the gallows was utilized by every segment of society. Making the benefit plea available to all made considerable sense as juries were asked (told) to condemn felons to hanging for thefts that they themselves might well have committed. On one hand clergymen provided vital social services to parishioners. On the other they provided some of the most egregious examples of vile criminality yet still they walked free and were back in the pulpit after a brief appearance before a very suspect tribunal of their peers. At the same time as the nation the Church too was in turmoil. Much of its powers had eroded and an increasingly questioning laity posed difficult questions about life, death and mortality that the Church found hard to answer. Blind obedience was waning in place of cynicism, satire and doubt. Monks had never been immune from the temptations of crime but now this too increased. The numbers of men leaving the protections of the

[34] Selden Society, *Northamptonshire*, Supra. p. 165. JUST 1/635 m. 89

cloister increased; some joined the secular priesthood, many left the religious life altogether and married. But leaving was not easy and having spent much time in poverty theft was at times necessary just in order to run away. Others, like their secular brothers, were just criminals in habits. In this chapter there is an example of when monks, priests and laymen colluded in the abduction of nuns. The culprits received an unusual blend of spiritual and temporal sentence. The lands of the defendants were seized by the crown. Their bodies were dealt with by the bishop; 'To appear barefoot and bareheaded dressed in penitential dress among the sinners in Salisbury cathedral and, with them, to be ejected, not to be readmitted until Holy Thursday. On three holydays he was to be flogged around Salisbury Cathedral and on three Tuesdays through the marketplace at Salisbury'. The ringleader was also to be flogged in Wilton (the scene of the crime) and Amesbury and he was required to spend three years in the Holy Land.

The chapter also contains evidence of the amelioration of the laws spiritual and temporal and of bishops and abbots working actively with secular authorities to secure the return of errant monks. There are examples too of bishops beginning to be a little more discerning in establishing the veracity of (some) clericus claimants. Roger Martival, bishop of Salisbury, goes as far as to give written directions to his envoys. One of his concerns is that the claimant may be a bigamist. Once a preserve of the Church in 1344 inquest of bigamy became a task of the secular authorities at statute law.

Throughout the century use of the Reading Test was increasing though many claimants stumble and mumble rather than read. With laicization Psalm 51 would become the standard text and gain the accolade of the 'Neck Verse'. And when a bishop's representative is not present in court the secular tribunals now increasingly asserting authority to administer the test. The ultimate arbiter of clerical authenticity is no longer the bishop's ordinary it is the temporal judge and jury. At this point divisions between the laws of England are perhaps as murky as they would ever be. Clarity was needed and the crown would provide the direction.

# Chapter 9. Untenable Legal Dilemmas: The Bishop and The Monk

Much of this chapter is about two extreme examples of abuse of the Excusory Quartet. A bishop, Thomas De Lisle, who could rightly be described as a mafia and ended his life in exile after the king personally found him guilty of crime. And a priest, Peter Dene, who became a monk while on-the-run (from the king). He then stole from his Brothers in order that he could leave the monastery and return to the life of luxury he had previously had in the secular world. Both men provided great challenges for the Church. Should they be allowed a hearing and be found 'not guilty' even though the king had been the presiding judge at one hearing? Should a former priest who stole from his own monastery be held 'not guilty' and then return to the same monastery? How could the Church possibly endorse the exclusivity of immunity pleas in the face of such flagrant abuse?

But these cases are exceptional. The vast majority of cases used in this book are not exceptional they are crimes that were common to England in the turbulent Middle Ages: murder, sex crimes, crimes of violence, kidnapping, property crimes. The clergymen offenders mirror secular society at every level; robber barons, murdering lords, common thieves. What set the criminous clerics apart was not the temporality of their crimes it was that in addition to offending the criminal laws of England they also offended the laws of god. In a sense the criminal cleric was more an outsider than the outlaw because the criminal cleric was an outcaste, spiritual and temporal. Fortunately for these criminals (thanks to purgation and absolution) the human interpreters of the laws spiritual most often found their brothers not guilty. And whereas the secular outlaw remained a social outcast for life the miscreant cleric was frequently returned to 'good standing' promptly (as seen in the examples of rapist and child abuser chaplain Thomas Porter, murderer William de Middleton, burglar John le Quaynte or robber cleric William Pernill, retrieved by his brothers on route to the scaffold).[35]

---

[35] All cited in the chapter, Infra

## Chapter 10. Immunity For All

The final chapter draws together the transformation of benefit of clergy from exclusive to inclusive, from ecclesiastical to secular, from an 'evil' legal fiction to congruent Common Law. By the third quarter of the fourteenth century the Reading Test is commonly in use and the number of clerics claimed by their ordinary had diminished significantly. The fiction of recidivist criminal defendants being claimed by the bishop had passed, a token branding on the brawn of the thumb was soon to become the only mark of clergy. Secular courts now accepted the reading of a psalm as a legitimate mitigatory plea; a legal excuse, a plea bargain, a reprieve from certain death.

What took place over the two hundred years covered in this book is more than examples of the transition of one prized plea from church ownership to secular. It is a commentary on the organic nature of the law brought about by the dynamic changes in society that occurred during the late Middle Ages. The narrower focus taken by previous commentators has limited the importance of benefit of clergy to an anomaly. But it does not belong in a backwater of legal history. Benefit of clergy is an integral part of the social history of one period in England's history; a time when the power and influence of the Church was decreasing as society expanded. The clergy were to become 'teachers, preachers and pastors of souls'[36] not just to village parishioners but urbanites, a (burgeoning) leisure class, consumers and bourgeoisie.

This concluding chapter explores the evidence of social change that impacted the Church and why it no longer fought to retain clericus: the changes in church architecture, civic architecture, the growth of towns, guilds and merchants. The growth in literacy, civic art, fashion and consumerism. Changes in the curriculum of universities and the manner in which the Church supported the development of a better

[36] Duffy, E. in Horrox, R., & Ormrod, W.M.,(eds) *A Social History of England 1200–1500*, Cambridge, Cambridge University Press, 2006. p. 302

educated clergy[37] (and society).[38] The advent of criticism through satire and vernacular ridicule (The walls of St. Paul's Cathedral and Westminster Abbey were subjected to graffiti).[39] This complex, challenging, rich environment did not reduce crime, it stimulated it. Clerics continued to participate in heinous felonies; they continued to be gang members, they continued to murder, rape, steal, rob and extort. Forum shopping had become a well-established practice too as clerics moved in and out of the available lawful options. The pace of abhorrence for criminal clerics multiplied concomitantly, of course it would. People were better informed. All the while genuine clerics, often local parish priests, worked alongside their parishioners helping them to make sense of harsh laws and harsh times. The criminal relationships that (sometimes) developed between these men and their parishioners is well articulated; they harbored them, took stolen goods from them and sometimes they committed crimes with them. They provided assistance to avoid the reach of harsh laws. These men, England's clergy, were not unique and they did not deserve unique legal protections. They were a product of their time. Extending benefit of clergy to the entire population was a natural development.

Finite dates can cause problems. They bring boundaries to subjects that are not absolute. As such the dates circa 1170 to 1377 are my choice. The two centuries I discuss are, like the benefit of clergy plea, not self-contained. They are representative of the most dynamic period of clerical immunities. They are the period of time over which most changes occurred and they are important because this period takes the benefit of clergy discussion from a high point within one legal system to a general application and acceptance within another. Benefit of clergy is not, and I will argue never was, a legal farce.

---

[37] By the end of the thirteenth century one sixth of the clergy instituted at Exeter cathedral were university graduates. Duffy, Supra. Ibid. p. 304

[38] For example bishop Wykeham's establishment of Winchester School and New College, Oxford

[39] Strohm, P. in Horrox. Op.cit. p. 461

benefit of clergy is an important indicator of the synthesis of canon law and ecclesiastical practice into the life of everyday people and the laws that governed the citizens of England during the Middle Ages.

I became fascinated by this topic about 5 years ago. I consumed all (most) that I could find on the subject and along the way was particularly inspired by the works of Leona Gabel and George Dalzell. Benefit of clergy in England and George Dalzell's work on benefit of clergy in America. I am so grateful to them both. What I found in reading their books was that there were (inevitably) gaps in the story. This book is an attempt to fill one of those gaps (and to tell the story from a different point of view). Why? Well because I think that what has been said about the clergy plea is a limited view. Some 40 years after her book was first published Leona Gabel said much more needed to be said. It still does. I found that most authors commenting on this plea considered it a bit of a farce or just plain evil. I do not. I also found that most works on the topic are about the one topic of clericus. I view it as one of four pleas that many (hundreds maybe thousands) of clergymen in the Middle Ages used, abused and manipulated. So it was time to share my version. Am I right? Well I am sure there are commentators that will disagree with me. But if you are now reading this introduction then perhaps you too are interested and maybe you will be motivated to read Gabel, Dalzell, Aberth and the many others I respectfully defer to. If so then this modest contribution has been worthwhile. I hope you enjoy the read.

Errors are mine. If I misquoted, you I am sorry. If I omitted to quote you I am very sorry. Please accept my apology. I have not mistreated your work with intention. It is not my intention that any of my comments offend. The actions of men known as clerics centuries ago should be viewed in the context of the times in which those actions took place and not as a reflection upon today's clergy. I have received many levels of support throughout this journey. Dr. Eric Fritsch, Chair of the Department of Criminal Justice at the University of North Texas, has supported me in every way possible. I am grateful to the University of North Texas for allowing me Faculty Development Leave for the period January 2016 until May 2016 in order that this book could be completed on time. My final word of thanks goes to Jay Cavalier at Kendall Hunt. He has become a trusted advisor and a friend. Thank you.

PJ

St. Jacut Du Mene

2016

# 1

# Establishing the Clerical Plea: Privilege or Benefit?

Benefit of clergy was probably most powerful as an expression of the Church's legal authority immediately after the death of Thomas Becket and until shortly after the Fourth Lateran Council of 1215. Following which there was a slow but progressive shift away from the importance of the Church in the everyday lives of the laity and a growing discontent with the manner in which criminal clerks, bogus and genuine, were permitted to flout the law and be deemed innocent by the ecclesiastical process of purgation. But the progression and amelioration of what started as an ecclesiastical privilege into mainstream secular law were not a singular event, they were part of the larger struggles taking place for control over the law and lives of the laity. The eventual result was that the cleric's plea became available to all Englishmen and not just 'mine anointed'; such that as sanctuary was a church asylum for the laity and abjuration civil death for the commoner, benefit of clergy too became one of the suite of options within the reach of all felons. And just as benefit of clergy had never really been a privilege available exclusively to legitimate clerics, neither had sanctuary, abjuration or even outlawry ever been the particular preserve of the secular law. Clerics of every hue, contrary to or with the support of the Church hierarchy, had always taken sanctuary, been permitted to swear their guilt and abjure or flee from laws spiritual and temporal to become an outlaw. To treat benefit of clergy as an exclusive plea is to only tell part of its history. In this book *privilegium fori* is discussed alongside sanctuary, exile and outlawry. This is not to say they are of equal status, benefit of clergy was far more widely abused than any of the other three. It is though an integral part of the quartet of mitigatory options spanning laws spiritual and secular from the period of most significant development, Becket's death in 1170, until secularization during the latter part of Edward III's reign (1327–1377).

After an evaluation of the sometimes grotesque and certainly numerous examples of abuse of benefit of clergy, consideration is given in the later chapters to a number of influential factors that impacted upon the changing status of the plea. These include: the growth of a merchant class, the demise of religious houses and expansion of secular clerics, the important changes in literacy which enabled courts temporal to assume authority to permit a layman to recite, or at least mumble his way through, the neck verse, and the demonstrable change in the status of the secular world through civic architecture, the explosion in the building of towns, the establishment of guilds, the bestowment of 'freeman' status on new city dwellers and the growth in satire and literary criticism as authorship of written work became established in place of anonymous monk scribes. Combined these influences provide an understanding of how the clergy plea evolved from the ecclesiastic high point of the first quarter of the thirteenth century through to secularization by the end of the third quarter of the fourteenth century.

Benefit of clergy, *Privilegium clericale,* is the term used to describe the opportunity for members of the clergy to avoid secular trial for criminal matters and as an alternative appear before an ecclesiastical judge at specially held courts Christian.[1] The term benefit of clergy is also often referred to as *Privilegium fori,* which indicates the privileged forum, the bishop's court, to which criminous clerks were required to appear once released by the secular tribunal. At English Common Law the benefit exempted clerics from secular courts in certain criminal matters. At canon law the privilege was based upon the notion that the clergy could not be judged by the laity. Initially restricted to anointed ranks of the clergy over time it grew to include every level, from the humble to the supreme. As the advantages of avoiding the death sentence became better known the volume of benefit of clergy abuse grew. This resulted in the true identity of many claimants becoming obscured. The Church sought to retain ownership over all criminal disciplinary matters pertaining to churchmen and was inclined towards a liberal interpretation of the term clergyman. Lay society wanted to stem the tide of abuse and hold clerics accountable as laymen. The introduction of universities throughout Europe, as well as the explosion in

[1] The classic interpretation of *Privilegium clericale* is Blackstone: 'I. Clergy, the privilegium clericale, or in common speech the benefit of clergy, had its origin from the pious regard paid by chriftan princes to the Church in ity's infant ftate; and the ill ufe which the popifh ecclefiaftics foon made of that pious regard. The exemptions, which they granted to the Church, were principally of two kinds: I. Exemption of places, confecrated to religious duties, from criminal arrefts, which was the foundation of fanctuaries: 2. Exemption of the perfons of clergymen from criminal procefs before the facular judge in a few particular cafes, which was the true original and meaning of the privilegium clericale'. Blackstone, W. *Commentaries on the Laws of England: A Facsimile of the First Edition of 1765–1769,* Chicago, The University of Chicago Press, 1979. Book IV Public Wrongs Chapter the Twenty Eighth. On the Benefit of Clergy. pp. 358–367. p. 358 *et sec*

men joining the Church as a means of securing some level of employment stability, meant that clergy pleas would increase in use alongside growing skepticism about the veracity of the claimants. This was particularly clear in the criminal atrocities committed by student 'clerics' at Oxford University who at one point held the dubious accolade of being the most prevalent murderers in the city.

Benefit of clergy is one of a number of privileges extended to the clergy that commenced after Roman Emperor Constantine's (272–337) alleged conversion to Christianity. Whether he became a practicing Christian or not he was demonstrably accepting of Christianity (he ended persecution of Christians) whilst also remaining tolerant of pagan worship.[2] Teachers, rhetoricians and pagan priests had long held immunity[3] status granted by Roman emperors on the basis that they should be free to serve the public without the hindrance of law. In a letter to Anulinus, Proconsul of Africa,[4] Constantine added Christian clergy, *omnibus omnino publicis functionibus*, to this list. He also authored Constitutions 321 and 331 which instructed laymen as to when cases should be heard before the bishop's court and

---

[2] The Synod of Milan, 354, authorized Christian worship. Under the Edict of Thessalonica, 380 A.D. *Cunctos populous*, made Christianity the state religion of the Roman Empire. Grant, M. *Constantine the great: the man and his time*, New York, Scribner, 1994. Brundage, J.A., *Medieval Canon Law*, London, Longman, 1997 at pp. 1–5. For contemporary evaluations of Constantine: Stephenson, P., *Constantine: Unconquered Emperor, Christian Victor*, London, Quercus, 2011, Barnes, T., *Constantine: Dynasty, Religion and Power in the Later Roman Empire*, Chichester, Wiley-Blackwell, 2014

[3] *Immunitas*: an exemption from a legal obligation. Generally, immunity follows the same rule as a legal privilege and exempts ecclesiastics and Church property from secular jurisdiction. Immunity is also commonly used in association with the idea of asylum and sanctuary

[4] Ockler, C., Augustine, Episcopal Interests, and the Papacy in Late Roman Africa, *The Journal of Ecclesiastical History*, Vol.42. No.2 (Apr., 1991) pp. 179–201

to confirm that cases heard before the Courts Christian once adjudicated were final and not subject to appeal. In matters that were exclusively spiritual the Christian court had absolute jurisdiction and civil authorities had no legislative nor judicial competence.[5] Personal inviolability, (physical injury upon a bishop resulted in excommunication and then secular trial and punishment)[6] special forums and immunity from a range of burdens[7] together amounted to a level of protections available to the Church that came to separate some of its members from secular society. Although the source of much dispute in future centuries many of the provisos amounted to an extension of liberties granted to pagan priests in Rome: exemption from holding municipal office, military service, trusteeships and guardianships. Injuring the body of a cleric, male or female, remains in force today as a crime at canon law. It is of note that despite the violent protestations of Thomas Becket (he fervently believed that submitting churchmen to the secular law and then the bishop's court was double jeopardy) the Church has remained silent throughout two millennia on the matter of laity being judged twice when they assault a cleric.

---

[5] Schaff, P. & Wace, H. (eds) *Eusebius: Church History, Trans in Nicene and Post-Nicene Fathers,* 2nd Series, Grand Rapids, MI, Eerdines, 1955. pp. 380–384. This was confirmed by Code Theod, de religion XVI, 2. An, 39; VII, De epsicop. Audentia, C. (I. 4). C.f. www.newadvent.org

[6] *Privilegium canonis.* 'Si quis suadente diabolo'. A person wounding a bishop was *ipso facto* excommunicated. Personal injury to a lower order cleric was punished with severe canonical penance. This privilege remains in existence today and is also extended to nuns. C.f. Ecclesiastical Privileges. www.newadvent.org

[7] E.g. *Privilegium immunitatis* is the exemption of the clergy from a range of obligations such as paying taxes and certain public burdens such as jury service

In time and perhaps unsurprisingly a number of these accommodations were abused and criminals who were also clergymen were able to thwart sanguinary temporal sanctions and instead appear before the bishop,[8] plead their innocence and be released. On those rare occasions that the accused cleric was found liable for his criminal actions he was excused secular bloodletting penalties and was instead sentenced to an appropriate penance by his prelate. As the reach of clerical sanctity expanded the Roman Empire invested the clergy with exemption from liability to torture and required the criminal prosecutor to take a pledge when accusing a priest. If the matter was acquitted the prosecutor was liable to pay compensation.[9] The expansion of benefit of clergy during the latter Roman period represents growth in the stature of the Church and an opportunity for it to exert a degree of representation in the development of a broad range of criminal legislation.[10] Ironically the ability of the Church to claim jurisdiction over an extended range of moral and social crimes meant the Church began to demand the death penalty in cases for which it had not been previously proscribed. For example, it was the Church that demanded the death penalty for adultery and for the crime of incest.[11] Endorsement of Christianity was confirmed by emperor Theodosius (379–395) who advised citizens that to reject the

---

[8] The Third Council of Carthage (397) deals with clerical appeals and the Fourth Council (398) prescribed the manner of judicial authority granted to bishops. The subsequent Apostolic Constitutions are the early source for mode of trial and procedure and the designation of certain days as appropriate for trials

[9] Boyd, W. *The Ecclesiastical Edicts of the Theodosian Code*, New York, AMS Press, 1969. p.100

[10] Permitting episcopal courts secular jurisdiction was unprecedented and unique in Roman jurisprudence. C.f. Boyd, W., Supra. p.92

[11] Von Bar, L. *A History of Continental Criminal Law*, Boston, Little Brown, 1916. p. 55 and Brundage, J., *Medieval Canon Law*, London, Longman, 1997. p. 17

tenets of the Church would be subject to imperial retribution.[12] He also viewed non-believers as demented and insane.

Protections for the clergy expanded contingently so that by the middle of the 6th century[13] the Church had obtained complete exemption for virtually all criminal actions committed by its members. The involvement of bishops in the administration of secular criminal law was so established by the 6th century that Emperor Justinian (483–565) decreed in 554 that even provincial governors, *iudices*, should be selected by bishops and secular magnates. He subsequently extended this further to permit bishops to be included as potential nominees for provincial governorships.[14] The 83rd Novell (Justinian) clearly delineates the spheres of temporal and spiritual law to provide that if the offense is spiritual the offender will always and exclusively answer to his bishop. If criminal (123rd Novell c.21) he shall appear before his bishop for deposition and then as laity before the courts temporal. Clerical status included all members of the Church, even minor order doorkeepers. Generally and importantly the growth of the Church also meant a growth in Christian communities who in time would become large and wealthy property owners. Within time the imperial concessions of Roman emperors had become established cotumal law effectively exempting all bishops from secular criminal jurisdiction

[12] Cod. Theod. 16.1.2.1 Norland, E., *From Four Royal Persian Stars to Jesus and the Sun*, Bloomington, IN, iUniverse LLC, 2013. p. 155

[13] Further gains were made throughout the fourth, fifth, sixth and seventh centuries e.g. *Constitutiones apostolicae* probably compiled around 380, *Statuta ecclesiae antiqua* in the fifth century, the *Dionysiana*, probably the early part of the sixth century and the *Hispana* (*Chronologica* and later *Systematica*) from the seventh century. Murray, A. Immunity, Nobility and the Edict of Paris, *Speculum*, Vol.69, No. 1 (Jan., 1994), p.28

[14] Murray, Supra. p.28

(with the possible exception of offences of *lese majeste*).[15] In 614 Chlothar II's (584–629) Edict of Paris[16] extended *emunitas*[17] from civic punishment to every grade of clergy and confirmed the right of every order to have all criminal charges heard exclusively by the bishop's Consistory Court.[18] Effectively the episcopal court now became the court of first instance for all criminal matters involving *clericale* defendants. This *de facto* included monks and deaconesses.[19] As Brundage noted this effectively provided canon law with a vested coercive power and moral authority.[20]

Throughout the remainder of the first millennium and into the early Middle Ages, imperial legislation[21] was viewed as subordinate to sacerdotal and in particular that members of the clergy should never be answerable to the laity.[22] In reality

---

[15] Von Bar, Supra. p. 29. Note 5. Also, The Council of Orleans, 511, *Concilium Aurelianense*, Oulton, J.E. and Lawlor, H.J., (eds) Eusebius, *Ecclesiastical History* 10.7, Cambridge, Mass, 1973 cited in Murray, A. Supra. p. 20. Note. 9. The Third Council of Orleans confirmed further. See: Baker, N. F., Benefit of Clergy-A Legal Anomaly, *Kentucky Law Journal* Vol. XV. No. 2 (Jan., 1927) pp. 85–115. p. 86

[16] Noted by Murray, Supra. p. 22 to be the 'so called' Edict of Paris after Clothar's (Chlothar) victory over Brunhild

[17] *Emunitas* is the Merovingian form of *immunitas*. For an extensive discussion of the use of this term see: Murray, Supra. pp. 18–39

[18] For commentary on the various ecclesiastic courts see: Blackstone, W., *Commentaries on The Laws of England in Four Books*, New York, Harper & Brothers, 1852. Vol. III. Chapter V. 'Of Courts Ecclesiastical, Military, and Maritime'. pp. 61–67

[19] C.f. Boyd, W., Supra who cites Nov. cxxx, 31 at p. 227. Note 4. The origin of this jurisdiction was the *audentia episcopalis* explicitly created under Constantine I. (Cod. Theod. 1.27.1–2)

[20] Brundage, J.A., *Medieval Canon Law*, London, Longman, 1997, p. 12

[21] E.g. Laws of Holy Roman Emperor Frederick II Statimus 1139 ad. I 33, C. de episc. I,3 www.newadvent.org/cathen/12437a. This is not to say that the burgeoning secular states were accommodating and there remained resistance to spiritual supremacy

[22] C.f. Lea, H.C., *Studies in Church History*, London, Sampson Low, Son, & Marston, 1869 p.62 et sec

there were two great, competing, institutions in Europe, the Church and the burgeoning secular state; each seeking to be supreme. A result of this struggle for dominance meant interpretation of the term benefit of clergy fluctuated as the Church and secular courts viewed the privilege differently. The ecclesiastical position was absolute; temporal courts were not competent to hear matters involving clerics. Priests were superior in status and dignity to laymen and it would be inappropriate for them to submit themselves for judgment before an inferior. By the early 6th century the episcopate were exempt from the death penalty for treason; bishops, cardinals and the Holy See were subject (only) to deprivation of office, excommunication and banishment to a closed order.[23] The secular view of *privilegium clericus* was that it was not a privilege but a benefit, that is, the secular courts permitted clerics to have cases against them heard by the courts Christian so that the trial and punishment of the criminous clerk would result in being judged by his peers. In one case it is a clerical right and in another a benefit allowed by the secular law.[24] As benefit of clergy penetrated Anglo-Saxon life attempts to exclude clergy from criminal trials was recorded in various early laws e.g. King Wihtread of Kent (690–725) held a clerk should be heard exclusively before four of his peers.[25]

---

[23] Von Bar, Supra. p. 29

[24] Legislation throughout the second half of the millennium confirmed this; the Edict of Clothar (614). Carolingian laws confirmed the privilege and extended it to censure clerics from appearing before civil tribunals (789)

[25] For a chronology of early use see: Boyd, W.K. *The Ecclesiastical Edicts of the Theodosian Code,* New York, AMS Press, 1969. And: Dalzell, R., *Benefit of Clergy in America,* Winston-Salem, NC, Blair Publishing, 1955. p. 11. Also Baker, N. F., Benefit of Clergy-A Legal Anomaly, *Kentucky Law Journal* Vol. XV. No. 2 (Jan., 1927) pp. 85–115. p. 85

Canon law[26] increased in stature and impact from the fifth century continuously throughout the first millennium such that by circa 11th century it comprised of a considerable body of rules. These rules regulated the lives of the clergy and laity across a broad range of daily life; morality, wealth, crime, legitimacy, religion and inheritance.[27] Canons regulated the liturgical calendar; feast days, ceremonies, fasting, as well as events, marriages, baptisms and funerals. Importantly canon law proscribed Christian doctrine. From an administrative point of view canon law provided the mechanism to devolve power from the papacy to local districts, the diocese. The enumeration of these powers meant that bishops had considerable authority to interpret the laws and apply them. As the Christian community became a large landowner across Europe canon law defined the rules for the management of the Church's material wealth. Disagreements between the Church and temporal authorities increased in volume and impact as the desire to gain control of land and people grew with the establishment of nation states. In many respects the pope was a prince of Europe himself and like his

---

[26] The word canon derives from the Greek καvοωv meaning a rule

[27] On the topic of canon law and the Church in England: Brundage, J.A., *Medieval Canon Law*, London, Longman,1997 is clear and concise. Brundage, J.A., *The Medieval Origins of the Legal Profession*, Chicago, University of Chicago Press, 2008 is an excellent resource for understanding the origins of the legal profession, spiritual and secular. Van de Weil, C., *History of Canon Law*, Louvain, Peeters Press, 1991, Hamilton, B., *Religion in the Medieval West*, London, Arnold Press, 1986, Logan, F.D., *A History of the Church in the Middle Ages*, London, Routledge, 2002. There are five chapters dedicated to the Church in Rigby, S.H., (ed) *A Companion to Britain in the Later Middle Ages*, Chichester, Wiley-Blackwell, 2009, also, Helmholz, R.H., *The Oxford History of the Laws of England: Volume I The Canon Law and Ecclesiastical Jurisdiction form 597 to the 1640's*, Oxford, Oxford University Press, 2004, Evans, G.R. *The Church in the Early Middle Ages*, London, Tauris, 2007, Deansley, M., (7th Edition) *A History of the Medieval Church 590–1500* London, Methuen, 1951, Duggan, C., *Canon Law in Medieval England, The Becket Dispute and Decretal Collections*, London, Variorum Reprints, 1982, Swanson, R.N., *Church and Society in Late Medieval England*, Oxford, Oxford University Press, 1989

secular counterparts was rarely minded to acquiesce power or wealth to others, especially when the ultimate power, entry to the afterlife, was vested in the pontiff rather than a mere glorified feudal lord.

Bishops, with the authority of Rome, were involved in many layers of dispute resolution. They also typically held high secular office and as a consequence this duality made them some of the wealthiest members of Middle Age society. In many instances they acted in a judicial capacity in both courts temporal and spiritual. From the twelfth century onwards the Church depended upon agreed and authoritative sources of canon law, the first of these being the *Decretum* of Gratian. Use of Gratian marked a turning point in canon law as it saw an interdependency and synergy with the Roman law based Civil Law of Europe[28] and a division between canon law and the Common Law of England. The Church was clear, it wanted full and exclusive jurisdiction over all crimes committed by clerics, regardless of how loosely defined the term clericus.

Across England individual parishes varied enormously in terms of their wealth and the contributions they could make to the upkeep of churches, priests and the diocese. This diversity meant that many parish vicars were so poor they were hard pressed to maintain a minimal standard of living. At the diocese level ownership of parishes, particularly the wealthier, led to frequent and bitter disputes between abbots and bishops and between lords secular and spiritual. Many of the seventeen bishops of England were themselves secular lords and landowners; it was in their own personal interests to ensure that the laws co-existed in a state of relative harmony. Matters of

---

[28] See further Brundage, 1997, Op.cit. pp. 44–69

ownership over tithes, farms, manors and estates were liable to be brought before both jurisdictions depending upon the status of the claimant. When not resolved amicably these disputes often erupted into violent and sometimes fatal skirmishes.

The establishment of parishes[29] becomes important in understanding the transition of clerical immunities to the general public because parishes became the mainstay of the daily relationship between a priest and his parishioners. It was here that abuse of benefit of clergy, sanctuary and abjuration were most visible. It is also at this close point of contact that the clergy were available to provide physical protections to fleeing felons under the expansive provisions of sanctuary. It is ironic that on one hand the clergy was criticized for its abuse of privileges that afforded clerics immunity from criminal prosecution before the courts temporal and at the same time were required by both secular and spiritual laws to house known criminals before they were exiled or prosecuted.

Throughout the Middle Ages the interface between members of the English Church and secular society was constant and evolving. The courts spiritual of England became the regular forum for all manner of disputes related to; probate of wills, marriage, divorce or annulations, illegitimacy and contested inheritance, legacies and bequests, sexual crimes; fornication, adultery and all manner of incontinence. Plus any felony committed by a priest as well as virtually any male who had an association with the Church or Oxford University.[30] The

---

[29] See: Hamilton. Supra. pp. 15–25

[30] Bishops and uniquely the chancellor of the University of Oxford, who may or may not have been a bishop. The Chancellor held exclusive jurisdiction over a broad range of crimes committed within the city of Oxford when the victim or offender was a student or faculty member (clerk) of the university

canon law truly permeated every level of life and social order in the Middle Ages.

The period 1140–1378 is sometimes referred to as 'classical period of canon law'. This can be misleading as the impact of canon law started to decline after the second quarter of the thirteenth century.[31] In many respects the influential zenith of canon law occurred in 1215 at the Fourth Lateran Council.[32] At this event Innocent III (1198–1216) banned clerical involvement in judicial ordeals and introduced a simplification of procedures in cases where the actions of a criminal priest were clear to all (and a protracted public trial would be damaging to the Church). In England this meant that the infallibility of God would be removed from the criminal trial process and juries comprising of the defendant's peers would become central to the trial process. In terms of benefit of clergy it accelerated the laicization of the plea because the strength of the jury meant it could now facilitate a mitigatory plea. That mitigatory plea was benefit of clergy and it would become available for all men in order that the reach of sanguinary legislation could be averted and fewer felons would be hanged for crimes they may not have committed. In terms of the changing nature of benefit of clergy the distinction between what took place with canon law in Europe and England is important as unlike mainstream Europe in England clericus became part of secular

[31] The period of the 'Great Schism' experienced no new decretals at all

[32] C.f. Brundage, 1997, Supra. p.145. It would be wrong to assume that after the ban on participation in ordeals that the clergy were never involved in blood- letting sentences. Bishops had broad sentencing discretion and were known to impose ritual flogging alongside the more usual sentences of pilgrimage, fines, donning of penitent clothing, fasting and abstinence (from food and sex) and degradation and excommunication

law and practice.[33] However different the absorption of clericus into Europe's legal systems may have been though the abuse of *privilegium fori* was similar in France and England during the late Middle Ages. In both kingdoms clericus claimants were required to be tonsured and wear clerical garb. In both they were brought before the criminal trial courts first and then claimed by the bishop's envoy for trial before the courts spiritual. France[34] did have a form of appeal (England did not) and in those instances where clergy was disputed the bishops could appeal the matter before the secular Provost's court at Châtelet, Paris.

---

[33] For a comparison with France during the period: Genestal, R., *Le Privilegium Fori en France du Décret de Gratien à la Fin du XIVe Siècle,* Paris, Le Roux 1921 and 1924 (2 Vols). Genestal notes that the practice of double jeopardy so objectionable to Becket continued in France into the 13th century. p. 115. Vol. 2. De Lepinois, E and Merlet, L., (eds) *Cartulaire de Notre Dame de Chartres,* Chartres, Garnier, 1865. 3 vols. Translated by Richard Barton at www.fordham.edu/source/1224chartres.asp Brooke, Z.N., *The English Church and the Papacy: From the Conquest to the Reign of John,* Cambridge, Cambridge University Press, 1989 esp. Chap XIII . Mansfield, M.C., *The Humiliation of Sinners: Public Penance in Thirteenth-Century France,* Ithaca, Cornel University Press, 1995 provides an interesting examination of the relationship between the Church in France, its clergy and the laity and the penances given when either appear before the consistory courts. Turner, R.V., Richard the Lionheart and the Episcopate in His French Domains, *French Historical Studies,* Vol. 21. No. 4 (Autumn, 1998), pp. 517–542. The state of morality and behavior of the cleric students of Europe in the Middle Ages is discussed in Rashdall, H., *Universities of Europe in the Middle Ages,* Oxford, Clarendon Press, 1895 (2 Vols) as is clerical violence generally: Smith C.E., Clerical Violence in the Pontificate of Innocent III, *Journal of Religion,* Vol. 24. No. 1. (Jan, 1944), pp. 37–41. Also see: Bellamy, J.G. *Criminal Law and Society in Late Medieval and Tudor England,* New York, St. Martin's Press, 1984. Esp. Chapter 6. 'Benefit of Clergy in the Fifteenth and Sixteenth Centuries' pp. 115–172. Also, Sherman, C.P., A Brief History of Medieval Roman Canon Law in England, *University of Pennsylvania Law Review and American Law Register,* Vol. 68, No. 3 (Mar., 1920), pp. 233–258, Duggan, C., The Reception of Canon Law in England in the Later Twelfth Century, *Proceedings of the Second International Congress of Medieval Canon Law, Boston College, 12–16 August, 1963,* Donahue, C., A New Synthesis of the History of the Canon Law in the Classical Period 1140–1243, Zeitschrift der Savigny-Stiftung fűr Rechtsgeschichte. Kanonistische Abteilung, Vol. 127, No. 96 (2010), pp. 609–615

[34] For discussion about the courts and procedures in France and across Europe: Dean, T., *Crime in Medieval Europe 1200–1500,* London, Pearson, 2001. Chap. 1. Courts, Crimes and Causes

By the thirteenth century canon law was a specific academic discipline across Europe (the first canon law degrees were awarded around 1230)[35] all the while ensuring that university professors, scholars and students were given beneficial clerical status. As a result the milieu of criminous students was by no means restricted to Oxford University; the clerk students at Paris University also engaged in a wide array of crimes as they moved in and out of mainstream Parisian life: privileged, autonomous and intellectually separate from urban life they were also an integral part of it.[36] Much like their English counterparts the less fortunate students; those who achieved access to university through ability rather than wealth and nobility, were not always guaranteed a beneficed parish at the conclusion of their studies and many resorted to crime and vagabondage as they inhabited the marginal world of pseudo-clergy. In France (and England) during this time the act of tonsure was common. It was not restricted to those entering monastic life or attending university and many families recognized the potential for special treatment associated with tonsure. For example; the Bishop of Rouen's register shows that between December 1390 and June 1392, 1642 tonsures were performed. On Palm Sunday 1397, 737 children were tonsured.[37]

---

[35] Brundage. 1997, Op. cit. pp. 63–64

[36] Geremek, supra, provides twenty-three pages of discussion around the activities of criminous university students and *privilegium fori* in Chap. 5. pp. 135–159. His work also includes material about the infamous criminal cleric gang led by Le Brun. It is interesting to me that Gabel. L. *Benefit of Clergy in England in the Later Middle Ages*, New York, Octagon Press, 1969 (reprinted) wrote her work in the 1920's around the same time as Genestal produced his celebrated volumes, she revised her work in the early 1960's around the same time Geremek produced his monograph, both Gabel and Geremek reference Genestal but neither reference each other

[37] Genestal, Supra. Vol. I, p.4, No. 4. Cited in Geremek, B., *The Margins of Society in Late Medieval Paris*, Paris, Editions de la Maison des Sciences de l'Homme, 1987 (Reprinted 2006), p.137. N. 7

Even with the advent of canon law degrees it was never the case that there was a distinct line drawn between canon law and secular law and to ignore the important role of canon law in the development of two of the major legal systems in place in the world today is to miss the point. In the dynamic world of the later Middle Ages the changing status of the two laws as seen through the lens of benefit of clergy (and the associated immunities) goes to the heart of understanding another piece of the social conditions that constructed medieval life. By the 1300s the power of bishops was declining across Europe[38] so much so that by the end of the Middle Ages there was a general sense that the Church had lost much influence; clerics were poorly controlled, a range of prelatory powers had been subsumed within the secular law, the pope had diminished in stature and reach and the local clergy were held in low regard if not contempt by many parishioners.[39] Explaining natural disasters was a challenge for the medieval clergy. When attempted by an overfed drunken felon, a 'waster',[40] who abused his position to avoid accountability, it became unsustainable. Literary condemnation of the clergy gained momentum also. At times enhanced further as satire entered the lexicon thanks to authors such as William Langland.[41] It would seem to be of little wonder, therefore, that the most protected privilege of the priesthood, the right to exclusive ecclesiastical trial for felony,

---

[38] Hamilton. Supra. p. 23

[39] The sometimes precarious position of medieval clergy in attempting to explain natural disasters is discussed by Logan. Supra. pp. 275–296

[40] Coss. P., 'An Age of Deference' in Horrox, R. and Ormrod, W.M., (eds) *A Social History of England 1200–1500,* Cambridge, Cambridge University Press, 2006. pp. 31–73. p. 60

[41] Coss. Op.cit. p. 56. Gorski, R., 'Justices and Injustice? England's Local Officials in the Later Middle Ages' in Appleby, J.C. and Dalton, P., (eds) *Outlaws in Medieval and Early Modern England: Crime, Government and Society, c. 1066–c.1600,* Farnham, Surrey, Ashgate, 2009. pp. 38–55

was itself diminishing as more and more lay felons managed to hide behind the term clerk and benefit of clergy morphed from (eventually) an exclusive spiritual right to a general common law plea reliant entirely upon a person's ability to read.

The importance of the Church in the lives of all civilians was enormous in the twelfth century. It peaked around the time of the Fourth Lateran Council 1215 and then started a slow but sure descent up to the general devastation caused across Europe by The Plague. The extent of the Church's power lay largely in its ownership of land and property, at one point amounting to around 25 per cent of the entire wealth of England.[42] Despite the fortunes and misfortunes of individual bishops, deacons and priests and the transference of some degree of legal authority to the crown, overall the English Church (*Ecclesia Anglicana* as it became known as during the period) remained important if less powerful throughout the later Middle Ages.

The organizational structure of the English Church followed that established by Rome; the parish, rural deanery, archdeanery, diocese and province. Since Anglo-Saxon times England's Church was divided into two provinces, York and the larger Canterbury. Each was headed by an archbishop. After years of bickering and visible disputes for supremacy York and Canterbury were declared autonomous in 1353. There were seventeen dioceses. Ely and Carlisle being the last, created in 1108 and 1133 respectively. The wealth of the dioceses varied greatly, Winchester was traditionally one of the richest and by the middle of the fourteenth century Ely had become the country's second wealthiest bishopric.

---

[42] Lepine, D., 'Church and Clergy' in Rigby S.H., (ed) *A Companion to Britain in the Middle Ages*, Chichester, Wiley-Blackwell, 2009. pp. 359–380. p. 359

Bishops were at the top of ecclesiastic administration. They were supported by archdeacons. These men represented a crucial part of the organizational structure of the Church. Archdeacons were appointed by bishops and reported directly to them often acting on behalf of the bishop in his absence. They frequently ran the lower consistory courts. Archdeacons were expected to act as supervisors to the local parish priests and chaplains; they were supposed to set an example to them in matters of behavior and morality. This was frequently not the case. By the late twelfth century archdeacons were often the butt of criticism and disapproval due their absenteeism, greed and criminality (especially extortion). At the local parish level were priests and chaplains. By 1291 there were about 9,500 parishes in England, each with a priest and many with a chaplain as well.[43] The parish priest had three possible avenues from which to make an income. Offerings made by the parishioners, a glebe (an endowment of land) and tithes. Tithes were a levy of one tenth applied to all agricultural produce within the parish. Priests were also able to supplement beneficed income by earning fees for baptisms, marriages and funerals. A good number of local priests were poor and when payment for services was not quickly forthcoming it was not unknown for them to resort to offensive and sometimes blatantly criminal recourse such as removing the baptismal clothing from children or taking items of value from the deathbed of a parishioner. Instances of such need and greed can have done little to endear parishioners to their clerics.[44]

More than one third of all English parishes were 'appropriated' that is adjoined to a monastery, nunnery or friary.

[43] Lepine, Supra. p. 361

[44] Bishop, M., *The Middle Ages*, Boston, Mariner Books, 2001. p. 154

Rectors were priests who received the full benefice from their parish. Vicars only received a portion of the benefice as part was taken, appropriated, by the ecclesiastical corporate body. Many parish priests had more than one benefice; these were technically impossible and contrary to canon law but in practice a common event. The problem with pluralist benefices was that it meant there were fewer available benefices to spread around amongst the large number of clerics who needed an income. This resulted in huge discrepancies between what one pluralist cleric could earn *per annum* and another unbeneficed cleric who was waiting for a benefice. Needless to say the latter category became those most tempted to engage in crime to supplement their lack of income. The former was most prominent in crime in using force to retain their benefices. Chapels were also an important part of the medieval church and as the fashion for endowing chantries grew many were located within chapels. The growth of chantries also represented a further opportunity for priests to earn a regular income but often at the expense of the monastic houses. Throughout the period it was generally the case that as secular chantries gained popularity the support for traditional religious establishments decreased.

Religious houses were establishments where traditional monastics, the regular clergy,[45] could live a life removed from the pressures and temptations of everyday life. At its height (the mid-twelfth century) there were nine new monastic houses being established every year in England.[46] From the early part of the eleventh century onwards Cluniacs, Cistercians, Benedictines, Augustinians and Premonstratensians came

[45] Also occasionally referred to as the 'religious' clergy

[46] Lepine. Op. cit. p. 363

to Britain from Europe. In the early thirteenth century this move was followed by friars. This group was distinguishable by their rejection of material wealth and preaching. The friars were mendicants and embraced poverty.[47] In time tensions arose between the religious orders. This sometimes erupted into physical violence as the various entities sought to establish ownership of lucrative lands and potential benefactors or in the case of the friars they fought with parish priests over pastoral work. Squabbling over land, property and financial support or over who had authority to preach and administer burials was rightly viewed as demeaning and vulgar by England's laity. Inevitably war-waging clergy, regular and secular, would become the victim of jokes and satire. So too would drunken friars, gambling monks, priests with insatiable sexual appetites and displays of depravity more in keeping with common criminals than clerics. The hierarchy of the Church made various attempts at curbing the decline in standards of behavior. One problem though was that many bishops lived a life of luxury and unaccountability themselves.

The jurisdiction of bishops was complex and often contested. In their absences, which were frequent due to a complexity of commitments secular and spiritual, a suffragan bishop was normally appointed to oversee matters spiritual. A vicar general was appointed to deal with day-to-day administrative operations of the diocese and to preside at the consistory court. All secular clergy were answerable to their bishop some religious orders (such as Cistercians) were exempt from diaconal jurisdiction. The regular clergy in the later Middle Ages can be sub-divided into monks such as Benedictines,

---

[47] For further commentary see Kerr, J., *Life in the Medieval Cloister*, London, Continuum, 2009

Cistercians and Cartusians, canons regular; Augustinians and Premonstratensians and the Friars such as Franciscans, Dominicans, Augustinian Hermits and Austin friars. There were also 'peculiars' that comprised of areas outside of the jurisdiction of the bishop; many Priors were exempt from diocesanal jurisdiction. And there was the constant competition for supremacy between bishops themselves. Though not restricted to the prelates of York and Canterbury their behavior was occasionally far from exemplary. In 1176 when papal legate Huguccio visited Westminster Abbey Richard of Dover, archbishop of Canterbury (1173–1184) sought to confirm supremacy by sitting to Huguccio's right. Roger De Pont L'Eveque, archbishop of York (1154–1181) promptly came to the same seat and sat down on top of the archbishop of Canterbury. He was violently removed by Dover's supporters and forced to sit elsewhere. The inability of the Church to unify, even during times of crises, is part of the reason for its reduction in status and the ease with which benefit of clergy became secularized. At the beginning of the middle ages the Church held absolute authority to punish clerics when they committed a crime. But this was not the only area in which the Church interacted with laws secular. Marriage, morality, matters of intestacy, some contracts and defamation cases, all caused both legal systems to interact and establish the appropriate forum. In every sense the Church and the secular law had the opportunity to impose societal control.

In principle clergymen were separate from secular society. They dressed differently, regular wore habits, secular dressed in a sober manner, and clerics wore the tonsure. As such the lower orders were encouraged to give the appearance of being separate from the temporal world. Their masters did not. Bishops were sometimes drawn directly from the nobility and frequently held high secular office as well as a diocesanal See. They lived in luxury. All had a palace, numerous manor houses and a sumptuous residence in London. Bishops dressed in the latest fashion and were in every sense part of the ruling elite. Most clerics entered the Church at the lower level where they remained. Exceptionally a few would be elevated to a bishopric. Walter Bronescombe, bishop of Exeter (1258–1280) Adam Orleton, bishop of Hereford, Worcester and Winchester (1317–1334) and Robert Grossesteste, bishop of Lincoln (1235–1253) are such examples.

The seven stage ordination process is what most clearly separated clerics from the laity. It started with entry to the four lower orders. These positions were largely ceremonial; lighting candles, guarding church doors (janitor), reading liturgical scripture, delivering messages on behalf of a bishop and singing in a choir. These were positions of support. Belonging to the lower orders did not imply entry to a full clerical career, importantly though it did attract the protections of *privilegium fori*. The major orders comprised of subdeacon, deacon and priest. These represent the sacramental positions[48] and full membership of the clergy. Regular clergy; monks, friars and nuns lived according to a Rule and lived within fully or partially confined religious houses. Secular clergy lived alongside their parishioners in the temporal world. Benefit of clergy extended to all; religious and secular, lower and higher orders. The number of regular clergy was around 12,000 in the early thirteenth century.[49] During the same period there were in the

[48] A bishop, who is also a priest, has the full range of sacramental powers as it is he who ordains a priest

[49] Lepine. Op.cit. p. 368

region of 33,000 secular clergy. The total number of clergy represented about 1 per cent of the population of England at the time.[50]

Control over the English Church was controversial and contested throughout the two hundred years covered in this book. The autonomy of the Church was in gradual decline and the opportunity for the crown to challenge and gain supremacy was a constant feature of life for all orders. The parallel legal systems, royal and ecclesiastical, did little to help ease the complexities. Although King John (1199–1216) managed to achieve excommunication he also gained considerably from his relationship with the Church which included gaining substantial revenues from vacant sees. His son and successor Henry III (1216–1272) managed to exert considerable influence over the appointment of England's bishops. The ability of the English crown to tax the Church at the end of the thirteenth century was a significant gain.[51] In 1317 Pope John XXII (1316–1334) grieved that the 'liberty of the church was more crushed in England than anywhere else'.[52] English supremacy over the Church was confirmed in 1305 when at Edward I's (1272–1307) request the pope suspended archbishop Winchelsey (1293–1313). The papal retreat from Rome to Avignon in 1309 (it was viewed as a pro-French statement) further eroded the strength of the Church in England. Some concessions were made by the crown though, *Articuli Cleri* in 1316 and *Pro Clero* in 1352, but the ultimate outcome was clear. Eventually the

---

[50] Ibid

[51] 1297. Later during the reign of Edward III taxation of the clergy provided almost half a million pounds of revenue for the crown

[52] Lepine. Supra. p. 374

shift in the balance of control brought about by the crown meant that the integration of the English Church into secular life generally was less difficult that it could have been. In return the crown depended upon the Church to supply manpower for high state positions and to serve as final arbiters in judicial appeals alongside secular peers. Bishops (and some abbots and priors) also had important roles to play in attending the Lords and scrutinizing legislation. The lower orders too were involved in the legislative machinery in the Commons. The Church also remained responsible for the supply of information, news, laws and propaganda. As one avenue for the dissemination of royal needs (and aspirations) was through the pulpit it followed that patronage of the Church by the crown was advantageous to both parties.

Control over the clergy was an important matter and there needed to be a balance struck between the assertion of absolute authority (by bishop or crown) and allowing local priests some degree of autonomy in the daily running of their parish. Whereas the regular clergy (in theory) lived a life of austerity, they were fully provided for. The secular clergy were not and remained entirely dependent upon gaining a benefice, a paid position. Priests, rectors, vicars, chantry priests and the minor clergy of cathedrals and collegiate churches were all eligible to receive a benefice. Competition for a benefice was aggressive and sometimes physically violent. Once obtained a benefice was both job security and a pension upon retirement. According to canon law a priest could not hold more than one benefice. In practice many did. So too did bishops and other higher order clergy. Possessing more than one benefice, pluralism, made the beneficed cleric disproportionately wealthy and it prevented an unbeneficed clergyman the opportunity of a stable income. Appointment to a benefice was by patronage; papal, primate, prelate or royal. Appointment to a bishopric was in theory the exclusive preserve of the pope but over time (and much contested language) the crown also bestowed bishoprics. Royal service was the most normal and likely route to securing a diocesanal see; John Waltham and Robert Hallum are such examples, both achieved the bishopric of Salisbury (1388–1395) and (1407–1417) after significant careers in civil administration.[53] Many of England's prelates were second sons and ineligible to inherit; a bishopric was a viable alternative which provided status and wealth. The next level of church administrator; archdeacons, suffragan bishops and vicars-general frequently came from the middle ranks of English society; parish gentry, county squires and increasingly from the burgeoning merchant classes and the yeomanry. Archdeacons often retained the benefice they were granted as a parish priest and along with other remuneration they could achieve a good standard of living. Pluralism, absenteeism (brought about by no longer living amongst parishioners) and financial irregularities were the three most common complaints levied against archdeacons and deacons.[54] Although the spiritual crime of simony, buying and selling ecclesiastical office, had been dramatically curbed by the end of the twelfth century, the practice of pluralism looked remarkably similar. In some instances benefices were actually sold and traded between clerics.

---

[53] Maddern, P.C., 'Social Mobility' in Horrox. Op.cit. p. 130–131

[54] Lepine, Op.cit. p. 370–371

Unbeneficed clergy were numerous. They were the majority and they did the majority of the work. It was the unbeneficed clergy who had most interaction with parishioners. Unbeneficed clergy outnumbered their beneficed colleagues by roughly two to one. In some dioceses it was far higher, as much as 83 per cent.[55] Much like the functions of the archdeacon to substitute for his bishop at the local level chaplains (assistant clergy) often served in place of absent priests. Chaplains were also utilized for personal service in wealthy households and eventually town guilds. Living and working at the lowest end of the clerical hierarchy unbeneficed chaplains were the most susceptible members of the clergy to succumb to crime. In the region of just 15 per cent were likely to ever secure a benefice.[56] The social origins of the lower orders were mixed; few were graduates, though many did have basic education. They were often recruited from the local community where they lived. Their relatives were typically craftsmen, laborers, merchants and peasants with some financial stability. It is this clerical rank, the chaplain, that not only undertook the majority of the parish work, he also lived in closest proximity to the community he ministered to. He was both one of them and apart from them. When it came to lechery, sex and gluttony, or conspiring to commit crime, hiding the profits of crime or participating in crime these lower order clerics were the most active. By the end of the fourteenth century much of England's clergy were viewed as mediocre and having far too many attachments to the secular world (at the expense of devotion to the spiritual). However, these observations should not obscure the very good work many religious

---

[55] Lincoln and Worcester. Lepine. Supra. p. 371

[56] Ibid

men (and women) undertook during this time. Although their high levels of immorality became a factor in a general depreciation of the clergy (and another good reason to secularize some clerical privileges) these men were the backbone of the English Church.

The period between Becket (died 29 December 1170) and the Black Death (1346–1353) was one of intense transformation for the English Church. At first it was one of reform, a shifting from contemplative to active monasticism (the friars) and secular clergy, a dwindling in the influence of Rome, developments in canon and secular law that impacted both worlds, the rise in the influence of the parish and the establishment of royal domination over a number of matters that had previously been exclusively ecclesiastic. It was followed by a period of consolidation of the national *Ecclesia Anglicana*; standards of clerical morality, education and pastoral care all increased. Sermons and prayers were more structured and relevant to its parishioners (during the thirteenth century clerical handbooks were produced as teaching aids and for the preparation of sermons) and the English language was employed throughout parishes so that priests and chaplains connected better with the people they served.

To date benefit of clergy commentary has been largely restricted to a discussion of the development of the plea in history and criticism of its perpetuation as some kind of legal embarrassment that expired in the nineteenth century. This only informs part of a broader discussion. Benefit of clergy is one of four provisions alongside sanctuary, abjuration and outlawry that felons, including legitimate and bogus clerics, moved in and out of depending upon the particulars of the crime they committed and the best option available to them at the time. How many of these priestly claimants viewed their crimes as excusable on the basis that they were immune from secular prosecution will never be known but immunity from criminal prosecution does not render the offender incapable just unprosecutable.

The cleric's plea was a part of the life of the Middle Ages. It was a living manifestation of the changes that took place throughout the period as society moved towards a more secular world with the role of the nation state becoming dominant in place of the Church.

The next chapter deals with the growth of benefit of clergy in England; early divisions and realignment under William I and the use and abuse that led to Clause 3 of the *Constitutions of Clarendon*[57] and the subsequent Becket murder. The chapter will conclude with an evaluation of the impact of Innocent III's (1198–1216) papal bull banning clerical involvement in blood trials and how this helped shape the course that *privilegium* would take over the next two hundred years in England. At face value clerics were banned from involvement in a system that condemned a man to death; in reality many clerics served dual roles in secular and spiritual courts. Withdrawal from this role necessitated the establishment of an independent jurisdiction for the courts Christian, one that would enshrine and protect clerics from the vagaries of an arbitrary temporal blood-letting system. But access to one was inextricably linked to the other and so it became necessary

[57] For a thorough discussion see: Hudson, J., 'Constitutions of Clarendon, Clause 3, And Henry II's Reforms of Law and Administration' in Jenks, S., Rose, J., and Whittick, C, *Laws, Lawyers and Texts: Studies in Medieval Legal History in Honour of Paul Brand,* Leiden, Brill, 2012

that in order that the law functioned the two systems worked in some degree of harmony. What the close of the period confirmed was the need for pragmatism; the protection of clerics even when they committed secular crimes but not to absolve them without question.

# 2

# The Church, Churchmen and the Benefit of Clergy in England

In this chapter I explore the development of benefit of clergy in England between the fifth and twelfth centuries; how it was incorporated into the language of the law and recognized as a legitimate privilege available exclusively to clerics. The chapter will then move into a discussion of the important influence of William of Normandy and his early *Ordinance* which established the foundations for the division of laws spiritual and secular. It is also a point at which the intention of the Norman and Angevin kings, to divide the laws and in doing so establish secular supremacy, commence. William I (1066–1087) is the author of legislation that attempts to control the role, function and jurisdiction of the bishop's consistory courts. Henry I (1100–1135) is best known for his contribution *Leges Henrici Primi* through which he acknowledged the exalted status of the clergy and confirmed their right to the privilege. Stephen (1135–1154) followed this with the *Oxford Charter* although ultimately he was to usurp the spirit of the provisions. The importance of Henry II (1154–1189) upon the development of an English common law is significant. This is often overshadowed by the killing of the archbishop of Canterbury and former Chancellor, Thomas Becket. For the purposes of the history and setting of *privilegium fori* the argument that erupted between Henry and Becket is pivotal to the entire benefit of clergy discussion. The proposals within, and subsequent rejection of, the provisions of the *Clarendon Constitution* became the *cause célèbre* for Becket and in no small part accounted for the speed with which he was canonized. At this point the first of many cases that demonstrate the excessive abuse of benefit of clergy are introduced. In this chapter these cases span the period from immediately after the introduction of *Clarendon* in 1164 until the conclusion of Henry II's reign in 1189. The examples are taken (mostly) from the Selden Society's *English Lawsuits from William I to Richard I*. Included within these cases is one of the exceptionally rare examples of when a cleric failed his purgation. It happened when Becket was archbishop. He ordered the cleric to be held in monastic solitary confinement for life. The chapter concludes with recognition of the important role Henry II performed in bringing definition to English legal procedure as the country transitioned from tribalism to an (infant) nation state. A country where at the close of this period clerics were still held in high regard albeit the number of criminals (cleric and lay) that attempted to abuse the privilege of immunity from the temporal law was increasing significantly. The final part of this chapter sets the scene for chapter 3. It contains a large number of examples that confirm the variety of felonious behavior clerics religious, secular and students engaged in during the thirteenth century.

As the Roman state progressively lost influence across its Western Empire the Church stepped in to assume jurisdiction over greater and greater levels of criminality.[1] By the seventh

---

[1] See: Von Bar, L. *A History of Continental Criminal Law*, Boston, Little Brown, 1916. p. 20. Note. 9. Citing violence by the Monachi, Theodos. 9. 40. (AD 398)

century benefit of clergy was well established. It would remain a feature of political, social and legal dispute for a further thousand years. At its zenith the privilege would allow murderers to walk free (whether they were clergymen or not) and it would attract such scorn and condemnation that kings were forced to intercede at the risk of humiliation, public penance and countrywide excommunication. The prominence that the plea achieved eventually worked in favor of the common man though and not those in authority who sought to manipulate it. For it was not clerics that were to ultimately profit from the legal anomaly but peasants and humble working-class citizens. It was the common man of England who would be able to circumvent bloody codes and excessive use of the death penalty by claiming that they were members of an elite and privileged class of protected persons.

When a criminal clergyman was released by the temporal tribunal to the bishop he would remain in custody until appearing before the diocesan consistory court. Here all proceedings followed the Inquisitorial model with bishops leading the proceedings.[2] The outcome was most frequently that the cleric was cleared of all wrongdoing. In those (few) instances where he was held guilty a number of remedies were available to the bishop. Degradation was viewed as the most serious penalty that the spiritual courts could impose. Bishops were forbidden from imposing the death sentence[3] which meant that the Church became a jurisdictional asylum[4]

---

[2] The only matters not justiciable at the diocese level were those against the See, *Roma Rota* cases (cases against heads of religious orders) and cases against cardinals or the Holy See himself

[3] This was not always followed. E.g. Isabel Bury. Infra

[4] Baker, J.H., The English Law of Sanctuary, *Ecclesiastical Law Journal*, Vol. 2. No. 6 (Jan., 1990) pp. 8–13

for criminals of every description as well as a literal asylum for those claiming sanctuary from arrest. Sanctuary (the right of asylum) provided a local immunity from arrest if a fleeing felon could arrive within the confines of the Church (churchyard) before apprehension. At the conclusion of forty days asylum the felon could be tried, executed or he could promise (swear on oath) to abjure the realm immediately.[5] At which point he was directed by the coroner to make for the nearest port and without delay take the first vessel leaving England (or make a foot crossing to Scotland).

> *You will cast off your own clothing, which will be confiscated and sold. You will wear only an ungirdled garment of crude sackcloth and you will walk bareheaded, carrying a wooden cross before you, made with your own hands from wood in the churchyard. You will tell passers-by what you are and you must take care not to stray from the highway nor stay in one place more than one night. If you fail, people are justly entitled to treat you as the wolf and behead you. And if you ever set foot in England again, you will be outlaw and your head forfeit to any man who can lift a sword".*[6]

Maitland[7] suggested that exile was a daily event as England shipped its felons to France[8] and (fewer) to Flanders to wreak further criminal havoc in those jurisdictions. Some sanctuaries were exceptional; Westminster Abbey and Beverley

---

[5] Jones, T. and Ereira, A., *Medieval Lives*, London, BBC Books, 2004. pp. 78–80 and Maitland, F.W., *The Collected Papers of Frederic William Maitland*, Vol. 2, (Ed. H.A.L. Fisher) Cambridge, Cambridge University Press, 1911

[6] Jordan, W.C. From England to France: Felony and Exile in the High Middle Ages, Princeton, Princeton University Press, 2015. Note 65. Chap. I. Disputes that sackcloth or similar was ever worn

[7] Maitland, Supra. p.127

[8] Jordan, supra. p. 5. Proposes that the French village of Wissant was the most common entry point English exiles

Minster provided perpetual (life) sanctuary. Abuse of sanctuary was frequent such that in 1402 the Commons referred to St. Martins le Grand, London, as a refuge for 'murderers, traitors and disturbers of the king's peace'. Previous commentators on the subject of benefit of clergy have given light attention to sanctuary. This can be explained in part because in theory neither sanctuary nor the associated abjuration and exile were available to clerics. They were banned at canon law. In practice this was never the case. Monks, friars, secular clergy, students and bogus clerics all took sanctuary and many then abjured the realm or fled and became outlaws. I believe that it is central to a more complete understanding of the secularization of *privilegium fori* that church sanctuary and the secular provisions of abjuration and outlawry are included in the discussion as they represent the interconnectivity of the two laws during the period under discussion and help explain why laicization of the benefit of clergy was inevitable rather than exceptional.

"Touch not Mine anointed, and do My prophets no harm" is contained within the first book of *Chronicles*, chapter sixteen.[9] Who was 'mine anointed' became a point of disagreement. During early usage clericus applied to those tonsured.[10] Wearing the bare spot on the head was meant to symbolize the host and was a requirement for male clerics until the late 20th century. Failing to maintain tonsure was itself tantamount to

---

[9] Psalms 105:15 and I Chronicles 16:22. This most famous penitential psalm originates from King David's admission of his affair with Bathsheba and prays for forgiveness

[10] In some countries; England and the USA most notably, Catholic clergy were permitted to remain un-tonsured due to the risk of persecution. Some holy orders employed a full tonsure e.g. Carthusians and Trappists and shaved the entire head except for a 'Monastic crown' of hair

self-excommunication. Miscreants were permitted one month in which to re-establish tonsure or face loss of clerical status and formal laicization (removal of power of orders).[11] The Synod of Ravenna (877), forbade clerks, nuns, orphans and widows under the guardianship of bishops from being brought before a secular court with threats of 'dread anathema any potentate who may dare infringe the rule'.[12] Over time a more liberal interpretation prevailed to include all secular clergy, ordained and minor orders[13] as well as the monastic orders. Tonsuring was a prerequisite for receiving the minor and major orders and obtaining the protections associated with clerical status. Failing to appear *tonsure clericus* or *ornamentum clericale* would (could) result in the secular tribunal denying clerical status. The advantage of being classified as clericus did not escape secular criminals and increasingly they adopted pseudo-clerical attire when appearing before temporal justices.

> The increasing frequency of faked first tonsures,[14] forged Holy Orders, and the wearing of stolen clerical vestments placed an additional burden on the court's determination

---

[11] I have not found evidence of nuns using the clergy plea

[12] Lea, H. C., *Studies in Church History*, London, Sampson Low, 1869. p. 184. 'This exemption included all who had been tonsured and wore the ecclesiastical dress, and was shared in by monks and nuns' www.catholiccity.com/encyclopdia/benefit_of_clergy.html Benefit was extended to women in larceny cases where the value of property stolen was not greater than 10 shillings by 21 Jac. I c.6 (1623) and to 'any person' (men and women) by 3 W & M. c. 9 (1691). 15 years later the Reading Test was abolished. Tonsure was no longer conferred after the *Ministeria quadedam* 1972 of Pope Paul VI

[13] Ordained clergy: diaconate, the presbyterate and the episcopate. In contemporary use clergy does not include monks unless they have received Holy Orders. It also does not include nuns, friars and religious Brothers. Holy Orders are the seven sacraments of Divine institution. www.clerus.org

[14] Gabel, L. *Benefit of Clergy in England in the Later Middle Ages*, New York, Octagon Books, 1929, p. 64. "A gaoler himself might confer a 'tonsure'!" Gabel cites the example of Robert de Neuby who acquired tonsure from his prisoner guard before appearing in court

> of clerkship and called for the institution of a new mode of proof, one that was less available to fakery and forgery...[15]

A literal interpretation of *privilegium* meant that blind men and bastards were not permitted clergy as they were *de facto* ineligible to become priests.[16] It is conceivable though that a bastard or blind man who was able to speak Latin would be able to convince the temporal court that he was a cleric and demand that the bishop's representative, known as the Ordinary, receive him.

Anglo-Saxon refers to the period of history between 400 and 1066 to describe the people and language of England before the Norman Conquest.[17] It is a time when the Church represented one of the few unifying factors in Western civilization and educated, literate clergy increasingly became a focal point in the community as canon law (genuine and fake) continued to grow in use and stature. The Pseudo-Isodorian Decretals, an aberration of *Isodore Mercator,* were introduced to enhance the influence of the diocese of Reims, France. They were a fraud. Nevertheless, the influence of the Decretals was

---

[15] Kendall, C., "Nooses and Neck Verses: The Life and Death Consequences of Literacy Testing" in Bizzell, P. (ed) *Rhetorical Agendas: Political, Ethical, Spiritual,* New Jersey, Lawrence Erlbaum, 2006. p. 100. Poole, A. L., 'Outlawry as a Punishment of Criminous Clerks' in *Historical Essays in Honour of James Tait,* (eds. Edwards, J.G., Galbraith, V.H., Jacob, E.F.) Manchester, 1933. pp. 239–246. p. 240 note. 5 cites the capture of a man in 1221 at Kidderminster who pretended to be a deacon and afterwards confessed he was not an ordained cleric

[16] 'Nor could any man who had a physical disability which would prevent his becoming a priest. Blindness was not held such an impediment as long, that is, as the prisoner could speak Latin congruously'. Bellamy, J. G., *Criminal Law and Society in Late Medieval and Tudor England,* New York, St. Martin's Press, 1984. p. 116

[17] Reynolds, S., What Do We Mean By "Anglo-Saxon" and "Anglo-Saxons"? *Journal of British Studies,* Vol. 24, No.4 (Oct., 1985), pp. 395–414 and Wormald, P., *The Making of the English Law: King Alfred to the Twelfth Century. Vol. 1. Legislation and Its Limits,* Oxford, Blackwell, 1999 (2001 reprint)

substantial and facilitated an entire new layer of hierarchy within the Church. The authors also managed to create bogus procedures and forms that were used extensively by the medieval church throughout Christendom.[18]

Early Anglo-Saxon laws placed considerable reliance upon the purgative oath.[19] Also called 'Wager of Law' it was a method of settling issues of fact that utilized a number of witnesses (most commonly twelve). The defendant was required to produce witnesses who would swear to his character and to the effect that he was telling the truth regardless of whether or not the witnesses had any knowledge of the alleged offence. It became the practice that in real terms this was restricted to those of known good character and increasingly only members of the nobility, aristocracy and the clergy. The oath was a forerunner to more awe inspiring ecclesiastical involvement in trial processes that involved divine, rather than human, responsibility for the pronouncement of guilt, the Ordeal. Though infamous in time, ordeals were a creation of need in a world that did not want to force witnesses to take responsibility for judgment of their peers. Shifting the responsibility for finding guilt to God relieved small communities from the uncomfortable burden of testifying against their neighbors. As the power of monarchs and the Church increased both entities sought to take a greater stake in the administration of justice and in doing so forced the citizens of Europe to

[18] The forgery was uncovered by David Blondel, a Calvinist minister (1591–1655). Whitman, J.Q., *The Origins of Reasonable Doubt: Theological Roots of the Criminal Trial,* New Haven, Yale University Press, 2008 and Pollock & Maitland, Supra. p. 455. Note I. Between 1000–1025 Burchard, bishop of Worms produced the outstanding canonical collection of the century, Burchard's *Decretum.* Brundage, J.A., *Medieval Canon Law,* London, Longman, 1997. pp. 32–34

[19] Compurgation was used in criminal cases until the 16th century. www.britannica.com

rely on established and centralized courts to resolve disputes rather than local, tribal and custom practices. The greatest manifestation of the decline of the Ordeal was the Fourth Lateran Council 1215 and the 'Judgments of Blood' that condemned outright the Ordeal process in its famous eighteenth canon.[20]

Aethelbert of Kent (601–616) issued the earliest recorded Anglo-Saxon laws (dooms) 601–604.[21] They included a number of provisions that articulate favorable treatment towards the Church and its members. For example: stealing from the Church or a person in holy orders was punishable by compensation from three to twelve times the value of the property taken; yet theft from the king was punishable by a fine up to a maximum of nine times the value stolen.[22] Later the Laws of King Wihtraed (690–725) declared that 'Let the word of the bishop and the king be, without an oath, incontrovertible'[23] and for the lower clerical orders "Let the clerk clear himself with four of his fellows, and he alone with his hand on the altar, let the others stand by, make the oath'.[24] The Council of Valence (374) had already declared that a cleric who committed a mortal crime should be removed from holy orders and the Council of Lerida (524) declared that a cleric who shed blood should abstain from communion for two years. The Fourth Council of Toledo (633) c.45 had forbidden church

---

[20] Infra

[21] For commentary on the development of laws throughout the Dark Ages and into the early Middle Ages: Jeffrey, C.R., The Development of Crime in Early English Society, *Journal of Criminal Law and Criminology*, Vol. 47, Issue 6, 1957 pp. 647–666

[22] Jones, M., and Johnstone, P., *History of Criminal Justice* (5th Edition) Waltham, Mass, Elsevier, 2012. p. 43

[23] The Laws of King Wihtraed, 690–725 A.D. 16. www.fordham.edu

[24] The Laws of King Wihtraed, 690–725 A.D. 16. Law 17. www.fordham.edu

members to shed blood. Those found guilty were required to purify themselves through forty days of fasting. [25]

King Alfred (871–901) made specific reference to offences committed against nuns to the effect that if a man committed fornication with a nun, without the king's or bishop's consent,[26] the offender should pay one hundred and twenty shillings compensation to the bishop.[27] There is little evidence of bishops being directly involved in running brothels during this period. Notably though the diocese of the Kingdom of Wessex transferred to Winchester in 660 A.D. it was to become one of the richest dioceses in England. By the 13th century Southwark Cathedral in London was part of the see of Winchester and it gained fame for its ownership of the brothels (Bankside Stews) and its prostitutes known as the Winchester Geese (after the Bishop of Winchester). The brothel owners were required to pay rent to the bishop. Alfred also held some reservations about clerical immunity; he apparently wanted the clergy to be justiciable before the secular tribunal in matters of murder. He sought to have the homicidal priest suffer degradation at the hands of his bishop and then face trial before the king's

---

[25] Whitman, Supra, p 41

[26] It is an interesting idea that the monarch could grant permission for intercourse with a nun (who like their monastic male colleagues were viewed by the crown as legally 'dead'). More generally for a discussion relating to prostitution in Saxon-England see Ross, M.C., Concubinage in Anglo-Saxon England, *Past and Present*, No. 108 (Aug., 1985) pp. 3–34

[27] The Laws of King Alfred, 871–901 A.D. Medieval Sourcebook: The Anglo-Saxon Dooms 560–975 at www.fordham.edu and also Rev Prof. Dr. Lee, F.N. *King Alfred the Great and Our Common Law*, http://www.dr-fnlee.org/docs6/alfred/alfred.pdf Edmund I (921–946) "He who has intercourse with a nun, unless he makes amends, shall not be allowed burial in consecrated grounds any more than a homicide'. Jeffrey, C. R., Development of Crime in Early English Society, *Journal of Criminal Law and Criminology*, Vol. 47. Issue 6. Article 2. (1957) pp. 647–666. p. 659

justices unless the convicted party's lord paid wergild.[28] In respect of the lower regular clergy it was long established that they could not profit from wergild as they held the same status as an outlaw in that the monk had no civil life, he was effectively dead in terms of matters of ownership and intestacy.[29] On another occasion Alfred ordered a secular judged hanged for executing a cleric because the king's justice 'must have known' the temporal judge had no authority over clerks.[30] Three centuries later degradation (de-frocking) followed by secular trial was viewed as double jeopardy and the cause of the most famous argument of the Middle Ages. Across England clear delineation between the criminal courts had not yet been established, commonly bishops sat in jurisdiction at courts temporal and spiritual. It was not until benefit of clergy had matured to the levels of use experienced before the courts of William the Conqueror (1066–1087) that a distinctly separate forum occurred.

By the close of the first millennium the Church had an important role to fulfill in the justice of the laity; both during life and the afterlife. Blind obedience was expected of all men regardless of their social rank and the Church viewed canon law as supreme. This inevitably stimulated rivalry between the emerging monarchs of Europe and the papacy as territories coalesced into provinces and provinces into sovereign states. For England jurisdictional vacillation was addressed

---

[28] White, E.J., Benefit of Clergy, *The American Law Review*, Vol. 46, (1912), pp. 78–94. p. 82. In certain instances part of the *wergild* was paid to the king and to the lord having lost, respectively, a subject and a vassal. www.britannica.com/EBchecked/topic/639839/wergild Blackstone, Supra, pp. 400–436 "Public Wrongs Book IV'

[29] Pollock, F., and Maitland, F.W., *The History of English Law Before the Time of Edward I, (2nd Edition)* Volume I. Cambridge, Cambridge University Press 1968. p. 434 and p. 438

[30] White, Supra. p. 82

by William I and succeeded by the emergence of a Common Law in England and Civil Law in continental Europe. Between 1072 and 1076 William of Normandy issued an Ordinance. It was in many respects a foundation charter for the Church courts of England.

> "William by the grace of God King of the English... I command, and by royal authority decree, that no bishop or archdeacon shall any longer hold, in the hundred court, pleas pertaining to the episcopal laws, nor shall they bring before the judgment of secular men any case which pertains to the rule of souls; but whoever shall be summoned, according to the episcopal laws, in any case or for any fault, shall come to the place which the bishop shall choose or name for this purpose, and shall there answer in his case or for his fault, and shall perform his law before God and his bishop not according to the hundred court, but according to the canons and the episcopal laws..."[31]

William had taken the crown of a country that already held widespread concerns about the activities of its clerics. Many monks entered the monastic life under compulsion, they were members of the nobility who as second or third born sons would not inherit (and therefore a viable and meaningful career needed to be fabricated for them). A number of religious establishments were little more than extensions of the regal court with all of the concomitant excesses[32] in eating, drinking and sex; but of most concern was the legal lacuna that permitted clergymen to avoid temporal justice and seek

---

[31] http://avalon.law.yale.edu/medieval/ordwill.asp The actual date of the Conqueror's Ordinance has been narrowed to a probable date of April 1072. Walker, C.H., The Date of the Conqueror's Ordinance Separating the Ecclesiastical and Lay Courts, *The English Historical Review,* Vol. 39, No. 155 (Jul., 1924) pp. 399–400

[32] Brundage, 1997, Supra, p.34. and Jones, T. and Ereira, A., *Medieval Lives,* London, BBC Books, 2004. pp. 169–171

refuge and sanctity behind the veneer of justice provided by the courts Christian.

As early as the eleventh century two popes attempted to intervene in the excesses displayed by many clergymen, Pope Leo IX (1049–1054) summoned a council in 1049 to adopt a number of canons designed to address higher standards of clerical discipline and the requirement that subdeacons and the ranks above to be celibate. This was followed by Pope Alexander II (1061–1073) with canons forbidding clerical concubinage and simony.[33]

William's approach was to divide the responsibilities of church and courts secular. He ordained that no bishop should administer episcopal laws in the secular hundred court, *curia,* nor bring to the secular tribunal any matter involving the cure of souls. If and when the courts Christian, *coram episcopo,* excommunicated an offender in William's view he would then be liable for trial before the temporal justices. In those instances when a defendant was rightly tried before the secular court and there was to be an Ordeal, the Church was the party responsible for the administration and oversight of the Ordeal process.[34] What should not escape commentary is that what William was also achieving here was a clear statement to the effect that it was the responsibility *and right* of the English monarch, not Rome, to designate the role, function and jurisdictional boundaries of the bishop's court. Gabel[35] has suggested this was a deliberate move to create two categories

---

[33] His successor, Gregory VII (1073–85) was even more zealous in his pursuit of errant clerics and temporal subservience to papal authority. Brundage, 1997. Supra. pp. 39–41

[34] Morris, C., William I and the Church Courts, *The English Historical Review,* Vol. 82. No. 324 (Jul.,1967) pp. 449–463. p. 449–450

[35] Gabel, L., *Benefit of Clergy in the Later Middle Ages,* New York, Octagon, 1969

of clergyable cases; spiritual cases and spiritual persons. Spiritual cases being those justiciable before the bishop's court regardless of the status of the offender, spiritual persons were those tried before the bishop's court regardless of the offence. By interpretation this would comprise of instances of heresy, simony, sacrilege, adultery, fornication, usury and Nicolaitism; all are matters of a spiritual nature. Spiritual persons would be clerics who regardless of the crime; murder, robbery or burglary, would be held accountable exclusively before the courts Christian.[36]

Nothing in William's edict suggests that prelates should not retain their jurisdictional function as temporal justices when sitting at the king's court; after all many of the bishops also held high secular office and were related by blood or marriage to the court. Archbishop of Canterbury Lanfranc (1070–1089) a close ally of William I, was a prime example of combined secular and prelatory power. On one occasion Lanfranc ordered that the monks of Glastonbury sing chants approved by Rome rather than the traditional Gregorian style. They refused so he had twenty-one of them shot by arrow. William elected not to intercede. (Allegedly William even bowed to Lanfranc in public).[37] William famously arrested his own half-brother, Odo, Bishop of Bayeux (1049–1097) who pleaded immunity from secular justice on the basis of his clerical office, 'I am a clerk, a minister of the Lord. It is not lawful to condemn a bishop without the sentence of the Pope' William responded 'I do not meddle with clerks or prelates. I do not seize the Bishop of

[36] Gabel, Supra. p.12

[37] Jones, T. Supra. p.95 and Brooke, Z.N., *The English Church and the Papacy from the Conquest to the Reign of John*, Cambridge, Cambridge University Press, 1989

Bayeux, but I do seize the Earl of Kent'.[38] Later during the $14^{th}$ century only five chancellors from a total of thirty eight who served in this capacity throughout the century did not hold a joint bishopric and chancellorship.[39]

The status of the criminous clerk is to be problematic for some time though as through William's intervention it has become necessary to establish jurisdictional authority between two competing tribunals. If the spiritual courts were to henceforth have exclusive jurisdiction over a range of moral offences committed by laymen and clerics, then the law of the realm was effectively being administered by the Church. Whereas this might become acceptable with practice in cases of no monetary value it cannot have been William's intention that he permit the Church competence to hear all spiritual offences that would also involve property rights and hereditary titles that evolved out of cases of matrimonial dispute, bastardy and fornication.

William the Conqueror's separation of the temporal and spiritual courts in 1072 caused significant changes to the balance of power that had existed in England between the Church and state since Anglo-Saxon times.[40] At the Council of Rheims, 1049 (at which England and Normandy were present) and at the later Council of Lillebonne, 1080, bishops were unable to prevent extended lay ownership of some episcopal rights and

---

[38] Baker, N. F., Benefit of Clergy-A Legal Anomaly, *Kentucky Law Journal*, Vol. 15. No. 2 (Jan.,1927) pp. 85–115. p. 90 citing Pollock and Maitland, Supra. pp. 450–451. Odo held both the bishopric of Bayeux and the Earldom of Kent

[39] Pollock & Maitland, Vol. 1. Pollock, F. & Maitland, F. W., *The History of English Law Before the Time of Edward I (2nd edition)* Cambridge, Cambridge University Press, 1968. Vol.1. p. 205

[40] Ogle, A., *The Canon Law in Mediaeval England: An Examination of William Lynwood's "Provinciale", in Reply to the Late Professor F.W. Maitland,* London, John Murray 1912. p. 23

temporalities.[41] Disputes between the competing jurisdictions could of course ultimately be decided by the king; neither the archbishop of Canterbury nor any bishops were permitted to 'enact or prohibit anything but was agreeable to his will and had first been ordained by him'.[42] This would assume that the pontiff was of a mind to acquiesce power to kings. The ensuing two hundred years indicate this was not to be the case in England as the Holy See sought to (periodically) demonstrate he was prince of both *sacerdotium* and *regnum*.

In William's homeland of France the situation differed in that the temporal courts had authority to hear criminal cases against criminous clerks (papal juridical supremacy was not achieved without recourse to the threat of excommunication). This changed after the early medieval period once the grip of the Inquisition took place across Europe.[43]

Upon the death of William the Conqueror his brother assumed the English throne. William II, known as Rufus (1087–1100) demonstrated little enthusiasm for extending the range of diocesanal power in England. Lanfranc remained archbishop of Canterbury after the death of William's brother and he

---

[41] Morris, C. William I and the Church Courts, *The English Historical Review*, Vol.82. No.324 (Jul.1967.), pp. 449–463

[42] Eadmer, *Historia Novoru in Anglia*, Rule, M. (ed) Rolls Series 81: London, Longman, 1884 cited in Jones, W.R., The Two Laws in England: The Later Middle Ages, *The Journal of Church and State* Vol. 11. No. 1 (1969) pp. 111–131 p. 122. Note 33 and. Cited by Gabel, Supra. p. 15. Note 18

[43] Of the situation in France and Germany and the 'prolonged struggles' between the Church and state see: Pollock & Maitland, *The History of English Law Volume 1*, Supra, pp.124–125. Williams, A.,(ed) *Old Church Life*, William Andrews & Co, London, 1909. p.19–20. Lea, H.C., *Studies in Church History*, London, Sampson Low, 1869 pp. 180–183. Walker, C.H., The Date of the Conqueror's Ordinance Separating the Ecclesiastical and Lay Courts, *The English Historical Review*, Vol.39. No. 155 (Jul., 1924), pp. 399–400

appeared to continue to exercise some considerable degree of influence (if not extending clerical privilege at least holding it firm). Two instances are recorded that involve William II and clerical privilege. One in 1088 against William of Calais, Bishop of Durham (1080–1096) when he was accused of treason (traditionally unclergyable). Lanfranc represented the interests of the crown and the Church. Durham refused to plead and in keeping with traditional secular law his estates were forfeited. William Rufus was present in court during the exchange between Lanfranc and Durham. An event that must have confirmed the allegiance Lanfranc held for the monarch (as he did for his brother William I). The second incident involved Anselm (1093–1109) successor to Lanfranc in the see of Canterbury. Anselm found himself charged by Rufus with failing to discharge his feudal obligations. Although strongly supported by his spiritual brothers, the Bishop of Durham and Bishop of London, Anselm elected not to fight Rufus and made no claim of immunity or privilege.[44] William II had a fractious relationship with Anselm and accordingly with the Church. He was keen to install fiscal levies upon the Church and when vacant bishoprics occurred he was slow to fill them (as during the period of inoccupation the taxes and revenues of the see went directly to the crown). Anselm felt defeated by William and eventually he gave up and exiled to France.

William's unexpected death placed Henry I (1100–1135) on the throne. His claim was weak and he sought endorsement from the Church and his own nobility. He proceeded to renounce the ways of his recently deceased older brother and embark upon a period of relative stability that indicated support for

---

[44] Baker, N. Supra. pp. 90–91 and Pollock, F. & and Maitland, F.W. *The History of the English Law before the Time of Edward I (2nd Edition) Vol. I*, Cambridge, Cambridge University Press, 1968, p. 451

established Church practices. Anselm was re-instated as archbishop of Canterbury. His asylum in France had equipped him with greater knowledge of canon law and the rights of the clergy and a firm commitment to the idea that the trend towards lay investiture and increased homage to secular kings over God was unacceptable.[45] Henry's best known contribution to the articulation of English law appear in the *Leges Henrici Primi* (compiled between 1108 and 1118 by an unknown author(s). The work draws together from a variety of sources to state the law as it stood at the commencement of Henry I's reign.[46] Fashioned after the legislation of Ethelred, Cnut and Alfred, the *Leges* acknowledges the exalted status of the clergy.[47]

Chapter five *Concerning the characteristic of causes*; at 5.4 through to 5.11 covers a number of situations pertaining to clerics and forum. 5.11 informs the reader that a bishop shall not be condemned except on the evidence of 72 witnesses. 5.11a The pope shall not be judged by anyone and 5.11b a priest *cardinalis* only on the evidence of 44 witnesses, a deacon *cardinalis* only on the evidence of 26 witnesses, a sub-deacon and below only on the evidence of 7 witnesses. 5.7 states that 'It has been decreed that in a cause touching the faith or

---

[45] At the synod of 1099 (the Investiture Controversy) Pope Urban II (1088–1099) announced that investiture of clergy by the laity was subject to excommunication for the lay person and the cleric. Visser, S., and Williams, T., Anselm: *Great Medieval Thinkers*, Oxford, Oxford University Press, 1965 also Green, J., *Henry I, King of England and Duke of Normandy*, Oxford, Oxford University Press, 2006

[46] Downer, L.J., *Leges Henrici Primi*, Oxford, Oxford University Press, 1972 and in passing: Pollock and Maitland, Supra. pp. 99–101. As Downer notes p.10, it sits and one end of the century with Glanvill at the other. The work is divided into 94 chapters of which Chap. 5 deals most extensively with matters relating to the Church and jurisdiction of bishops and the status of the clergy

[47] Gabel, Supra. p. 18 and Pollock and Maitland, Supra pp. 99–101

any ecclesiastical order judgment must be made by a person who is neither inferior in office nor of different status in law' and at 5.8 Laymen ought not to permit ecclesiastics to make their charges or accusations against them, just as ecclesiastics should not permit this for laymen. 'If anyone accuses any cleric of fornication, then according to the injunction of Paul the apostle two or three witnesses shall be required of him; but if, when the witnesses have been produced, he has not been able to prove his assertion, the accuser shall suffer the excommunication which would have befallen the accused'.[48] It would seem that clerics are entitled to be notified of pending actions anyway for at 5.22 'Anathema on him who ever lays a charge against a priest before his own judges before giving a friendly warning, or who lays a charge at any time before temporal judges'.[49]

Bishops (always at the forefront of exceptional privileges it would seem) if accused of any crime shall be 'Heard by all the bishops who are in the province' and his accusers have to be personally present at the hearing.[50] Ecclesiastical matters that transcended spiritual and secular jurisdiction are dealt with in chapter eleven. 'There are certain other pleas being pleas in the jurisdiction of the Christian faith in which the king

---

[48] *Leges Henrici Primi* Chapter 5 at 5.16

[49] Note also that the clear direction contained in this sub-section is that matters concerning the clergy are only to be heard 'before his own judges' *Leges Henrici Primi* C. 22

[50] This would be quite a logistical feat. For a division of dioceses and numbers during this period see: *The Dioceses of England: An Outline History* www.churchofengland.org/media/40668/chapter2.pdf. *Leges Henrici Primi* C. 5.24. Should the complainant be a monk he would need the authority of his abbot to give evidence, unlikely given the relationship between abbots and bishops. C. 5.35 The oath of a son or daughter, without the father's knowledge, and the vows of a monk, without the abbot's knowledge, and the oaths of a child, are void

has a share in the following way'.[51] Homicide committed in a church warranted compensation to Christ first and then the king.[52] Commoners withholding tithes permitted the priest to accompany the sheriff and take property to the value of the tithe by force; plus an extra ten per cent.[53] If a married man committed adultery, 'The king or lord shall have the man, and the bishop the woman, for the purpose of exacting penalty'.[54] Anyone causing injury to a man in holy orders (no mention here of nuns) shall pay compensation in accordance with the clerics rank and if he cannot pay the offender will be liable to forfeiture of all his property.[55]

Chapter twenty, *Concerning soke,* deals with manorial privilege; 20.2 addresses the rights and privileges of bishops, sake and soke,[56] to maintain order over their lands and to hold accountable not only clerics but any tenants of the bishop in respect of misdemeanor offenses. However, the authority of the bishop is not supreme in these matters as Henry has final jurisdiction over all serious matters relating to right of soke, 'over individual barons and great men, whether clerical or lay...[57] Sections 8–9 of Chapter sixty four *Concerning the conducting of accusations according to their nature* defines the value of oath testimony by priests. One priest's oath is

---

[51] *Leges Henrici Primi.* C. 11.1

[52] Ibid C. 11.1a

[53] Ibid C. 11.2

[54] *Leges Henrici Primi.* C. 11.5

[55] Ibid C. 11.12

[56] An Anglo-Saxon term that denotes the right of a lord to exercise jurisdiction over his lands. The king has in theory a right of sake and soke over the entire kingdom but this is transferred to barons, knights and bishops through the bestowment of estates and privileges. Toll and Team is another form of expression that denotes the authority of a lord to fine and punish and hold moot courts.

[57] *Leges Henrici Primi* C. 20.3

sufficient to clear himself against one accuser and two clerics of his rank are sufficient to disprove three lay accusers.[58] A deacon can clear himself of an accusation by swearing an oath with assistance from two other deacons but he needs six deacons to disprove the word of three lay accusers;[59] whereas a priest accused by a bishop or archdeacon needs five other priests to swear with him.[60]

Homicidal clerics are dealt with in chapter sixty six at section two where we are informed that any minister who kills another man shall be deprived of office and go on a pilgrimage as directed by the pope.[61] Importantly this makes it very clear that Henry I does not assume that he has jurisdiction over the murderous cleric; it is within the purview of the pope. Clerics that are victims of violent crime, fatal or not, are dealt with in chapter sixty eight with the usual degree of preferential treatment; if an ordained priest were slain one third of the compensation went to the bishop, one third to the altar and one for a religious community.[62] A layman foolish enough to kill a bishop was answerable directly to the king; slaying a monk or priest, intentionally or not, required entry into the service of god, after payment of any compensation due, and in cases of intentionally killing the murderer was required to do penance 'until his life's end';[63] a particularly

---

[58] Ibid C. 64 8

[59] Ibid C. 64 8 a

[60] Ibid C. 64 8 c

[61] *Leges Henrici Primi* C. 66.2

[62] *Leges Henrici Primi* C. 66.5 d

[63] Ibid C. 68.7. Pugh, R.B., *Imprisonment in Medieval England,* Cambridge, Cambridge University Press, 1968. Chapter III "The Imprisonment of Clerks, Serfs, and Jews". For an alternative use see: Pollock & Maitland, Supra, pp. 444–445 and: Maitland, F. W., The Deacon and the Jewess; or; Apostacy at Common Law, *The Collected Papers of Frederic William Maitland,* by Fisher, H.A.L., (ed) Cambridge, Cambridge University Press, 1911. Vol. I

depressing prospect as one manifestation of this meant solitary confinement for life and a diet of bread and water (when a monk killed another brother). Variations included: incarceration in windowless pits accessible by ladder, the wearing of chains, repeated floggings and being required to go on pilgrimage to the Holy Land. The Church used the term Immuration, *inter alia*, to describe a voluntary solitary confinement with access only to food and water and perhaps a line of sight to an altar. We are immediately reminded of the lofty status of those who are voluntary clerics for if a deacon or priest commits homicide he shall be removed and do penance in accordance with the judgment of his bishop.[64] Later in the reign of Henry I homicide is addressed as a topic generally and the law relating to the punishment of ordained clerics specifically. This is not to say that Henry assumed any jurisdiction over criminous clerks, *Leges Henrici Primi* are not the laws written by Henry but rather more a statement of the laws applicable in England at that time as written by the anonymous author.

At chapter seventy three 'Concerning ordained persons who commit homicide' one can see that a bishop who commits homicide shall be removed from office and do penance for twelve years; seven years on bread and water and for the remaining five he shall fast three days each week.[65] In somewhat of a turnabout in ecclesiastical hierarchical preferences the homicidal priest now gets away with just ten years penance; six on bread and water and four years on a three day each week fast. The murderous deacon has to serve a mere seven years penance, four years on bread and

---

[64] *Leges Henrici Primi* C. 68. 8

[65] Ibid C. 73. I

water and the remainder at three days of fasting each week. Unordained clergy who murder are subject to six years penance, three years of bread and water followed by two years of three day each week fasting. Differentially though the bishop is allowed to eat the food of his brothers during his last five years of penance whereas the priest or monk has to supply their own food for the last four years.[66] Ordained clerics who wound or inflict other serious bodily harm are liable to fast for one hundred days and pay compensation.[67] The value of a lost limb, a man's genitals, shoulder or his arm are equal. So too is loss of a leg, below the knee. Each are worth eighty shillings.[68] Anyone committing a homicide inside a church cannot offer to pay compensation for the crime unless they receive permission from the king. If a homicide is committed in the house of a bishop the accused is liable to lose his limbs or pay compensation; to the bishop.[69]

The *Leges* appear to be most supportive of England's clergy. This did not mean that tensions between Henry and England's bishops abated. The reform movements within the Church that had started in the eleventh century sought to improve the image and behavior of the lower orders not acquiesce power to monarchs.[70] Those advocating change wanted the clergy to be seen to live a moral life. In part this

---

[66] Ibid C. 73. 2, 73. 3, 73. 4

[67] See: Leges Henrici Primi C. 93

[68] *Leges Henrici Primi* C. 73. 2 a

[69] Ibid C.80. 8

[70] Bartlett, R., *England Under the Norman and Angevin Kings*, Oxford, Oxford University Press, 2000. pp. 377–412. Also Helmholz, R. H., *The Oxford History of the Laws of England: Canon Law and Ecclesiastical Jurisdiction from 597 to 1640s*, Vol. I. Oxford, Oxford University Press, 2004, Chap. 2

meant involvement of the Church in secular juridical practices that shed the blood of humans was increasingly viewed as anathema. In England the tensions between Henry and the Church were (in part) due to the history that had long supported the appointment of prelates and abbots to high temporal office. These tensions came to a head in 1107 when Henry sought to exercise his right to invest prelates and Pope Paschal II (1099–1118) responded with a threat of excommunication. The matter was resolved in the Church's favor by the Compromise of Bec ratified in London on August 1, 1107.[71] This document saw Henry I formally surrender the royal right of investiture to the Church.

As the Chuch and its dioceses expanded through Europe its wealth grew exponentially;[72] it was an appropriate time to formalize ecclesiastical law into a *Corpus iuris canonici*.[73] A key ecclesiastical legal issue in England was not so much who had jurisdiction over criminal clergymen but rather more who had control over the wealth of the clergymen and their parishes. Under the Anglo-Saxons the English Church had gained a considerable amount of land and property. God's appointed landlord in Rome had no intention of relinquishing its worldly gains to any temporal prince.[74] Whereas a miscreant cleric

---

[71] Hence also known as the *Compromise of London*

[72] Somewhat dramatically described as "The rise of the Papacy, from the persecuted head of an insignificant local church to the supreme domination over both the spiritual and temporal hierarchy of Europe is one of the most curious problems in history" Lea, H.C., *Studies in Church History*, London, Sampson Low, 1869. p. 104. It is certainly a fascinating study in power struggles between Rome and monarchs of which benefit of clergy sits firmly at center stage

[73] Brundage, J., *Medieval Canon Law*, London, Longman, 1997

[74] Fleming, R., *Domesday Book and the Law*, Cambridge, Cambridge University Press, 1998 p. 54 estimated that one quarter of all the land in England was owned by the Church during the time of William I

who could be treated as laity meant potential revenue for the crown if the same clergyman was tried before the courts spiritual his benefice[75] and personal estate remained in the see.[76] The establishment of separate courts could have clarified jurisdictional loci and removed any rational excuse for double jeopardy. Yet this remained contentious as courts temporal and spiritual disagreed over the venue for first appearance. Before the end of the 12th century this issue would develop into an international furore.

In 1135 Stephen (1135–1154) seized the throne with help from his brother Henry of Blois, Bishop of Winchester (1129–1171).[77] He was crowned king of England on December 22. His uncle's[78] daughter, Matilda, was direct in line and somewhat inevitably civil war followed. Stephen's reign was tarnished with the label 'The Anarchy', it was a good time for the English Church to make gains in status and influence, to align itself more closely with the common laity and to continue to exert its influence over the sphere of matters justiciable before the courts spiritual.[79] Stephen's tenuous claim to the throne meant he would seek

---

[75] Churches and their parishes were awarded to a clerk from which they gained income in terms of tithes, letting of farms, taxes and money from baptisms, marriages and burials. The complex procedure for appointing to and awarding parishes (or bishoprics) known as advowson was contested frequently

[76] For discussion of these issues see: Thompson, H., *The English Clergy and Their Organization in The Later Middle Ages*, Oxford, Oxford University Press, 1947

[77] Henry of Blois was also a monk and Abbot of Glastonbury. He retained Glastonbury upon elevation to the bishopric of Winchester. As prelate he consecrated Thomas Becket to Canterbury on 3rd June 1162 and he presided over the subsequent trial of becket at Northampton castle 8th October 1164

[78] Stephen was Henry I's nephew. Matilda was Henry's daughter and heir apparent

[79] Berman, H.J., *Law and Revolution: The Formation of the Western Legal* Tradition, Cambridge, Mass, Harvard University Press, 1983. Notes that 'As the Papal revolution gave birth to the modern Western state, so it gave birth also to a modern Western Legal system, the first of which was the modern system of canon law'. p. 115. And see pp. 434–459

papal support for his kingship, which he received. The favor was returned in Stephen's *Oxford Charter*, 1136.[80]

In June 1139 Stephen took the unusual step of attempting to seize the lands and estate of Roger, Bishop of Salisbury (1102–1139).[81] The king was taking advantage of a disturbance that had occurred between Roger's son and nephews and Earl Alan of Brittany. Stephen determined the incident to be a (criminal) breach of the king's peace. Salisbury sought to utilize his benefit of clergy but to no avail as Stephen ignored this in much the same manner as his grandfather, William I, had done with bishop Odo. Stephen's actions were censured by the Church, and his own brother Henry (bishop of Winchester) and the king were required to do penance for their actions. Salisbury had apparently annoyed the king by his overt display of prelatory wealth by building two new castles, Sherborne and Devizes, and supporting his nephew in the building of a third. To Stephen this represented a (vulgar) threat to sovereignty and a visual manifestation of the wealth of secular clergy.[82] Stephen having confiscated the bishop's estates never returned them' even though the crown had confirmed the right of ecclesiastical privilege in the Oxford Charter just three years previously.[83] Towards the end of

[80] Where he specifically mentioned his anointment was confirmed by the holy Church. *Statutes of the Realm* I.3 Exeter version *Domini M.C. XXXVI set regni mei promo*

[81] Roger was a village priest in Caen, France who found favor with Henry I and was brought to England. He served as Lord Chancellor and is credited with establishing the Exchequer system

[82] Chron. Sax. p. 238. Cited by Hume, D. *The History of England from the Invasion of Julius Caesar to the Revolution in 1688* at www.olllibertyfund.org

[83] 'I permit and confirm justice and power over ecclesiastical persons and all clerks and their effects and the distribution of ecclesiastical goods to be in the hands of the bishops…' Oxford Charter, Supra and Baker, N.F. Supra. p. 92

his reign[84] relationships with the Church soured as Stephen sought to have his son Eustace crowned king. Archbishop of Canterbury Theobald of Bec (1138–1161) refused, the decision was supported by Rome.

In the year of his death Stephen attempted secular authority over churchmen one last time. The matter involved a homicidal cleric, Osbert of Bayeux. Osbert was archdeacon of York and avidly opposed to the return of the previously deposed archbishop William Fitzherbert (1141–1147). Fitzherbert was reinstated May 1154. On June 8th 1154 archbishop Fitzherbert died after consuming poison from the chalice. Osbert was arrested and requested to have the matter adjudicated before the Christian court in accordance with established rights of *privilegium.* Stephen refused on the basis that the nature of the crime was heinous and the charges had been proffered in the king's presence. He held that Osbert should be tried before the temporal justices and had the defendant held in secular custody pending trial. Stephen died before the matter was tried and the issue of Osbert's immunity carried over into the reign of Henry II (1154–1189). In the second year of Henry's reign he permitted the matter to be transferred to the papal courts in Rome.[85] Osbert is also of interest because he represents the increase in the influence of cathedral (secular)

---

[84] Before leaving this decade mention should be made of the arrival of the Gratian decretals, *Concordia discordantium cononum,* which became the authoritative source for canon law in the Middle Ages. Of Gratian little is known. The work itself is regarded as the beginning of the 'classical' period of canon law (1140–1375). For a thorough discussion see: Brundage, 1997, Supra. pp.44–69

[85] Pollock & Maitland, Supra. pp. 449–450. The case is reported in detail at Van Caenegem, R.C.(ed) *English Lawsuits from William 1 to Richard 1,* Vol. 107 (I and II), London, Selden Society, 1991 Case 520 pp. 571–578

clergy over monastics in matters spiritual.[86] The trend towards appointing secular clergy to bishoprics had been gaining momentum. By 1123 just one monk held a bishopric in England, Ernulf of Rochester (1114–1124).

As the century progressed the source of offence to England's lay population; the privilege that permitted clerics emancipation from secular justice, was in no sense ameliorated by the increased status of secular clergy. Canonical compurgation[87] was viewed as an escape from justice; impunity for crimes that rendered the layman liable to death and the cleric a meagre penance. By the middle of the 12th century each diocese held a consistory court presided over by the chancellor of the diocese (Commissary-general at Canterbury) or other official appointed by the bishop. All bishops retained the right to withdraw cases from the appointee and hear them personally if they so elected. Appeal from the consistory court lay to the provincial court of the archbishop. William I had removed ecclesiastical pleas from the secular hundred court and in addition to the consistory court archdeacons held a court. Appeal from the archdeacon's court lay to the consistory court.[88] Henry II soon recognized the tensions this preferential situation created and he embarked upon reform; the results were historic.

---

[86] E.G. Bethel, D. L., English Black Monks and Episcopal Elections in the 1120's, *The English Historical Review*, Vol. 84, No. 333 (Oct., 1969) pp. 673–698

[87] Purgation was the formal method of proof used in criminal cases heard before the spiritual courts as prescribed by a number of canon law texts including the authoritative *Decretum Gratiani*. C.f. Helmholz, Supra. p.622. He further points out that there was considerable similarity between canonical and secular juridical procedures during the 12th and 13th centuries; the use of inquests, the importance of public fame and proof by means of *purgatio*. Helmholz, Supra pp. 623–624

[88] Holdsworth, W. S. *The Ecclesiastical Courts and Their Jurisdiction-Select Essays in Anglo-American Legal History*, Vol. 2 [1907] Boston, Little Brown, 1908

# 3

# Dissention, Discord and Double Jeopardy

Henry, Duke of Normandy, Aquitaine and Count of Anjou became the unopposed king of England on 25 October 1154.[1] King Henry quickly moved towards bringing leadership and stability to government of the country. He utilized the services of a number of men who had previously worked with Stephen.[2] At the suggestion of archbishop Theobald of Canterbury (1138–1161) Thomas Becket was brought in to serve as Chancellor; keeper of the king's seal and to act as a personal confidant of the crown. Becket was often the sole witness to royal writs and charters and soon became an intimate friend and advisor to Henry. When Theobald died in April 1161 Henry announced his intention of elevating Thomas to the episcopate of Canterbury. After an initial *noli episcopari*

---

[1] Stephen I had recognized Henry as heir and *justiciar* the previous year by the treaty of Wallingford. The title *justiciar* implied that as monarch he also had control over all business of the realm, including judicial. Bury, J.B., *Cambridge Medieval History: The Contest of Empire and Papacy.* Vol. 5 Dalen, P. (ed), Cambridge, Cambridge University Press 1911 at www.cristoraul.com/ENGLISH/MedievalHistory/Cambridge. It is noted the publication of Luscombe, D., and Riley-Smith, J., (eds) *The New Cambridge Medieval History Vol. 4. C. 1024–1198 Part I and 2,* Cambridge, Cambridge University Press, 2004 and the coverage given to the Angevin empire (Part 2) as well several chapters that deal with the Church and clergy in the central Middle Ages (Part I)

[2] Robert, Earl of Leicester, Theobald Archbishop of Canterbury, Richard de Luci, Nigel Bishop of Ely

Thomas accepted. Thomas Becket now jointly held the second highest secular and the highest spiritual offices in the realm. Once consecrated Becket soon resigned his chancellorship[3] and started to attempt to secure the return of lands and rights to the diocesanal see that had been lost to Stephen.[4] On October 1, 1163 the issue of criminous clerks was discussed at length at the Council of Westminster. At this meeting Henry announced his desire for criminal clerics to appear first before the courts temporal and then be handed over to the bishop's court for trial. Crucially Henry announced that after trial and degradation the layman, as he now was, should be returned to the secular court for sentence. Becket retorted *Nec enim Deus iudicat bis in idipsum.*[5] Henry moved for papal assent to his proposals and Thomas appeared to acquiesce. With the hope of a legally binding agreement Henry summoned council to meet at Clarendon on 25th January, 1164.[6] The attending English bishops were presented with sixteen Constitutions which Henry asserted to be established customs of the realm.[7]

---

[3] He did not, however, give up his beneficed archdeaconry of Canterbury until forced to so by Henry

[4] Bury, J.B., *Cambridge Medieval History: The Contest of Empire and Papacy*. Vol. 5 (Dalen, P. ed), Cambridge, Cambridge University Press 1911 and Barlow, F., *Thomas Becket*, Berkeley, University of California Press, 1990. P. 49

[5] 'God will not judge a man twice for the same offence'

[6] There are a number of erroneous references to the *Assize of Clarendon* and the *Constitutions of Clarendon* as being the same event. The *Constitutions of Clarendon* took place in 1164 and is the event which stimulated the rift between Henry and Thomas and Becket's subsequent martyrdom. It is this document that contains numerous references to the relationship between criminous clerics and the crown and rights of appeal. The *Assize of Clarendon* occurred in 1166. It contains 22 paragraphs none of which relate to benefit of clergy

[7] Gabel. L. *Benefit of Clergy in England in the Later Middle Ages*, New York, Octagon Press, 1969 (reprinted) p. 19 and https://openlibrary.org/books/OL23378300M/A_history_of_crime_in_England Pollock, F., and Maitland, F.W., *The History of English Law Before the Time of Edward I, (2nd Edition)* Volume I. Cambridge, Cambridge University Press 1968pp. 447–449

The first of these gave the king authority to have matters of disputed advowson and church land titles to be adjudicated before the courts temporal. The best known of these disputes involved an inter-church dispute, case 360, between the abbot of Battle and the bishop of Chichester that was adjudicated at the courts temporal before the king. During the proceedings Henry was so infuriated by the bishop he reminded him personally of his fealty and binding oath to his lord king. The bishop procured a letter from Rome behind Henry's back. Theobald attempted to mediate the worsening situation but the king refused his intervention. The bishop rescinded and publically denounced his claim before the king. A victory for Henry in the ongoing battle for fealty over the pope. This event is what led, in chief, to article 8 of the *Constitutions of Clarendon*.[8]

In recognition of the tensions that existed between the courts spiritual and secular, Henry's opening statement to the Constitutions proclaimed 'And on account of the dissensions and discords which had arisen between the clergy and the Justices of the lord king, and the barons of the kingdom concerning the customs and dignities, this inquest was made in the presence of the archbishops and bishops, and clergy and counts, and barons and chiefs of the kingdom.'[9] The third, fourth and eighth paragraphs proved to be contentious: Clerks charged and accused of anything shall appear before the king's justices and if it is determined he should then respond before the bishop's court upon having done so "If the

[8] Van Caenegem, R.C.(ed) *English Lawsuits from William 1 to Richard 1*, Vol. 107 (I and II), London, Selden Society, 1991

[9] Henderson, E. F., *Select Historical Documents of the Middle Ages*, London, George Bell & Sons, 1896 Constitutions of Clarendon (114) p. 11–12

clerk shall be convicted, or shall confess, the Church ought not to protect him further'. Paragraph four stated that it was not lawful for archbishops or bishops to leave the kingdom without permission of the king. This linked to paragraph eight which stated that 'Concerning appeals...if the archbishop shall fail to render justice, they must come finally to the lord king'. *De facto* appeals would not proceed to Rome without 'consent of the lord king'.

Henry held the belief that Becket would sign the Constitutions; he refused. The subsequent and well-rehearsed argument between two powerful men is pivotal in the history of benefit of clergy. Henry was tired of the flagrant abuses that clericus permitted. In particular, the inability of the Church to effectively punish criminals and the commonly held view that members of the clergy, however loosely defined, were immune from the secular law, regardless of the crime committed. Thomas appears to have taken a position from which he could not back down; a trial before the king's court and a second trial before the bishop's court followed by returning a criminous clerk to the king's court after degradation was double jeopardy.[10] In Henry's view the secular proceeding was not a trial *per se* but rather more a venue to establish jurisdiction. The proceedings at the courts spiritual were a trial from which the convicted felon was now, as a layman, sentenced before the courts secular.

Papal reaction to the initial proposal at Westminster had been favorable. Pope Alexander III (1159–1181) was in exile from

---

[10] Paragraph three of the Constitutions held that a representative of the king would be present at the bishop's court to observe the proceedings and claim the degraded clerk for punishment

Rome and no doubt was aware that offending Henry could further destabilize his own tenuous position. As the divide between Henry and Becket grew the pope remained largely silent; caught in an invidious situation Alexander needed Henry's support and he needed to support the episcopate. The king pursued Becket with fervor and summoned him to appear in answer to a charge of failing to discharge his court Christian in a matter where Becket had presided over a land ownership dispute.[11] Becket failed to appear and was held in contempt. On November 2, 1164 Becket fled the country as a fugitive. Henry responded by exiling Becket's family and relatives and seizing his estates. By 1166 Alexander III was back in Rome and ready to lend more support to Becket. A number of excommunications followed: John of Oxford, Richard of Ilchester, Richard de Luci, Jocelin de Balliol followed by Ranulf de Broc, Hugh de St Clare and Thomas fitz Bernard. All significant in the support of the Constitutions and seizure of Becket's estates.[12] But these moves had little impact upon Henry who continued to ignore the diocesanal authority of Becket. When reconciliation between the two men was agreed a meeting was set for 22nd July, 1170 at Fréteval, France. The adversaries met but Henry refused to give Thomas the significant kiss of peace; little had changed except Thomas was now permitted to return to England and assume his diaconate responsibilities. Becket arrived back in England on December 1st 1170. He was murdered inside Canterbury cathedral during the early evening of December 29th the same year. Henry was

---

[11] See: Van Caenegem, R.C., (ed) *English Lawsuits from William I to Richard I*, Vol. 107 (I and II) London, Selden Society, 1991. Case 420. p. 423

[12] Duggan, C., Richard of Ilchester, Royal Servant and Bishop, *Transactions of the Royal Historical Society*, Vol. 16 (Dec., 1966) pp. 1–21 and Knowles, D., *The Episcopal Colleagues of Archbishop Thomas Becket*, New York, Cambridge University Press, 1951

informed of the murder on 1st January 1171. He was reportedly deeply moved by the death of his close friend and spent three days in solitude. The pope had previously sanctioned an interdict on Henry's continental lands if Becket were arrested. His murder clearly violated this provision. But England's bishops refused to implement the papal mandate. Henry was sanctioned personally (but only mildly) he was forbidden from entering a church.

Discord between Rome and England continued throughout the first four months of 1171. So too did the status of Becket as mourners across the country started to report witnessing miracles. The first took place in Sussex just three days after Becket's death.[13] By Easter 1170 'miracles came in crowds'.[14] In April 1172 Henry II left Ireland to appear before the papal legates at Avranches[15] and receive pontifical judgment for his involvement in the murder of Becket. He received absolution. On return to England the king was required to attend Canterbury cathedral and lay prostrate before the monks who would flog him. This visually powerful sign that earthly princes were subservient to heavenly kings took place on July

[13] Miraculous intervention was a common event during the Middle Ages E.g. Godric is consulted about an upcoming judicial battle, Case 412, St. Thomas Becket intervenes in Case 463 and again in case 502. Case 503 is interesting as it involved unclergyable forest law offences, presumably even after death St. Thomas Becket did his utmost to defeat Henry's wishes and apply benefit of clergy as broadly as possible. Bury, Supra

[14] Bury, Supra. Divine intervention is well recorded throughout the Middle Ages and even forms the basis of official court documents e.g. Case 403. and Van Caenegem, Supra. A case of trial by judicial duel and the prophetic role played by St. Godric

[15] Thorne, S.E. The Assize "Utrum" and Canon Law in England, *Columbia Law Review*, Vol. 33. No. 3 (Mar., 1933) pp. 428–436 note 21 states that Henry's reconciliation required two concessions. Thorne points out that the English bishops were in general ignorant of the punishments they were required to enforce on Henry which resulted in a mass of excommunications between the English episcopate and Rome

12th 1174. In addition to his public penance Henry also vowed to undertake a crusade[16] and he pardoned those associates of Becket's he had exiled. In real terms this was a light sentence.[17] The true cost to Henry was that he had to submit all matters pertaining to criminous clerics to the authority of the Christian courts. Subsequently he did attempt to restrict this to those holding higher orders only; subdeacon and above and thereby exclude acolytes, porters, lectors, exorcists, cantors, curates, gravediggers and vicars.[18] In reality Henry's position was not as extreme as Becket wanted to portray. Nor was the distance between England's competing legal systems.

The implications of the Clarendon[19] debacle have been subject to much discussion in subsequent centuries. It is generally accepted that Henry did not intend an outright abolition of *privilegium fori* but more that he wanted to rein-in clerical abuse and have criminous clerks returned to the *curia regis* for punishment. Whether his reliance on cotumal precedent would have sustained judicial inquiry is a moot point. What William's *Ordinance* and Stephen's *Oxford Charter* provided Henry with was the basis upon which he could build the *Constitutions* and submit the English clergy to accept

---

[16] Which he never did. He built three monasteries instead

[17] And seemed to make little impact upon Henry's continuing efforts to curb the excesses of the Church e.g. 1176 *Assize of Northampton* c.45 Henry managed to provide immunity from secular prosecution to 'all punishable acts except those against forest laws and non-fulfillment of feudal obligations'. And cited in Baker, Supra. p. 104

[18] Per 1176 Assize of Northampton at c. 45. And for a discussion of the seven orders: Firth, C.B. Benefit of Clergy in the Time of Edward IV, *The English Historical Review*, Vol. 32, No. 126 (Apr., 1917), pp. 175–191, p.180 citing British Museum Add. MS. 12195. f. 74

[19] http://avalon.law.yale.edu/medieval/assizecl.asp and Helmholz, R.H. The Early History of the Grand Jury and the Canon Law, 50 *University of Chicago Law Review* 613 (1983) pp. 613–627

temporal authority over a range of matters previously and predominantly within the domain of the church.[20]

A number of cases from throughout Henry's reign demonstrate the sometimes fractious and sometimes amicable bipartisan relationship with the courts spiritual and the king as lay judges and bishops jointly administered justice across the realm. Evidence of these endeavors as well as some attempts to gain jurisdictional traction can be seen in the cases that follow below.[21]

Case 371 involved a rural dean who failed to exculpate himself before the king's court and the temporal court consented to the matter being dealt with by the bishop even though the crime transgressed a royal edict. At trial Richard de Lucy (Luci) asked "And what judgment will you give as far as the lord king is concerned, against whose constitution this man acted?" "Nothing", said John, "since he is a cleric". Then, said Richard, "I shall not party to this sentence". In turn the king declared the ecclesiastical sentence to be false and demanded the matter be returned to his court.[22] Case 409 is an example of the growing tension between Henry and Becket. Becket had been ordained priest on June 2, 1162 and the following day consecrated as archbishop of Canterbury. It therefore probably came as a surprise to Henry that Becket should so

[20] Thorne, S.E., The Assize "Utrum" and Canon Law in England, *Columbia Law Review*, Vol. 33, No. 3 (Mar., 1933) pp. 428–436

[21] The cases cited span the period after the *Constitutions of Clarendon 1164* until the end of Henry II reign in 1189

[22] This did not happen as Henry was informed of his brother Geoffrey's death in France and left England before the matter was resolved. Case 383 is another example of Henry claiming jurisdiction over the Church when he issued a writ to the bishop of Norwich requiring the bishop to allow an advowson of the Church at Repps to go to abbot William of St. Benets, Hulme

quickly (and forcefully) embrace his ecclesiastical office given the short time that he had been in holy orders. In this example Henry informed Becket that he wanted a cleric, who had seduced a girl and killed her father, to be tried before the king's justices. Becket, to the clear annoyance of the king, refused. This was followed in Case 410 when Henry demanded a cleric accused of theft; a silver chalice from the church of St. Mary-le-Bow, London, appear before the lay justices. Again Becket refused and proceeded to have the cleric appear at the courts Christian where he was degraded and branded.[23] The case note contains the commentary that 'Another [estrangement] occurred because of a cleric...Apparently the branding was only administered as an appeasement to the king also'.[24]

The prosecution of Philip de Broi for murder was particularly irksome to Henry. The notation to Case 411 starts, 'Not long afterwards another violent quarrel broke out between [Henry II and Thomas Becket]...'[25] De Broi was canon of St. Paul's, Bedford and was alleged to have murdered a knight. He had claimed his clergy and successfully purged himself before his bishop.[26] Simon fitz Peter, a secular judge of the region, was outraged at the outcome and sought to have the matter reopened with a view to prosecuting de Broi before the secular court. De Broi refused to stand trial on the basis that he was

---

[23] This is one of just two examples that I have found of clerical branding. Infra

[24] Van Caenegem, R.C.(ed) *English Lawsuits from William 1 to Richard 1*, Vol. 107 (I and II), London, Selden Society, 1991. p. 405 Case 410

[25] Van Caenegem, Supra. p. 405. Case 411

[26] This case may be linked to the change in demographics of the Priory at Newnham for around this period the former monastery became a secular priory with financial support for the new building coming from Simon de Beauchamp about 1166. The de Broi case attracted such attention that very soon after the disgraced canon was relieved of his prebend the monks left and the new building, and name, began. www.British-History.ac.uk

not answerable to the secular courts and secondly, the matter had been adjudicated. Fitz Peter reported the incident to the king who himself became furious, 'and swearing awfully by God's eyes as was his custom, maintained that it was as if abuse which Philip heaped upon his knight had been heaped upon himself'.[27] Henry confirmed that de Broi should answer before a secular court. Becket pronounced 'this will certainly not be done, for a layman cannot be judges of clerics'.[28] However, he did permit a meeting of bishops and lay justices at Canterbury. At this hearing it was held that de Broi should relinquish his prebend for two years and that although this amounted to punishment more than he deserved it was imposed because of the king's peace and honor. The king responded, 'By God's eyes, you are going to confirm to me under oath that you have given a just judgment and have not spared this man because he is a cleric'.[29]

In case 413[30] we see a stern rebuke from Gilbert Foliot, Bishop of Hereford (1148–1163) to Elias de Say, Lord of Clun and king's justice, for hearing a case against a priest and dean known as William. Foliot states, '...but I am much more astounded to hear that you subject to the judgment of your court a priest of ours and a dean and that you claim against the Church this power which kings and emperors, in spite of much sweat and labour, have not been able to obtain against her until this day'. He continues, 'we therefore order you,

---

[27] Ibid. p. 406 Case 411

[28] Ibid. p. 406 Case 411. In the narrative of Ralph de Dicero *Imagines Historiarum* p. 410 he adds that de Broi was also banished from the kingdom for two years. This is not substantiated elsewhere

[29] Ibid. p. 407 Case 411

[30] This is one example among six involving criminous clerks that neither Henry nor Becket were directly involved in

dearest, that you shall let us judge our clerics'. Foliot concludes by telling Lord Clun that if he does not comply the bishop will pronounce sentence against him and his goods.[31] Quarrelling between the clergy and laity is the issue in case 415; William, earl of Arundel sent a number of his representatives to the abbey of Wymondham to secure ownership rights that he disputed. Ralph de Neurs, a monk, who was himself not adverse to violence, was so enraged a brawl ensued between the earl's men and some monks.[32] Abbot Robert was unable to resolve the issue and took it up with the founder's family, William d'Aubigny. D'Aubigny refused to attend the matter and Becket stepped in, threatened d'Aubigny with excommunication and assumed jurisdiction. It transpired abbot Robert was unable to show full ownership title but with due influence upon the parties from both ecclesiastical and royal interests, the earl ceded his claim and turned to abbot Robert with the comment, 'By the lance of God, your name will henceforth be changed and you will be called "Robert Matefelone', taking and keeping your name from your accomplishment'.[33]

A rare example of a cleric failing his purgatory oath appears in case 416. A priest in the diocese of Jocelin, Bishop of Salisbury (1142–1184) was accused of manslaughter and arrested; he claimed his clergy. Before the bishop he sought purgation and failed. Jocelin wrote to Becket for advice on sentencing (perhaps itself a clear indication of how rarely a priest failed his purgation). Becket ordered deprivation of every ecclesiastical benefice

[31] Van Caenegem, Supra. p. 405. Case 413

[32] Doors were broken, locks forced and fences attacked by representatives from both sides. Ibid. Case 415. p. 415

[33] Ibid Case 415. p. 419. The contemporary translation being that Robert was a 'make felon' i.e. one who commits felonies

and the offender to be held in monastic solitary confinement for life.[34] In 1163 Becket degraded a criminous clerk and then required he abjure the realm. Henry was infuriated on the basis that exile was not punishment at all and anyway that permission to abjure was a royal privilege not ecclesiastic. Becket responded he represented God who was above all kings.[35] Case 419 is another example of the declining relationship between Henry and Becket and the core issue between them: jurisdiction over criminous clerks. The case starts with the note that 'as the king molested the Church and ecclesiastical men even more vehemently than usual and was resisted constantly by the archbishop'.[36] Apparently a group of clerics was arrested for a number of crimes including murder and theft. Becket insisted they all appear before the courts Christian to which, with considerable reluctance, Henry agreed and handed them over on condition that once condemned and degraded they would be returned to his justices for sentence. Becket maintained that they were not to be punished twice and degradation would be sufficient. He did however introduce a new element into the discussion to the effect that should the clerics commit further crimes 'It would be no concern of his by what judgment they were condemned'.[37]

In case 432 king Henry takes jurisdiction in accordance with his interpretation of *Clarendon* when by way of an exception and temporary measure (and with the approval of the bishop of Durham) royal justices exercised jurisdiction over a particular group of thieves, and robbers and murderers, 'not that

---

[34] Ibid Case 416. pp. 419–420

[35] Poole, A.L. 'Outlawry as Punishment of Criminous Clerks' *in Historical Essays in Honour of James Tait*, (eds. Edwards, J.G., Galbraith, V.H., Jacob, E. F.) Manchester, 1933 at p. 239

[36] Van Caenegem, Supra. p. 422. Case 419

[37] Ibid Case 419 p. 423

I want this to be turned into a custom in my time or that of my heirs'.[38] In case 449 Gilbert Foliot, now Bishop of London (translated 1163–1187) sent a rebuking letter to Robert, earl of Leicester (as he had previously to Lord Clun) for assuming temporal jurisdiction over the canon of St. Paul's, London.[39] Foliot concludes his remonstration with the words, 'We wish that you are well in the Lord and that to Caesar will be rendered what is his, so that you will also render to God what is God's'.[40] Young Henry, crown-prince, son of Henry II[41] had his first encounter with benefit of clergy in Poitiers, France when Adam, deacon and vice-chancellor, appeared before him charged with treason. Adam had been part of the group that sided with the young king to overthrow his father. Adam was charged with treason (executable and non-clergyable). He was tried before the Young Henry and permitted to claim his clergy. His life was spared and he was handed to the bishop's court. Presumably the bishops court felt that Adam needed to be made an example of. He was found guilty and sentenced to be whipped (naked) in the squares and streets of every French village and town between Poitiers and his final destination, prison at Argentan, Normandy.[42]

---

[38] Van Caenegem, Supra. p. 405. Case 432. p. 466

[39] This case also appears in Duggan, Supra. p. 12. Richard of Ilchester is further admonished by Foliot, bishop of London, at Duggan, Supra. pp. 14–15 Ilchester rose to the See of influential Winchester after Beckets death. It would not have occurred during Beckets lifetime as although a bishop Ilchester was viewed as a strong supporter of the king and endorsed the contentious contents of Clarendon. See also Brooke, Z.N., *The English Church and the Papacy from the Conquest to the reign of John,* Cambridge, Cambridge University Press, 1989

[40] Ibid Case 449 p. 485 At note 2 it is pointed out that Leicester was probably acting as royal *justiciar* in the absence of Henry II who was at the time in France

[41] Crowned June 1170 while Henry II was still alive. Henry the Younger died in 1183

[42] Van Caenegem, Supra Case 490 pp. 534–535

The high level of revulsion at the murder of Becket was no doubt a contributory factor in the speedy canonization of the former archbishop.[43] The sheer volume of pilgrimages to Canterbury itself set an English precedent; a concession from Henry was inevitable so that some normality could return to relations between the English king and Latin Christendom.[44] Quite why the issue of criminous clerks took on such major proportions for Becket will remain unclear. He embraced the life of a priest with vigor right from ordination; he wore sackcloth under his bishop's attire, attended mass daily and resigned his secular office with haste. Perhaps Thomas experienced emotional evangelism, perhaps entrenchment for a cause, perhaps he backed himself into a corner with Henry and martyrdom was a release (if not relief). Overall martyr St. Thomas achieved more by his death than he had in his lifetime for it was Henry, not Thomas, that made the lasting impact upon the establishment of an English criminal justice system, *regnum* and *sacerdotium*.[45] The *Constitutions* were a strong statement from a strong monarch; not a fatal blunder. They were an attempt to exert authority over a legal excuse that was crashing into disrepute.[46] For the time being religious authorities would maintain their dominance over most aspects of human conduct (birth, marriage and

---

[43] A mere two years after his death to full sainthood

[44] In 1172 Henry formally renounced his intention to force clerics to answer to secular courts for felonies. C.f. Berman, H.J., *Law and Revolution*, Cambridge, Mass, Harvard University Press, 1983 p.263

[45] For commentary upon some of the many impacts made by Henry II, Helmholz, R.H., The Early History of the Grand Jury and the Canon Law, *The University of Chicago Law Review*, Vol. 50, No. 2, Fiftieth Anniversary Issue (Spring, 1993) pp. 613–627

[46] Brooke, Supra. at p. 206 'On the other hand, I think that Henry II committed a fatal blunder in publishing the Constitutions, which was a novelty'

death) but the civil courts had now been given the tools to establish their right to define the boundaries of canon law.[47] As a result of what Henry II developed secular concessions to the courts Christian would become a vestige of the past in English criminal law and benefit of clergy would become a mitigatory plea for clerics and laity alike rather than a legal sanctuary for tonsured outlaws. This is not to say that the Church was one entity and the secularization of benefit of clergy would apply uniformly. The structure of the medieval church was fragmentary and highly localized. Some parishes and diocese were extremely wealthy and others very poor. In terms of canon law there were a number of unifying features though such as authority to hear matters pertaining to established ecclesiastic law and marriage, sex and family and prominently, of course, the protections afforded to clerics accused of committing a felony.[48]

Henry II remained respectful of the Church throughout his life. He consistently sent matters from his *curia* to the bishops when it was a matter of established canonical jurisdiction. Without exception all matters of bastardy and marriage appeared before the bishop's court in Henry's reign[49] and the *Constitutions of Clarendon* made clear and explicit reference to the holy mother Church.[50] The great battle between Henry

---

[47] E.g. until 1215 on matters of consanguinity canon law decreed that marriage within seven degrees of kinship was forbidden. This rule was modified by the 4th Lateran Council C.f. Brundage, J.A., *Medieval Canon Law,* London, Longman, 199. pp. 70–91

[48] Brundage, 1997, Supra, p. 86

[49] Van Caenegem, Supra. Vols. I and II

[50] Henderson, Supra. p. 16 'There are, moreover, many other great customs and dignities of the holy mother church…And may they be preserved to the holy church, and to the lord king, and to his heirs, and to the barons of the kingdom, and may they be inviolably observed forever'. *Constitutions of Clarendon*

and Becket[51] represented more than a dispute between two large egos; it represented the power struggle that was taking place between the Church and State on a platform that traversed all of medieval Europe. In fewer than fifty years pope Innocent III would decree that the clergy shall not participate in any judicial proceedings that caused the spilling of blood. He would, in effect, create the pivotal division between English common law and continental European civil law that remain today.

Over the period from the 5th through to the 13th century England transitioned from tribalism through feudalism to the early years of being a nation state.[52] As the authority of kings evolved and they focused upon the interests of the civil estate so too the bishop of Rome and his episcopate nurtured and grew the gravitas of the Church and its sphere of influence over temporal and dogmatic interests. What emerged was a dual legal system of overlapping canon and secular law where the ambiguous quality of each system would be tested time and again. William I had made significant headway in separating conflicting jurisdictions with the *Ordinance*.[53] Under Henry England experienced

---

[51] Of the many works written about this issue and the life of Becket, including those cited, see : Duggan, C., 'The Becket Dispute and the Criminous Clerks', *Bulletin of the Institute of Historical Research*, Vol. 65 (1962) pp. 1–28, Staunton, M., *Thomas Becket and His Biographers*, Woodbridge, Suffolk, Boydell and Brewer, 2006, Barlow, F., *Thomas Becket*, Berkeley, University of California Press, 1990 and Davis, H.W. C., *England Under the Normans and Angevins* 1066–1272, New York, Putnam, 1905 and Brundage, 1997, Supra. pp. 70–97

[52] See Jeffrey, C.R., The Development of Crime in Early English Society, *Journal of Criminal Law and Criminology*, Vol. 47, Issue 6, 1957 pp. 647–666. p. 665

[53] Lea, H.C., *Studies in Church History*, London, Sampson Low & Marston, 1869.pp. 180–183. Walker, C.H. The Date of the Conqueror's Ordinance Separating the Ecclesiastical and Lay Courts, *The English Historical Review*, Vol. 39, No. 155 (Jul., 1924) pp. 399–400

the establishment of a centralized secular judicial system that was no longer reliant upon feudal manors. Law became common to all Englishmen as custom gave way to statute. For now the Church retained control over morality, souls and felonious clerics, even those who conspired to murder their own (Jocelin, Bishop of Salisbury famously cleared himself of alleged complicity in the murder of Becket by claiming his clergy).[54]

But a clear division of legal systems, temporal and Christian, was not possible. They were not separate of each other; the Church did not operate outside of secular life but rather more as an integral part of it. Clergymen lived in the secular world; they contracted with it, bargained with it and committed crimes with it. Of course many aspects of medieval life touched both the laws of the Church and of the state; concomitantly not in isolation. However, the clergy of the 12th century was indeed privileged; they had absolute immunity from trial where they might themselves have their own blood spilled. They were soon to be barred from engagement in any secular criminal processes that might cause the spilling of blood of another and they could exempt themselves if the cause of the trial was the establishment of sins against God; in these matters torture, blood-letting, mutilations and excruciating death were acceptable procedures before the secular courts. It is not surprising therefore that criminals bent on avoiding temporal liability flocked to the Church for protections under the guise of being clerks. The succeeding two centuries were

---

[54] Pollock and Maitland, Vol. I, Supra. p. 443 and Osbert, archdeacon of Richmond who allegedly poisoned his archbishop William of York, Supra and Van Caenegem, R.C.(ed) *English Lawsuits from William I to Richard I*, Vol. 107 (I and II), London, Selden Society, 1991 Case 520 pp. 571–578

testimony to the excessive use and abuse of this quirk of legal history known as benefit of clergy as the term itself shifted from meaning those in Holy Orders to all who were literate; even bastards, blind men and gangs of robber clerics.[55] It is the history of the growth and transition of the clerical exemption throughout the thirteenth and fourteenth centuries that is discussed next.

[55] See: Blackstone, W., *Commentaries on the Laws of England A Facsimile of the First Edition of 1765–1769 Volume IV of Public Wrongs (1789)*, Chicago, The University of Chicago Press, 1979. Chapter 28 pp. 358–367

# 4

# The Prostitution of Oaths, Self-Slaughter and Judgments of Blood

Throughout the thirteenth century the number of serious crimes being committed in England increased. In response to the problem the Church and the crown made specific efforts to bring good order back into society. For the most part the courts spiritual and secular disagreed on how best to achieve this and in doing so criminal offending by laymen and those who could claim the title clergy grew further. Amongst legitimate society contempt and disapproval for the immunities that the clergy had access to increased also and in some notable instances the local population took extreme measures against murderous clergy and attempted to conduct lynchings, kidnappings (from churches where the clergy had taken sanctuary) and in a few cases they even stormed prisons as the laity sought to bring clerics to justice. The first quarter of the century also represented the zenith of pontifical power. It is when Innocent III held the famous 4$^{th}$ Lateran Council and the entire clergy of Christendom were banned from involvement in ordeals and criminal sanctions that resulted in the spilling of a convicted person's blood. The translation of his intentions in England was largely undertaken by the newly formed mendicant orders.

The Dominicans arrived in 1221 and became a major force in the life of Oxford, the Franciscans landed in 1224 and were more scattered across the country. Generally, the friars made a significant impact on English parish life, licit and illicit. The word parliament had not entered the English lexicon when Innocent made his proclamations but soon would. In doing so it represented another key stage in the slow but meaningful progression from a country of lords and established wealthy families to a unified nation state under the leadership of one monarch. For the English Church this represented the acquiescence of legal authority over a number of criminal actions and the eventual acceptance of the domination of the state over church. One manifestation of greater secularization was the transition from tonsure and garb to the Reading Test. The effect being that even more borderline (quasi) clergy claimed their privilege as they learnt to limp through the recitation of a standard religious work, psalm 51. It is also the time when offences began to be categorized as 'clergyable' or 'unclergyable' by secular lawmakers and some felonies, even when committed by clerics, could no longer attract immunity from prosecution before the king's justices. As the century progressed there was clear evidence of clergy claimants starting to consider their jurisdictional options more carefully; claiming benefit of clergy, sanctuary, abjuration and outlawry. The thirteenth century concluded with England at war with France and Scotland and Edward I's futile attempt to tax the clergy resulting in *Clericis laicos*.

Clerical privileges and the abuse of them had been the subject of tensions between the Church and England's monarchy since the Thomas Becket affair. Some degree of calm was achieved towards the close of the of the twelfth century by

Richard I (1189–1199) the warrior king.[1] He demonstrated his support for the priestly classes by endorsing the continuation of the clericus plea and the use of the legal process of compurgation. But compurgation was a process full of bias and it favored the tonsured classes at the expense of the laity. When a compurgator sided with a cleric who was found guilty the compurgator suffered no penalty. However, when an unfortunate layman swore his non-cleric countryman was innocent and this was found not to be the case, the secular compurgator suffered loss of limb. By 1300 this archaic method of proof had lost currency in France in exchange for torture. The Common Law never favored torture and the compurgatory oath remained on the statute book until 1833.[2] Its continued support by Richard must have done little to convince the common man that the law was applied equally throughout the realm and it no doubt added to the growing abhorrence for all clerical immunities that would mature further over the next hundred years.

Within England's changing legal landscape there was confusion about how and when the secular courts should determine clerical status. Was the benefit plea to be entered at

---

[1] He achieved the sobriquet 'Lionheart' as a young prince due to his courage and military ability. For a recent discovery piece with regard to the heart of the Lionheart see: http://www.scientificamerican.com/article.cfm?id=forensic-exam-of-king-richard-the-lionheart-reveals-embalming-practices

[2] 3 and 4. Will IV, C. 42, sec.13 and see: Committee of the Association of American Law Schools, Select Essays in Anglo-American Legal History, by various authors, compiled and edited by a committee of the Association of American Law Schools, in three volumes (Boston: Little, Brown, and Company, 1908). Vol. 2. Chapter: PART III. PROCEDURE Accessed from http://oll.libertyfund.org/title/2082/158495. For numerous examples of the range and scope of canonical abuse see: Hovvland, A. C., (ed) *Ordeals, Compurgation, Excommunication and Interdict*, Philadelphia, University of Pennsylvania Press http://archive.org/stream/ordealscompurgat0404howl/ordealscompurgat0404howl_djvu.txt

the commencement of temporal proceedings? If so it averted a trial and required immediate transfer of the suspect to the bishop's envoy, or did the benefit occur at the conclusion of the secular hearing, when guilt had been determined, but prior to sentence? Apparently over the breadth of the thirteenth century both procedural conditions were accommodated and clearly some defendants put themselves 'upon the country' and had their case heard before their lay peers and if found guilty then assumed the fallback position of claiming clergy and purging themselves before their clerical peers. This extraordinary situation was itself in some flux however as the method of establishing a genuine cleric moved from *could read* to *must read*.[3] Associated with this legal obtuseness was the manner in which the clerk was handed to the ordinary; as *clericus convictus* or *non convictus*. If a clerk was released to the bishop before a trial had taken place he was *non convictus* and the bishop was required to keep his clerk until the secular hearing upon which he would be delivered, tried and then returned to the bishop. His status upon return to the bishop was not formalized under statute law until the reign of Edward III[4] nevertheless prior to this it was customary for a cleric who had been found guilty of a heinous crime by the courts temporal to be released back to the bishop as *absque purgatione;* without the option of purgation. Subsequent convictions of the same defendant also rendered him *absque purgatione*. If a clerk confessed to the facts before the courts temporal he could

---

[3] Gabel. L. *Benefit of Clergy in England in the Later Middle Ages*, New York, Octagon Press, 1969 (reprinted) cites a number of examples of this situation and the testing of literal competency E.g. John, chaplain of Kynton. He was found guilty of murder by the jury and then handed to the ordinary. pp. 32–33 and pp. 46–47

[4] 25. Edw. 3. St. 3. C. 4. The statute *Pro Clero*, infra

not then deny the crime before his bishop. What followed in the absence of a purgation hearing was possible degradation and sentence (penance). In this case a clerk was not claimed by the ordinary he was delivered to him by the secular judges. If claimed or 'demanded' by the bishop the clerk could swear his innocence, an event Blackstone viewed as 'This scandalous prostitution of oaths and the forms of justice in the almost constant acquittal of felonious clerks by purgation'.[5] If he failed purgation the clerk was deemed to be corrigible (a first time offender) or incorrigible, a recidivist.[6] The final years of Richard's reign contain many examples of clerical abuse and complicity of the higher orders as they sought to retain exclusive authority over a number of criminal matters.[7] In 1195[8] a chaplain ordained by the bishop of Coventry was indicted for murder. Curiously the priest was apparently ordained after his arrest which implies the bishop knowingly claimed a layman as clergy and then altered his status to ensure the man could not be returned to the king's justices. If this is the case

---

[5] Blackstone, W., *Commentaries on the Laws of England: A Facsimile of the First Edition of 1765–1769*. Vol. 4. p. 362

[6] See further Rex v Dwyer. *The English Reports* Vol. 25. p. 188. Gabel, Supra. p. 60 and note.110 cites an interesting example where a clerk dies in the bishop's prison before purgation and questions who then gets the goods and chattels, the crown or the bishop

[7] One of his first acts was *Laws of Richard I.* (Coeur de lion) *Concerning Crusaders Who Were To Go To Sea. 1189 A.D. Roger of Hoveden. III. p. 36 Rolls Series;* 'Whoever slays a man on shipboard shall be bound to the dead man and thrown into the sea. But if he shall slay him on land, he shall be bound to the dead man and buried in the earth…A robber, moreover, convicted of theft, shall be shorn like a hired fighter, and boiling tar shall be poured over his head, and feathers from a cushion shall be shaken out over his head, so that he may be publicly known; and at the first land where the ships pull in he shall be cast on shore'

[8] He was released from custody of Duke Leopold upon payment of 100,000 marks, a huge sum that represented twice the gross domestic product of England at the time. Richard returned to England late February after two years of imprisonment and ransom negotiations. C.f. *Three Rolls of the Kings Court in the Reign of Richard the First A.D. 1194–1195*, xxii-xxiii

it is perhaps the only example of such criminal complicity by an English bishop recorded throughout the strange lifetime of *privilegium fori*.[9]

King John (1199–1216) was also not averse to personal involvement in the ordination of criminals. He permitted Robert of Rushock, a murder suspect, to take holy orders and enter a monastery in Worcester before conviction so that once at trial he could secure his clergy.[10] Rushock and his wife Alice were both permitted to 'self-slaughter' meaning to enter a monastery for life. The Rolls do not say whether or not Alice accepted this opportunity. Robert did and his estate escheated to the crown. He died as a monk. John's indifference towards establishing continuity in matters involving the clergy was further demonstrated when he provided amnesty to a layman who killed a priest and then in 1209 (during the Oxford University debacle) he imprisoned the archdeacon of Richmond and Geoffrey of Nantwich.[11] The eventual

---

[9] *Three Rolls of the Kings Court* (Pipe Roll Soc., xiv) p.2. http://archive.org/stream/piperollsociety33pipeuoft/piperollsociety33pipeuoft_djvu.txt C.f. Cheney, C.R. The Punishment of Felonous Clerks, *The English Historical Review*, Vol. 51, No. 202 (Apr., 1936), pp. 215–236. p. 227. Note that the spelling of felonous also exists as felonious. The latter is employed throughout. It is most likely this event occurred in 1195 as the work of Hugh Nonant, bishop of Coventry (1195–1198) who inveighed in against the monks of the cathedral priory, *'Monachi ad diabolos'* and installed secular clergy. A man of distinctly political rather than spiritual objectives Nonant was reportedly refused absolution on his deathbed due to the number of crimes committed by him.

[10] *Rolls of Justices in Eyre for Lincolnshire (1218–1219) and Worcestershire (1221)* (Selden Society Publications) pp. 558–9. No. 1141 also cited in Cheney, Supra. pp. 227–228

[11] Cheney, C.R., *The Papacy and England 12th-14th Centuries*, London, Variorum Reprints, 1982 pp. 300–303. For further reading about the creation of the second university, Cambridge see: Zutshi, P., The Dispersal of Scholars from Oxford and the Beginnings of a University at Cambridge: A Study of the Sources, *English Historical Review*, Vol. 127. N. 528 (2012) pp. 1041–1062

resolution of the latter was that: any clerk arrested by the town (Oxford) authorities would be immediately handed over to the bishop of Lincoln, the rents of lodgings for ten years would be held at half what they had been prior to the hangings and those citizens who had been involved in the hangings were to go to their graves barefoot and unbelted, without caps or cloaks. The city of Oxford continues to pay (in perpetuity) fifty two shillings per annum to the university for the benefit of poor scholars and it provides dinner for one hundred poor scholars each year.[12] Throughout his reign John attempted in vain to exert great authority over the secular legal system; he did achieve some success in centralizing and expanding the remit of the *curia regis* and written records of court proceedings increased under him as well.[13] He was less successful in is relationships with Rome. In 1209 he became the second English king, Harold II (1066) was the first, to be excommunicated after he refused to accept the appointment of Stephen Langton to the vacant archbishopric of Canterbury. In 1214 John paid homage to Innocent, the interdict was lifted and John was absolved.[14]

During the early part of the thirteenth century about 2 percent of the English population was eligible to claim some form of

---

[12] The annual dinner takes place on December 6th each year as this is believed to be the anniversary of the day of the hangings. http://news.bbc.co.uk/local/oxford/low/people_and_places/history/newsid_8405000/8405640.stm

[13] In no small part due the influence of Hubert Walter who had already served as chief justiciar under Richard I. Walter went on to serve as Lord Chancellor (1199–1205) and jointly archbishop of Canterbury (1193–1205) under King John. C.f. Adams, N., and Donahue, C., *Select Cases from the Ecclesiastical Courts of the Province of Canterbury, c. 1200–1301*, London, Selden Society, 1981. Vol. 95

[14] Cheney, C.R., *The Papacy and England 12th-14th Centuries*, London, Variorum Reprints, 1982. Chap. IX. 'King John and the Papal Interdict'

clerical status.[15] Of these it has been estimated that at least 1000 each year escaped secular justice by use of the clergy plea.[16] Accurate numbers of clergy vary but there were at least 9,500 parishes and in the region of 8,100 beneficed (those in receipt of temporalities) and 16,000 unbeneficed clerks. Additionally there may have been as many as 7000 nuns.[17] By the end of the century episcopal registers indicate more than 5000 ordinations were taking place in just one diocese alone over a 20 year period.[18] It is reasonable to assume the pattern of investiture was similar across the seventeen dioceses throughout the realm which would mean an average of 1700 ordinations each year. The number of lower orders that were counted as clerics by the Church would have added to this figure considerably. By the *Statute of Marlborough* 1267[19] Henry

---

[15] Maxfield, D. K., St. Mary Rouncivale, Charing Cross : The Hospital of Chaucer's Pardoner, *The Chaucer Review*, Vol. 28, No. 2 (1993) pp. 148–63. Estimates a total population of between three and four million of which 26,500 (one or two per cent) were ordained priests, a further 6,500 monks and 'For each priest there were several members of the six lower clerical orders…' totaling between 132,500 and 159,000 in all. p. 150. For a thorough discussion see: "The maddeningly imprecise term of *clericus*" (p. 930) Turner, R. V., The *Miles Literatus* in Twelfth-and Thirteenth Century England: How Rare a Phenomenon? *The American Historical Review*, Vol. 83. No. 4 (Oct., 1978), pp. 928–945. Estimated figures for the later period are cited by Lander, J.R., *Government and Community: England, 1450–1509*, Cambridge, Mass, Harvard University Press, 1980. pp. 128–129

[16] Cox, J.C., *The Sanctuaries and the Sanctuary Seekers of Mediaeval London*, G. Allen & Sons, 1911. p. 33 estimates 1,000 clerics each year escaped secular justice during the late medieval period due to the benefit of clergy plea

[17] Powicke, M., The Thirteenth Century 1216–1307, Oxford, Clarendon Press, 1953 pp. 445–447

[18] Gabel, L. *Benefit of Clergy in England in the Later Middle Ages*, New York, Octagon, 1969. p. 74 Citing the registers of Godfrey Giffard and Thomas de Cobham, bishops of Worcester

[19] 52 Hen. III. 1267. Henry III was recovering from recent internal turmoil (it was just two years since De Montfort's Parliament had been disbanded) and it is very likely that he knew extending *clericus* would achieve widespread approval from the bishops and in doing so bring a measure of stability to the realm. It is the oldest surviving active legislation in England and 4 articles of the *Statute of Marlborough* remain in force; c. 1,4,15 and 23

III (1216–1272) extended the term *clericus* to all clergy; first tonsure (psalmist) and higher orders. In terms of committing serious crime the majority of felonious clerics were from the lower orders. For example when 175 defendants appeared before the Wiltshire Eyre in 1249, 21 of the defendants were classified as clerks, *clerici* or *capellini,* 'Several of them were said to be members of gangs, charged with violent robbery'.[20] Some years before in 1201 at Wells three brothers were accused of murder, Henry and Roger were outlawed but the third, Hugh, a subdeacon, pleaded his clergy. A commission was issued by the bishop and Hugh was taken by the ordinary.[21] In 1202 at Bedford four men stood accused of murder; one abjured after sanctuary, two were outlawed and the fourth, Gilbert, a subdeacon, claimed his clergy.[22] Also in 1202 Ralph of Nettleham and his brother, William, one a clerk the other a subdeacon, were accused of the murder of Reginald, son of

---

[20] Given, J.B., Society and Homicide in Thirteenth-Century England, Stanford, Stanford University Press, 1977, Lawrence, C.H., 'The English Parish and its Clergy in the Thirteenth Century' in Linehan, P. and Nelson, J.L., (eds) *The Medieval World,* London, Routledge, 2001 at Chapter 37. p.667. Note 5

[21] Cited by Cheney, *The Papacy and England.* Supra. p. 228. Note 6 and 7. I have been unable to verify the reference. The process of issuing an episcopal commission during the Middle Ages is described by McHardy, A.K. 'Church Courts and Criminous Clerks in the Later Middle Ages' in Franklin, M.J. and Harper-Bill, C., (eds) *Medieval Ecclesiastical Studies in Honour of Dorothy M. Owen,* Woodbridge, Suffolk, Boydell Press, 1995. pp. 165–183

[22] Cheney, Supra. Also in 1202 at Northampton Thomas a clerk was claimed by the ordinary in a case of violence. His two accomplices were outlawed. Stenton, D.,(ed) *The Earliest Northampton Assize Roll A.D. 1202 and 1203,* Northampton, Northants. Rec. Soc. 1930 Vol. 5. Entry No. 78. The same case is probably being referred to by Helmholz, R.H., The Early History of the Grand Jury and the Canon Law, *University of Chicago Law Review,* Vol. 53 (1983) pp. 613–627 at p. 624. Note 50 and Poole, A.L., 'Outlawry as Punishment of Criminous Clerks' in Edwards, J.G., Galbraith, V.H., and Jacob, E.F., (eds) *Historical Essays in Honour of James Tait,* Manchester, Manchester University Press, 1993. pp. 239–246 at p. 244–245 and p. 240. Note 3. A possible reference to the same case *Willelmus clericus de Harewedon, Select Pleas of the Crown* (Selden Soc.) p.185

Picot. The clerics pleaded their clergy. Ralph was degraded and then outlawed, his brother only degraded.[23] The sentence applied to Ralph may represent the first example of a clerk being degraded and then outlawed; itself unusual as it would amount to a clear effrontery to the Becket issue of double jeopardy. An alternative and plausible explanation is that one brother was degraded and the other fled thus making himself an outlaw. The court records are unclear on this point.[24] It was established canon law that degradation was a complete sentence in itself. The only exception to this was in cases of apostasy where the degraded cleric was burnt in the hand by the temporal tribunal having already been degraded.[25]

Not all criminal clerics came from humble backgrounds. At Oxford University all students held the status of clerk and perhaps not dissimilar to some contemporary students they too were prone to excessive consumption of alcohol and generally riotous behavior; much of which resulted in crime, particularly assault and homicide. Between 1241 and 1261 a massive 10.3 per cent of all murder defendants were Oxford students claiming to be clerics.[26] Many murder victims were students as well, such as David de Trempedhwy. He was murdered by a group of clerics on December 10, 1296 while attempting

---

[23] Stenton, D., (ed) *Lincolnshire Assize Rolls A.D. 1202–1209,* Lincolnshire Rec. Soc. 1926 Vol. 22. Entry No. 923 and 924 and Cheney, Supra. p. 233 and again at p. 235 where he appears to contradict himself by stating that one brother cleared himself and the other suffered degradation

[24] Cheney, Supra at p. 235 and notes 4 and 5. Further examples of clerics being outlawed are recorded in 27 Henry III, infra, and Cheney, Supra at p. 235 note 7. cites *Somerset Pleas,* i, No. 939

[25] Poole, Supra. p. 240 and Note. 1. cites Bracton, *De legibus, de placitis coronae* (ed. Woodbine), ii. 348, fol. 123

[26] Given, Supra. p. 85

to solicit a prostitute.[27] In 1298 when inside a public house cleric student John Barel started a verbal dispute with John of Suffolk and Nicholas de Uilers, also a clerk. The argument continued outside and Barel attacked de Uilers with his sword. De Uilers and Suffolk responded by planting an axe in Barel's head, killing him.[28] It was in the same year that a group of students entered Oxford high street with bows and arrows and slings and swords. They attacked a group of local citizens and then proceeded to rob and loot from nearby shops.[29] In self-defense Edward de Erkalewe, who was not a student, shot an arrow through the eye of rioting cleric Fulc Neyrnyt. The dead student was clearly prepared for battle as he died with sword and shield in hand.[30] Instances such as these highlight the challenge for the medieval legal system at this time as it facilitated one law for the commoners and another for society's elites; in particular the clergy who seemed immune from almost any level of accountability before the courts secular.

At times the anger that lay society felt towards criminal clerics meant that they took matters into their own hands. In 1208 a group of Oxford clerics accidentally killed a woman of the city; three of the suspects then attempted to plead their clergy but were taken by the townsfolk and hanged. In 1252 at Faversham in Kent there was an attempted lynching of cleric John le Noreys. Le Norreys along with Thomas de Hauekenese (Hauekeneye) murdered a commoner, Hugh de Shope (Shape). Both Hauekenese and Noreys were detained

---

[27] Given. Supra. p.85

[28] Given, Supra. pp. 85–86

[29] There is no reason to think students at continental European institutions behaved any better. See: Hastings, R., *Universities of Europe in the Middle Ages,* Oxford, Clarendon Press, 1895. Vol. II, Part I. esp. 'Student Life in the Middle Ages'

[30] Ibid

and held in the bishop's prison at King's Mill to await spiritual trial. Whilst in custody a group of local villagers broke in and seized le Noreys. The archbishop of Canterbury attempted to secure the cleric's return. However, the locals of Faversham refused to surrender their captive and they proceeded to erect a makeshift gallows on which to hang him. In response the entire village was excommunicated.[31] The local abbot, who by custom as Lord of the Manor had jurisdiction over a large number of felonies,[32] was so outraged by the total disregard for the Church's jurisdictional authority that he held all the Faversham townsfolk liable for the 'murdrum' of Noreys and they were forced to pay the friar a compensatory fine. Four years before the incident in Faversham another clerk named le Norreys was appealed for robbery and the rape of a woman in Wolverhampton.[33] It was held by the justices that being without chattels or goods, le Norreys was outlawed. This case of 1248 is important because it represents one of the early examples of the secular courts outlawing a cleric, a resolution which the Church forbade and yet the secular law applied anyway. Also before the same justices Nicholas de Nodariis was found guilty of murder and theft. He too was a cleric. He held no benefice and therefore had no chattels or goods to be taken

---

[31] Murray, K.M.E., Faversham and the Cinque Ports, *Transactions of the Royal Historical Society (Fourth Series)* Vol. 18 (Dec., 1935) pp. 53–84

[32] E.g. All offences committed in the fair or market place (which the abbot owned); he also had authority to appoint ale-tasters and held the weights and measures for the town and authority to hear all cases of stranger's pleas and breaches of the assizes of bread and ale. C.f. Murray, Supra. pp. 58–59 and cited in Given, Supra. p. 94

[33] *The Roll and Writ File of the Berkshire Eyre of 1248*, Clanchy, M.T. (ed), London, Selden Society, 1973. Vol. 90. No. 868. p. 344. Cited in Stewart, S., 'Outlawry as an Instrument of Justice in the Thirteenth Century' in Appleby, J.C. and Dalton, P., (eds) *Outlaws in Medieval and Early Modern England: Crime, Government and Society, c. 1066-c.1600*, Farnham, Surrey, Ashgate, 2009

by the sheriff. De Nodariis was proclaimed a clerk and an outlaw.[34] In terms of the general laicization of the laws of England these two cases represent an important progression as the secular courts apparently feel sufficiently empowered to apply a temporal sanction even though it is formally impossible under church law. This is also a time when the secular courts are seen to be attempting to apply the developing common law in matters of wealth disbursement and the disposal of the goods and chattels of criminals; both secular and unpurged clergymen.

It was not only laymen in Kent who carried out prison breaks though as the cleric students of Oxford University demonstrated. In 1285 clerics Hugh de Bolre and William of London were being held in Headington prison, Oxford, on suspicion of theft. A large group of students came to the prison and forced the release of Hugh, William was fortunate enough to be let out by the bailiff. There is no record of either suspect ever standing trial.[35] Following this event six men; John, son of Walter de Hayle, Henry Helle, Thomas de Fres, Reginald de Stretle, Henry Somer de Stoke de Insula and Simon de Wayetyng, were all condemned to death for

---

[34] *The Roll and Writ File of the Berkshire Eyre of 1248*, Clanchy, M.T. (ed), London, Selden Society, 1973. Vol. 90. No. 872. p. 345–6. Cited in Stewart, Supra. p. 44

[35] Given, J.B., *Society and Homicide in the Thirteenth Century*, Stanford, CA, Stanford University Press, 1977. p. 116 Further examples of episcopal prison escapes are provided by McHardy, A.K., *Church Courts and Criminous Clerks in the Later Middle Ages in Medieval Ecclesiastic Studies in Honour of Dorothy M. Owen*, Woodbridge, Suffolk (UK), Boydell & Brewer, 1995. pp. 165–183, p. 173. *Privilegium fori* hearings, sometimes referred to as *in foro ecclesiastico,* were at the discretion of the bishop. Venues included local churches, cathedral chapels and formal consistory courts. The same venues were also available for use by the secular courts. Pugh, R.B., *Imprisonment in Medieval England,* Cambridge, Cambridge University Press, 1968. Chapter III 'Imprisonment of Clerks', Chapter VI 'Bishop's Prisons' and Chapter XVIII 'Monastic Prisons'

murder. On route to the gallows they were rescued by a group of clerics, took sanctuary in the church of St. Giles and subsequently abjured the realm. It is assumed that the murderers were unable to establish a claim of clerical privilege at trial.[36]

Taking of sanctuary by clerics was not permitted by the Church. That did not mean that it did not happen. Long established as a means of respite for secular criminals this was now being used increasingly by fleeing felonious clerics. So too was abjuration, also not available to clergymen, being utilized with the explicit assistance of the secular office of coroner. The fourth commonly applied legal option was outlawry. Proclaimed (by the courts) or self-selected outlawry is now in greater use as many clerics opt for societal exclusion rather than face perpetual ecclesiastical solitary confinement. By the third quarter of the century it can be seen that the declinatory pleas of clericus and sanctuary along with exile and outlawry are now being attempted by greater numbers of felons generally and particularly by unbeneficed clerics living on the margins of the two worlds they inhabited. As these ranks of 'underpaid and unstable clerical proletariat'[37] continued to rise greater numbers were unlikely to have the secured income of a parish. Resorting to crime was an inevitable concomitant of this beneficial lacuna.

---

[36] Given, Supra. p. 116 citing Homans, G.E. *English Villagers of the Thirteenth Century*, Cambridge, Mass, Harvard University Press, 1941. p. 118. For a discussion of the use of the term 'privilege' Boureau, A., 'Privilege in Medieval Societies from the Twelfth to the Fourteenth Centuries, Or: How the Exception Proves the Rule' in Linehan, P. and Nelson, J.L., (eds) *The Medieval World*, London, Routledge, 200. Chap. 35

[37] Lawrence, C.H., 'The English Parish and its Clergy in the Thirteenth Century' in Linehan, P. and Nelson, J.L., (eds) *The Medieval World*, Supra. Chap. 37. p. 656

Innocent III[38] was elected pope in January 1198[39] He assumed the papacy as *mater et magistra* of all churches.[40] The pontiff did not favor the Angevin dynasty and his lack of support led to king John's humiliating fealty (and eventual abdication).[41] In being forced to hand over England and Ireland to the pope John incurred the displeasure of his barons. This resulted in the meeting at Runnymede on June 15, 1215 and *Magna Carta.* As former adversaries John and Innocent now worked together to defeat the great charter. The pope issued a papal bull annulling it on August 24, 1215.[42] Three months later[43] Innocent III opened the 4th papal council at the basilica of St. John Lateran in Rome. 70 canons (decrees) were agreed by the council. Decree eighteen forbade the clergy from involvement in command of low soldiery, men of blood, 'nor let any subdeacon, deacon, or priest practice any office of surgery which requires

---

[38] For commentary on the papacy of Innocent III Tierney, B., *The Crisis of Church and State in 1050–1300,* Englewood Cliffs, N.J., Prentice-Hall, 1964 Chap. 4. 'The Reign of Innocent III'. pp. 127–138. Logan, F.D. *A History of the Church in the Middle Ages,* London, Routledge, 2002. Chapter 10 pp. 184–201. For influence upon the establishment of legal systems: Whitman, J.Q., *The Origins of Reasonable Doubt: Theological Roots of the Criminal Trial,* New Haven, Yale University Press, 2008. Chapter 4. pp. 92–157. For a brief overview of clerical violence during his papacy; Smith, C.E., Clerical Violence in the Pontificate of Innocent III, *Journal of Religion,* Vol. 24, No. 1 (Jan, 1944), pp. 37–41

[39] Deansley, M., *A History of the Medieval Church 590–1500,* London, Methuen, 1951 (7th Edition) p. 143

[40] Cheney, C. 'England and France' in Powell, J. (ed) *Innocent III Vicar of Christ or Lord of the World,* Washington, DC, Catholic University of America Press, 1994 (2nd edition) pp. 153–156. p. 153

[41] For examples of some of the many attempts made by John to assert authority over the English episcopate and the consequences see: Smith, C.E., Innocent III, Defender of the Faith, *The Catholic Historical Review,* Vol. 32, No. 4 (Jan., 1947), pp. 415–429. pp. 424–426

[42] *Magna Carta* was reissued in 1216 after the deaths of King John and Innocent III. Both the charter and the papal bull are available to view, alongside each other, in the British Library. Logan, Supra. p. 188 and Duggan, C., *Canon Law in Medieval England,* London, Variorum, 1982. Chapter XV 'From the Conquest to the Death of John' pp. 65–115. p. 95

[43] 11 November, 1215

burning or cutting. Nor let anyone pronounce over the ordeal of hot or cold water or glowing iron any benediction of rite of consecration, regard being also paid to the prohibition formerly promulgated respecting the single combat or duel'. The 'Judgments of Blood' were a strong reiteration of the established canonical position posited by Burchard (Burkhardt), Ivo of Chartres and Gratian, *curia a cruore*.[44] Henceforth, no cleric was permitted to be involved in any trial proceedings that might result in a death sentence. They were also banned from attending executions. "If anyone in consequence of this prohibition (*hujusmodi occasions statuti*) should presume to inflict damage on churches or injury on ecclesiastical persons, let him be restrained by ecclesiastical censure."[45]

Although there are many factors that led to benefit of clergy eventually being owned by the temporal courts one of the most significant was the unavoidable pressure of societal change that gave the common layman a voice in their own lives. In large part this voice was achieved through literacy.[46] In 1212 Innocent III had decreed that a married acolyte was entitled

---

[44] 'Court comes from Blood' a crib from the Pseudo-Isidorean Decretals. Whitman, J.Q., *The Origins of Reasonable Doubt: Theological Roots of the Criminal Trial,* New Haven, Yale University Press, 2008. pp. 46–49 and Clark, J.K., 'Of Kings and Popes and Law: An Examination of the Church and State Relationship in England During the High Middle Ages and the Influence of that Relationship on the Structure and Processes of English Law' MA Thesis, University of Victoria, 2012 (Unpublished)

[45] Rowland, A.C., (ed) 'Ordeals, Compurgation, Excommunication and Interdict' in *Original Sources of European History,* Philadelphia, Pennsylvania University Press, Vol. IV. No. 4. C. 9. Abolition. p. 9 Corp. Jut. Can., c. 9, Extra III, 50 (Can. 18. Ann. 1215) https://archive.org/details/translationsrepr01univiala also: CANON 18 Text. http://www.fordham.edu/halsall/basis/lateran4.asp

[46] McHardy, A.K., 'Church Courts and Criminous Clerks in the Later Middle Ages' in *Medieval Ecclesiastic Studies in Honour of Dorothy M. Owen,* Woodbridge, Suffolk (UK), Boydell & Brewer, 1995. pp. 165–183 at p. 182 and Johnstone, P., *Benefit of Clergy in Colonial Virginia and Massachusetts,* Dubuque, IA, Kendall Hunt, 2015

to benefit of clergy but could not be forced to wear tonsure;[47] within 60 years the first known case of reading as a means of proving clerical status appeared before the *curia regis*.[48] The requirement that every cathedral and other parish churches of sufficient wealth appoint a master of grammar to instruct, *gratis*, clerics and poor students was contained within Canon eleven.[49] For the remaining life of benefit of clergy the application of this provision meant that literacy would substitute the wearing of religious regalia.[50] In England by the middle of the fourteenth century capital punishment for the illiterate was decided by a defendant's ability, or not, to quote a standard text, Psalm 51. "Have mercy upon me, O God, according to Thy Loving kindness; according unto the multitude of Thy tender mercies, blot out my transgressions".[51] Not surprisingly *Miserere mei Deus*, David's prayer for the remission of sin, became known as the Neck Verse.[52] Confirmation of laicization of the plea came in 1350 when Edward III (1327–1377) promulgated laws that permitted the use of benefit of clergy

---

[47] Lea, H.C., *Studies in Church History*, London, Sampson Low, Son, & Marston, 1869. p. 198

[48] Gabel, Supra. pp. 65–66. *Gaol Delivery Rolls* 35, m 36d, Newgate. 6 Edward I

[49] CANON 11. SUMMARY In every cathedral church and other churches also that have sufficient means, a master is to be appointed to instruct *gratis* the clerics and poor students. The metropolitan church ought to have a theologian who shall teach the clergy whatever pertains to the *cura animarum* (i.e. care of souls). http://www.fordham.edu/halsall/basis/lateran4.asp

[50] Gabel, Supra. p. 67

[51] Williams suggests that 'each prison had its own neck verse', Williams, A., (ed) *Old Church Life*, William Andrews & Co, London, 1909. p. 14. I am not able to confirm this assertion and the general view appears to be that psalm 51 was widely used throughout England, this is certainly the position proposed by Gabel, Supra

[52] The first recorded use of the reading test is Gaol Delivery Rolls 6 Edward I. a case involving the escape from prison by Thomas le Blake. Source. Gabel, Supra. p. 65. For a discussion of the 'neck verse', Kendall, Supra. pp.99–107 and Johnstone, P. *Benefit of Clergy in Colonial Virginia and Massachusetts*, Dubuque, IA, Kendall Hunt, 2015 pp. 35–36

for all men regardless of social station in matters of treason and felony that 'did not touch the king's person'.[53]

But the transition was not clear-cut and for many decades the courts vacillated between habit and tonsure, reading and habit and variations between. In 1300 cleric William Asshendene was not granted clergy for murder although he successfully read from the bible. He did not appear in *habitum et tonsuram clericalem*.[54] In 1305 before the Eyre of Middlesex a defendant appeared without tonsure or clerical habit but was able to read. This was deemed insufficient at the time and the defendant who had been claimed by the ordinary, was required to be returned to the king's prison.[55]

The decretals of the 4th Lateran Council of 1215 did not include specific references to the issue of benefit of clergy. Pope Lucius III (1181–1185) in *Ad abolendam* (1184) decreed that laity *and clerics* found guilty of heresy should be executed. Clerics would be defrocked and then as a civilian face the death sentence. Pope Celestine (1191–1198) followed this by handing incorrigible criminal clerks over to the secular courts for sentencing and in 1201 Innocent III decreed that clerks found guilty of forging papal documents should be punished by the temporal courts. Clearly eternal damnation was insufficient punishment for those who dared to mimic the papal signature.[56] Any

---

[53] 25 Edw. 3. St. 3. C. 4. 1350

[54] Kendall, C., 'Nooses and Neck Verses: The Life and Death Consequences of Literacy Testing', in Bizzell, P., (ed) *Rhetorical Agendas: Political, Ethical and Spiritual*, New Jersey, Erlbaum, 2006. pp. 99–107. p. 106. Note 10 citing Gabel, Supra, p.65 (This page number is an error by Kendall as the reference is Gabel p. 66. Note 21)

[55] Gabel, Supra. p. 66. Includes two further examples where the defendants appeared tonsured and read successfully

[56] Baldwin, J.W. *The Government of Philip Augustus: Foundations of French Royal Power in the Middle Ages*, Berkeley, CA, University of California Press, 1986. p. 326

member of the laity foolish enough to injure or kill a cleric ordinarily faced extreme punishment. During the 11th century in Caithness, Scotland a group of locals tortured and removed the tongue of the bishop. The pope sentenced the offenders to 'Walk around the diocese for fifty days, clad only in trousers and a sleeveless woolen coat and carrying a green bough. During the fifty-day period, his tongue was to be kept extended by twine, except when he ate his meals, limited to bread and water. Upon conclusion of the penitential perambulations, the culprit was to prostrate himself before the cathedral of the mutilated bishop to undergo a severe flogging with the bough he carried. Then, he was ordered to go to the Holy Land for two years, to perform such hard labor for the benefit of the holy places as might be directed by the local ecclesiastical authorities'.[57]

As far as the papacy was concerned *privilegium clericus* was indisputable. This was never the position taken by the crown or secular courts in England where bishops and kings spent many years defining and redefining the parameters of spiritual authority and the determination of what offences were 'clergyable' and those that were 'unclergyable'. Misdemeanors and the felony of treason excluded, as these were never clergyable, all others could become unclergyable by royal decree, statute, or implied custom. For example between 1276 and 1547[58] English law held that if a man married a widow or took a second wife after the death of the

---

[57] Smith, C.E., Innocent III, Defender of the Faith, *The Catholic Historical Review*, Vol. 32. No. 4 (Jan., 1947), pp. 415–429. p. 418. For further discussion of violence committed by the clergy see: Smith, C.F., Clerical Violence in the Pontificate of Innocent III, *Journal of Religion*, Vol. 25 (Jan., 1944), pp. 37–41

[58] In 1547 Edward VI enacted a statute that forbade Jews, Turks, blind men and pirates from claiming clergy regardless of the law concerning other users of the benefit. Egyptians and vagabonds had already been marginalized by Henry VIII in 1531 (22 Hen VIII, c.10)

first wife any offence committed by him that was otherwise clergyable became *de facto* unclergyable. The reasoning was that because the benefit applied only to clerks and canon law forbade bigamous marriage to a widow any clerk committing bigamy was subject to degradation and therefore it was impossible to claim clergy.[59] The church's position was supported by Edward I when he promulgated 4 Edw. 1 'Men twice married, whom the Bishop of Rome hath excluded from all Clerks Privileges...shall not henceforth be delivered to the prelates, but Justice shall be executed upon them, as upon other lay people.'[60] This example of unity between the laws Christian and secular[61] was applicable to all the lower clerical ranks. The higher orders of subdeacon, deacon or presbyter were forbidden to marry after ordination.[62] Under Edward's I and II[63] the courts temporal had authority

---

[59] Three types of bigamy existed at cannon law; true, interpretative and similar. C.f. www.newadvent.org/bigamy. And 'By marrying a second time, or by marrying a widow, the clerk, who thus became *bigamus* forfeited his immunities'. Pollock and Maitland, Supra, p.445 and Hall, J., *Theft, Law and Society*, Indianapolis, Bobbs-Merill, 1935. p. 356

[60] 4. Edw. I, St. 3. C. 5 (1276) *Statutes of the Realm, De Bigamus*

[61] Per Second Council of Lyon 1274 16. Article 22 'Putting an end to an old debate by the present declaration, we declare that bigamists are deprived of any clerical privilege and are to be handed over to the control of the secular law, any contrary custom notwithstanding. We also forbid bigamists under pain of anathema to wear the tonsure or clerical dress.' http://www.papalencyclicals.net/Councils/ecum14.htm#16.

[62] Ancient Epitome of Canon VI. 'If any ordained person contracts matrimony, let him be deposed. If he wishes to be married he should become so before his ordination. This canon annuls the tenth canon of Ancyra, which allows a deacon and even a presbyter to marry after ordination and continue in his ministry, provided at the time of his ordination he had in the presence of witnesses declared his inability to remain chaste or his desire to marry. This present canon follows the XXVIth of the Apostolic canons.' The last clause of this canon, limited in its application to subdeacons, is found in the *Corpus Juris Canonici*, Gratian's Decretum, Pars I., Dist. XXXII., c. vi. http://www.fordham.edu/halsall/basis/trullo.asp

[63] Gabel, Supra. p. 90 who cites: (Selden Society) Eyre of Kent 6 and 7 Edw II, Vol. 5. 140–141

to establish bigamy. Edward III reverted this to the courts Christian.[64] The involvement of the ordinary in bigamy tests post 18. Edw. III. c. 2 is haphazard in some instances; the ordinary took the bigamist before the courts spiritual and then returned him to the secular justices and in other cases the lay jury proceeded with a determination; with or without the presence of the bishops ordinary.[65] This situation remained the applicable law in England until the sixteenth century when a bigamist was once again permitted to claim his clergy under Edward VI (1547–1553).[66]

Procedurally thirteenth century courts temporal viewed the handing over of a clerk to the bishop's ordinary as a temporary release until the matter before the ecclesiastical court was finalized. This made sense to the secular law as a defendant might well return to the justices for sentence having been deemed to have committed the alleged felony. Consequently the clerk was released to the ordinary on bail to appear before the Christian court or he was remanded into the custody of the ordinary that was responsible for holding the defendant in prison until a purgation hearing.[67] Instances of bishops refusing to hear purgation are extremely rare. One did occur in 1278 when Geoffrey (Godfrey) Giffard, bishop of Worcester (1268–1302) ordered the archdeacon of Worcester not to hear the purgation of Roger de Malton. The motivation may have not been entirely without bias though as Roger was held in prison on the orders of Geoffrey's brother, William Giffard,

---

[64] 18. Edw. III. 3. C. 2

[65] Gabel, Supra. p. 90 and notes 110, 111, 112 for case examples

[66] Edward VI, 1547–1553, 1 Edw. VI, c.12

[67] Gabel, Supra. p.105 and citing Register of Godfrey Giffard. Bishop of Worcester 1268–1302. Willis, J.W., (ed) Worcester Historical Society. 2 Vols. Oxford, 1902. p.97. n.77

archbishop of York (1266–1279) for offences committed against the provincial see.

In February 1221 Pandulf Masca, bishop of Norwich (1215–1226) managed to override the king's objections in respect of Geoffrey the Chaplain. Geoffrey was imprisoned at his bishop's castle at the behest of the crown. When he was summoned to appear before the judges temporal for conspiracy the bishop refused to surrender his clerk on the basis that whilst in Bedford prison Geoffrey had celebrated mass while under an order of excommunication. This, according to Pandulf, meant that the gravity of the ecclesiastical offence trumped the secular and Geoffrey would remain his. King Henry disagreed and wanted Geoffrey to exile the realm. In this instance *privilegium fori* triumphed and the king withdrew his complaint.[68]

Over the course of his reign Henry III (1216–1272) succeeded in encouraging his parliament to require that bishops return unsuccessful clerical purgators to the secular courts. Relations between the Church and Henry deteriorated generally though and clerical remonstrations, collectively referred to as *gravamina,* became a regular feature of his monarchy.[69] The tension between the crown and the Church provided an ideal environment for clerics of all ranks to manipulate of the available legal systems. In 1238 the William, bishop of Exeter (1223–1244) took the unusual step of providing sanctuary to

---

[68] Cheney, C.R., The English Church and its Laws 12th-14th Centuries, London, Variorum Reprints, 1982. p. 226 Rot. Lit. Claus (ed Hardy), ii. 97a (Rotuli Litterarum Claurums)

[69] See: Jones, W.R. Bishops, Politics, and the Two Laws: The Gravamina of the English Clergy, 1237–1399, *Speculum: A Journal of Mediaeval Studies,* Vol. 151. N. 2 (Apr., 1966) pp. 209–245. Commentary on the Gravamina is best known in the works of Bishop Grosseteste of Lincoln. Grosseteste was of the view that no spiritual matter should be judged by an inferior (the secular courts)

an outlawed subdeacon who had abjured the realm. The felon returned from exile without securing a royal pardon (an offence for which hanging without trial was the punishment) and the bishop allowed the clerk's purgation. Royal censure ensued as no original secular trial had ever taken place to establish clerical status. Bishop William had usurped the law in two ways; by harboring an outlaw and permitting the consistory trial after exile. Under the protocols of *Clarendon* a heinous cleric villain should abjure the realm if he first purged himself before the bishop. In this instance the purgation was after the period of exile and illegal.[70] Prior to this in 1221 the abbot of Bordesley, Worcestershire decided to apply his own version of law when he entered the parish church of Stone and rescued William de Bracy (Brasey) from the local community. De Bracy was a suspected felon. Although the offenders clerical status is not known the abbot and fellow monks took it upon themselves to dress de Bracy in the habit and grant him perpetual sanctuary at the nearby monastery. A subsequent attempt by the crown to amerce the abbot failed as well.[71] Also in 1221 Nicholas the Bigot was arraigned for murder. The secular jury found that Nicholas had stabbed his victim inside the porch of a church.[72] Benefit of clergy was not available to felons who committed sacrilege and therefore Bigot should have been denied ecclesiastical immunity. Nevertheless, he pled

---

[70] Gabel, Supra. p. 113–114, Poole, Supra. p. 245. Cheney, Supra. p. 226 citing *Close Rolls 1237–1242*. p. 122. Per 4. Hen VII c.13 (1489) Abjuration was limited to first conviction only. This of course presumes that an exile received permission or a pardon to return to England so that committing a second or subsequent offences was possible

[71] Cheney, Supra. p. 227. *Pleas of the Crown* (Selden Soc.) Vol. 86. No. 135. and *Rolls of the Justices in Eyre* No. 1141 pp. 558–9, Bullen, W.R., The Right of Sanctuary in England, *The Tablet*, 19 May, 1923. p. 6

[72] All felonies committed inside churches became unclergyable, except to those in Holy Orders, under 4. Hen. 8. C.2. (1512)

his clergy before the justices and was claimed by the ordinary. He then purged himself before the archdeacon of Coventry.[73]

Fluid interpretation of established laws appear again in 1249 when in the county of Suffolk five clerics[74] were held *clerici convicti*. This was repeated in 1250 when chaplain Thomas de Calceto of Mendham, Suffolk, appeared before the temporal justices accused of robbery and arson.[75] After trial he pleaded his clergy and was handed to the bishop of Norwich's ordinary.[76] A few years later John of Pipewell, a lay-brother from the Cistercian Abbey at Sawtry, was accused of killing his servant, Simon of Warden. The jury found that Simon had attacked Brother John and the cleric had responded by axing the servant to death. It would seem an acquittal on the basis of self-defense was appropriate but in fact John was handed over to the ordinary for purgation.[77] There is probably more to this outcome than is recorded as the law at the time held that until a cleric had successfully purged himself his lands and titles were held by the sheriff. If purgation was successful personal possessions were (eventually) returned. If purgation failed and was followed by diocesanal imprisonment or degradation and secular sentencing the offenders' valuables remained in the possession of the crown. In reality this was rare and bishops spared little time in demanding the return of benefices

[73] Poole, A.L., 'Outlawry as Punishment of Criminous Clerks' in Edwards, J.G., Galbraith, V.H., and Jacob, E.F., (eds) *Historical Essays in Honour of James Tait,* Manchester, Manchester University Press, 1993. pp. 239–246. p. 241 *Select Pleas of the Crown* (1225) pl. 160 and pl. 185

[74] Gabel, Supra. p. 36 cites Assize Roll 1177, m. 4d and 7d. *Suffolk Gaol Delivery.* Three more cases appear in 1264. *Suffolk Gaol Delivery* 1197, m.14. Gabel, Supra. p. 36

[75] Arson was not yet, but would eventually become, unclergyable. 4 & 5 P & M. c. 4. (1557)

[76] Poole, Supra. p. 241

[77] Poole, Ibid. p. 241

after a priest had cleared his name. In fact amongst the many grievances[78] the Church took against Henry III one was that undue delay in returning goods and chattels amounted to a second punishment. Robert of Trevoret, Cornwall, is a case in point. He was committed for murdering his wife. He pleaded his clergy and was handed over to the bishop of Exeter. He made his purgation before the court Christian and then promptly demanded the return of his goods and chattels from the sheriff.[79]

An unusual dispute between the clergy and laity took place between 1255 and 1260 when Walter (William) Kirkham, bishop of Durham (1249–1260) and John Baliol (John de Balliol) Scottish landowner and Lord of Barnard Castle, embarked upon a bitter dispute over land titles. The outcome led to the establishment of Balliol College, Oxford and the personal involvement of the king who ordered the release of clerics held in a civilian prison. After Kirkham and Balliol were unable to resolve the land title dispute amicably the bishop excommunicated Balliol and ordered the arrest of Balliol's men. Balliol responded by forcibly taking some of the bishop's clerics and holding them in Barnard Castle. Henry III became involved. He found that Balliol did not hold title to the disputed lands and his detention of the clerics was unlawful. Now resolved bishop Kirkham imposed a penance on Balliol; to maintain sixteen poor scholars at Oxford University. Lord Balliol died in 1269 and his widow, Dervogilla, Lady Galloway

---

[78] Another of the grievances of 1257 was the outlawing of fugitive clerks as the law was unclear; Burger, M., *Bishops, Clerks and Diocesan Governance in Thirteenth-Century England: Reward and Punishment,* Cambridge, Cambridge University Press, 2012. p. 13, 53 and 72

[79] Poole, Supra. p. 242 and Note. 3 where it is noted that the Church viewed to retention of goods and chattels as a second punishment

continued and extended the works of her husband by endowing the building of a college and creating a code of statutes that remains in place today.[80]

From the entries for the 1256 Eyre Roll of Shropshire it is clear that the volume of serious crime being committed by felons who then claimed clergy was significant. Hugh of Ludlow murdered his father and (unusually) was tried *in absentia* by the secular courts where he was found guilty; his goods and chattels were forfeited before he was granted his clergy.[81] William Pimley was found guilty of the executable crime of burglary at nighttime; he pleaded his clergy and was handed to the ordinary.[82] Giles of Norfolk, parson of Burford, was an accomplice to the murder of Reginald de Gaugy; he was found guilty by the courts temporal and handed to the ordinary.[83] Four monks; William of Brompton, John of Bratford, William of Brettenwald and William Little of Notton were all found guilty of wounding and robbery. They had no chattels to confiscate and were all handed to their abbot.[84] William of Brompton appeared before the justices a second time the following year, from this one

---

[80] Powicke, M., *The Thirteenth Century 1216–1307*, Oxford, Clarendon Press, 1953. p. 466 and Close Rolls, 1254–6. p. 217, also; Brooke, C., Highfield, R. and Swan, W., *Oxford and Cambridge*, Cambridge, Cambridge University Press, 1988. p. 62

[81] Harding, A., (ed) *Roll of the Shropshire Eyre 1256*, London, Selden Society, 1981. p. 208. All of the following cases cited are at Crown Plea with exception of those cases that resulted in abjuration

[82] Harding, A., (ed) *Roll of the Shropshire Eyre 1256*, London, Selden Society, 1981. 566. p. 215

[83] Ibid. 673. p. 243. Entry 934. p. 308, deals with William of Bridgnorth who stood co-accused with Giles of Norfolk. Both defendants were found guilty of being accomplices to murder and both claimed their clergy and were released to the ordinary after their goods and chattels had been secured by the sheriff

[84] Ibid. 741. p. 259

must assume he successfully purged himself the first time, on this occasion he appeared with five brother monks and his abbot. Brompton, Hugh de Graham, Pain of Brompton, Robert of Campden, Hugh of Nantwich and Robert of Eyton who along with abbot William of Combermere were all indicted before the crown to answer a charge of conspiracy to murder.[85] It is worth recalling that monks were regarded as being dead before the common law and at canon law were frequently not granted the opportunity to purge themselves; a monk *convictus* faced perpetual solitary confinement, so their motivation to abscond was even greater than for lay clerics.[86] In the same Roll a priest, Adam of Norton, was convicted of harboring thieves; he too was handed to the ordinary.[87] So too was Walter Palmer, indicted on two counts, one for harboring outlaw Roger of Kniver and the second for murdering a local woman in his parish. Palmer was acquitted of the harboring charge and found guilty of murder. He pleaded his clergy and left court with the bishop's ordinary.[88] Roger the Parson appeared charged with assault, the court record does not indicate whether or not he was found guilty before the secular justices before he was released to the ordinary. William, a clerk and William de Baskerville were also charged with assault, in their cases both were found guilty before the king's court before release to the bishop.[89] In addition there are twenty-one cases of clerical abjuration of the realm.

---

[85] Ibid. 742. p. 260

[86] This is not an absolute as Gabel cites a number of examples where monks have purged themselves. See: p 109 Walter Northlache and Brother John Burdet

[87] Ibid. 749. p. 263

[88] *Roll of the Shropshire Eyre of 1256.* 861. p. 290

[89] Ibid. 791. p. 273, 794. p. 275, 901. p. 299

By 1257 Henry was in need of money to support his ambitious foreign policies and to pay for an army to quell domestic discontent.[90] Increased taxation of barons and the clergy was one solution; a solution set to fail, which it did in 1258.[91] In the environment of instability created by Henry it was important that the Church and secular justices worked together; they needed to cooperate, share best practices. A clear distinction between the role and function of England's bishops had not been achieved and many continued to serve as justices at canon and common law. Some level of inconsistency as well as desire for ownership of the law was inevitable. The king was aware of this as were his secular judges. Yet he was pragmatic and promulgated a number of statutory provisions[92] more favorable to the Church than those that existed at the commencement of his monarchy. His courts[93] also demonstrably endorsed the existence of the clericus plea[94] and provided for the well-being of clericus defendants.[95]

---

[90] Jones, W.R. Bishops, Politics, and the Two Laws: The Gravamina of the English Clergy, 1237–1399, *Speculum*, Vol. 41, No.2 (Apr., 1966), pp. 209–245. at p. 213. Hereafter Jones, W.R. 'The Gravamina'

[91] Jones, W.R., 'The Gravamina' Supra. p. 215

[92] Hoskin, P. *De vi laica amovenda: Testing the bounds of secular and ecclesiastical jurisdiction in the reign of Henry III.* Fine Rolls Project Henry III, 1.1. C 60/48 Fine Roll 35 Henry III (28 October 1250–27 October 1251), m.7. http://www.finerollshenry3.org.uk/content/month/fm-01–2011.html. *De vi laica amovenda* is a writ to remove lay force. This is one of many examples of where Henry was tested in the civil courts as well as the criminal courts in respect of jurisdiction and temporal authority

[93] Harding, A., (ed) *Roll of the Shropshire Eyre 1256*, London, Selden Society, 1981. p. xxxix per. Substitution of misdemeanor trespass to felony false imprisonment and the case of Roger of Dustone and associates pleading benefit of clergy

[94] Cheney, Supra. p. 227 *Close Rolls*, 1254–6. p. 96

[95] Cheney, Supra. p. 227 at Note. 4 who cites the case of John Attestan, a clerk being held on suspicion of murder and awaiting trial and then presumably being claimed by the ordinary. A royal mandate ordering the sheriff of Devon to take good care of Attestan. *Rot. Lit. Claus* ii. 188a For commentary on the clerical protestations *non bis in idipsum*: Cheney, Supra. p. 234 and Poole, Supra, p. 244

The sticking point was the clerical atrocities, the extreme examples of abuse and the blatant disregard for the Common Law. These are what so irked the king and his justices. A murder committed by Henry the Summoner of Southwark in 1263 was just such an example. Summoner had been convicted by lay jury of the murder of a local man, Nicholas le Porter. He had killed the victim with a scythe. The incident was witnessed by a number of locals. Henry took off immediately after the crime and was designated an outlaw and his chattels were confiscated by the sheriff. Shortly afterwards Henry the Summoner decided to submit himself to the Eyre with the intention of pleading his clergy. His clerical occupation was that of messenger; he delivered summonses on behalf of the bishop, sufficient however for benefit of clergy. Summoner appeared at his secular trial and was found guilty of murder. The court recorded that 'He says he is a priest and that he cannot answer here. And upon this comes the dean of Guildford, proctor of the bishop of Winchester, who was present, and claims him as a clerk'.[96] Summoner then appeared before his lord bishop and successfully purged himself of a murder that had been witnessed by a large crowd 'not a few rectors, vicars and priests of churches'.[97] In May of the same year the king issued orders to the sheriff of Surrey to restore the lands, house and chattels of Henry le Summoner 'without delay by our special grace'.[98]

---

[96] Stewart, S., 'Outlawry as an Instrument of Justice in the Thirteenth Century' in Appleby, J.C. and Dalton, P., (eds) *Outlaws in Medieval and Early Modern England: Crime, Government and Society, c. 1066-c.1600*, Farnham, Surrey, Ashgate, 2009. pp. 37–54. p. 44 and Stewart, S., (ed) *The 1263 Surrey Eyre*, Surrey Record Society, 2006. no. 537, p. 259

[97] Carpenter, D.A., Magna Carta 1253: The Ambitions of the Church and the Divisions of the Realm, *Historical Research*, Vol. 86, No. 232 (May, 2013), pp. 179–190. p. 187

[98] *Close Rolls of the Reign of Henry III 1261–64*, p. 230 and Stewart, Supra. p. 44. Note 32

On October 5, 1270 the regular and secular clergy were again at odds with each other. The issue was money and land. Hugh Bossard of Knotting asserted advowson and possession of Souldrop Church, Bedfordshire. A local monk, Hubert of Chelsham, disputed the claim and sought to repossess the Church. Matters quickly disrupted into conflict and Hugh's men attempted to evict the monks by setting fire to the Church. The monks responded with arrows fatally wounding Roger le May, one of Hugh's men. Privilegium clericus was not disputed; both sides had a claim (or not since the entire sequel of crimes were sacrilegious).[99]

In 1276, before the justices sitting as the Eyre of London, Geoffrey the Clerk stood accused with three others of the brutal murder of John le Jovene. Geoffrey had taken sanctuary in his church St. James Graschirche, and then submitted himself to the secular tribunal to plead his clergy. Whereupon, 'Richard de Herwes minor canon of London comes and claims him as a clerk by letters of the bishop of London testifying that the bishop entrusted him his authority to claim clergy. But that it may be known for what he is to be handed over, let the truth be ascertained by the forty-two men; the jury say on their oath that he is guilty, so as such let him be handed over to the bishop'. His guilt was clear to the jury who were required to witness, with no doubt some degree of reluctance, Geoffrey being released to the ordinary.[100]

Around the same time City of London alderman Ralph Crepyn gained considerable notoriety for his dual life; daytime doyen

---

[99] Fowler, G.H., *Calendar of the Rolls of the Justices in Eyre at Bedford 1247*. pp. 52–54 cited in Given, Supra. p. 71

[100] Crown Pleas: I Edward I - 4 Edward I (nos 238–294), *The London Eyre of 1276* (1976), pp. 66–83. URL: http://www.british-history.ac.uk/report.aspx?compid=35999

of respectability as an elected representative of the City of London and at night a criminal entrepreneur working out of the public house owned by his mistress Alice (Atte) Bowe. One of Crepyn's associates was goldsmith Lawrence Duket. In 1276 Duket killed a man, William de Leffrement. Alderman Crepyn managed to secure Duket a king's pardon and he was released from prison. Shortly afterwards the two men argued which resulted in Duket injuring Crepyn with a sword. This time Crepyn had no intention of assisting his former associate turned adversary and knowing this Duket took sanctuary at St. Mary le Bow Church. During the course of his sanctuary Duket appeared to commit suicide by hanging. However, a local boy hidden inside the church at the time revealed that Crepyn's mistress, Atte, had entered the church with a number of Crepyn's gang and murdered Duket and made it look like suicide. Atte, Crepyn and six members of Crepyn's gang were arrested. At trial Crepyn and two of the gang successfully pleaded their clergy; the others were sentenced to death. Atte was the most unfortunate for as a woman she was ordered to be burned at the stake. Crepyn, now an innocent man according to law, resumed his public functions as alderman for the ward of Aldgate.[101]

At the conclusion of Henry III's reign royal power prevailed in spite of denunciations and verbal hostility from the prelates of England. Bishops continued to assert authority through

---

[101] Thornley, I., Sanctuary in Medieval London, *Journal of the British Archaeological Association*, Vol. 38, (1932–33), pp. 293–315. p. 298, Given, Supra. p. 184. Also citing: Williams, G.A., *Medieval London: From Commune to Capital*, London, University Press, 1970. (2nd Edition) pp. 248–254. Crepyn was also known as Ralph de Alegate and Ralph Crepin. This event is fictionalized again by Doherty, P., *The Great Crown Jewels Robbery of 1303: The Extraordinary Story of the First Big Bank Raid in History*, London, Constable, 2005 in Chapter 4 with the startling title 'Satans at St. Mary's'

a number of remedial options; purgation, degradation,[102] excommunication and episcopal imprisonment. Temporal justice sought to provide a balance and relinquished proven clerics to the spiritual jurisdiction in a variety of ways; pre and post findings of guilt. The differences were not irreconcilable but the divisions these disputes created would continue to facilitate forum shopping by criminals of the cloth for another hundred years.[103]

---

[102] In an interesting interpretation of canon law; perhaps a last attempt to usurp the dying king, in 1271 archbishop William Giffard (not to be confused with his brother Geoffrey Giffard, bishop of Worcester) degraded a man for stealing church ornaments. The value is not known so this could be a misdemeanor, *transgressio*, for which Giffard would have no jurisdiction, more likely a felonious theft. Giffard held that nobody should punish him further. Cheney then refers the reader to a further forty cases of degradation from the registers of Romeyn, Corbridge and Greenfield. Cheney, Supra. p. 234 and citing: *Reg. J. Romeyn. i. 395–6 ii. 55, Reg. T. Corbridge, ii. 17,23; Reg. Wm Greenfield, i. 228, 245, 255, 256, 265* and notes all of the clerks degraded were in minor orders

[103] C.f. Jones, W.R., The Two Laws in England: The Later Middle Ages, *The Journal of Church and State*, Vol. 11. No. 1 (1969) pp. 111–131

# 5

# Custody Pending Trial, Immuration and Clerics as 'Jailbirds'

In England all crime increased throughout the later stages of thirteenth century. The most troubling were; roving bands of robbers, homicides associated with robbery and cases of arson. The population of the country had grown exponentially and a mobile workforce meant many commoners were away from their villages and towns; they were susceptible to being victims of crime as well as resorting to crime to make ends meet. Also many menfolk were away from family fighting campaigns for Edward I (1272–1307). This too contributed to a break in social and community ties and an increase in vagrancy (and crime) once the military were unemployed. Edward responded in 1285 with the *Statute of Winchester*.[1] Itself cited as an admission of 'the lawlessness of the thirteenth

[1] 13 Edw. I. St. 2. He had already, 3. Edw. I. cap. 2 ruled that all felonious clerics delivered to the ecclesiastical courts must be subjected to purgation and should the bishop fail to conduct this procedure Henry might find it necessary to intervene. Lea, H.C., *Studies in Church History*, London, Sampson Low & Marston, 1869. p. 188

century'.[2] In many instances felons were a mixture of laymen and clergymen acting in concert with full knowledge that if caught the gallows were avoidable if the bishop's ordinary held the ecclesiastic 'legit'.

It had been the case for many years that the secular trial judge was permitted to explore the legitimacy of the ordinary's claim of *legit*. If found to be in error the ordinary was subject to repercussions; reprimand from the lay court and (potentially) loss of his temporalities by the bishop.[3] When a genuine clergyman defendant appeared before the temporal court and was found not guilty he was acquitted as *clericus quietus* and handed to the bishop's court for them to deal with any vicarial issues.[4] An alternative, taken by a number

---

[2] Summerson, H., The Enforcement of the Statute of Winchester, 1285–1327, *The Journal of Legal History*, Vol. 13, No. 3 (1992), pp. 232–250. p. 232. One reason for the clearways of greenery that are seen today alongside the main highways of England relates to the requirement under this statute that 200 feet either side of every public highway shall be cleared to prevent ambush. Another clause permitted the 'Savoyard custom' of allowing victims of crime to claim compensation from the authorities who failed in their duty to pursue robbers within forty days of the crime

[3] Bellamy, J.G., *Crime and Public Order in England in the Later Middle Ages*, London, Routledge, 1973 cites two pertinent examples. pp. 120 and 166. (26 Edw. III. Year Books no. 19) and White, E.J., Benefit of Clergy, *The American Law Review*, Vol. 46, (1912), pp. 78–94. p. 84 note 18. By 16th century the ordinary's responsibilities increased further as Chief Justice Fineux ruled claimed clerks awaiting spiritual trial were 'lay prisoners' and therefore subject to the same conditions of imprisonment as secular prisoners. This had the effect of making the ordinary responsible, upon payment of a one hundred pound fine, that the prisoner did not escape, nor was granted bail and that he was held in conditions neither less, nor more-harsh, than a prisoner in the secular system. Year Books, Trinity 15 Hen. VII nos. 1 and 10. McHardy, A.K., 'Church Courts and Criminous Clerks in the Later Middle Ages' in *Medieval Ecclesiastic Studies in Honour of Dorothy M. Owen*, Woodbridge, Suffolk (UK), Boydell & Brewer, 1995. pp. 165–183, pp.169–71

[4] For operation of the consistory courts, in particular the court of the archbishop of Canterbury, the Court of Arches; Logan, D.F., (ed) *The Medieval Court of Arches*, The Canterbury and York Society, Woodbridge, Suffolk, Boydell Press, 2005 and Brundage, J. 'Sin, Crime and Pleasures of the Flesh' in Linehan, P. and Nelson, J.L., (eds) *The Medieval World*, London, Routledge, 2001 at Chapter 17. p. 305 the 'Official's Court'

of clerics,[5] was to live a temporary or permanent life of outlawry. Insecure though this might be,[6] as one's status was that of a dead man in terms of goods, chattels and forfeiture, it was possible to be in-lawed again and retrieve the rights and privileges of licit society. During the interim the capricious nature of the criminal law was averted and the felon retained his neck.

Clashes between spiritual and temporal jurisdictions were a feature of Edward I's reign. Archbishops of Canterbury, Pecham (1279–1292) and Winchelsey, (1294–1313) were rarely averse to direct and inflamed confrontation with Edward in their attempts to guard the rights and juridical privileges of the Church.[7] Pecham held the view that the king was subservient to the Church and a harmonious society was one in which secular power was subordinate to spiritual. Edward was equally forceful in claiming the financial benefits that were associated with vacant sees and parishes; upon the death of a bishop or beneficed cleric or for the duration of time that a criminous cleric was in prison awaiting trial the temporalities reverted to the crown (and the financial benefits were not insignificant). During Edward's reign vacant sees created by

---

[5] Pollock, F., and Maitland, F.W., *The History of English Law Before the Time of Edward I, (2nd Edition)* Volume I. Cambridge, Cambridge University Press 1968. p. 478 state that for every one man hanged ten escaped justice through outlawry. There is no source cited by them for this claim

[6] An outlaw was executable on sight if he resisted arrest. Pollock and Maitland, Vol. I., Supra. p. 477. In the counties of Gloucestershire and Herefordshire outlaws were executable at any time

[7] Millon, D., (ed) *Select Ecclesiastical Cases From The King's Court 1272–1307*, London, Selden Society, 2009. Vol. 126. p. xv. *Select Ecclesiastical Cases From The King's Court 1272–1307*, p. xv. For an example of clerical harmony during the period see: Greatex, J., Monks and Mendicant in English Cathedral Cities: Signs of a Mutual Benefit Society? *The Friars in Medieval Britain: Proceedings of the 2007 Harlaxton Symposium.* (2010) pp. 97–106

the death of a bishop amounted to an income for the crown of £60,000.[8] For his part Pecham took issue with Edward over the practice of convicting clerks in the temporal court and then, before sentence, allowing them to claim clergy. The king disagreed perhaps in part to ensure that claims of secular forfeiture were not tested.[9] Ecclesiastic vacancies did not always result in conflict though and each legal system was capable of demonstrating liberal judicial flexibility and compromise when necessary. The trial against the rector of Kingston is such an example.

It had long been established law that clergy was not available as a plea in trespass cases even when physical force was alleged.[10] Before the King 's Bench sitting at Michaelmas term of 1279[11] William Joye complained that Guy de Mortimer, rector of Kingston, and Thomas le Clerk of Harrington together with William de Knolley of Kent and William de Cotes of Leicestershire attacked Joye tearing his lip. Joye sought 100 pounds as compensation for this trespass. Guy and Thomas denounced the jurisdiction of the temporal court and claimed the right to clergy; they refused to answer questions or enter

---

[8] Heath, P., *Church and Realm 1272–1461 Conflict and Collaboration in an Age of Crisis,* London, Fontana, 1988. p. 27

[9] Cheney, C.R. The Punishment of Felonous Clerks, *The English Historical Review*, Vol. 51. No. 202, (Apr., 1936), pp. 215–236. p. 229 and Cheney, C.R. The so-called Statutes of John Pecham and Robert Winchelsey for the Province of Canterbury, *The Journal of Ecclesiastical History*, Vol. 12, Issue 1 (March/April, 1961), pp. 14–34

[10] *Select Ecclesiastical Cases From The King's Court 1272–1307*. p. cxvi and Frank, T. and Plucknett, T., *A Concise History of the Common Law* Chapter Three: Misdemeanors, Trespass and Tort , [1956] Edition used: Indianapolis: Liberty Fund, 2010 http://oll.libertyfund.org/?option=com_staticxt&staticfile=show.php%3Ftitle=2458&chapter=243120&layout=html&Itemid=27

[11] KB 27/49, m. 13 ( 1279. Cambridgeshire). This was not the first clergy case to be tried in Edwards reign the Calendar Rolls of 1275 record a commission from the bishop of Lincoln to the Justice of Gaol Delivery to deliver a clerk to his ordinary. Cal. C.R. 1272–1279, pp. 354–5 cited in Gabel, Supra. p. 37

a plea. The king's court held the injury was not of sufficient severity to warrant designation as a felony. Guy and Thomas were found guilty of trespass and each of them was ordered to pay 100 pounds to Joye. They were then committed to gaol as enquiries were made as to how the culprits might pay such a huge amount. A financial comprise was reached and Guy and Thomas were handed over to Geoffrey de Mortimer, archdeacon of London. This appears a complex outcome as the two were deemed ineligible to claim their clergy on the basis that the assault was a trespass and unclergyable and yet their status as clerics was not disputed as after secular disposition they were handed to the ordinary, presumably for ecclesiastical censure having brought the diocese into disrepute.

At canon law no cleric was to be subjected to the punishments of blood or death save for the rare times when a felonious cleric might dare to forge the pope's signature (in which case he was scourged and excommunicated). That said England's bishops clearly thought that it was appropriate to inflict corporal punishment on the laity and they did. In 1279 a mandate issued by the archbishop of York ordered that the king's bailiff, Robert de Berley, be flogged for allowing clerks charged with murder to be beheaded before the bishop had the opportunity to claim them.[12] Later the same year William Wickwane (Wygwane) (1279–1285) succeeded Giffard[13] as archbishop of York. Wickwane was a frugal, austere and severe man who expected all within his suffragan to adhere to his

---

[12] Brown, W., (ed), *Register of William Wickwane Lord Archbishop of York 1279–1285*, London, Surtees Society. 1907. Vol. 114. pp. 37–38

[13] William Giffard died April 25, 1279. Wickwane received 18 votes during the first round of episcopal elections at St. Albans on June 22nd, 1279. In the following round he was unanimously chosen. *The Register of William Wickwane: Lord Archbishop of York, 1279–1285*. 1907. Reprint. London: Forgotten Books, 2013. 1–2. Print. pp. 9–10

uncompromising standards; he soon annoyed the diocese, the sees of Canterbury and Winchester and the crown.[14] Soon after his elevation he moved to take action against his own brothers if irreligious, immoral[15] or criminal activities were suspected.[16] However, his pietistic approach was not entirely without the support of his inferiors as the archbishop resolutely defended the right of the Church to admonish its own.[17] Throughout his period in office he punished clergymen severely when necessary.[18] Notwithstanding his achievements Wickwane took refuge in France[19] for the last three years of his life. The pressure exerted upon him by other English prelates (and Edward I)[20] culminated in a troubled episcopate supplemented by no shortage of felonious clerics continually testing the bounds of clerical privilege. 1285 was the year of Wickwane's death, it was also the year during which at the Easter parliament king Edward issued his general edict refuting the *gravamina* and condemning the advancement of ecclesiastic courts into the secular domain.[21]

---

[14] Brown,Supra. No. 480, 483, 505

[15] Ibid. No.216, 310, 402 and 312, 340 and 512

[16] Ibid. No. 505, 513, 606

[17] Per the incident relating to sheriff Robert de Berley, No. 122 and the excommunication of persons for assaulting clerics. No. 236

[18] E.g. Richard de Vescy excommunicated by Wickwane in 1272. *Register of William Wickwane* No. 320 and *Calendar of Patent Rolls 1281–1292.* p. 193

[19] Pontigny, the Cistercian Abbey north of Auxerre, also where Thomas Becket had taken refuge during his estrangement from Henry II. William Died there after a short fever on August 26th, 1285

[20] Edward readily agreed to Wickwane's request to leave England and gave him letters of protection. In his absence Hugh of Stapleford and Robert of Tadcaster represented the diocese

[21] Jones, W.R. *Bishops, Politics and the Two Laws: The Gravamina of the English Clergy, 1237–1399,* Supra. p.220

Strong sacerdotalist beliefs were also the hallmark of Robert Winchelsey's episcopate[22] (1293–1313) as he too fought to preserve the erosion of ecclesiastical rights. Like Wickwane he was living in a time of rising clerical criminality; it was during his episcopate that the monks of Westminster colluded with a former priest to steal the crown jewels.[23] He was also the archbishop who was to experience the indignation of being labeled an outlaw.[24] Winchelsey was not the first prelate to self-impose exile nor was it restricted to clerics; a number of England's noblemen and ranking justices took temporary refuge abroad as they worked through the stages of being granted and paying for a royal pardon.

1289 was the year that the former Lord Chief Justice of England was implicated in a murder. Thomas Wayland (Weyland) had served in the highest judicial office for eleven years before he was removed for corruption. On 20th July 1289 two of his servants committed a murder at a village fair; some viewed this as an outcome of a drunken brawl; others suspected that Wayland was behind the event as the murdered party held allegiance to the Earl of Norfolk with whom Wayland had a long term dispute. Wayland became an accessory as he knew of the murder yet failed to give up his servants to the crown and he was duly indicted for harboring felons. Wayland knew he would likely face the death penalty and he fled to the Franciscan priory at Babwell where he took sanctuary and holy orders. Wayland was now faced with a secular trial at which he could attempt to

---

[22] He was consecrated at Aquila on September 12, 1294 and returned to England January 1st, 1295

[23] Pudlicott *et al*, infra

[24] 1306–1308. In his case though it was the strong support of *clericis laicos* that landed him in proverbial kingly hot water. C.f. Denton, J.H., *Robert Winchelsey and the Crown 1294–1313*, Cambridge, Cambridge University Press, 1980. pp. 102–104

claim his clergy and risk a penance of perpetual imprisonment at the priory or abjure. He chose the latter; swore his guilt before the coroner and on 20th February 1290 he left the realm for Paris. Wayland received a royal pardon one year before his death and returned home in 1297.[25] Wayland's case is another example of criminals who crisscrossed between ecclesiastic and secular options. He was of course well placed to profit from legal lacunae having held the highest secular judicial office in the country; he would be familiar with the close intersection between temporal and Christian criminal liability and he used his knowledge and opportunity to the full. Deposed judge, fleeing corrupt felon, accessory to murder, sanctuary seeker, tonsured monk and finally exile rather than monastic prison.

A fascinating entry exists from the same records as Wayland. It is an example of one of the last instances of the old system of trial by battle. It is of note because the monks involved must have known that papal canons banned the spillage of blood. Notwithstanding the applicable law they hired a knight to fight on their behalf. Monks John de Creyk, Godfrey de Beaumont and Ralph de Berners were embroiled in a lawsuit over ownership of the manors of Semer and Groton. Fearing they might lose they elected to defend their rights by judicial combat. A champion, Roger Clerk, was then hired to fight for the clerics. They paid him 20 marks in advance and 30 more to be paid if he were the victor. The fight took place on 14th

---

[25] Spitzer, A.L. The Legal Careers of Thomas of Weyland and Gilbert of Thornton, *The Journal of Legal History*, Vol. 6, Issue 1, (1985) pp. 62–83. For an entry relating to the corruption of Weyland before the case of feloniously harboring murderers: Riddell, W.R. Erring Judges of the Thirteenth Century, *Michigan Law Review*, Vol. 24, No. 4, (Feb., 1926), pp. 329–343 and 'The king held a Parliament in Westminster to discuss the wrongdoings of some Justices. Among them was Thomas Wayland, who had all his property confiscated, and was sent into exile. He had held the manor of Onehouse from St Edmund's abbey, and had been an important East Anglian landowner'

October 1287 in London. Roger Clerk was killed and the abbey lost the manors of Semer and Groton.[26]

In the year 1300 William, a cleric of lower orders, was accused of homicide. Ralph, a relative of the deceased, alleged that William had fatally strangled his wife. William pleaded his clergy.[27] The trial court was not convinced of the legitimacy of William's claim to clerical privilege and it remanded him into the custody of the secular prison. One year later no bishop had claimed William and he pleaded his clergy a second time before the courts temporal. The king's court held that in response to a recent papal decree,[28] which distinguished cases of clergy that should be handed to the bishop's ordinary and those that should be held before the courts secular, it would further remand William into secular prison until the following Easter. Presumably the king's justices took this course of action in order that Edward I could consider the matter personally and decide whether or not to claim jurisdiction or permit William his clergy (even though he had not appeared tonsured and was for all practical purposes a married layman). Again no bishop stepped forward to claim William and he was

---

[26] Entry 1287. http://www.stedmundsburychronicle.co.uk/Chronicle/1216–1539.htm

[27] Common Pleas 40/131, m. 21d (1300)

[28] *Liber Sextus* promulgated by Pope Boniface VIII in 1298 which decreed that married clerks must be tonsured and wearing clerical habit at the time of appearance before the secular justices if they are to be granted clerical privilege. *Liber Sextus* 3.2. Boniface also decreed that 'Although it is known that prisons were specially instituted for the custody of criminals, not for their punishment, yet we shall not find fault with you if you commit to prison for the performance of penance, either perpetually or temporarily as shall seem best, those clerics subject to you who have confessed crimes or been convicted of them, after you have carefully considered the excesses, persons and circumstances involved in the case'. *Boniface VIII. Cap.' Quamvis', iii, 'de poen', in. 6* http://www.newadvent.org/cathen/12436a.htm and Hamilton, S., 'The Unique Favour of Penance: the Church and the people c.800–c.1100' in Linehan, P. and Nelson, J.L., (eds) *The Medieval World*, London, Routledge, 2001. Chap 13. pp. 240–242

subsequently tried before the secular court, found guilty and hanged. This case may be exceptional though as the defendant William had committed a heinous crime that attracted no sympathy from the church or the crown and both were most likely content to see William hang as a commoner. The fact that the courts referred the matter to the king for a decision as to whether or not a papal edict would be considered binding on a secular court in England is of significance as it supports the pattern of legal supremacy that the Common Law was achieving. Prior to this in 1285 a cleric was hanged in Oxford but in his case he had been subjected to degradation for a previous offence and his attempt to claim clergy a second time was dismissed by the court and not objected to by the bishop.[29] Conversely one year later the bishop of Lincoln was successful in claiming cleric Richard of Scarborough who had informed the secular court he wished to abjure. Permission to abjure was an uncontested right of the king. In this instance Edward agreed to release the clerk to the bishop until the justices had made a determination and decided whether or not to permit exile.[30] The king appears to have sought to work with his bishops in this instance but of note is that the determination as to whether or not to *permit* exile remained with the crown. In 1292 Oliver de Sutton, bishop of Lincoln (1280–1299) excommunicated Edward St. John and a number of his men for seizing the Church of Thame, setting fire to it and killing Peter of Wyresdale who was inside at the time. In an attempt to nullify the announcement of his excommunication St. John then attacked the church of Long Creton and a local monastery. In

---

[29] Oxford City Documents. p. 223. Cited in Cheney, The Punishment of Felonous Clerks. Supra. p. 234 and Note. 4

[30] *Cal. Close Rolls,* 1279–1288. p. 399 cited in Cheney, The Punishment of Felonous Clerks. Supra. p. 225 and Note. 3

this instance St. John did not need to rely upon his dual status as cleric and royal appointee as the matter never came to trial. Edward I pardoned St. John and his followers for the murder.[31] What this case invites is consideration of a situation where a clerk could claim clergy but would refuse to do so as his canonical sentence would undoubtedly be perpetual ecclesiastical imprisonment. St. John was apparently aware of the strength of his royal patronage and was secure in the knowledge that a temporal trial for murder was not forthcoming.

In 1301 a successful clergy claimant was refused subsequent suit in the king's court against his two accusers. The defendant turned claimant appealed his clergy after the secular criminal trial court had held its usual inquiry into guilt prior to handing the defendant over to the bishop's court for purgation. However, the secular trial court found the defendant not guilty. He now attempted to sue his accusers for defamation. The king's court refused to allow his suit on the basis that as a cleric he had *ipso facto* refused to accept the jurisdiction of the secular court and therefore had no right to benefit from secular statutory provisions.[32] In the same year the Exeter justices refused benefit of clergy to Hugh of Cornwall. Hugh pleaded his clergy in a case of rape. The ordinary claimed Hugh but the justices refused to hand him over on the basis that he had lost his clergy when he married a local widow, Hugh was a bigamist. Hugh objected on the basis that he claimed his widow wife was a virgin when he married her and therefore this did

---

[31] *The Rolls and Register of Bishop Oliver de Sutton, 1280–1289.* 6 Vols. Hereford, Lincoln Record Society, 1948–49. Cited by Given, J.B., *Society and Homicide in Thirteenth-Century England,* Stanford, Stanford University Press, 1977. pp. 71–72 and 224

[32] Easter 1301, Richard son of Henry of Shafton v Richard of Sotwell. *Select Cases in the Court of the King's Bench Under Edward I. 1272–1307.* Selden Soc. Vol. III. m. 63

not offend the canonical provisions of the Council of Lyon 1274. Having failed to convince the court he should be allowed his clergy Hugh then attempted to evade trial by claiming he was a knight and that he should be tried by his peers. He was and they acquitted him. The judge tersely and perhaps with some degree of misbelief commented, 'My lord Hugh, because these men acquit you, we acquit you'.[33]

Towards the end of Edward's reign one of the most daring robberies ever recorded took place in London when Richard Pudlicott, a former tonsured cleric, along with a large number of secular and clerical accomplices stole the kings jewels, silver plate and valuables; collectively valued at £100,000.[34] Allegedly the crime started during the first four months of 1303 when Pudlicott and others cut a hole through the thirteen feet thick walls of Westminster Palace. On the night on April 24 entry was gained and by April 26 the crown jewels, silverware, artwork and a number of saintly relics, had been stolen. It was immediately apparent that the criminals had been assisted by people working inside the palace; the prime suspects were: William Palmer (William of the Palace and deputy warden of Fleet prison), John of St. Albans, a priest and John of Rippingdale, another priest. The king appointed John Droxford, Keeper of the Wardrobe, to investigate. On June 25$^{th}$ Pudlicott and Palmer were arrested. This was quickly followed by the arrest of John of St. Albans and John of Rippingdale and all forty-two Benedictine monks of Westminster Abbey. Pudlicott, perhaps with a pang of clerical guilt, attempted to convince Droxford

---

[33] Year Books in the Reign of King Edward the First 30–31 (ed) Horwood, A.J. London, 1863–79 pp. 529–62 cited in Powicke, M., *The Thirteenth Century 1216–1307*, Oxford, Clarendon Press, 1953. p. 463. The event occurred in 1301

[34] King Edward was residing in York at the time of the crime

he acted alone and had secured entry via the hole made in the exterior wall. It was manifestly clear that this was impossible and the hole was most likely an exit point; entry having been gained by an open door courtesy of Palmer. Monastic complicity was obvious but the arrest of an entire abbey was politically very difficult for Edward I. In 1304 Edward relented to domestic and pontifical pressure and released the suspected monks except Pudlicott; who in spite of his clerical protestations was tried and convicted before the secular justices. In October 1305 Richard Pudlicott, former tonsured cleric and wool merchant was hanged for the highest value burglary ever recorded in medieval English history. Once declared dead his cadaver was removed from the scaffold. It is has been suggested that his skin was flayed and then nailed to the doors of Westminster abbey.[35] The issue of the crown detaining all the monks from Westminster was probably an illegal act by the crown but it was never tested in the courts canon or secular.[36]

---

[35] For the most complete version of this event see, Tout, T.F., The Human Side of Medieval Records, *Transcripts of the Royal Historical Society Fourth Series, Vol. II* (1928) pp. 1–16. Also: Pike, L.O. *A History of Crime in England* Illustrating the changes of the laws in the progress of civilization, London, Smith Elder, 1873. Vol. I. pp. 199–203. https://openlibrary.org/books/OL23378300M/A_history_of_crime_in_England A contemporary discussion appears as a footnote in Gregory-Abbot, C., 'Sacred Outlaws: Outlawry and the Medieval Church' in Appleby, J.C. and Dalton, P., (eds) *Outlaws in Medieval and Early Modern England: Crime, Government and Society, c. 1066–c.1600,* Farnham, Surrey, Ashgate, 2009. At p. 78. Note 16. This brief entry relies on the version supplied by Bellamy, J.G. *Crime and Public Order in England in the Later Middle Ages,* London, 1973. pp. 50–53 the date supplied is 1303 per Doherty, infra, and there is no commentary relating to the disposition of the case to the effect that a clerk was hanged despite his benefit of clergy plea. Also for a more exhilarating portrayal: Doherty, P., *The Great Crown Jewels Robbery of 1303: The Extraordinary Story of the First Big Bank Raid in History,* London, Constable, 2005. This is a work of fiction that draws upon numerous criminal events that took place in medieval London *viz* Ralph Crepyn

[36] Tout, T.F., The Human Side of Medieval Records, *Transcripts of the Royal Historical Society* Fourth Series, Vol. II (1928) p. 19

Holding clerks in secular custody was not of itself an unusual event and many clerics were detained in secular prisons awaiting the outcome of an initial hearing at which they would seek to achieve clericus. William de Pavely appeared before the king's justices in 1304 accused of murdering his father. He allegedly entered his father's home and 'there feloniously and in premeditated assault wounded his father in the head resulting in his immediate death'.[37] William claimed his clergy and John, dean of the Court Christian of York presented letters patent in the words, '...we commit to you jointly and separately with power of canonical coercion our office for requesting and receiving all clerks, religious *as well as others* (my emphasis) accused of any crime before our lord king...and John by virtue of this commission claims William as a clerk.[38] Bishops were singularly rare in their condemnation of miscreant clergy regardless of whatever efforts the culprits made to avoid liability. One of the few exceptions appears in the register of Oliver, bishop of Lincoln (1280–1299) who excommunicated John de Clipston, a cleric, in 1299 for his involvement in a theft.[39] In 1294 Michael de Leigh, clerk to the bishop of Exeter forged his lord's signature. Contrary to papal decrees Michael was not excommunicated and then tried by the secular courts, he was given episcopal penance to perform.[40] Edward I attempted

---

[37] CP 40/149, m. 389 Michaelmas Term, 1304

[38] Per CP 40/149, m. 389 presented 16th December 1304. In 1293 William and Galfridus de Charlewode had pleaded as layman in one trial and then claimed their clergy in another. 21 Edw I Gaol Delivery Roll 36, m.39, m. 44. Gabel, Supra. p. 47. Note 59

[39] Burger, Supra. p. 144 at *Episcopal Register of Oliver Sutton, Bishop of Lincoln,* Rolls and Regs. Sutton. VI. 163–4

[40] Burger, M., *Bishops, Clerks and Diocesan Governance in Thirteenth-Century England: Reward and Punishment,* Cambridge, Cambridge University Press, 2012. Chap 9 nn. 1–2 and p. 147 Note 54 citing Reg. Bronscombe. No. 103

meaningful development of the common law in his lifetime but his impact upon stemming the rise of criminality committed by clerics was not significant and the ease with which clerks could exonerate themselves before the bishops' courts remained largely unchanged.

During the reign of Edward II (1307–1327) secular justices asserted far greater control over a defendant's effort to select *loci.* In two separate instances before the Eyre of Kent judges dealt with felonious clerics attempting to try their hand at secular trial and if that failed resorting to the bishop's court. Justice Spigurnel was resolute in his opposition when he demanded of the accused, 'Will you hold by your clergy or go to jury? You must make your election of one or the other for you cannot have both'.[41] This was followed in 1313 when one of William de Asshenden's co-accused, John, put himself on the country and saved his clergy plea to later. Justice Beresford was apparently uncomfortable with this double dipping and told John, '...so you must choose definitely yourself between being Church's man and not Church's man'. The matter continued, 'Sir, we understand from you and my other lords that a clerk may put himself on the country yet saving his clergy' Beresford responded. 'Then you have understood us very badly. What you suggest applies only in case of an appeal by private party, and you will never get it allowed in both...No, no, stick to one or the other'.[42]

In principle defendant clerics were held pre-trial in civilian prisons and once claimed by the ordinary would be held

[41] Gabel, Supra. p. 50. Cites. Maitland, F.W. and Turner, G.J. (eds) *1–4 Edw II. Eyre of Kent, Year Book, V. I* London, Selden Society, 1907 p. 151

[42] Gabel, Supra. p. 49. And Maitland, L.W. Harcourt, V. and Bolland, W.C. (eds) *6 and 7 Edw. II. Eyre of Kent, Year Book,* Vol. V. London, Selden Society, 1909. p. 113

exclusively in diocesanal custody. In reality it was not so straightforward; medieval prisons were often franchised and despite Boniface's decree of 1261 bishops used an assortment of venues to hold benefit of clergy claimants,[43] convicted clerics, *absque purgatione* and those (few) who failed episcopal purgation and needed securing to serve out the standard solitary life imprisonment.[44] As wealthy landowners and occupants of diocesanal palaces bishops were well placed to build or convert suitable premises into prisons. This did not necessarily translate into action though and a number of dioceses were without bespoke premises. The bishop of Hereford borrowed his prison from the sheriff, so too did the bishop of Chichester who used Amberley castle and seven years prior to the Canterbury decretal the bishop of London requested that Newgate prison house his clerk John of Frome who was suspected of murder.[45] Conversely some dioceses had more than one prison, Norwich

[43] 'Let every bishop in his diocese have one or two prisons' Constitutions of Archbishop Boniface 126, Helmholz, R.H., *The Oxford History of the Laws of England: The Canon Law and Ecclesiastical Jurisdiction from 597–1640s.* Vol. I. Oxford, Oxford University Press, 2004. p. 512. Boniface had himself built the magnificent palace at Lambeth which remains the official London residence of the archbishop of Canterbury today. The bishop of Salisbury was perhaps the first to precede this decree, he had a prison since 1200. The bishop of Worcester had a prison in 1216. Pugh, Infra. pp. 134–135. During the first half of the thirteenth century more than one hundred commissions were executed to establish gaol deliveries. Bishops prisons at Otford (Canterbury), Leominster, Reading and St. Albans are all examples. Pugh, R.B., *Imprisonment in Medieval England,* Cambridge, Cambridge University Press, 1968. p. 258

[44] Although already in existence this sentence was encouraged by archbishop Pecham in his dilatory purge of miscreant clerics. Notwithstanding it was still the case most purgatory hearings resulted in release. Clerical imprisonment did become more severe under *Pro Clero* (1352), infra

[45] The sheriff of London was subsequently admonished and the warden of Newgate prison, Alan of Shoreditch, was outlawed for complicity in the escape of John of Frome. *Fine Rolls Henry III. 39. Hen. III* (28 Oct 1254–27 Oct 1255) Membrane 13. 74. 13th January 1254 at Westminster. http://www.finerollshenry3.org.uk/content/calendar/roll_052.html#it074_013 also Pugh, Supra. p.134

had three[46] and eventually London had three in addition to the penitentiary tower in St. Paul's cathedral.[47] Mixed clerical and secular usage was also familiar; the bishop of Lincoln had both a spiritual and temporal prison, the archbishop's prison at Maidstone accommodated lay and clerical inmates as did the castle at Eccleshall, prison to the bishop of Coventry and Lichfield.[48] Westminster Abbey was unusual in that it housed lay prisoners for a fee and clerks claimed within the liberty of Westminster. Noticeable is that Puddlicott and his burglarious companion monks (of the Abbey) were not housed in the prison here after their involvement in the theft of the crown jewels in 1303. Academic clerics claiming their clergy were housed in a variety of locations; lay prisons, bishop's palaces and castles. By law as of 1231 the townsfolk of Oxford were required to supply a building suitable for housing student clerics who committed crimes; they were clearly a perennial problem as the chancellor of the university not infrequently sought the assistance of the sheriff to house his scholastic charges.[49] Lay criminals were not beyond the reach of the University either as they too were liable to receive prison sentences from the chancellor and vice-chancellors through delegated diocesanal authority.[50]

---

[46] Norwich, North Elmham and Thetford

[47] For a fascinating account of the genuine 'Lollards Tower' of St. Paul's see: Sparrow Simpson, W., *Chapters in the History of Old S. Paul's*, London, Elliot Stock, 1831. Chapter VII. pp. 113–126

[48] Pugh, R.B., *Imprisonment in Medieval England*, Cambridge, Cambridge University Press, 1968. p. 136 and further Gabel, Supra. p. 110 re: Worcester and Gloucester and McHardy, A.K., Church Courts and Criminous Clerks in the Later Middle Ages in *Medieval Ecclesiastical Studies in Honour of Dorothy M. Owen*, Woodbridge, Suffolk, Boydell Press, 1995. pp. 165–183. p.170

[49] E.g. 1236, 1244 and 1254 per Pugh, Supra. pp. 137–138. By 1431 both university towns utilized lay and bishops prisons

[50] Pugh, Supra. p. 51 citing *Documents Illustrative of Academical Life and Studies at Oxford* (Roll Series) I.94. Cambridge followed suit in 1327. *Calendar of Patent Rolls 1327–30.* 183–4

Speedy trial was not a feature of medieval justice and some clerks spent months or years in prison pending a purgation hearing.[51] John de Hoyville waited four years,[52] Walter de Ermythwayt three years;[53] John Clerk (a horse thief) was imprisoned by the bishop for thirteen years before his trial.[54] William Touicere, convicted by the secular courts of stealing a robe, waited twenty five years for his purgation hearing.[55] William Brone of Kingstead spent twenty six years in prison before he was permitted his purgation hearing.[56]

With prisons come escapes. In 1268 the bishop of Lincoln's prison at Thame was broken into and a number of clerical inmates released. The prison was in the cellars of the Bird Cage Inn. Two other clerics had escaped from the same public house (prison) in 1247.[57] In the following century fourteen clerics escaped Newbury and nine from Banbury.[58] But prison-breaking was always a very dangerous pastime. The statutory sentence at common law[59] was beheading without further

---

[51] Pugh, Supra. p. 49 suggests two to four years as not being uncommon

[52] Gabel, Supra. p. 109

[53] McHardy, Supra. p. 172

[54] Ibid. p. 172 citing Storey, R.L. (ed) *The Register of John Kirkby, Bishop of Carlisle, 1332–1352* and *The Register of John Ross, Bishop of Carlisle, 1325–1332,* Canterbury and York Society, 2 Vols. 1993–1995. 79, 81 and further examples of 5 years (2), 6 years, 10 years, 14 years, 15 years, 16 years, 17 years (2)

[55] Ibid

[56] McHardy. Supra. p. 172

[57] Lobel, M., (ed) *A History of the County of Oxford: Dorchester and Thame Hundreds.* Vol. 7. Oxford University Press, London, 1962. pp. 113–116

[58] For further examples see inter alia: Burger, Supra. p. 139. John de Arden's bond for allowing two clerks to escape from bishop Swinfields prison at Ross in 1307 and McHardy, Supra, p. 173. Fourteen clerks escaped from Newbury, December 24, 1381, nine from Banbury, July 29, 1389

[59] Until statutory provisions prevailed in 1295 under 23. Edw. I. Stat. Realm. I. 113

trial, priest or not.[60] The precise status of clergymen prison breakers was unclear until Henry VIII (1509–1547) determined that all escapees, irrespective of status, committed an unclergyable felony.[61] Assisting a cleric to escape from prison was treated differently than helping a civilian escape from prison. Regardless of whether or not there was any degree of complicity for every cleric that escaped his bishop was liable to a £100 fine.[62] The Patent and Close Rolls contain examples; the bishop of London was fined for allowing twelve prisoners to escape, the bishop of Winchester also fined for allowing two clerics to escape and the bishop of Norwich was fined £200 for allowing two clerks to escape.[63] During his period in custody a clerk's benefices and chattels became crown property (before the inevitable commission from the bishop demanding restoration of successful purgation). Also, unlike sheriffs and lay wardens, bishops themselves could not be removed from

---

[60] Per two men who escaped from the Tower of London and were captured inside the graveyard of St. Paul's cathedral, no doubt intent upon claiming sanctuary. They were beheaded at the scene. Also Henry de la Mere, 1315, executed for escaping. Pugh, Supra. p. 227. There are however, numerous examples of escapees being captured and held again until trial. E.g. Two escapees from Canterbury castle who were flogged and by contrast two escapees from Warwick Eyre, 1221, who had been on the run for so long the justices decided that they had been convicted of the original crime *in absentia*

[61] Before this an Oxford academic cleric was outlawed and expelled from the university for springing another clerk from the bishop's prison in 1421 whereas in the same year a group of academics joined their fellow student escapees and rode around the county participating in hunting trips. Overtime it seems to have become the case that the issue was whether or not the escapee had broken out of prison or 'wandered abroad' that is walked out due to the inefficiencies or connivance of the warden. C.f. Pugh, Supra. p. 229–230. 23. Hen. VIII. C. II, s. I

[62] Gabel. L. *Benefit of Clergy in England in the Later Middle Ages*, New York, Octagon Press, 1969 (reprinted) p. 111

[63] Gabel, Supra. p. 11. Citing: *Cal. P.R.* 1266–1272. p. 43. (Norwich), *Cal. P.R.* 1413–1416. p. 198 (Chichester). *Cal. P.R.* 1354–1358, p. 355 (London) and *E 401 Receipt Roll* 909, 14 Nov. 12 E. IV (Winchester)

office, imprisoned or executed for allowing escapes; a severe financial penalty was one of the few remedial options available to the monarch and it was always rescindable through the process of royal pardon.[64]

England was many years away from establishing a penal policy and establishing institutions that focused on reform and rehabilitation. The medieval prison, secular or spiritual, was a dismal affair with all prisoners reliant upon eleemosynary provision. It was the intention of England's prelates that clerics would have individual accommodations, in reality segregation was not always possible and clergy and laity often shared quarters as the odious terms 'dungeon' and 'pit' crept into the English lexicon. The Lying House at Durham was referred to as a dungeon in 1385, the term was also employed to describe Stafford prison in 1391, Hereford in 1462 and Hertford in 1508. In 1334 Newcastle gaol was called the 'pit', York castle a dungeon (1360) so too; Colchester (1373), Leicester (1411) and Nottingham (1532).[65] Later nicknames include: 'The Cowhouse', used to describe the bishops prison in Wells (1439), 'The Bullpit', Clarendon Palace (1445), and being a 'jailbird' is probably attributable to the Bird Cage Inn, Thame, Oxon.[66] Monastics kept a tight rein on felonious brothers and

---

[64] In 1382 the bishop of Lincoln was pardoned for allowing fourteen clerks to escape. Also in 1382 the bishop of Winchester was pardoned for allowing an escape. Five pardons were granted to the archbishop of York between 1386 and 1413 for escapes. Bishops of Chichester, Exeter and the abbots of St. Albans and Westminster were all recipients of pardons. Pugh, Supra. p. 246

[65] Pugh, Supra. p. 354

[66] Pugh, Supra. p. 354. Bocado is a term used in Oxford to describe the borough prison it has been suggested there is a Latin heritage in the declension of 'privy' for a broader commentary see; Pugh, Supra. pp. 360–361. For an overview of the monastic prison Pugh, Supra, devotes a chapter to the topic (XVIII) 'Monastic Imprisonment'. Bocardo is also employed by McHardy, Supra. p 173. Note 2

their detention facilities were more austere and confining than either the bishop's prisons or secular. While serving a custodial sentence the criminal Brother was appointed a guardian who was often the only source of conversation for the penitent; 'hard commons and in chains should he not repent', followed by a meagre diet. Perpetual solitary immuration[67] was the prospect for many criminal monks in the thirteenth century.[68] The rational was simple; punitive custody was non-violent and provided the perfect blend of 'misery and spiritual growth'.[69]

For all the imperfections that existed between courts Christian and temporal in mode of trial, custody and sentencing outcomes significant progress had been achieved by the end of the thirteenth century. The way was now open for the adoption of a reading test (piecemeal and organic as it would remain)[70] that could successfully supplant tonsure as the definitive means of establishing clericus.[71] Benefit of clergy would be open to all men including aliens and those of non-Christian religions. Foreigners were permitted to use a bible in their own tongue; by inference this meant that Latin[72] was not required for the purposes of the reading test. *De facto* the authenticity of the

---

[67] See: Pollock & Maitland, *The History of the English Law,* Supra. p. 444

[68] 1283, Bishop Giffard instructing Prior Secunda on how to provide the appropriate custodial environment for a miscreant canon. Cited in Pugh, Supra. p. 382

[69] Geltner, G., Medieval Prisons: Between Myth and Reality, Hell and Purgatory, *History Compass,* Vol. 4, Issue 2, (March, 2006), pp. 261–274. P.5

[70] Per Edw. III, Infra. 25. Edw. 3. St. 3. C.4, 1350

[71] Gabel. Supra, p. 76–77. I cannot find a definitive source that specifies a date at which there was a transition from any bible text to wholesale use of the *misère.* Certainly by the time that Edward III enacted legislation in 1351 to extend the benefit to the laity all records indicate that psalm 51 was in widespread use by the courts. Gabel. Supra. p. 66. The exact date from which that Psalm 51 was recited in English is not recorded. It was being used from at least the eighteenth year of Elizabeth's reign onwards

[72] Bellamy, J., *Criminal Law and Society in Late Medieval and Tudor England,* New York, St. Martin's Press, 1984. p. 116

claimant as a priest was no longer an issue for the Common Law. Being able to read would be all that mattered. And whereas all clerics were supposed to be *literatus* rather than *illiteratus*[73] this was certainly not always the case. By requiring the reading of a text it now meant that those clerics who were unable to read would have to be schooled to do so. It also erased the fiction of all clerics being highly educated and in its own subtle way would confirm the ordinariness of the parish clergyman. Minima figures support this for as few as 14 per cent of clergy held a baccalaureate degree.[74] It was not until the massive expansion of grammar school education in the fifteenth century that levels of literacy across every social class would improve noticeably.[75] Even as late as the mid-sixteenth century 106 of 311 clergy in the diocese of Gloucester could not recite the Ten Commandments; 10 could not say the Lord's Prayer and 34 of them were not even able to identify the creator of the work.[76] As Lander has noted the small English intellectual avant-garde, comprising mostly of clerics, was indeed a minority.[77]

Once in use the ability required to convince a secular tribunal of literacy was exceptionally low. The negative aspect of this meant that since proving clericus was such a low threshold clergymen were now in danger of being perceived as little

---

[73] Pope Gregory VIII declared that literary knowledge was important to all ranks not only bishops and both Alexander III and Innocent III permitted masters and students to exempt themselves from their benefices to pursue study. Luscombe, D., and Riley-Smith, J., (eds) *The New Cambridge Medieval History*, Cambridge, Cambridge University Press, 2004. Vol. IV c. 1024–1198. pp. 435–436

[74] Lander, J.R., *Government and Community: England, 1450–1509*, Cambridge, Mass, Harvard University Press, 1980. p. 131

[75] Lander, Supra. pp. 131–134

[76] Lander, Supra. p. 133

[77] Lander, Supra. p. 133

more than laymen. For the criminal clergyman this probably made little difference to their perception of themselves or the criminal law and they had made extensive gains; the strict interpretation of canon law that forbade sanctuary, abjuration and outlawry had been continuously flaunted (and with active approval of bishops).[78] If viewed as a positive development in the life of legal excuses then by the close of the century criminal defendants, cleric and lay, had four established mitigatory options available to them. Given the arbitrary nature of the criminal law this may not have been such a bad thing.

---

[78] For a discussion of canonical courts and procedures see: Brundage, J.A., *Medieval Canon Law*, London. Longman, 1995. Chapter 6. pp. 120–153. Also Purvis, J.S., *An Introduction to Ecclesiastical Records*, London, St. Anthony's Press, 1953

# 6

# Sanctuary, Abjuration and Exile

As law and order deteriorated[1] across medieval England criminous clerks oscillated between the sanctioned immunity of clericus and prohibited, but frequently utilized, provisions of sanctuary, abjuration[2] and outlawry. At canon law sanctuary was reserved for lay criminals who sought the protections of the Church for a specific period of time before the laws temporal interceded. This temporary respite was followed by either abjuration (swearing guilt and exile from the realm), submission to the courts secular and a trial or the criminal sentence (or self-infliction) of outlawry. Until 1261 bishops were permitted to impose sentences of abjuration and outlawry upon clerics; after this time clergymen were prohibited from seeking any form of abjuration or outlawry as this *de facto* subjected churchmen to the provisions of the secular law. The nexus between the legal (excusory) quartet; benefit of clergy, sanctuary, abjuration and outlawry is demonstrated in the number of cases where defendants moved between each and the authorities spiritual and temporal accommodated them. As this chapter will show regardless of established canon law

---

[1] Lebow, R.N., *A Cultural Theory of International Relations,* Cambridge, Cambridge University Press, 2008. pp. 256–257. For an alternative position, Burt, C., *Edward I and the Governance of England 1272–1307,* Cambridge, Cambridge University Press, 2013, pp. 7–8

[2] Abjuration is the English term that was applied to any felon who admitted their crimes and were then permitted to exile England

clerics passed freely between all these excuses. Instances of diocesanal objection or direct interference are extremely rare. What more frequently occurred was the intervention of the bishop when a layman or cleric was forcibly removed from a holy place and a sacrilegious crime was then committed by those seeking forcible extraction of the sanctuarian.

The intertwining of legal options and jurisdictional cooperation through sanctuary and abjuration also demonstrates how the functions of the Church and secular legal society overlapped, principally through the office of the coroner. In some instances the Church did not support the sanctuary seeker, layman or cleric, and took active steps to remove the protections of church asylum and return the offender to temporal authorities. What we are seeing at this point is evidence of the significant overlap between what the laws Christian and temporal proclaimed and what in practice was taking place. Sanctuary and abjuration are commonplace across the spiritual and secular divide and outlawry (which of itself was more extreme; outlaws immediately bore the 'wolves head') was imposed by the courts secular, the coroner, and self-imposed by criminals. Although prohibited at canon law; there are many recorded instances of clerics being outlawed and later pardoned.

What is striking about the uptake of the Excusory Quartet by English clergy is the objective nature of their decision making, the weighing up of the likely outcomes, the strategic planning. Felonious clerics do not view benefit of clergy as one single immunity but one of a range to be used (and abused) as best suits the circumstances of the felon concerned. Nowhere is this clearer than in the actions of the growing number of gangs of bandits that started to terrorize the countryside towards the end of the thirteenth century and the early part of the fourteenth (Two of the most infamous gangs; the Cotterals and the Folevilles feature in the following chapter). The range of crime conducted by the crime gangs is typical of contemporary organized crime groups; kidnapping, extortion, murder, arson. What is unique is that in some cases the gang contained members who throughout their criminal careers remained beneficed clergymen. It is therefore important to document this involvement and the attempts by the gang members to usurp justice, secular and spiritual, and to recognize the implicit acceptance of the flexible interpretations of laws available. Outlawry was denied at canon law yet commonplace and much as clerics who had abjured were eligible to seek a royal pardon so too were outlaw clerics. Both the provisions and any pardon were an effrontery to laws Christian and yet both co-existed even to the point of declarations of outlawry being made in St. Paul's cathedral, London. Within the class structured society of medieval England the financial tariff for obtaining a king's pardon was set at £1000 for an archbishop and £200 for a regular clergyman; secular pardons to criminal clergymen was established common law. The expansive use of legal provisions that straddle laws spiritual and secular by clergymen gang members provides concrete evidence of the merging of licit and illicit lifestyles. It also answers in part why the response to criminal gangs that took place in the first quarter of the fourteenth century was so expansive and all-encompassing, regardless of the status of the offender. England's monarchs had to respond to the unrest in society. The English Church was largely impotent to assist; a number of its members were criminals themselves and those that were not allowed the manipulation of the law to provide the best possible outcome. As this chapter will demonstrate the English Church was an implicit and explicit partner in the use and abuse of England's porous legal boundaries as benefit of clergy moved ever closer to being a temporal remedy alongside sanctuary, abjuration and outlawry.

Clergymen who engaged in crime might interact with secular judicial officials at a number of points during pre-trial and trial proceedings.[3] If remanded into custody they could be housed in either secular or spiritual gaols. If secular they were under the custody of the sheriff. Initial trial hearings were before judges secular and in many instances the trial proceeded and upon conclusion a determination of clericus was established. Some clerics having weighed up their options decided on sanctuary and then; either abjuration or outlaw status. During these alternative processes the cleric was subjected to interaction and determination by secular authorities not spiritual. A key player in non-court processes was the coroner; he was at the very intersection of the laws spiritual and secular and would have frequently come into contact with clerics who themselves had succumbed to worldly pressures and skirmishes with crime. Association between temporal and spiritual authorities was a fact of life for criminous clerks, the office of coroner was frequently the conduit for this. And just as benefit of clergy appeared to provide an opportunity for criminal clerics to avoid the consequences of their actions so too did sanctuary facilitate another mechanism for

---

[3] Clerics were not immune from prosecution in civil matters. Helmholz, R.H., *The Oxford History of the Laws of England. Volume I The Canon Law and Ecclesiastical Jurisdiction from 597–1640s*, Oxford, Oxford University Press, 2004

clerics, and the laity, to avoid the reaches of the courts temporal. In addition to the role of hearing abjuration oaths[4] the coroner recorded inquests into deceased persons and heard presentments of felonies. Some coroners held responsibility for the production of financial accounts pertaining to wealthy landowning ecclesiastical benefices (such as the palatinate of Durham and liberties of Ely and Hexham).[5] In many respects the work of the coroner represented a bridge between England's two legal systems, Christian and temporal.

As this chapter will demonstrate one example of legal discord was over the issue of clerics claiming sanctuary and then abjuring the realm. The civil law permitted this, canon law did not. Another was when local citizens ignored sanctuary rights and kidnapped escaped felons to administer summary justice. In one extreme example (Hubert de Burgh 1234) the Church claimed that killing this felon on route to exile was sacrilege as he was still under the protection of the Church. This is of dubious validity though as it was established law that those abjuring the realm were under the protections of the crown and never the Church. Compromise was inevitable too and together the coroner and the bishop, through local clergy, cooperated to administer a range of immunities that transcended life secular and Christian.[6]

---

[4] In England by the late twelfth century abjuration became a regular practice associated with sanctuary. Logan, W., Criminal Law Sanctuaries, *Harvard Civil Rights-Civil Liberties Law Review*, Vol. 38 (Summer, 2003) pp. 321–391. p. 327

[5] Infra. Secular sanctuaries also existed for example Chester, Hoole Heath, Overmarsh and Rudhealth all provided sanctuary to fleeing felons and all were perpetual as well. Bellamy, J. *Crime and Public Order in England in the Later Middle Ages*, London, Routledge, 1973. p. 106

[6] Helmholz, Supra. p. 62. N. 173 Also, there are examples of where criminals were permitted asylum even though the crime from which they fled was not a felony. Given, J.B., *Society and Homicide in Thirteenth-Century England*, Stanford, Stanford University Press, 1977, p. 116

Sanctuary has its roots in pre-Christian society.[7] It was taken up as church asylum through the establishment of holy places introduced by Emperor Constantine (306–337) and the construction of the Holy Sepulchre Church in Jerusalem at the presumed site of the tomb of Christ.[8] This provision was confirmed by Emperor Theodosius (379–395) in 392 A.D.,[9] the 441 Council of Orange and again by the Synod of Orleans, 511, (which extended the privilege to bishops' residences and thirty five paces beyond).[10] Located in the idea of refuge it was intended that sanctuary, *salvatio*, was an area free from: oppression, service to secular lords, violence and conflict.[11] Jews, Germanic tribes, the Romans and

---

[7] Helmholz, R., *The ius commune in England: Four Studies,* Oxford, Oxford University Press, 2001. Chapter One 'The Law of Sanctuary' p.23

[8] Rubin, M. and Simons, W., *The Cambridge History of Christianity Volume 4 Christianity in Western Europe c. 1100–c. 1500,* Cambridge, Cambridge University Press, 2009.

[9] Pope, S., Sanctuary: The Legal Institution in England, *University of Puget Sound Law Review,* Vol. 10. (1986–1987) pp. 677–697. p. 680

[10] Cox, R., *The Sanctuaries and Sanctuary Seekers, of Medieval England,* London, George Allen & Sons, 1911, reprinted by Forgotten Books 2012.p. 4., Logan, W., Criminal Law Sanctuaries, *Harvard Civil Rights-Civil Liberties Law Review,* Vol. 38 (Summer, 2003) pp. 321–391, Helmholz, R., *The ius commune in England: Four Studies,* Oxford, Oxford University Press, 2001. Chapter One 'The Law of Sanctuary', Pryce, H., *Native Law and the Church in Medieval Wales,* Oxford, Clarendon Press, 1993, Chapter 7, Pope, S., Sanctuary: The Legal Institution in England, *University of Puget Sound Law Review,* Vol. 10. (1986–1987) pp. 677–697, Rosser, G., 'Sanctuary and Social Negotiation in Medieval England' in Blair, J., and Golding, B., *The Cloister and the World; Essays in Medieval History in Honour of Barbara Harvey,* Oxford, Clarendon Press, 1996. Clovis 511 c.1. provided '…criminals who take refuge in a church may be taken from this refuge only if the injured person or his relatives promise to abstain from vengeance and to be satisfied with penance' Wallach, L., *Alcuin and Charlemagne: Studies in Carolingian History and Literature,* New York, London-Johnson Reprint, 1968. p. 129

[11] The physical parameters of sanctuary were set by a number of methods e.g. at Meunet in the diocese of Bourges it was established by shooting an arrow in all directions from the choir of the Church. Where the arrow landed established the limits of sanctuary. Constable, G., 'Religious Communities 1024–1215' in Luscombe, D. and Riley-Smith, J., (eds)

later Merovingian, Carolingian and Scandinavian codes all provided for protected status of those who had fled to the immunity of a church.[12] Specific reference to sanctuary appears in England soon after Ethelbert (590–616) converted to Christianity in 597. By 688 under Ine, king of Wessex (688–726)[13] two forms of sanctuary, general and chartered, appear to have been available. Of chartered the most famous were Westminster Abbey, Durham and Beverley. Generally chartered sanctuaries provided larger geographic areas than consecrated asylum and longer periods of protection than the standard forty days.[14] In 1496 three canons of the Premonstratensian abbey of Eglestone and a servant together took asylum at the great priory church of Durham. They had been involved in an affray in Stretford that resulted in the death of a man. They arrived at sanctuary twelve days after the crime and were still permitted entry.[15] Beverley was unique in that the limits of perpetual sanctuary extended to the extremities of the town itself.[16]

---

*The New Cambridge Medieval History, Volume IV, c. 1024–1198, Part I.* Cambridge, Cambridge University Press, 2004. p. 359

[12] Helmholz, Supra. p. 24

[13] E.g. the privileges of the liberties of the minster at Beverley, Infra, translated from Saxon English into Latin by the sacrist Master Alured. Cox, Supra. p. 130. N. 1. Also Riggs, C. H., 'Criminal Asylum in Anglo-Saxon Law', *University of Florida Monogrpahs,* Social Sciences, Vol. 6. No. 18 1963 'If anyone renders himself liable to the lash and flees to the church, he shall be immune from scourging' cited by Logan, W., Criminal Law Sanctuaries, *Harvard Civil Rights-Civil Liberties Law Review,* Vol. 38 (Summer, 2003) pp. 321–391. p. 321

[14] Cox, Supra. p. 326. And Olson, T., 'Sanctuary and Penitential Rebirth in the Central Middle Ages' in Musson, A., (ed), *Boundaries of the Law: Geography, Gender and Jurisdiction in Medieval and Early Modern Europe,* Aldershot, Ashgate, 2005. pp. 38–52

[15] Cox, Supra. p. 109

[16] Cox, Supra. pp.126–149. The record of perpetual claimants at Beverley for the period 1478–1539 is held at the British Museum and shows two clerks and one chaplain

Further codes followed in 887[17] and 930[18] so that by circa 1000 a sanctuary seeking felon could either pay wergild compensation or face perpetual life imprisonment. Upon committing a subsequent felony the culprit was barred from any further resort to church asylum.[19] In 1070 William I enacted laws pertaining to 'Criminals fleeing to the Church' which held that a felon who repeatedly sought sanctuary in a church or priest's house had to leave the province.[20]

Alongside these secular developments the number of sanctuaries frequented by pilgrims increased.[21] In many instances it became popular to place tombs near to where the Eucharist was offered. As this preferred burial space became a premium the zone around the Church, *circuitus ecclesiae,* increased giving rise to the establishment of consecrated burial sites. Cemeteries were soon to become *de facto* sacred places and presence in such a place afforded a sanctuary.[22] By the thirteenth century sanctuary was understood to mean a place of refuge for criminals trying to avoid judicial vengeance.[23]

---

[17] Under Alfred the Great. Cox, Supra. p. 7 also referring to Alfred's laws, Wormald, P., *The Making of the English Law: King Alfred to the Twelfth Century. Volume I Legislation and It's limits,* Oxford, Blackwell, 1999 (Reprinted 2000) p. 272. "If he then reaches a church, then let it be according to the church's privilege…'

[18] King Athelstan. Cox, Supra. p. 7

[19] Cox, Supra. p. 8

[20] The province stipulation being a forerunner to banishment from the realm. Pope, Supra. p. 684–685 and N. 31. William also extended special sanctuary status to the Abbey of St. Martin at Battle after a vow made at the Battle of Hastings. Cox, Supra. pp. 196–197. An alternative discussion on the establishment of chartered sanctuary of Battle, Rosser, Supra. p. 75. He claims that the right of mobile sanctuary vested in the abbot is located in 1160

[21] Many now in Europe not just the Holy Land e.g. St. James of Compostela, St Foy of Conques in Rouergue, St. Mark's in Venice, St. Thomas Becket at Canterbury Cathedral

[22] Rosser, Supra. p. 63 esp. N. 23

[23] Jordan, W. C. A., 'Fresh Look at Medieval Sanctuary' in Karras, R.M., Kaye, J., and Matter, E. A., (eds) *Law and the Illicit in Medieval Europe,* Philadelphia, University of Pennsylvania Press, 2008

Some commentators have viewed this as an 'irrational gift' from the state.[24]

Church asylum was not incompatible with medieval justice it was a fundamental part of it that provided all manner of unfortunates the opportunity to repent for their crimes and face the consequences; perpetual exile. Exceptionally clerics too took this extreme option (*infidelis*).[25] The first stage in the process was to admit one's criminal wrongdoing and then through penitential suffering ask for forgiveness. For the Christian church mercy prevailed at this point, for the secular law justice was satisfied once the oath of abjuration[26] or committal to trial had taken place. For the criminal cleric either was a potential soft option and the forty day[27] delay (barrier) provided plenty of time for an assessment of his options.

Many who achieved the privilege of sanctuary (the legal entitlement to the Church's protection) were willing to go into exile rather than stand trial before sanguinary secular laws. Occasionally felonious clerics also took the option of abjuration rather than face the prospect of failing their clergy or more likely failing purgation and then receiving the sentence

---

[24] Olson, Infra, p.39 citing Hyams, P., Feud and the State in Late Anglo-Saxon England, *Journal of British Studies*, Vol. 40 (2001), pp. 1–43. p.27

[25] Not 'law worthy'. Until the middle of the twelfth century in England and France once a fleeing felon reached sanctuary there were a number of ways in which he might resolve the situation, e.g. by proposing compensation for the wrong or having his crimes forgiven by the victim or participating in a particular public penance. See: Olson, Supra. p. 41 and the famous St. Ursmer incident. Those crimes that were so heinous that compensation was not permissible or unamendable, *botles* crimes, subsequently became (in England and France) felonies

[26] To swear an oath of perpetual exile from the realm

[27] Any person providing respite, food or assistance to a felon after the forty day period themselves committed a felony; this included clerics. Gross, C., (ed) *Select Cases from the Coroners' Rolls A.D. 1265–1413: With a brief account of the history of the office of coroner*, London, Selden Society, 1896.Volume IX. pp. 86–87 and 1316. 9. Edw. II. c. 10

of perpetual diocesanal imprisonment in solitary confinement. A cleric prisoner was required to petition for his purgation. As seen previously there was no guarantee of a speedy hearing particularly if the bishop thought the clerk to be notorious or the prelate had a personal stake in the outcome. To deny purgation invariably sentenced the would-be claimant to perpetual solitary confinement. Prior to commencement of a purgation hearing the bishop ordered an enquiry into the claimant and the offence. This was normally, though not exclusively, conducted by twelve rectors or vicars appointed by the bishop.[28] Others, often career criminals, who abused the privilege of benefit of clergy because they were able to claim clericus even though their association with the Church was minimal, decided on the more hazardous status of outlaw. Combined; benefit of clergy, sanctuary, abjuration and outlawry form the totality of privileges available to felonious clerks to avoid capital punishment during the Middle Ages.[29]

In England general sanctuary was attached to all churches, priests' houses, conventual buildings, church hospitals and many episcopal palaces.[30] For the majority of these premises the immunity extended to forty paces beyond the walls of the Church, sometimes less if a smaller church.[31] If a monastery or priory had a chapel then sanctuary applied to those parts of the

---

[28] Bellamy, Supra. pp. 153–154 and Helmholz, Supra. p. 296

[29] Logan, Supra, notes that despite the formal abolition of sanctuary in the seventeenth century the 'spirit of sanctuary' lived on through benefit of clergy as a way of mitigating the severity of the secular criminal law. p. 329

[30] Wormald, Supra. p. 280. In France it extended to fortified churches. Jordan, Supra. p. 21. Olson, T., 'Sanctuary and Penitential Rebirth in the Central Middle Ages' in Musson, A., (ed), *Boundaries of the Law: Geography, Gender and Jurisdiction in Medieval and Early Modern Europe*, Aldershot, Ashgate, 2005. p. 39

[31] Helmholz, Supra. p. 29 and Abbiot de bello, Cox, Supra. p. 197

establishment but not ordinary lodgings or storage facilities within the monastery. Private chapels and oratories were not places of sanctuary. The special status of Westminster Abbey was confirmed in 1222 by Henry III (1216–1272) when he freed the abbey from the jurisdiction of the bishop of London and the archbishop of Canterbury. In effect Westminster reported directly to the pope. This unique status has over the years transformed into the current situation where each new bishop of London and archbishop of Canterbury confirm the uniqueness of St. Peter's as soon as they make their first visit to the cathedral church (former abbey).

Sanctuary could also be chartered, that is granted by the crown as was the case with Battle Abbey, Gloucester Abbey, the Cathedral Church of Lincoln, all Cistercian Abbeys. St. Peter's Westminster,[32] St. Martin Le Grand,[33] Durham[34]

---

[32] The Dean (as this is now a cathedral church and no longer an abbey) is formerly considered to be a 'Royal Peculiar' and is appointed directly by the crown. Shepherd, R., *Westminster: A Biography*, London, The National Archives, 2012. p. 51. The special status of Westminster derives from two sources, it is the pilgrimage and center for St. Edward the Confessor and it holds 'special' sanctuary status because the monarch waives his right to assert the laws in favor of the local lord, in this case the abbot. The abbot therefore held the franchise on the sanctuary and determined it to be perpetual. Shepherd. Ibid. pp. 98–99. So frequent was the use that one of the streets is named 'Thieving Lane'. Also Cox, Supra. p. 148 re: the restoration of Westminster privileges by Queen Mary 1553–1558. A further special feature of Westminster was that the names of those in sanctuary were not ordinarily revealed. Of note is that the UK Supreme Court is now located on the site of the Abbey's sanctuary. Shepherd. Ibid. p. 103

[33] Founded in 1056 as a college of secular canons under the leadership of Ingelric. From consecration St. Martin's was exempt from all episcopal and archdiaconal jurisdiction. Cox, Supra. p. 81. Riley, H.T. (trans) *Memorials of London and London Life in the XIIIth, XIVth, and XVth Centuries: Being a Series of Extracts, Local, Social, and Political, from the Early Archives of the City of London*, A.D. 1276–1419, London, Longmans, 1868. p. 57

[34] Neville, C.J. "The Bishops Ministers": The Office of Coroner in Late Medieval Durham, *Florilegium*, Vol. 18. Issue 2 (2001) pp. 47–60 and Cox, Supra. pp. 95– 125

and Beverley[35] are the most famous.[36] Christ Church Canterbury was granted Liberties in 1017 by king Cnut(1016–1035).[37] St. Martin Le Grand was a primary sanctuary location in London and the venue for the nightly ringing of the curfew bell that applied across the capital. "At every Parish church, a curfew is to be rung at the same hour as at St. Martin's le Grand...".[38] The curfew denoted that the city gates should be locked, ale houses were to be closed and no one was to walk the streets. Citizens found to be out walking after curfew committed a crime recorded as being a 'Nightwalker". In 1304 John Blome, a cleric, was indicted for affray and riot committed after the curfew hour, he was detained in secular prison to await trial.[39] The particular attraction of chartered sanctuaries was that they offered permanent refuge, mostly within the confines of the physical buildings. In the case of the Minster of St. John of Beverley sanctuary extended one and one half miles in every direction.[40] Some sanctuaries were combined spiritual and secular. The Knights Hospitaller's Paris Garden and The Clink,[41] (both in Southwark, London) were known as

---

[35] Truly exceptional as the sanctuary extended to the limits of the Yorkshire town and sanctuary seekers could claim the privilege three times. Upon third usage the seeker was bound in perpetuity to the confines and service of the minster. Cox, Supra. pp. 124–149. Beverley represented the personification of the ecclesiastical control of sanctuary rather than secular

[36] For a complete list see Cox, Supra. pp. 183–214

[37] Harmer, F.E. (Trans and Ed) 'Cnut's Confirmation of the Liberties of Christ Church, Canterbury (1017–1020)' in Harding, A., *The Law Courts of Medieval England,* London, Allen and Unwin, 1973. pp.130– 131

[38] 10. Edw. I. 1282. Letter Book. Also Riley, Supra. p. 4

[39] Riley, Supra. p. 57 and in 1311 and again 1320 clerics Richard Heryng, Riley, Supra, p. 70, and John de Sloghtre Riley, Supra, p. 93 were arrested for 'nightwalking'

[40] For a comprehensive discussion of Beverley see: Cox, Supra. pp. 126–149

[41] It is believed that the Clink first achieved sanctuary status in 1181. It was a 'liberty' meaning it comprised of a number of manors the lords of which were granted privileges by the crown and from which, importantly, the sheriff did not have authority or jurisdiction. Brandon, D., & Brooke, A., *Bankside: London's Original District of Sin,* Stroud, Amberley, 2011. p. 104

'bastard sanctuaries' due to holding joint secular and spiritual legal statuses.[42]

Exceptionally it was claimed that sanctuary was attached to a person rather than a building. St. Hugh, bishop of Lincoln (1186–1200) asserted that church immunity extended to wherever he was present; flight to the body of a bishop was in essence a form of 'expiratory pilgrimage'.[43] In the spring of 1199 while travelling through St. Albans on route to Normandy Hugh arrived as a hanging was about to take place. The condemned man pleaded for the bishop's intervention. Hugh responded that a bishop and his entourage were the Church and sanctuary attached to him wherever he travelled.[44] On another occasion bishop Hugh excommunicated[45] a group of men who had forced a felon from the sanctuary of a parish church and lynched him. It transpired that one of the offenders was a cleric. Four of the men submitted to the authority of the church and were given penance (much like bishop Giffard ordered in the following century) which required that they exhume the body and carry the remains to the local church for Christian burial. The offenders were then ordered to walk barefoot between Brackley and Lincoln;

---

[42] Brandon. Supra. p. 70. This area is also frequently referred to as 'Bankside' and at times was viewed as an 'outlaw borough'. Ibid. pp. 89–90

[43] Thornley, I., Sanctuary in Medieval London, *Journal of the British Archaeological Association*, Vol. 38. (1932) pp. 293–315. p. 301

[44] Cox, Supra. p. 210

[45] Excommunication can be equated with the secular proclamation of outlawry as both pronounce death upon the incumbent. "By the authority of God the father omnipotent, the Son and the holy spirit and by my own I tear from you your clerical habit and depose, degrade, despoil and strip you of all orders, benefits and privileges of clergy" Brown, W. (ed) *The Register of Walter Giffard, Lord Archbishop of York*, London, Surtees Society, 1904. p. 64. For further discussion see: Logan, F.D. *Excommunication and the Secular Arm in Medieval England*, Toronto, Pontifical Institute of Medieval Studies, 1968

to be beaten by the local priest at every church on route. The sole cleric among this group of felons fled from the realm as he '...preferred to leave England rather than make the angels rejoice by a fitting show of penance'. According to the record this cleric did eventually repent and was sentenced by the bishop to seven years penance.[46] Occasionally monks claimed mobile sanctuary.[47] In 1364 Abbot Robert de Bello of St. Martins Abbey, Battle applied the prerogative of personal sanctuary to a felon awaiting the gallows at Marshalsea prison, London.[48] Itinerant sanctuary attached to an archbishop until the statutory ending of all church asylum in the seventeenth century.[49]

Royal sanctuary existed in principle as far as 'the verge' (twelve miles). It was limited in distance though when applicable to those on route to an abjurers port of departure (or if the abjurer strayed off the king's highway).[50] An interesting

---

[46] Douie, D.L. and Farmer, D.H. (Eds) *Magna Vita Sancti Hugonis: Volume II The Life of St. Hugh of Lincoln* (Oxford Medieval Texts) Oxford, Oxford University Press, 1962. pp. 197–199, Myers, A.R. (ed) Punishment for Violation of Sanctuary, *English Historical Documents*, Vol. IV c. 1327–1485 Part III. Sec. 4. and Richardson, H.G. and Sayles, G.O.(eds) Fleta II, Seldon Society, Vol. 72 (1955) pp. 76–77 being Fleta, Book I, chap. 29 in Rothwell, H. (ed) Sanctuary and Abjuration of the Realm, and Outlawry, *English Historical Documents*, Volume III c. 1189–1379 Part 3. Document 110 both at www.englishhistoricaldocuments.com/document/view.htm?id=723

[47] E.g. those of Glastonbury. Rosser, Supra. p. 62

[48] For commentary: Helmholz, Supra. p. 29. N. 55. There are a number of exceptions also for example Battle Abbey, Sussex sanctuary was set at a distance of one and a half miles from the choir. Pope, Supra. p. 685. N. 31 and Olson, Supra. p.44. Abbots of Battle Abbey were also given permission by William I to free robbers or thieves from hanging. Olson, Supra. p. 44

[49] 16 April, 1697 William III. Hertzler, J.R., The Abuse and Outlawing of Sanctuary for Debt in Seventeenth-Century England, *The Historical Journal*. Vol. 14. No. 3 (Sep., 1971) pp. 467–477

[50] Harding, Supra. p. 103

example of the scope of royal itinerant sanctuary occurred in 1347 when Edward III (1327–1377) was in Calais and his son, Lionel, was placed as Keeper of England. On Good Friday 1347 Margery de la Beche was abducted, during which two of her servants were murdered. The abductor was Sir John Dalton. Both the king and his son Lionel were outraged at the event and the timing of it. The crime was held to be committed within 'the verge of Marshalsea' to the terror of the *king's* household.[51]

By the thirteenth century sanctuary was only available to those suspected of committing a felony. One exception was that a felon who committed the crime inside or within the curtilage of a church had also committed sacrilege[52] and therefore, in theory, sanctuary was not available to them.[53] In one instance a fornicating cleric fled to a church to avoid the woman's father. The priest claimed responsibility for a minor theft in order that he could gain asylum. He was subsequently allowed to abjure albeit he should have stood before the bishop's court. Apparently the priest at first refused to confess which rendered abjuration impossible. He then pled guilty to the fictitious crime of stealing eight pennies (which was a felony) and was granted abjuration and later granted a pardon.[54] A further example of creating a felony to facilitate

---

[51] Bellamy, J. *Crime and Public Order in England in the Later Middle Ages*, London, Routledge, 1973 p. 59 and Ormrod, W.M., 'Law in the Landscape: Criminality, Outlawry and Regional Identity in Late Medieval England' in Musson, *Boundaries of the Law*, Supra. p. 9

[52] In the case of Rex v Bury (1321) a woman sought sanctuary after she killed a man in a churchyard. The secular courts held that she should be removed and stand trial. This was not disputed by the Church and the woman was found guilty and hanged. *Rex v Bury*, Eyre of London, 14 Edward II. Vol. I. cited in Helmholz, Supra. p.66–67. N. 189

[53] Wormald, Supra. pp. 159–160, N. 153 citing LS 178 *The Waltham Chronicle* 24. pp. 62–65

[54] Rosser, Supra. p. 68. Also cited in Hunnisett, R.F. *The Medieval Coroner*, Cambridge, Cambridge University Press, 1961. p. 45

exile took place in May 1301 when Richard Mandeville and his brother Nicholas were playing and a stone hit Nicholas resulting in his death. Richard immediately fled to the local church, St. Peter of Watford, and from his sanctuary confessed that he was a thief and had previously stolen a coat worth eight pence. Richard abjured the realm from the port of Dover.[55] Jordan states that in those instances where a cleric sought sanctuary and it was granted; the ecclesiastical authorities were subsequently repudiated by the courts temporal.[56] Reprimands of any form are rare. Church immunity applied to all laymen and married women[57] other than Jews, heretics, excommunicates and serfs.[58] Slaves could not seek freedom through church asylum.[59] Women could not claim sanctuary as a means to escape their husbands.[60] However married men and women could use sanctuary with abjuration for the purposes of divorce. Once declared an abjurer the felon was legally dead and therefore the husband or wife was now a widow and free to marry again.[61] Pope Innocent III (1198–1216)decreed that the 'nocturnal highway robber and pillager of fields' should be excluded from sanctuary. This was extended further by Pope Gregory IX (1227–1241)[62] who held that those committing mayhem or murder within

---

[55] Gross, Supra. pp. 68–69

[56] Jordan, Supra. p. 21. N. 16 citing Helmholz, R., *The Ius commune in England, Four Studies*, Oxford, Oxford University Press, 2001,pp. 60–61 and Cox, C., *The Sanctuaries and Sanctuary Seekers, of Medieval England*, London, Allen & Sons, 1911, pp. 19–21

[57] Clergy were permitted to claim sanctuary in France. Jordan, Supra. p. 23

[58] Serfs were returned to their lord masters for punishment. Heretics and excommunicates were barred until such time as they might be readmitted to the Church

[59] Helmholz, Supra. p. 33

[60] Helmholz, Supra. p. 33

[61] Rosser, Supra. p. 68

[62] *De immunitate ecclesiarum X. 3.49.10* Helmholz, Supra. p. 34

the Church or churchyard excluded themselves from the protections of church immunity. The logic for this exclusion was founded on the graphic example of the sacrilegious murder of archbishop Thomas Becket (1162–1170) inside Canterbury cathedral on 29th December 1170. In principle sanctuary was not available to a felon who had been convicted of the crime for which he sought sanctuary and no defendant was eligible for sanctuary once formal proceedings had commenced. A contested area of sanctuary was around the crime of rape. At canon law sanctuary was permitted for rape. By the late Middle Ages it was not available at common law.[63]

Once a fugitive had managed to enter the curtilage of a church he was required to state the reasons for his flight from justice and the circumstances surrounding the alleged offence. The sanctuary seeker was required to give the full names and as much detail as possible of the persons injured by the criminal actions. (This may have been a form of proof that ensured the true offender was identified rather than a person acting as a substitute and being prepared to exile for the culprit). In order that over-zealous lynching parties were thwarted local villagers were responsible for preventing the escape[64] of the sanctuary seeker and ensuring his safety until expiration of the

[63] Musson, A., 'Crossing Boundaries: Attitudes to Rape in Late Medieval England' in Musson, A., (ed) *Boundaries of the Law: Geography, Gender and Jurisdiction in Medieval and early Modern Europe*, Aldershot, Ashgate, 2005. Chap. 7. pp. 85–101.p. 95 and Hunisett, R.F., *The Medieval Coroner*, Cambridge, Cambridge University Press, 1961, Brundage, J.A., *Law, Sex, and Christian Society in Medieval Europe*, Illinois, Chicago University Press, 1987, p. 210, 250. Alternatively Olson, Supra, refers to the charter of Battle Abbey and in this the issue of rape is silent '…or anyone other guilty [person] flee from fear of to this church, let him in no way be hurt… p.44

[64] Sanctuary watch was required of the men from the four nearest villages to the Church in which the felon rested. If these men allowed a fugitive to escape they were liable to a fine. Bellamy, Supra. p. 108

sanctuary period. Whereas escape from sanctuary might seem counterintuitive felons who were not entitled to sanctuary could attempt escape before their illegal status was revealed. The provision of food and shelter inside the Church was the responsibility of the clergy. Failure to provide sufficiently exposed the cleric liable to excommunication. Sanctuary was limited to forty days[65] after which the sanctuary seeker was required to abjure the realm or 'place himself upon the country' (secular jury trial). Sometimes a fleeing felon demanded the right to remain in the Church for the full forty days. In 1377 John Philpot fled to the sanctuary of St. Andrews church, Northampton. When swearing his guilt before the coroner he was asked if he wished to abjure and responded 'not before the forty days'.[66] The idea of perpetual exile was another reason why the English Church rejected the option of sanctuary for clerics[67] as the sentence of enforced banishment was viewed as punishment, which of course could only be meted out by the Church and not a secular tribunal. In France sanctuary seekers who elected for exile were branded with the fleur-de-lys.[68] Such visual identification methods were very rarely employed in England; there is one example from Waltham Abbey when four thieves tunneled beneath the Church and stole silverware.

---

[65] There is evidence to the effect that under Alfred the Great it was limited to seven days but certainly by the period under discussion it was established to be forty days. Pope, Supra. p. 677. N. 3

[66] Gross, Supra. p. 86 and the case of Rochard Spelby, 1362. Cox, Supra. p.27 and pp. 277–278

[67] 9 Edward II. 1315–1316 *Articuli Cleri.* s.15 provided that a clerk should not be *compelled* to abjure

[68] Clerics who abjured after sanctuary were not required to be branded. Jordan, Supra. p. 23. For the extent of sanctuary across Europe Helmholz, R. Supra and Duclaux de Martin,P. T., *Le droit d'asile* Paris : Librairie du Recueil Sirey (société anonyme), 1939 esp. pp. 268–286

The villains then made for London where they attempted to sell the stolen property to a goldsmith. Unfortunately their chosen receiver was the artist who made one of the stolen items. He immediately notified the authorities and the four were returned to Waltham for trial. Three were executed; the fourth claimed his clergy. He was 'branded in the face with a red-hot key of the church'.[69] Illegally returning from exile rendered the felon liable to summary beheading by any member of English society.

A felon who fled from justice was immediately viewed as an outlaw under English custom and his property was forfeited by the crown (as he was legally a dead man).[70] Much like the returning exile the outlaw could be executed with impunity. Whereas the sanctuary fugitive who elected to abjure was a protected person under the crown[71] a declared outlaw had no such protections and could be killed at will. Notwithstanding the legal provision abjuring felons were occasionally attacked. In one recorded instance a Frenchman convicted of murder sought to abjure the realm and return to his native Brittany. 'He took the cross (*cruce in manu*) and foreswore the king's land' upon which locals who knew the victim took stones and

---

[69] Watkiss, L., and Chibnall, M., (Eds and Trans) *The Waltham Chronicle*, Oxford, Oxford University Press, 1994. pp. 62–65

[70] Rosser, G., 'Sanctuary and Social Negotiation in Medieval England' in Blair, J., and Goldong, B., (eds) *The Cloister and the World: Essays in Medieval History in Honour of Barbara Harvey*, Oxford, Clarendon Press, 1996. Chap 4. pp. 57–79. Esp. p. 64 and Pope, S., Sanctuary: The Legal Institution in England, *University of Puget Sound Law Review*, Vol. 10. (1986–1987) pp. 667–697. Esp. p. 689. Abjuration in Normandy followed the rest of France after the re-conquest of 1204. Jordan, Supra, p. 27

[71] E.g. Under *Articuli Cleri* 9. Edward II 1315–1316, referring to felons who escaped to the sanctuary of a church, declared that "They abjure the Realm so long as they be in the Common way, shall be in the King's peace, nor ought to be disturbed of any Man...'

gutter dung and ended the murderer's life'.[72] Later in the Middle Ages the cross was substituted for branding; an A on the brawn of the left thumb. In part this was to prevent felons from being mistaken as pilgrims.[73] The declaration of the status outlaw or abjurer marked an important legal distinction consequently both involved the office of coroner.[74] The well-established right to the protection of the 'sacred boundary'[75] was denied to recidivists in 1467[76] and radically reduced by Henry VIII (1509–1547).[77] Henry also introduced the requirement that those granted sanctuary did not abjure the realm but were to remain in domestic sanctuary; this new class of felon was required to wear an identifying mark on their clothing and were prohibited from going outside during

---

[72] Rosser Supra. p. 68. This event is also recorded in Myers, A.R. (ed) *Punishment for Violation of Sanctuary, English Historical Documents,* Vol. IV c. 1327–1485 Part III. Sec. 7. with a little more detail; the event occurred between Easter and Whitsuntide and sanctuary was sought at the Holy Church at St. George's, Southwark where he 'took the cross and foreswore the king's land' whereupon women of the parish took stones and gutter dung … and thus this false thief ended his life' p. 354

[73] Jordan. Supra. pp. 17–33. p. 25. And citing Bellamy, J. *Crime and Public Order in England in the Later Middle Ages,* London, Routledge, 1973. p. 112 and Hunnisett, R.F., *The Medieval Coroner,* Supra. p.54

[74] Hunnisett, R.F., The Origins of the Office of Coroner: The Alexander Prize Essay, *Transactions of the Royal Historical Society,* Fifth Series, Vol. 8 (1958), pp. 85–104

[75] 'Sacred Ban' was the term used by Cardinal Peter of Albano when describing the sacred boundaries of Cluny to warn people in the surround that the closer they lived to Cluny the more they should 'avoid injuring the servants of God'.Luscombe & Riley-Smith, Supra. p. 359

[76] Logan, Supra. p. 328

[77] 4 Henry VIII (1512) made it virtually impossible for a fleeing felon to seek sanctuary in a church outside of the county in which he committed the crime, 21 Henry VIII (1529) required that all sanctuary abjurers be branded with an A. 22 Henry VIII (1530) abolished abjuration of the realm to become exile within sanctuary in England, 26 Henry VIII prohibited traitors from claiming church immunity. 33 Henry VIII c.15 abolished sanctuary for murder, rape, burglary, robbery, arson, sacrilege and accessories to these felonies. It also abolished all chartered sanctuaries and replaced them with eight sanctuary towns: Derby, Launceston, Manchester (transferred to Chester the following year), Northampton, Norwich, Wells, Westminster and York

night hours. Sanctuary was abolished by the early Stuarts;[78] with the exception of the protected area of Alsatia and Savoy in London.[79]

The origins of the office of coroner are unclear. There is evidence of his existence in the Middlesex Eyre of 1194[80] when itinerant justices William de Stuttville and Geoffrey Fitz-Peter reported of two defendants who it was alleged had committed murder and "The coroners having been called to Westminster...the sheriff and men of the county confirm the testimony of the coroners...".[81] There is plausible commentary that the office existed before this time at least in London and some of the larger cities of England.[82] By the thirteenth century each county had four coroners, all assisted by a deputy. Qualifications for holding office were knighthood

---

[78] In 1603 sanctuary towns were abolished and then 1624 21 James I, c.28 generally and 1626 for London and the abolition of the special sanctuaries of the City of London, Westminster and the Borough of Southwark. Thornley, I.D., The Destruction of Sanctuary, *Tudor Studies , Presented by the Board of Studies in History in the University of London to Albert Frederick Pollard, being the work of twelve of his colleagues and pupils.* 1924. pp. 182–207, Baker, J.H., The English Law of Sanctuary, *Ecclesiastical Law Journal*: The Journal of the Ecclesiastical Law Society, Vol. 2, No. 6 (1990) pp. 8–13 and Logan, Supra. p. 329 and see Helmholz, Supra p. 19 N. 13. re: the 'long life' of sanctuary

[79] Both survived until 1727. Cox, Supra. p. 336. Bellamy, Supra. p. 111. For commentary on the role and function of the coroner and the use of Coroners Reports; Hanwalt, B., *The Ties that Bound, Peasant Families in Medieval England,* Oxford, Oxford University Press, 1989

[80] Gross, C., (ed) *Select Cases from the Coroners' Rolls A.D. 1265–1413: With a brief account of the history of the office of coroner,* London, Selden Society, 1896.Volume IX, p. xv and Rosser, Supra. pp. 77–78. N. 84 and Bellamy, J., *Crime and Public Order in England in the Later Middle Ages,* London, Routledge, 1973. Esp Chap. I Crime and Medieval Society

[81] Gross, Supra. p. xvii

[82] Gross, Supra. In 1247 Lawrence de Brock was retained by the crown as a permanent attorney at the King's Bench, this initial appointment became permanent and the records of this person were known as the *Controlment Rolls,* (which included details of confessions by approvers). Confusingly this person became known as the 'Coroner of England'. Harding, Supra. p. 110. Clerics were ineligible to become Approvers because it might entail them having to engage in trial by battle with a defendant who denied a crime alleged by the approver

and residency in the county that was served.[83] Coroners were appointed by the crown and served for life; office was served without financial reward. The City of London provided an exception as the mayor was authorized to appoint a coroner for Southwark after election by the independent Corporation of London. This coroner was known as a 'franchise coroner'.[84]

In addition to those responsibilities discussed above the coroner was required to: investigate all violent deaths, establish Englishry,[85] work with the sheriff to bring felons to justice, hold an inquest into all deaths by misadventure, establish the value of the deodand[86] and the crowns portion of estates, receive the declarations of approvers and maintain a record of exigents and outlaws. Having received the confession of felons fled to sanctuary the coroner proscribed the terms and conditions of departure for abjurers. Coroners also appraised

---

[83] It would appear that by the fourteenth century a knighthood was no longer required. Gross, Supra. p. xx

[84] Brandon, Supra. p. 63

[85] "Presentment of Englishry" was the procedure that identified the nationality of a deceased person. It started shortly after the Norman conquest when native Englishmen were known to murder Normans as revenge for occupying England. When a Norman was murdered the village was held responsible for paying a fine to the king for the loss of his subject. The Normans insisted that any man murdered was a Norman unless it could be proven to the contrary and the deceased was proven to be English (Anglo-Saxon). If Englishry was established then the village was not required to pay a fine. The 'murdrum fine' was hated by Englishmen and it was finally abolished in 1340 www.britannia.com/history/coroner3.html

[86] A Deodand was the object or instrument that caused a death e.g. an axe. The coroner was responsible for valuing the deodand which would (usueally) become property of the crown. Sometimes the family of the deceased would be permitted the article or its value in monetary compensation. Similar to 'Englishry' the Deodand was also viewed by many as another means of boosting the royal treasury. Deodand was abolished in 1846. The word derives from *Deo dandum* meaning "Giving to God' because the weapon used for a crime was believed to have become sinful (tarnished) and by giving the instrument to God its sinfulness would be removed www.britannia.com/history/coroner3.html

wrecks and treasure trove and were responsible for the safe custody of any valuables found. The coroner played a key role in the courts where he provided a necessary link between the crown and the people; he not only safeguarded the financial interests of the king but also the interests of justice by providing a crucial link between local and central administration throughout the country.[87]

In many respects the office of coroner is representative of the interests of all three segments of medieval society; the Church, the crown and the local communities. The preserved reports of the coroners, the Coroners Rolls, amount to 260 rolls containing approximately 2,140 membranes from Henry III to Richard II.[88] These Rolls were the sole record of confessions to the alleged crime and authority to abjure the realm. They were also the official record for proclaiming outlawry and the source for authority to hang or behead outlaws.[89] Sanctuary was temporary immunity from criminal prosecution, one that caused actors under the canon law and secular law to interface and laws to be compromised; sanctuary was a custom of the secular law but a process of both temporal and Christian officials. Once sanctuary had been achieved and the fleeing felon 'confessed' his crime to the coroner he exiled via a designated port. His safe passage on the kings' highway was guaranteed

---

[87] Coroners today remain responsible for treasure and shipwreck trove and they may substitute for the office of sheriff if called upon to do so. Contemporary coroners are remunerated for their services

[88] Henry III (1216–1272) Richard II (1377–1399). All are housed in the Public Record Office, Kew, Surrey under Assize Rolls of the Queen's Bench (Crown Side). For discussion of the Rolls: Gross, Supra. and Hunnisett,R.F., *The Medieval Coroner*, Cambridge, Cambridge University Press, 1961. Chap. VI. pp. 96–117

[89] Hunnisett. Supra. p. 110

at secular and canon law; the felon was deemed to be in joint safe custody. The cross he carried signified ecclesiastical protections and as long as the abjurer remained on the highway royal protection was implied.[90]

Over time the Church had successfully established a range of privileges to protect persons (and status) that in practice forced parish clergymen to provide accommodations to the laity far beyond the cure of souls. As the following cases demonstrate the lower orders were not only providing services that caused them to interface directly with criminal society they were not infrequently the beneficiaries of these liaisons. In exceptional circumstances prelates too afforded themselves the malleable options that traversed laws spiritual and secular.

The much recorded murder of Thomas Becket is not a case of clerics seeking sanctuary but is often cited as the most egregious example of abuse of the immunity. Equally compelling is the example of sanctuary abuse in 1191 when Geoffrey, archbishop of York (1191–1212)[91] having invoked immunity from arrest was forcibly removed from Dover priory by William Longchamp, bishop of Ely (1190–1197), the monarch's regent and chancellor.[92] This was followed in 1196 when Hubert Walter, archbishop of Canterbury (1193–1205) and royal justiciar, embroiled himself in the protests against taxation conducted by William Fitz Osbert (commonly known as Longbeard). The protests resulted in Longbeard attempting to avoid arrest and taking sanctuary in St. Mary

---

[90] Ibid.p. 48

[91] Half-brother to Richard I (1189–1199). Geoffrey provides another example of a prelate who also held high secular office during his career. He was Lord Chancellor from 1181–1190

[92] Cox, Supra. pp 35–37

le Bow Church, London. In direct breach of laws spiritual and temporal archbishop Walter set fire to the Church to force Fitz Osberts' surrender. Longbeard was subsequently hanged for his felonious actions.[93] It would appear that archbishop Walter held higher regard for his secular appointment than his ecclesiastic. His church arson was a sacrilegious crime at canon law.

An early demonstration of lower order clerics attempting to invoke church asylum took place in 1231 when a murder occurred in the grounds of St. Paul's cathedral, London. A clerk present at the scene ran off and took sanctuary at St. Peter's church, Cornhill. As we have seen canon law held that *all* clerics were prohibited from sanctuary. It transpired that local opinion was in the clerics favor and the community was of the view that the cleric was not one of the assailants. He was informed he could leave the confines of the church and departed.[94] In the same year at York a cleric named John achieved sanctuary within the liberty of St. Peter, York. He was permitted audience with the coroner and swore his oath of abjuration and exiled the realm from the port of Dover.[95] In 1232 Peter de Rivalis, nephew to Peter de Roches, bishop of Winchester (1204–1238) was appointed treasurer of the king's household. The following year de

---

[93] McEwan, J., William FitzOsbert and the Crisis of 1196 in London, *Florilegium,* Vol. 21 (2004) pp. 18–42

[94] Rosser, Supra. p. 66. Citing Chew, H.M. and Weinbaum, M., (eds) *The London Eyre of 1244,* London, London Record Society, 1970. pp. 28–29. In 1336 the parson of St. Margaret, Bridge Street and the parson of St. Benet, Gracechurch were considered to be 'sanctuary breakers' took further refuge in St.Paul's. Thornley, Supra. p. 298

[95] Shoemaker, K., *Sanctuary and Crime in the Middle Ages, 400–1500,* New York, Fordham University Press, 2011. p. 146 N. 185. 15 Hen. III. *Yorkshire Eyre of 1231. Roll of Civil and Crown Pleas.* 20 Oct 1230 – 27 Oct 1231 Rots 24. M. 20

Rivalis was made treasurer of the Exchequer. However, de Rivalis' attempts at fiscal reform were bitterly opposed and in February 1234 he was summoned to Westminster Palace to answer before the king. At his appearance the former Treasurer wore tonsure and clerical garb to emphasis his priestly status. Unsure of the likely final outcome he fled to his uncle the bishop at Winchester and sanctuary.[96] In 1256 a priest, William de Nutel (Nobel), fled from the scene of a murder he had committed and ran to sanctuary at Corebridge Church. He was permitted his oath of abjuration and exiled the realm.[97] This event was followed in 1262 when the church of Kingston-upon-Thames was utilized by robbers John de Marscall, Richard le Parmenter and cleric, Willam de Punfreyt. Subsequently de Punfreyt was claimed as a cleric by the bishop of Winchester. Later the same year and also at Kingston William de Braunton, a cleric, was arrested for theft of four cows and a horse. He was placed into secular custody but escaped and took sanctuary at the Church whereupon he admitted the crimes and was permitted to abjure the realm.[98] In 1265 an affray occurred in Hailbridge, Bedfordshire when two assailants attempted to rob a woman on her way to the local market. A young man known as William came to the rescue of the victim; he was attacked by the perpetrators and died of his injuries. A number of offenders were apprehended by locals at the scene. One, a cleric, Nicholas of Huntington, ran from the scene and took refuge in the church of Diddington where he claimed sanctuary.[99]

---

[96] Shepherd, R., *Westminster: A Biography*, London, The National Archives, 2012. p. 46

[97] Bain, J.,(ed) *Calendar of Documents Relating to Scotland 1108–1276*, Edinburgh, HMSO, 1881. Vol. I. p. 396

[98] Cox, Supra. pp. 290–291

[99] Cox, Supra. p. 274

Under the 1271–1272 Staffordshire Assize Rolls is the case of Robert Herberobur, a clerk. At the church of Tamworth he admitted theft and robbery and was permitted to abjure the realm. There is no further mention of his clerical status, any conflict with clericus, or any attempt by the bishop to claim him. In March 1276, John, clerk of St. Mary Magdalen, Southwark was playing at throwing tiles with John Fuatard (Futard) when a tile hit Fuatard; he died three days later. John the clerk did not wait for the outcome of the coroner's decision as to whether or not it was misadventure; he fled to the sanctuary of his church and from there escaped and lived out his life as an outlaw.[100] On May 5th, 1278 at St. Mary's Church, Staining Lane (Stanigeslane) in the City of London a group of local citizens were keeping watch over Richard de Cadisford (de Codesfold) who had put himself in the Church having committed a murder. Thomas, clerk of the Church, was present and heard a sound he believed to be a local citizen, Henry de Lanfare, attempting to forcibly remove de Cadisford from his sanctuary. In response to this Thomas thrust a lance out through a window towards de Lanfare and wounded him severely between the nose and the eye. On May 19th de Lanfare died of the injuries received. Cleric Thomas was arrested and rather than being placed in the bishop's gaol or fleeing to sanctuary was detained in Newgate prison to await trial. There is no record of the bishop of London seeking to secure Thomas into his custody. The sanctuary seeker Richard de Cadisford remained in church asylum at St. Mary's Church.[101] Also in

---

[100] Riley, H.T. (trans) *Memorials of London and London Life in the XIIIth, XIVth, and XVth Centuries: Being a Series of Extracts, Local, Social, and Political, from the Early Archives of the City of London*, A.D. 1276–1419, London, Longmans, 1868. p.36

[101] Cox, Supra. pp. 228–229. For full details see: Riley, Supra. pp. 41–42 and Thornley, Supra. p. 295

1278 William Cole, 'a citizen of London, was lying dead, by another death than his rightful death'.[102] The sheriff's investigation reported that on 25th July the deceased was in his field in Stratford when John, parish clerk of Stratford Church, entered the field and stole corn. William remonstrated and John departed only to return soon after with two accomplices, a fellow cleric, Richard, chaplain to the Prioress of Stratford and John de Scheld. The three attacked William and left him for dead. Local people reported that after the attack the two clerics and de Scheld ran from the scene to the sanctuary of Stratford Church; sometime soon after the three escaped from the Church and were never seen again, having chosen outlawry rather than the bishop's court or exile.[103]

In 1279 Godfrey Giffard, bishop of Worcester (1268–1301)[104] presided over the case of cleric, Richard de Walden. De Walden had been acting under the directions of the constable of Bristol Castle to arrest a fugitive, William de la Lay, who, having reached sanctuary in the churchyard of St. Philip and St. James, was dragged away and beheaded; cleric de Walden and four others were held responsible. On August 21st, bishop Giffard ordered the five men to exhume the body of the deceased, complete with decapitated head, take the remains to the church of St. Philip and St. James and there bury William de la Lay. Following this the five were ordered to walk barefoot, in breeches and shirts, from the burial site to the church of Friars Minors

[102] A commonly used phrase to describe an unnatural death. Riley, Supra. p. 42

[103] *18 Roll of Felonies and Misadventures 1281*. Edw. I. Letter Book. Riley, Supra. pp. 41–42

[104] Godfrey also held the chancellorship of the exchequer and in 1266 was appointed Chancellor of England. He was known to hold numerous benefices throughout his lifetime

every market day for five weeks whereupon on arrival they would be flogged by priests specially appointed to conduct the punishment. Initially this may appear to be an extreme example of diocesanal interference in a secular matter; but this is not the case.[105] The bishop had both spiritual and secular responsibilities and the offending cleric may have been a cleric in name only. Time and again these cases show the considerable overlap between the interests of the secular law and canon and that there is a sense of both legal systems working with local communities in an attempt to ensure justice prevails. Richard de Walden acted far beyond the parameters of acceptable behavior under the law, either law, and the very public punishment handed down was a clear signal from the ecclesiastical domain, not secular, that clerics were accountable for their actions when those actions were in concert with common criminals of either color, temporal or spiritual.

In 1283 the mayor of London, Henry le Waleys, was forced to implement emergency measures to deal with the capital's expanding crime problem.[106] Vagrant felons were a perceived source of crime yet the temerity of the criminal fraternity was often exemplified by men of cleaner cloth; the clergy. In 1294 Henry de Heapham was being held in the Tower of London for having forged the king's seal. Whilst in custody a parson, John de Ramsey of St. Andrew's Church, London, visited de Heapham and bribed him to appeal another cleric, Nicholas de Thorton. This event was stimulated by an initial

---

[105] Bund, J.W., (ed) *Episcopal Registers for the Diocese of Worcester, Bishop Godfrey Giffard, September 23, 1268 to August 15, 1301*, Volume I, Worcestershire Historical Society, 1902. p. lxvi
[106] Bellamy, Supra. pp. 10–11

criminal complaint of conspiracy and trespass made by cleric de Thornton against parson de Ramsey.[107]

The 1284–1285 Assize Rolls of Cornwall[108] contain an unusual case relating to clerical sanctuary; James, a clerk, mortally wounded Ralph with a knife. James fled immediately for the sanctuary of St. Michael's Mount, a Benedictine monastery. He then requested the attendance of the coroner and confessed his felony of murder. Following his admission of guilt James requested he be granted exile from the realm and this was granted. However, before the expiration of the forty day period James was taken into the custody of the Prior of St. Michael's, and immured; placed in a solitary confinement cell and presumably given a diet of bread and water every third day for perpetuity.[109] The following year, 1285, a number of unusual benefit of clergy and sanctuary related events took place in the university town of Oxford. John de Derby, put himself in the church of St. Michael at North Gate, and confessed to being a repeat offender thief. He remained at the Church for eight days and then 'by connivance of Hugh the present parson of the church', he escaped from sanctuary. De Derby was declared an outlaw and Hugh, the parson, was ordered to be arrested. Hugh had apparently also fled Oxford and he too was pronounced an outlaw. At the same Eyre Simon de Wanetynge

---

[107] Bellamy, Supra. p. 129. Sayles, G.O., (ed) *Select Cases in the Court of the King's Bench Under Edward I*, London, Selden Society, 1936. Vol. 2. 55.

[108] 12 Edw. I. 1283–4. Cox, Supra. p. 301

[109] The term 'Immuration' was utilized by the Church to describe solitary confinement with access only to food and water and perhaps a line of sight to an altar. For an alternative use see: Pollock, F. & Maitland, F. W., *The History of English Law Before the Time of Edward I* (2nd edition) Cambridge, Cambridge University Press, 1968. Vol.1. pp. 444–445 and: Maitland, F. W., The Deacon and the Jewess; or; Apostacy at Common Law, *The Collected Papers of Frederic William Maitland*, Ed by H.A.L. Fisher, Cambridge, Cambridge University Press, 1911. Vol. 1

was condemned to death by hanging. On route to the gallows, clerks of the University of Oxford, their names were not established, by force rescued Simon and delivered him to St. Giles' Church where he claimed sanctuary. Contrary to secular law (a convicted felon could not claim sanctuary for the crime he had been convicted of) his confession was accepted by the coroner. The court report does not record if Simon abjured or not. Also before the same justices Henry Somm of Stokes Island, a clerk, was condemned to be hanged. He too was rescued by force by a group of university clerics, one was known as Robert de Tursway. Somm was also taken to St. Giles Church. In this instance the escapee took the oath of abjuration and was permitted to exile the realm, which he did. The jury then considered the participation of Robert de Tursway who had fled. He was declared an outlaw. In another case Robert de Pennoby and John de Ardern fled to St. Giles Church. Robert confessed to having committed multiple thefts. He swore before the coroner and abjured the realm. John gave himself up to the sheriff and was placed in Oxford gaol to await trial. John was convicted before the secular tribunal and then claimed by the bishop as a cleric. At the same Eyre another cleric accused of murder, was claimed by his bishop, a second fled the scene of a murder was arrested and died in secular prison awaiting trial and a third, accused of theft, failed to appear before the courts temporal and was declared an outlaw.[110] Also at the same Eyre Henry de Hengestesey, a cleric, claimed his clergy for murder and was released to the bishop. Philip de Waley, clerk, fled the scene of a murder. He was later arrested and died in secular prison while awaiting trial. David de Hybernia,

---

[110] Proceedings of the Eyre of Oxfordshire 1285. J.E. Thorold Rogers, ed. *Oxford City Documents, Financial and Judicial, 1268–1665,* Oxford Historical Society, vol.18 (1891), 194–236

clerk, was accused of theft, failed to appear before the courts temporal and was adjudged an outlaw.[111]

These early cases are important because they capture examples of clerics committing felonies that would not necessarily attract sanctuarial protections; assisting a felon to escape from lawful custody or from sanctuary. And they demonstrate how flexible canon law and temporal law were in practice; clerics were allowed to abjure, clerics were declared outlaws and clerics were taken from sanctuary by the Church. This pattern of legal dexterity continues throughout the thirteenth century.

In 1286 a Lincolnshire cleric sought to abjure after securing sanctuary. Richard de Scardeburgh, a chaplain, had fled to the parish church of Marton shortly after committing the felony of larceny. His bishop, Oliver of Lincoln (1280–1299) sought to have the cleric returned to the courts Christian and requested the clerics abjuration not be allowed. Following the previous example of James from Cornwall the provisions of the secular law prevailed and de Scardeburgh was permitted his forty days and then exiled.[112] On the Feast of St. George, Friday April 23rd, 1289 London chaplain Walter Bacun fled to the protection of St. Paul's cathedral after he and others had stolen sixteen silver dishes. He requested the attendance of the coroner, William le Mazeliner, before whom he confessed his felony. The stolen silverware was recovered and returned to its owner. The final fate of the chaplain is not recorded but his confession was accepted by the coroner without interference from the bishop of London.[113]

---

111 Ibid

112 Cox, Supra. p. 20–21. *Calendar of the Close Rolls, 1286*, July 5

113 17. Edw. I. 1289 Letter Books in Riley, H.T. (trans) *Memorials of London and London Life in the XIIIth, XIVth, and XVth Centuries: Being a Series of Extracts, Local, Social, and Political, from the Early Archives of the City of London*, A.D. 1276–1419, London, Longmans, 1868. p. 45

On February 23, 1293 an unusual event was recorded in the Patent and Close Rolls for Staffordshire when cleric William de Tyssington was pardoned for the death of William de Lenton. De Lenton was in the process of pursuing an escaped felon from the local castle gaol into the parish church of Tutbury when the resident cleric mistook de Lenton for a thief. A scuffle ensued and de Lenton struck the clerk, in response the cleric hit de Lenton a mortal blow to the head. The matter of the clergyman's status and claiming his clergy did not arise as the lay justices held the matter to be misadventure. In February 1298 the students of Oxford University were again engaged in violent disorder. This time clerks Roger of Brecham and Henry of Brecham struck a sword through the body of Thomas Churchey of Iffley. The incident took place opposite the church of St. Mary the Virgin in Oxford high street, surprisingly the murder was not also classified as sacrilege. Roger and Henry appear to have made a quick assessment of the situation and decided that outlawry was their best option.[114] In spite of their clerical status the two fled and were never seen again. Under the circumstances this might not have been such a poor choice as the chancellor's commissary of the university of Oxford had recently sentenced clerk students David of Northampton and John Lawrence to prison for murder and in a separate incident students William Mitchell, Stephen of Duffield and Madoc of Belty also received imprisonment.[115] In 1292 Elyas, a chaplain, was in secular prison

[114] Gross, C., (ed) *Select Cases from the Coroners Rolls AD. 1265–1413: With a Brief Account of the Office of Coroner*, Volume IX, London, Selden Society, 1896. p. 90

[115] Gross, Supra. p. 89. February 1298 was also the month of the mayhem that involved a large number of Oxford students fighting and looting resulting in the death of cleric Fulk Nennunt. Gross, Supra. p. 90–91. In 1296 after the Oxford murder of John Meteschamp two of the five student clerks responsible decided to flee the scene and were declared outlaws, Michael of Bolehall and John of Scant, their three associates were all imprisoned. Gross, Supra, p. 88

awaiting trial for murder. He escaped and attempted to reach sanctuary at the local church. He did not succeed; the local townsfolk apprehended him and executed him by beheading on the spot.[116] On those occasions when a sanctuary seeker was unlawfully seized symbolic restoration to the Church was possible and occasionally requested.[117] In 1299 a reversal of the incident in 1286 with Richard de Scardeburgh occurred when John le Berner, clerk, fled to the church of Austin Friars near Ludlow. Le Berner was pursued by locals who forcibly removed him from the Church and placed him into the local gaol at Shrewsbury Castle. The bishop of Hereford, Richard de Swinfield (1282–1317) appealed the actions of the local townsfolk and demanded le Berner be granted his sanctuary. The bishop's request was approved and the cleric was handed back to the church of Austin Friars.[118]

The 1286 Assize Roll for Norwich has recorded the case of William de Loddon and Hugh Maydenlove. William was a cleric, both were sheep rustlers. The pair were arrested and broke the Tollhouse gaol and made good to the church of St. John of Ber Street. Cleric William carried his accomplice Hugh (who at the time was incapacitated). The following day William surrendered himself back to the sheriff and claimed his clergy. Hugh took the opportunity to confess before the coroner and abjure.[119] This event was followed in 1292 when parson Thomas

---

[116] 21 Edw. I. Staffordshire Eyre of 1293 Berwick's Roll of Crown Pleas, Gaol Deliveries and Jury Calendar. 12 Nov 1292 – 19 Nov 1293. National Archives. JUST I/806 m. 18

[117] See: Shoemaker, Infra. p. 141

[118] Cox, Supra. p. 21. Calendar of the Close Rolls 1299 and p. 249 and Trenholme, N.M., *The Right of Sanctuary in England*, Columbia, University of Missouri, 1903. p. 43

[119] Assize Roll for Norwich 1286. Cox, Supra. p. 238

de Pontesbury fled to the church of Cranfield, Bedfordshire after being found guilty of a number of felonies before the Bedford justices. The rector was deemed a convicted fugitive, he neither claimed his clergy nor was he claimed by the ordinary. However, he was permitted to make his oath before the coroner and abjured the realm. His goods and chattels valued at £24, 14s. 11d were distributed to St. Catherine's Hospital, London.[120] In 1302 at Cornwall Alan de Bloyon, rector of Ludwon Church murdered Michael, the steward. Thinking quickly the murderous priest ran to his own house, 'which is a sanctuary' and claimed asylum.[121]

During February 1302, the Prior of Worcester instructed the dean to excommunicate a group of local citizens who had pursued a fleeing felon into the crypt of the cathedral church. Of interest is that the man being pursued was cleric, Richard Kaye, a declared fugitive from justice. Kaye was not only permitted to remain in sanctuary but the Prior permitted his oath of abjuration before the coroner and Kaye exiled the realm. This case again demonstrates the flexible interpretation of the laws canon and temporal where a fleeing cleric, who under canon law is denied sanctuary and abjuration, is protected by the Church and then allowed secular remedy.[122] In 1311 William of Wellington, parish chaplain of Ylevertoft, struck and killed his clerk, John. William immediately fled to his own church and took sanctuary. He then confessed his

---

[120] Cox, Supra. p. 200

[121] Shoemaker, K., *Sanctuary and Crime in the Middle Ages, 400–1500*, New York, Fordham University Press, 2011. p. 128. N. 95 citing 30 Edw. I. Cornwall Eyre 1302. Rex Roll of Civil, King's and Crown Pleas, Goal Deliveries and Plaints. 20 Nov 1301–19 Nov 1302 National Archives. JUST 1/117A M. 68

[122] *Cox, Supra. pp. 247, 248*

crime before the coroner and abjured the realm.[123] Christian legal dexterity was not extended to Isabella Bury however, who in 1321 killed the chaplain of All Saints by London Wall Church. She sought sanctuary in the Church of her felony. Five days later the bishop of London sanctioned her forced removal to Newgate (secular) prison. She hanged for her crime. The death sentence was personally ordered by the bishop.[124]

In 1323 chaplain Geoffrey of Steventon was indicted for arson. He had set fire to the house of parishioner John of Ashton. The cleric was arrested by the sheriff and held in custody at the Northampton gaol awaiting trial. There is no indication of the bishop seeking to have Geoffrey released to the bishop's prison or claimed by his clergy.[125] Edward II (1307–1327) once ordered the arrest of the abbot of the Cistercian abbey at Vale Royal, Cheshire for harboring monks who were suspected of theft from the parish priest at Weverham. Richard de Sutton and Urian de St. Piere, serjeants of the peace, were clearly uncomfortable with the order and did not comply. Fortunately for the serjeants the king had a change of heart and withdrew; respectful no doubt of the special conditions of sanctuary that applied to Cistercians.[126]

---

[123] Gross, Supra. p. 69. In 1323 Geoffrey of Steventon, chaplain, set fire to two houses that belonged to his parishioners. He was arrested and whilst awaiting trial in prison at the castle of Northampton, he died. Gross, Supra. p. 80

[124] Cox, Supra. p. 230 and Gregory-Abbot, C., 'Sacred Outlaws: Outlawry and the Medieval Church', in in Appleby, J.C., and Dalton, P., *Outlaws in Medieval and Early Modern England; Crime, Government and Society, c. 1066–c.1600*, Farnham, Surrey, Ashgate, 2009. Chap. 4. pp. 75–89. p. 88. N. 62

[125] Northamptonshire Coroners Rolls, August 9, 1323. Gross, Supra. p. 80

[126] Even those who stole from priests. Cox, Supra. pp. 193–194 For the special status Cistercian sanctuary; Fletcher, J.S., *The Cistercians in Yorkshire*, London, Forgotten Books, 2013 (Original work published in 1919) pp. 156–158

In May 1343, Edward III (1327–1377) granted pardons to Richard de Pulham, clerk to the dean of Lincoln, Peter de Dalderby, canon of Lincoln, Walter de Stauren, canon of Lincoln, Robert de Landon, chaplain and penitentiary, the rectors of the churches of St. Peter at Arches, Croxton and Blankney and several unnamed chaplains and vicars. The band of criminous clerics had taken two convicted felons, Little John and Thomas de Bernelay from the cart in which they travelled to the gallows. The clerics then secured the escapees sanctuary inside the cathedral church of Lincoln.[127] Thomas soon fled from this 'lawful' sanctuary (perhaps in the belief that local citizens might extract him forcibly and behead him on the spot). The king's pardon extended to taking no further action over the matter of the escape[128] as well as the kidnappings of convicts. By contemporary standards a heist of convicted felons from the death chamber would be considered organized crime; clearly the pleas of the primate of England worked well in this instance. Pulham *et al* marks an interesting contrast with an event that occurred five months prior in January 1343. This incident also caused the intervention of archbishop of Canterbury. John Wentynburgh, a clerk, had ensconced himself in Ely cathedral as he believed his life to be in danger, a number of local citizens were after him for unspecified activities.

---

[127] *17. Edw. III Patent Rolls.* Part I. M. 23 and Cox, Supra. p. 212. Interestingly the bishop of Lincoln at the time, Henry de Burghersh, had recently secured from Edward III permission to extend the rights of sanctuary attached to Lincoln cathedral to: the bishop's palace, houses of the canons, the cemetery and grounds. Cox. Supra. p. 212

[128] At common law local laity were responsible for ensuring that those in sanctuary did not escape. Failure to do so resulted in a fine, amercements, being levied against the village. Ordinarily a watch was set up by the local menfolk. During the forty-day sanctuary period the fleeing felons were expected to perform work and tasks for the church e.g. at Beverley Minster they were required to perform bell ringing. Gregory-Abbott, Supra. p. 88

Neither the bishop of Worcester, nor the archbishop of Canterbury, appear to have believed him innocent either as they appointed Robert Flambard, serjeant-at-arms, to enter the cathedral and forcibly remove the fugitive and present him before the prelates.[129] Two years later there is further questionable use of privilege when a team of highway robbers were captured; Thomas de Blurtone and his partner, cleric Thomas Harmere. They had committed a number of robberies and horse thefts across the county of Sussex. De Blurtone hanged for his crimes. Thomas Harmere successfully claimed his benefit of clergy.[130]

The Coroners Rolls of Nottinghamshire for the year 1349 record six fugitives who having taken ecclesiastical sanctuary abjured the realm. The group included a priest.[131] All were guilty of murder. Of the chaplain, Irishman John de Kilkenny, the record does not state whether his crime was committed in Ireland and Kilkenny absconded to England or if the crime was local to the county of Nottinghamshire. His sanctuary was permitted, so too was his exile from the port of Dover.[132] The Wiltshire Coroners Roll for 1358 shows a cleric claiming sanctuary and then abjuring from the port of Bristol.[133] The Coroners Rolls for the city of York 1349–1359 contain a case that should have presented a challenge to the Church because the victim and the culprit were both clergymen; apparently it did not. Aldane, vicar of St. Laurence Church, Walmgate was murdered by Stephen de Burton, chaplain of the same

---

[129] Cox, Supra. p. 266
[130] 19 Edw. III Letter Book. Riley, Supra. p.131
[131] John de Kilkenny. Cox, Supra. p. 302
[132] Cox, Supra. p. 302
[133] Cox, Supra. p. 291

church. Stephen killed Aldane in the parish church and then sought sanctuary at the scene. De Burton was permitted to remain inside the sanctuary, he was permitted to confess to the coroner and he was allowed to abjure the realm from the port of Dover.[134] The Wiltshire Coroners Roll for 1358 contains the case of Roger de Ludynton and William, chaplains of St. Thomas, Salisbury. Both were charged with felony and fled to the parish church of St. Edith, Wilton. After one night they fled.[135] They were then apprehended by the bailiff of the abbess of Wilton. Two days later they were being escorted to the court of the abbess when as they passed the chapel of St. Thomas the Martyr, the bailiff took Roger de Ludynton inside and handed him over to the sanctuary of the resident chaplain. Roger then stayed in the Church until the next day when the coroner arrived. Before the coroner Roger confessed to stealing a psalter worth twelve pence from the church of St. Thomas, Salisbury six weeks previously. The coroner then heard his oath of abjuration and he was exiled from the port of Plymouth. All implications are that the abbess knew of the plan to secure Roger's exile and her bailiff was complicit as the abbess was held liable for the value of the alleged stolen goods.[136] Thomas Knapet, clerk of the church of St.Peter the Little, Poulsewharf, London had not committed a felony and therefore he probably never considered the need to seek

---

[134] Cox, Supra. pp. 295–296 including a facsimile of the original report *Coroners Roll of the City of York, 1349–59*

[135] It was the case until 1327 that local citizens were responsible for escapes from ecclesiastical sanctuary. Edward III changed this for London (and then the rest of the country) so that in future the local citizenry was not financially burdened with this. The result was that the number of nighttime escapes from sanctuary increased significantly. Thornley, Supra. Three quarters of the coroners rolls end with "afterwards he escaped by night". p. 296

[136] Cox, Supra. p. 292–293

sanctuary or self-proclaim outlawry. However, Knapet was arrested by the mayor of London for using disrespectful and disorderly words towards the Duke of Lancaster. The offender was committed to Newgate gaol pending trial. His bishop did not intercede.[137] Unscrupulous clerics surfaced again in 1382 when Walter atte Watre and Nicholas Somersete broke into a goldsmith's shop at nighttime and stole a large quantity of gold, jewelry and clothing. They were arrested before securing sanctuary, tried and found guilty. Fortunately for the offenders they were able to claim their clergy and the two were handed over to the ordinary.[138]

One of the most unusual clerical sanctuary cases took place at Westminster Abbey in 1388. This time the matter was not one of felony, at least it was not to start with. In principle it should never have become a sanctuary case, but Westminster was unusual as it had chartered status, which meant sanctuary was perpetual. The case involved a dispute between two beneficed clergy. The sanctuaried petitioner, William de Chesterton, was in dispute with the holder of a benefice and having petitioned his bishop in vain he took refuge at Westminster pending appeal to the pope. The appeal to Rome was intercepted by the Lord Chancellor, Thomas of Arundel, who construed the contents to be critical of him personally in his dual roles as bishop of Ely

---

[137] Riley, Supra. p. 215. And 2 Richard II. A.D. 1378. Letter Book at http://www.british-history.ac.uk/report.aspx?compid=57718. The incident may have come about due to the support that John of Gaunt had shown towards Wyclif. Goodman, A., *John of Gaunt: The Exercise of Princely Power in Fourteenth-Century Europe*, London, Longman, 1992 esp. pp. 242–247

[138] Riley, Supra. pp. 234–235. In 1406 William Hegge was tried for burglary and found guilty. He successfully claimed his clergy but at the time since no ordinary was present in the courtroom he was remanded to Newgate prison pending claim by the bishop. 7. Henry IV. A.D. 1406. Riley, Supra. p. 273

(1373–1388) and chancellor of England.[139] Arundel immediately brought the matter before parliament. The author of the letter was now charged with revealing secrets of the kingdom and making false charges against the king's officials. Sanctuary was not available for treason and therefore the chancellor petitioned for the forcible release of the clerk. The abbot of Westminster was summoned to explain why, if at all, the clerk should not be released to parliament. In May parliament ordered the release of the cleric. At this point Richard II (1377–1399) intervened and expressed his view that the sanctity of the Westminster abbey could not be violated and the cleric should be left alone. The cleric remained (perhaps perpetually) in the safe custody of the abbot of Westminster.[140] The monarch's intervention was seen again many years later in 1430. Thomas Bourchier, dean of St. Martin's, London[141] petitioned Henry VI (1422–1461) for the release of Henry Ciprian, canon of Waltham. Ciprian had been forcibly removed from the Church by the mayor of London and placed into secular prison. The king found in favor of the dean and Ciprian was returned to the sanctuary of the Church.[142] Contained within the muniment of Westminster Abbey for 1442 is the record of the sanctuary of the abbot of Westminster. The record indicates that the abbot and others had assaulted and imprisoned a prior in Kent and then taken ecclesiastical refuge within their own

---

[139] Arundel also served as archbishop of York and archbishop of Canterbury and twice as Lord Chancellor, 1399 and 1407–1410

[140] Cox, Supra. 53 and Shepherd, R. *Westminster: A Biography From the Earliest Times to the Present*, London, The National Archives, 2012. pp.99–100 and Thornley, Supra. pp. 306–308

[141] Bourchier went on to be archbishop of Canterbury 1454–1486

[142] Cox, Supra. pp. 82–83

abbey.[143] In 1457 the bishop of Chichester, Reginald Pecock (1450–1461) was deprived of his bishopric for the spiritual crime of heresy.[144] He was permitted to spend the remainder of his life in perpetual sanctuary in an abbey.[145] Another cleric of high office, Willam Grey, bishop of Ely (1454–1478) sought sanctuary at St. Martin le Grand, London in 1471; The War of the Roses having turned against him he took refuge until fortune changed in his favor.[146]

---

[143] Cox, Supra. p. 71. Edmond Kirton (Kyrton) (1440–1462) became abbot of Westminster in 1440 and was soon surrounded by accusations of mismanagement, and later of fornication, adultery, simony and being a dilapidator (1446 by the Bishop of Winchester) Kirton eventually resigned from office in 1462, probably due to ill health but his period of abbotship was marred with financial troubles. Certainly Kirton avoided standing papal trial for his alleged offences and he did remain within the chartered sanctuary curtilage of Westminster abbey throughout his life. Furthermore, on June 2, 1440, 18 Hen. VI records the revocation of the protections 'granted to our brother Edmund Kirton' for 'as intending to stay in the parts of Aquitaine on the king's service he tarries in the town of Westminster'. Hen VI. Calendar of the Patent Rolls. Vol. 46. M. 9. Pearce, E.H., *The Monks of Westminster: Being a Register of the Brethren of the Convent from the Time of the Confessor to the Dissolution, with the List of the Obendientaries and an Introduction,* Cambridge, Cambridge University Press, 1916, (2100 Reprint Ulan Press). The incident Cox, Supra, refers to may be the alleged imprisonment of monk Robert Alleyn which is mentioned by Galbraith, V.H., A Visitation of Westminster in 1444, *English Historical Review,* Vol. 37. (1922) pp. 83–88

[144] For commentary on the trial of Pecock; Catto, J., 'The King's Government and the Fall of Pecock 1457–1458' Chap.12 in Archer, R.E., and Walker, S., (eds) *Rulers and Ruled in Late Medieval England: Essays Presented to Gerald Hariss,* London, Hambledon Press, 1995, and for the life of Pecock, Green, V.H.H. *Reginald Pecock; A Study in Ecclesiastical History and Thought,* Cambridge, Cambridge University Press, 2014

[145] Davies, J.S., (ed) 'The Abjuration of Reginald Pecock, Bishop of Chichester, 1457', in, Myers, A.R. (ed) Punishment for Violation of Sanctuary, *English Historical Documents,* Vol. IV c. 1327–1485 Part III. Sec. 7. Doc. 516 and Rosser, Supra. p.68

[146] Cox, Supra. p. 93. And Haines, R.M. *Oxford Dictionary of National Biography,* Oxford, Oxford University Press, 2004–2014, House of York, *Chronicles of the White Rose: A Set of History Fragments Relating to the Reign of Edward the Fourth,* London, Stevens (2012 Reprint. Ulan Press). p. 60. N. 29. And pp. 92–94. Of note just one year previous the future Edward V (1470–1483) was born November 2, 1470, whilst in the sanctuary of Westminster abbey. Shepherd, R., *Westminster: A Biography,* London, The National Archives, 2012 esp. Chap. 13. 'Sanctity and Sanctuary'. pp. 97–103

Eventually the infamy of chartered sanctuaries as 'nests of corruption' grew such that they warranted special commentary by the king.[147] St. Martin's had already been subject to limitations in 1456 when ordinances were issued to control one of the capital's most notorious 'satellites of satan'.[148] It now became the case that on arrival sanctuary seekers were required to give up their swords and knives. The gates and church doors were to be secured - from nine at night until six in the morning- and 'pickers of locks', counterfeiters and utterers of silver and gold were no longer permitted to seek asylum.[149] Strumpets and bawds were also banned from entry.[150]

Criminal clergymen on-the-run did not always seek to be claimed by their bishop, Nicholas de Nodariis is a case in point. Nicholas was a cleric who fled from a felony trial. He had been convicted of homicide and larceny. He did not attempt to claim his clergy or flee to sanctuary, he accepted the fate of being outlawed; as a

---

[147] Richard II. Cox, Supra. p. 80–81

[148] Thornley, I., Sanctuary in Medieval London, *Journal of the British Archaeological Association*, Vol. 38. (1932) pp. 293–315. p. 298

[149] Ibid and Trenholme, N.M., *The Right of Sanctuary in England*, Columbia, University of Missouri, 1903. p. 55

[150] Cox, Supra. pp. 89–90. The special status of some sanctuaries such as St. Martin's meant that fleeing felons could remain beyond the purview of the secular law for the remainder of their lifetimes if they stayed within the confines of the Church. More unusual are examples of sanctuary seekers who waited years before claiming asylum Cox lists a number of examples throughout his book, one extreme example is Henry Stake who in 1488 murdered a man in London and twenty six years later claimed perpetual sanctuary at Durham. Cox, Supra. p. 117. The notoriety of St. Martins is commented upon by many authors of sanctuary. One of the more graphic contributions is cited by Thornley, Supra that it lay at 'the tone at the elbowe of the citie, the tother in the verye bowelles". p. 299

clerk he had no chattels for disbursement.[151] Walter le Norreys, a cleric who raped women, committed robbery and breached the king's peace also elected the life of an outlaw. There is no record of him ever seeking to claim his clergy or being claimed by the bishop or fleeing to sanctuary. Upon designation as an outlaw the court held he had no chattels nor was he in tithing because he was a clerk.[152] The Assize Rolls of Cornwall 1283–1284 contain one example of a clerk being refused abjuration. James, a clerk, fatally stabbed Ralph with a knife. James immediately fled to sanctuary at St. Michael's Mount Church. He sought the coroner to swear his oath but was instead handed over to the custody of the local prior.[153] Three years later Oliver, bishop of Lincoln (1280–1299) was attempting to prevent a cleric from exiling. His petition to Edward I (1272–1307) failed and the cleric was permitted to abjure (after he had followed the temporal law requirement that he returned to his church of sanctuary and from there abjure).[154]

One of the last examples of the benefit of sanctuary as it applied to clerics took place in 1519 when chaplain Thomas Ley misplaced a large quantity of money he had collected on behalf of his lord the Earl of Derby. He fled to sanctuary in the local church and confessed to the coroner.[155] Whether or not Ley had stolen

---

[151] Stewart, S., 'Outlawry as an Instrument of Justice in the Thirteenth Century' in Appleby, J.C., and Dalton, P., *Outlaws in Medieval and Early Modern England; Crime, Government and Society, c. 1066–c.1600,* Farnham, Surrey, Ashgate, 2009. Chap. 2. pp. 37–54 p. 44 quoting N. 33. Clanchy, M.T. (ed) *The Roll and Writ File of the Berkshire Eyre of 1248,* London, Selden Society, 1973. No. 872. pp. 345–346

[152] Stewart, Supra. pp. 44–45 and N. 34. Clanchy, Supra. No. 868. p. 344

[153] Cox, Supra. p. 301

[154] The case of Richard de Scardeburgh, July 5, 1286. *Calendar of the Close Rolls,* 1286 Edw. I. Cox, Supra. pp. 20–21

[155] Trenholme, Supra. p. 63

money or simply misplaced it is not clear. What the incident does exemplify is that use of sanctuary by clerics was so familiar to them that even in cases of potential criminal accusation they saw sanctuary as a temporary refuge in exactly the same way as did the laity.[156] There are no further examples of clerics claiming sanctuary and abjuration from the realm. The use (abuse) of sanctuary by civilians thrived for another two hundred years.[157] In the case of bad debtors it existed in various guises until 1727.

In order that the coroner kept records exigent[158] he needed to visit sanctuary seekers, administer the oath of abjuration and assign the exile a port of departure.[159] As seen above clerics frequently used sanctuary and in some cases swore the oath of abjuration.[160]

---

[156] It was also the case that when the Church sought to retain sanctuary generally and particularly around Westminster on the basis that eradication of sanctuary would cause a financial loss to the church… because property rentals in the immediate area would be less desirable. Thornley, Supra. p. 315

[157] General sanctuary was banned in 1624 and for a number of special sanctuaries in 1626. Cox, Supra. p. 336

[158] There is also a specific use of the term as it applied to felons who failed to appear three times before a criminal tribunal. On the fourth trial hearing date the coroner recorded that the alleged offender was a fugitive. The process of doing this, exigent, was a solemn legal procedure culminating in designation of outlawry. The procedure was only permitted in the county courts where outlawry was promulgated. Helmholz, Supra. p. 144. In London the proclaiming court was named The Hustings. Women and children under twelve could not technically be classified as outlaws. Women were outlawed though but the term employed was 'waived' or 'waivery' Hunisett, Supra. p. 62 and Musson, A., (ed), *Boundaries of the Law: Geography, Gender and Jurisdiction in Medieval and Early Modern Europe*, Aldershot, Ashgate, 2005. p.3

[159] There examples of the exile being permitted to elect his point of departure but this is rare. By far the most common port was Dover and in most instances it was the coroner who designated port, the route and the time for arrival at the departure point. C.F. Gross. Supra. p. 9 the case of sanctuary at Southoe Church, Huntington. Also Hunisett, R.F., *The Medieval Coroner*, Cambridge, Cambridge University Press, 1961. Chap III Abjurations of the Realm. pp. 37–54

[160] "The Abjuration and Oath of Thieves". 1235. Hen III. c.I. *Abjuration et Juramentum Latronum* and Cox, Supra. pp 13–15 for a version taken from Bracton's *De Corona*, 16th chapter

Although abjuration was always associated with ecclesiastical sanctuary it appears the coroner was not compromised by clergymen abusing the asylum. Those clerics who sought to utilize the entire extent of abjuration were designated a departure port and exiled in same manner as laymen. Acceptance of clerical abjuration[161] was given statutory authority under Edward II but contained safety measures not extended to the laity; commoners were subject to beheading if they returned from exile without a royal pardon, clerics could not be subjected to such summary justice and the 'Immunity or Privilege of the Church and Spiritual persons may be saved and unbroken'.[162] According to statute law a clerk could not be compelled to abjure, he could select from a range of options; benefit of clergy, sanctuary, perpetual ecclesiastical asylum, putting himself on the country, abjure and if the latter should he return without pardon did not wear the 'head of the wolf'[163] and risk summary beheading. For the fleeing criminal seeking sanctuary, layman or cleric, all felonies appear to have been within church asylum with the exceptions of heresy, witchcraft and necromancy.[164]

---

[161] Since the assize of Clarendon, 1166, it was clear that clerics who had claimed their benefit of clergy could not be forced to abjure. Bellamy, Supra. p. 112

[162] *Articuli Cleri* 9 Edward II 1315–1316. s.15

[163] The term 'wore the wolves head' applied to felons whose status as an exile that returned without pardon or was a designated outlaw, could be executed with impunity by local villagers. Hunisett, Supra. p. 67. N. 6 quoting Richardson, H.G., and Sayles, G.O. (eds) Fleta. Vol. II. Prologue, Books 1 & 2, Selden Society, 1953. Vol. 72. p. 70

[164] Cox, Supra. p. 59. For examples of the fate of exiled convicts returning without pardon as well interpretation of the law as viewed by *Fleta;* Richardson, H.G. and Sayles, G.O. (ed and trans) 'Fleta on Sanctuary and Abjuration' 'in Rothwell, H., (ed) Sanctuary and Abjuration of the Realm, and Outlawry, *English Historical Documents,* c. 1189–1379,Part III. Vol. III. Doc. 110 at www.englishhistoricaldocuments.com/document/view.htm?id=723

# 7

# Outlaws and Gang Members

During the last quarter of the thirteenth century justices visiting Gloucester reported 'an appalling tale of crime' it included three hundred and thirty murders. Yet of this number only fourteen men hanged and one hundred either failed to appear at all or were outlawed during the process. The pattern was the same across the country with large increases in the number of appeals for murder, robbery and extortion.[1] Of parallel concern was the number of those indicted that never appeared[2] and were proclaimed outlaws; few accused felons ever stood trial.[3] The pattern of lawlessness continued (largely

[1] Edward I made special reference to the deterioration of order in the preamble to the Statute of Winchester 1285. Summerson, H. The Enforcement of the Statute of Winchester 1285–1327, *The Journal of Legal History*, Vol. 13. No. 2. (1992) pp. 232–250

[2] For a breakdown of occurrences in most English counties see Bellamy, Bellamy, J.G., *Criminal Law and Society in Late Medieval and Tudor England*, New York, St. Martin's Press, 1984. pp. 157–159

[3] E.g. Shropshire 1256 of one hundred and eighty-six cases of homicide presented only nineteen resulted in conviction and execution. "Crime after crime was presented as committed by *malefactoess ignoti* [persons unknown]. The system was incapable of dealing with the hardened criminal who wandered from shire to shire'. Harding, A., The Origins and Early History of the Keeper of the Peace, *Transactions of the Royal Historical Society* (Fifth Series) Vol. 10. (1960) pp. 85–109. p. 86 citing Public record office J.I. 1/734 Shropshire Eyre. At the 1263 Surrey Eyre fifty-five per cent of defendants failed to appear (122 of 227). One hundred and sixteen of this group were pronounced outlawed. Stewart, S., 'Outlawry as an Instrument of Justice in the Thirteenth Century' in Appleby, J.C. and Dalton, P., (eds) *Outlaws in Medieval and Early Modern England: Crime, Government and Society, c. 1066-c.1600*, Farnham, Surrey, Ashgate, 2009. p. 41 citing Stewart, S., (ed) *The 1263 Surrey Eyre*, Guildford, Surrey Record Society, 2006. p. lxxx

unabated) into the new century. Of particular concern was the visible increase in the number of criminal gangs.[4] The crown was aware of the problems and attempted remedial measures, of varying success.[5] As early as 1305 supplementary judicial provision was introduced with the creation of Trailbaston courts; a body of itinerant justices specifically commissioned to deal with felonies in the counties.[6] Generally confidence in royal justice was waning though; individual members of the judiciary were corrupt[7] and at the same time susceptible to abuse and violence. Their lives were at peril and in one famous instance Richard Willoughby, justice of the king's bench, was kidnapped and held for ransom by the infamous Foleville gang.[8] Incredibly the culprits were themselves members of the English gentry who took organized crime as an opportunity created by proximity to the monarch. In 1336 a

---

[4] Harding, A., *The Law Courts of Medieval England*, London, Allen & Unwin, 1973. p. 88 referred to this as '...the great crisis of justice and order at the turn of the thirteenth century'. Many gangs were formed from the men who were returning g from military campaigns and now found themselves without income or employment. C.f. Stewart, Infra. p.p. 52–53

[5] See generally Bellamy, J.G., *Crime and Public Order in England in the Later Middle Ages*, London, Routledge, 1973 pp. 10–14. Esp. pp. 10–11 e.g. 1277, 1283, 1305 and information received by Edward II in 1314 and Edward III in 1335 and 1347 about complaints from the people pertaining to felons and criminal gangs and the enquiry instigated by Edward III into corruption 1349–1352. Also Edward III personally attended the trial of the Folevilles, Infra, at Stamford in 1332

[6] A. Harding, 'Early trailbaston proceedings from the Lincoln roll of 1305', in R. F. Hunnisett & J. B. Post (eds.), Medieval Legal Records Edited in Memory of C. A. F. Meekings, London, H. M. S. O., 1978. Ormrod, W.M., 'Law in the Landscape: Criminality, Outlawry and Regional Identity in Late Medieval England' in Musson, A., (ed) *Boundaries of the Law*, Aldershot, Ashgate, 2005. p. 10

[7] See Bellamy, Supra. p. 17. For evidence of corruption later in the century the case of Adam le Clerk is symptomatic. He was a lawyer who represented both the defendant and the aggrieved party in suit, took fees from both. His clients were the abbot of Pershore and the abbot of Westminster. Jury 'knobbling' or at least jury influencing by the gentry was also rife, so much so it was given a name; embracery

[8] Infra

Rutland gang murdered a justice and in 1350 a Hertfordshire justice was murdered whilst on route to the assizes.[9] Also in 1350 Lionel de Bradenham and two hundred armed accomplices besieged the entire town of Colchester; it was the second time Colchester had been overtaken by felons in seven years.[10] In 1358 a gross effrontery to the judiciary took place at the residence of justice Thomas Seton in Fleet Street, London when Thomas de Nesebit, a chaplain, murdered the judge in his home. The killing was particularly disturbing to the higher echelons of society because the felonious priest had been paid to conduct the homicide; it was a contract killing.[11]

Until 1341 it was common for the judiciary of England to compromise of spiritual and secular justices.[12] Professionalization of an entirely secular bench was a lengthy process, in part due

---

[9] 1336 Sir John Wittlebury. 1350 John Leggat. Bellamy, Supra. p. 20

[10] 1343 The Fitzwalter gang. Bellamy, Supra. p. 79. 1350. *Calendar of Patent Rolls under Edward III, 1364–1367.* Dec. 6. Vol. 13. m. 7. pp. 54–56. Fitzwalter was eventually imprisoned in the Tower of London and released after he secured a pardon and purchased back his confiscated lands from the king. Hanwalt, B., Fur-Collar Crime: The Pattern of Crime Among the Fourteenth-Century Nobility, *Journal of Social History*, Vol. 8. No. 10 (1975) pp. 1–17. p. 10

[11] *Calendar of Patent Rolls Before* Edward III, 1358–1361. m. 22d July 3, 1359. Vol. II. p. 280. "The like to William de Shareshull, William de Thorpe, Robert Westminster, de Thorpe, Henry Grene, William de Notton and John Lovekyn, mayor of London, touching certain satellites of the devil who plotting the death of Thomas de Seton ,one of the justices of the Bench retained by the king to be one of the secret council, hired Thomas de Nesebit, chaplain, to kill him, which Thomas ,when Thomas de Seton was of the king's council, entered his dwelling at Flete strete, London, in friendly fashion and uttering fair words to him there struck him in the belly with his knife and atrociously wounded him"

[12] Owen, D.M., *The Medieval Canon Law: Teaching, Literature and Transmission*, Cambridge, Cambridge University Press, 1990. pp. 21–23 and Owen, D.M., 'Ecclesiastical Jurisdiction 1300–1500: The Records and Their Interpretation' in Baker, D., (ed) *Studies in Church History, Vol. 11, The Materials, Sources and Methods of Ecclesiastical History*, Oxford, Oxford University Press, 1975. pp. 199–221. The reverse would eventually occur with doctors of civil law being empowered to exercise ecclesiastical jurisdiction by 1545. Owen, D.M., *The Medieval Canon Law: Teaching, Literature and Transmission*, Cambridge, Cambridge University Press, 1990. p. 43

to stagnation in judges salaries and in part because all members of the bench served at the king's pleasure. Change slowly took place. As it did the Church remained central to the lives of the citizenry, particularly at the local level. Priests had a role to play at the beginning of life, at death and at many stages between. Thirteenth century England relied upon the Church for many services that would today be taken up by the state; secular court trials were often held in churches[13] and other ecclesiastic venues[14] and churches were the most appropriate location for proclamations of temporal news and announcements (in English and French). The delivery of information by priests could accordingly be personalized to express significant support or mild disapproval for royal news and secular propaganda.[15] Those in high office in the Church were in theory controlled by Rome but in reality the king was an increasingly forceful voice in the selection of prelates. As lords of the realm bishops were confidants of the crown. Perhaps not surprisingly given the access that members of the Church had to and within society these men were also active criminals. They used their office to aid, abet, conspire and through their position as social superiors,[16] force others to commit a broad

---

[13] Harding, A., (ed) *Roll of the Shropshire Eyre 1256,* London, Selden Society, 1981 pp.114- 115 e.g. St. Bartholomew's Church, London was a location for clerks and attorneys to meet and develop legal practice

[14] Owen, D.M., *The Medieval Canon Law: Teaching, Literature and Transmission,* Cambridge, Cambridge University Press, 1990. pp. 23–24

[15] Musson, A. *Medieval Law in Context: The Growth of Legal Consciousness from Magna Carta to the Peasant's Revolt,* Manchester, Manchester University Press, 2001. pp. 226–227. p. 231

[16] Summerson, H., The Criminal Underworld of Medieval England, *The Journal of Legal History,* Vol. 17. No. 3. (1996) pp. 197–224 and Fryde, N. A Medieval Robber Baron: Sir John Molyns of Stoke Pages in Hunnisett, R., and Post, J. (eds) *Medieval Legal Records Edited in Memory of C.A.F. Meekings,* London, HMSO, 1978. pp. 197–221. Bellamy, Supra. pp. 17–18 with examples of corrupt court officials, lawyers, abbots, bishops. 'The king was well aware that many of those concerned with the administration of justice were corrupt'. p. 17

range of felonies.[17] When legal privileges and royal patronage expired some prelates resorted to outlawry.

Exactions and proclamations of outlawry[18] were vested in the county courts through the office of coroner.[19] Defendants who failed to appear before a criminal tribunal four times[20] were on the fifth occasion deemed to be outlaws. A fleeing felon could also be classed an outlaw. A sanctuarial who did not abjure the realm was also an outlaw. Outlawry was not a punishment[21] (as a trial had not taken place), It was rather more a declaration of status. Men were declared outlaws.

---

[17] It was not until 1377 that Edward III felt sufficiently confident that he could order the bishops not to continue the practice of allowing notorious clerical felons to purge themselves. Bellamy, Supra. p. 166. In addition to felonies outlawry also lost some of its stigma and impact so that whether by choice or judicial decree outlawry itself was not as shameful to the clergy as it had been in the past. Stewart, Supra. p.54 quoting Musson, A. *Medieval Law in Context: The Growth of Legal Consciousness from Magna Carta to the Peasant's Revolt*, Manchester, Manchester University Press, 2001. pp. 171- 172. Also, Musson refers to the poem *An Outlaw's Song of Trailbaston* as an indication of the change in the face of outlawry and the judicial institutions of the fourteenth century

[18] The term outlaw is used in its judicial sense and not as a term of reference for the mythical and romantic notions of Robin Hood. For a discussion of the development of the term outlaw, fictional and actual, and its implications, Keen, M., *The Outlaws of Medieval England*, London, Routledge, 1961 (Revised Edition 2000). See Bellamy, Supra. pp. 42–43 for a depiction of the real face of highway robbery in England during the late Middle Ages and pp. 87–88

[19] A proclamation of outlawry was possible at both civil and criminal law. Clerics were subject to the civil law of England and could be proclaimed civil law outlaws. Civil law outlawries are held Plea Rolls CP 40 at the Public Records Office. Criminal outlawries are to be found on the Eyre Rolls from the late twelfth to mid-fourteenth century are housed in the British National Archives (JUST 1) and the *curia regis* rolls (KB 26) and *coram rege* rolls (KB 27)

[20] In London it was after failure to appear three times. The proclamation of outlawry was then made at St. Paul's. Stewart, Supra. p. 40

[21] In her chapter 'Outlawry as an Instrument of Justice in the Thirteenth Century', Susan Stewart suggests that outlawry was a punishment for a felony. Appleby, J.C., and Dalton, P. *Outlaws in Medieval and Early Modern England, Crime, Government and Society, c. 1066-c.1600*, Farnham, Surrey, Ashgate,2009. Chapter 2. pp. 37–54. p. 37

Women,[22] who could not technically hold that criminal title, were exacted and waived. Children under the age of fourteen should not have been permitted to abjure or be outlawed.[23] Outlaws bore the 'wolves head'[24] however, obtaining a king's pardon was commonplace.[25] It suited the miscreant who was now able to return to licit society and offend again and it brought money, 'punishment by the purse' into the treasury. Cash settlements or service, normally military, were an option e.g. John Fitwalter, one time robber baron and besieger of Colchester amassed a royal pardon debt of £847 2s. 2¼d.[26]

---

[22] Children could be 'outlawed'. Women could abjure whereas children could not. Hunnisett, Supra. p. 62 and Bracton, Infra. Vol. 2. pp. 353–354. Only men over the age of fourteen years could be outlawed. (JUST/1/780. M.2). Also see generally : www.nationalarchives.gov.uk/records/research-guides/outlawry

[23] In 1272 an eight-year-old boy was permitted to abjure the realm after he swore guilt before the coroner. His twelve-year-old brother accomplice was hanged. Summerson, H., The Criminal Underworld of Medieval England, *The Journal of Legal History*, Vol. 17. No. 3. (1996) pp. 197–224. p. 212

[24] 'Henceforth they bear the wolf's head and in consequence perish without judicial inquiry; they carry their judgment with them and they deservedly perish without law who have refused to live according to law. This is so if they take to flight or resist when they are to be arrested; if they are arrested alive or give themselves up, their life and death will be in the hands of the lord king'. Woodbine, G.E. (ed) Thorne, S.E. (trans) *Bracton on the Laws and Customs of England*, Cambridge, MA, Harvard University Press, 1968–1977. 4 Vols. Vol. 2. p. 357

[25] Hunnisett, Supra. p. 68 and Stewart, Supra. pp. 42–43. Reversal of outlawry required the outlaw to appear in person before the Court of Common Pleas or the King's Bench an alternative was to plea a pardon. To plea a pardon required the outlaw to surrender himself to the Fleet or Marshalsea prison and then apply to have his matter heard before the Court of King's bench. If successful, the outlaw's goods were restored to him. In exceptional cases (serious felony or treason) an outlaw could petition to plead his case directly before Parliament. Edward I promised pardons to felons who would fight for him in France. Summerson, *Criminal Underworld*, Supra. p. 207.

[26] Furber, E.C. (ed) *Essex Sessions of the Peace, 1351, 1377–1379*, Essex Archeological Society Occasional Publications 3, Colchester, 1953.p. 76 quoted in Bellamy, Supra. p. 85. N. 43. And by Hanwalt, B., Fur-Collar Crime: The Pattern of Crime Among the Fourteenth-Century Nobility, *Journal of Social History*, Vol. 8. No. 10 (1975) pp. 1–17. p. 10 "Ten years of Pipe Rolls benignly enters payments to the king from his "dear and faithful" John Fitzwaleter". Nicholas Thornley, an esquire, married without obtaining a royal license paid a fine to the crown to be released and to be allowed the marriage. Bellamy, Supra, p. 165

Returning to favor, particularly for nobles and church hierarchy, was available throughout the reigns of Edward's I, II and III.[27]

Fines (payments in cash to the crown) could be made before arraignment or after finding of guilt. Justices were not authorized to pardon. Their role was to facilitate the arrangement for the crown and obtain sureties in instances where the pardon was military service for the king.[28] All pardons were an exclusive royal prerogative. Pardons were unpopular with commoners. They provided no opportunity for involvement in the judicial process and few laymen had the means to secure a pardon other than by providing their labor (life) as military service. In such a class structured society as medieval England even pardons were assessed based upon social rank; £1000 for an archbishop or a duke, a mere 200 marks for a criminous clerk.[29] A curious but important link between outlawry and the Church existed in London as the proclamation of a felon being deemed an outlaw was made in St. Paul's.[30] Moving between legal options (forum shopping) was potentially advantageous but also risky as it could expose criminal clergyman to the full extent of the secular law. Once proclaimed an outlaw he was, in theory, no longer under the protection of his bishop. He could achieve this precarious state because he had been degraded and held the status of a layman or he had not been claimed by the ordinary because he failed to appear four times and

---

[27] E.g. Bellamy, Supra. pp. 85–86 and p. 100

[28] Bellamy, Supra. pp.191–198

[29] The 200 marks normally included one year's imprisonment as well. Bellamy, Supra. p. 195

[30] Stewart, Supra. p. 40 esp. N. 12. Weinbaum, M (ed) *The Eyre of London 1276,* London, London Record Society, 1976. p. xviii. For an example of a less honorable connection between outlawry and the Church, Harding, Supra. p. 117 quotes the association between the Chapter of Lichfield cathedral and known gang members

was exacted; either way the criminal cleric was an outlaw until such time as he sought pardon or stood trial and attempted to claim his clergy.[31] By 1390 pardons were no longer granted for treason, rape, murder, homicide by ambush, or assault occasioned by malice.[32]

The earliest recorded occurrence of ecclesiastic outlawry probably occurred in 1163 when a cleric was degraded and then brought before the courts temporal. The felonious clerk was proclaimed an outlaw by the secular tribunal. It is not clear in this case whether outlawry was imposed as a sentence after trial or due to him being a fugitive.[33] In 1180 the village of Wymondham, Leicestershire was fined for receiving an outlawed cleric, the offending cleric was later pardoned after intervention by Ralph, archdeacon of Cornwall. Fugitive status was removed upon amercement of £100 and the offender

---

[31] Pollock, F., and Maitland, F.W., *The History of the English Law Before the Time of Edward I,* Cambridge, Cambridge University Press. 1968, Second Edition. p. 478 note the proximity of outlawry and excommunication and refer to the latter as 'ecclesiastical outlawry'. Logan, Supra, p.13, 15, 18–19. N.1 comments that when excommunication did not result in repentance then the Church turned to secular society for the imposition of service in a holy war, pilgrimage

[32] 13. Richard II. st. 2. C. 1. Further; Kesselring, K., *Mercy and Authority in the Tudor State,* Cambridge, Cambridge University Press, 2003. pp. 103–104

[33] It is also possible that the cleric was degraded and then sentenced by the courts Christian as before 1261 it was possible for the bishop's court to impose outlawry and abjuration sentences. After the Council of Lambeth, 1281, perpetual solitary confinement in a bishop's prison or monastery was substituted for the temporal punishment of execution or fugitive status. Poole, A.L., 'Outlawry as a Punishment of Criminous Clerks', in Edwards, J.G., Galbraith, V.H. and Jacob, E.F., (eds) *Historical Essays in Honour of James Tait,* Manchester, Manchester University Press, 1933. pp. 239–246. p. 239 and p. 244. N. 7. Bellamy, Supra.p. 163 For the secular convict terms of imprisonment varied from one week to life. By the reign of Edward I the term was calculated on the basis of one week's imprisonment for each one penny of value of goods stolen

being available to stand trial.[34] This was followed in 1202 by the appealing of a clerk for murder. Ralph of Nettleham, cleric, and his brother were suspected of murdering Reginald, son of Picot. Ralph was claimed by the bishop and released to the ordinary. He was then degraded and outlawed by the spiritual court.[35] This case clarifies that a cleric could be proclaimed an outlaw and it supports the view that outlawry was a sentence. (In this case it was imposed by a judicial tribunal and not as a result of the defendant having failed to appear a certain number of times previously). This case also confirms that outlawry was available to courts Christian and temporal. In 1221 a clerk from Cornwall was accused of the murder of a woman, he fled the scene and the court proclaimed him an outlaw.[36] Six years later another cleric, Ansell de Bray, was outlawed by the justices sitting at the Bedford Eyre.[37] This was followed in 1238 when a subdeacon was appealed for murder and either fled or escaped from custody. He had not been degraded or appeared before the courts Christian at this time. Subsequently the subdeacon returned from his self-imposed exile and was arrested by secular bailiffs. He appeared before the justices wearing clerical garb and was demanded by the bishop of Exeter, to whom he was released. The subdeacon then purged himself before his ecclesiastic peers. Clearly

---

[34] Poole, A.L. 'Outlawry as a Punishment of Criminous Clerks' in Edwards, J.G., Galbraith, V.H., and Jacob, E.F., (eds) *Historical Essays in Honour of James Tait,* Manchester, Manchester University Press, 1933. p. 244 and N. 2, 3,4 taken from 26 Hen. II. Pipe Roll, p. 102 and 28. Hen. II. Pipe Roll, p. 83

[35] Poole, Supra. p. 244 Esp. N.7

[36] Poole, Supra. p. 243. N. I. Citing Watson, E.G. (ed) *Pleas of the Crown at Bristol 1223.* p. 23

[37] 1227. Poole, Supra. p. 243 and N. I Fowler, G.H., *Bedford Eyre of 1227,* Bedford Historical Society, 1916. Vol. 3. No. 361

annoyed, the king remonstrated with the bishop but eventually backed down and no further action was taken against the re-instated cleric.[38]

In 1248 Nicholas de Nodariis, a clerk, along with six other men, were appealed by Berkshire justices for murder. Nicholas and two others failed to appear. The court found them guilty of homicide 'so they are to be exacted and outlawed'.[39] The defendants were found guilty *in absentia*, which technically did not exist at common law.[40] The same record shows that Walter le Norreys, a cleric, was appealed for the murder and rape of Alice of Wulvruehampton. He too was outlawed by the Berkshire justices.[41] Further evidence of clerics being proclaimed outlaws occurred in Oxford in 1285 when Henry de Makworth, Thomas de Sancto David, David Furlong, William Ousyn, Roger le Fletcher, William de Blithe, and Henry de Staumford, burgled the house of Ivo de Hackebourn. All of the suspects fled. The court held 'They are believed guilty, therefore they

---

[38] Exeter Close Roll 1237–42. P. 122 citied by Poole, Supra. p. 245 and N. 2. Poole, Supra. p. 245. N.3 citing Maitland, F.W.; Leveson, W.V.H.; Craddock Bolland, W. (eds). The *Eyre of Kent 6 and & Edw. II. 1313–1314*, London, Selden Society,1910. Vol I. No. 24. p. lxx. The issue of which prison an outlawed cleric should be housed in pending royal pardon was finally resolved during the reign of Edward II in favor of the secular prison. Poole, Supra. p. 245. N.3 citing Maitland, F.W.; Leveson, W.V.H.; Craddock Bolland, W. (eds). The *Eyre of Kent 6 and & Edw. II. 1313–1314*, London, Selden Society,1910. Vol I. No. 24. p. lxx

[39] Stewart, Supra. p. 44. quoting Clanchy, M.T., (ed) *The Roll and Writ File of the Berkshire Eyre of 1248*, London, Selden Society, 1973. Vol. 90. No. 872. pp. 345–346

[40] But as Bellamy, Supra, notes very often men were found guilty (and sentenced) in their absence. p. 104 citing the example of John de Clifford found guilty of rape *in absentia* in 1282. Sayles, G.O. (ed) *Select Cases in the Court of the King's Bench Under Edward I*, London, Selden Society 1936. Vol. I. 55.p. 102

[41] Stewart, Supra. p. 45 quoting Clanchy, M.T., (ed) *The Roll and Writ File of the Berkshire Eyre of 1248*, London, Selden Society, 1973. Vol. 90. No. 872. pp. 344

are to be outlawed.' The transcript continues 'Possessions of Henry de Staumford [are worth] 16s., for which the sheriff is to answer; Henry [de Makworth] and the others had no possessions, because they are clerks'. Six of the seven defendants were clerks and all were sentenced as outlaws.[42]

Fourteenth century priestly venality started in 1303 with the daring raid on the king's treasure at Westminster by Richard Pudlicott.[43] It was the beginning of a very active period of clerical criminality. On December 10, 1317 at Windsor justices indicted Brother William Sansemer and Brother Thomas de Monyngton, monks of Rufford Abbey, Nottinghamshire, for establishing a gang and committing felonies. The cleric gang had kidnapped Thomas de Holm and held him in ransom for £200.[44] In the same year John, son of William Tynhide, had been sentenced to be hanged by justices of Oyer and Terminer at Wiltshire. On route to the gallows he was freed by John de Mulford, William de Hulmerton, John de Bathampton, Francis Aubyn and John de Styntesford all of the Order of Friar Preachers. The monks were subsequently pardoned on

---

[42] Thorold Rogers, J.E., (ed) *Oxford City Documents, Financial and Judicial, 1268–1665*, Oxford Historical Society, 1891. Vol. 18. pp. 194–236

[43] An estimated heist of £100, 000 from the treasury at Westminster. Infra. Also Bellamy, Supra. pp. 50–53. N. 21 and Gregory-Abbot, C., 'Sacred Outlaws: Outlawry and the Medieval Church' in Appleby, J.C. and Dalton, P., (eds) *Outlaws in Medieval and Early Modern England: Crime, Government and Society, c. 1066-c.1600*, Farnham, Surrey, Ashgate, 2009. p. 78

[44] *Calendar of Patent Rolls Edward II. 1317–1321* Vol. III. m. 13d. p. 93. 'The Patent Rolls are the Chancery enrolments of royal letters patent. Those for the 11th to the 14th years of the reign of king Edward II (8 July 1317 to 7 July 1321) were edited for the Public Record Office by G. F. Handcock, and published in 1903. The main contents are royal commissions and grants; ratifications of ecclesiastical estates; writs of aid to royal servants and purveyors; and pardons. Most extensive are the commissions of Oyer and Terminer to justices to investigate complaints about specific crimes and wrongs in particular counties'. http://www.theoriginalrecord.com/database/search/search/annesley

January 6, 1318. The reason and monetary settlement figure of the pardon is not recorded.[45]

Counterfeiting was a dangerous but lucrative criminal trade in the Middle Ages. A skillfully copied seal (episcopal or royal) could assist or prevent a number of lawsuits, establish legal ownership of land or benefices and indict or pardon a felon. Some of the most skilled forgers in the country were those who also produced legitimate documents; clerics. Philip Burdon was a chaplain and forger. He formed a gang of criminous clerks that included Richard of Bourne, a parson of Wroxhall Church, and Richard of Harslade, clerk. Their case is not one that resulted in outlawry but is important because it exemplifies the level of organized crime that groups of clerics engaged in. Philip obtained a copy of the royal seal on a number of documents; a writ of novel disseisin and a writ of patent. The gang then copied the king's great seal into a metal die and used the forgeries to manufacture counterfeit writs. When asked by the justices what motivated his treason Burdon responded for revenge upon his enemies who had trespassed upon him. The priest was found guilty of felony and treason[46] before the Winchester Gaol delivery. He claimed his clergy and was released to Roger Poule, rector of Chessel Church, the bishop of Winchester's ordinary. Richard of Bourne's case was delayed and he was remanded into secular custody pending trial. Richard of Harsdale, claimed his clergy but was not claimed by the bishop; suggesting the bishop accepted the legitimacy of Burdon's claim but not Bourne or Harsdale's.[47]

---

[45] *Calendar of Patent Rolls Edward II. 1317–1321* Vol. III. m. 6. p.69

[46] Which was *de jure* unclergyable at common law

[47] *Select Cases in the Court of the King's Bench Under Edward II.* pp. 158–160. Also Sayles, G.O., (ed) Select Cases in the Court of the King's Bench Under Edward II, London, Selden Society,1955. Vol. 74

Less ambitious crimes were committed as well; in 1329 a chaplain was convicted of taking metal from tombs in St.Pauls cathedral.[48] A few years earlier a covering from an image of the Virgin Mary was stolen, the alleged response was 'her son is rich enough to give her a new one'.[49] It is not clear if the author of this was a cleric but it is suggestive of the general attitude many of the lower orders had towards petty theft and larceny generally, even to the point of adopting a sobriquet such as Thomas Midnygh, a cleric who specialized in house breaking at nighttime.[50]

Sir John Molyns of Stoke Poges was a landowner and criminal who supplied criminal services to the Church. He was charged with a variety of crimes throughout his lifetime including murder, extortion and theft. For the Church he supplied fear and the muscle to back it up. For a fee he would kidnap clergymen for other clerics and he would evict ecclesiastics from their benefices and install others at the behest of bishops. He was an entrepreneur and opportunist and like so many criminals of the era he saw a window of opportunity during the unrest created by the capture and abdication of Edward II; England suffered an explosion of looting and robbery during this tumultuous period and Molyns was available for hire as needed. In 1333 the prior of Christchurch Canterbury and his tenants at Monks Risborough engaged in a dispute. By 1335 the situation had deteriorated and Molyns was co-opted in to help. On May 20, 1336 Molyns and his men attacked Monks Risborough on behalf of the prior of Canterbury and destroyed homes and kidnapped a number

[48] Summerson, Supra. p. 208
[49] Summerson, Supra. p. 216
[50] Ibid. pp. 217–218

of men from the village. Molyns, his criminal churchmen and his thugs then fled and were outlawed.[51] In July 1340 Molyns sent a gang of his men, headed up by John Hay, vicar of Weston Turville and Molyns' closest friend, to attack a sheriff and his family who were presenting Molyns with a few problems. Afterwards the gang, still headed by the criminous vicar, ran amuck across the counties of Bedfordshire and Buckinghamshire, looting and causing mayhem as they travelled.

Receiving shelter and assistance from the clergy was common and applied to all walks of life, even the criminal. However, the hospitality of the Church was sometimes beyond charitable and reached levels of criminal complicity. The priors of Bristol and Holland, Lancashire willingly received Sir John Dalton in 1347 despite the fact that he was a double murderer who had abducted a lady and that one of his murder victims was the woman's chaplain. Even more vexing is the fact that the crime was committed on Good Friday and within the protection of the crown; nevertheless the monks of Bristol and Lancashire offered safe haven to Dalton.[52] Subsequently Dalton was outlawed but managed to find enough cash to pay the king for a royal pardon and he and his abducted lady, now wife, returned to court. The issue of committing a felony within the itinerant sanctuary of the monarch was not mentioned again. Further examples followed in 1348.[53]

---

[51] Fryde, N. A Medieval Robber Baron: Sir John Molyns of Stoke Pages in Hunnisett, R., and Post, J. (eds) *Medieval Legal Records Edited in Memory of C.A.F. Meekings,* London, HMSO, 1978. pp. 204–205

[52] Bellamy,Supra. p. 59

[53] Infra

Bands of criminous clerks, like most organized crime groups, diversified their portfolio of crime offerings. Some like Burdon[54] operated largely for their own means; others offered their services to criminal episcopates and secular lords. Conversely secular gangs offered their services to the lower clerical orders too. The canons of Lichfield cathedral hired the Coterel gang to remove Walter Can, vicar of Bakewell, the evictors took the opportunity to steal from the Church at the same time. The canon of Sempringham hired the Foleville gang to destroy a rival clerics watermill and the abbot of Our Lady of Bootham, York hired Lionel 'the ravener' (robber)[55] to threaten the parson of Huntington, Richard de Snaweshill (Snowshill).[56] In the same year six friars were arrested for creating felonious disturbances in Bury St. Edmunds. The mayhem was conducted in partnership with associates of Sir Robert Tuchet and Lord Markeaton, known patrons of both the Coterel and Foleville gangs.[57] Walter Musard made his extortion and eviction services available to the diocese of Worcester to evict Godfrey Crombe from the rectory of Weston-sub-Edge.[58]

Gangs of criminal clerics or illicit groups that had priests as members represented a significant threat to peace and good order in England during much of the fourteenth century.

---

[54] Summerson, Supra

[55] Ormrod, *Boundaries of the Law*, Supra. p. 17

[56] *Select Cases in the Court of the King's Bench Under Edward III. pp. 93–94.* Also G.O., (ed) *Select Cases in the Court of the King's Bench Under Edward III*, London, Selden Society,1957. Vol. 76 and Bellamy, Supra. p. 73. Bellamy quotes the abbot of being from St. Mary's, York. The court record states Our Lady of Bootham

[57] Bellamy, Supra. pp. 73–74. It was in the grounds of the estate of Lord Markeaton that the proceeds from the kidnapping of justice Sir Richard Willoughby (Wylughby) were divided up

[58] Bellamy, Supra. p. 79

These gangs were often formed as needed though some stayed together as a loosely defined unit for many years. Expert help was drafted in as needed. Hired thugs were periodically needed and readily available. But the crimes of criminous clerks was never restricted to thuggery, far from it. In 1348 a chaplain who was a member of a Suffolk organized crime gang forged a royal seal. He then secured employment with Queen Philippa[59] and forged documents in an attempt to obtain large sums of money from the treasury. He persevered and eventually obtained cash from the royal bailiff. This is not the first, nor was it the last case of clerics committing forgery but it was always a particularly dangerous crime because according to the law any counterfeiting was treason, which was not (theoretically) clergyable.[60] In the same year Nicholas Boyet appeared before the justices for obtaining money by presenting forged seals and documents. He did not claim his clergy but it was suspected that he had been a cleric due to his ability to write and forge documents so accurately.[61] Less erudite but financially effective this was followed in 1349 by the abbots of Sherbourne and Middleton and the prior of Horton, who together stole timber and game from the countess of Lincoln.[62] Around the same time Robert Helewell, clerk, was arraigned as an accessory to murder. His co-accused was the Folevilles. Alan of Baston, canon of Sempringham was indicted for harboring the Foleville gang.[63]

---

[59] Wife of Edward III. 1314–1369

[60] C.f. Bellamy, Supra. p. 65

[61] Bellamy, Supra. p. 65

[62] Gregory-Abbot, C., 'Sacred Outlaws: Outlawry and the Medieval Church' in Appleby, J.C. and Dalton, P., (eds) *Outlaws in Medieval and Early Modern England: Crime, Government and Society, c. 1066-c.1600*, Farnham, Surrey, Ashgate, 2009. p. 85

[63] Gregory-Abbot, Supra. p. 84 and Stones, E.L.G. The Folevilles of Ashby-Foleville, Leicestershire, and Their Associates in Crime, 1326–1347, *Transactions of the Royal Society*, 5th Series, Vol. 7. (1957) pp. 117–136

Illicit liaisons between criminal gangs and the clergy took many forms. In a number of instances middle and high ranking clerics paid gangs to apply coercion upon tenant farmers or the holders of benefices who refused to leave or hand over a wealthy parish. (This was not dissimilar to the use that the laity employed when feudal lords paid retainers and financial incentives to criminals to exert authority over their underlings). Bishops frequently held ecclesiastical and secular estates and employed many tenants and farmers. A band of thugs available at short notice to enforce prelatory control was an attractive and sometimes necessary requirement of fourteenth-century life (especially as the pattern of English life moved away from feudalism to the issuing of contracts and grants). This transition, sometimes referred to as 'bastard feudalism'[64] was as pertinent to prelates as it was to secular nobility; a concomitant of this was that the use of hired criminal help was a major social problem.

Of the groups that offered specialized contractual criminal services two are significant; the Coterels and the Folevilles (Folvilles). Not only because of the scope and longevity of their activities but because both gangs had established and long standing relationships with the Church; they were directly employed by churchmen to extort, murder, and kidnap and the gangs had members of the Church as active participants in their illicit enterprises. The political unrest that pervaded the monarchy of Edward II spilled over into the early years of Edward III's reign and provided the ideal environment for

[64] Spencer, A., *Nobility and Kingship in Medieval England: The Earls and Edward I, 1272–1307*, Cambridge, Cambridge University Press, 2013, Part II "The Earls in Local Society'

gangs to plunder, pillage and prosper.[65] The long established sanctuary of churches and the ease with which clerics could be tempted to provide shelter in conjunction with the periodic need that bishops and priors had for a mobile army of enforcers promulgated an invidious and criminally profane connectivity that worked in the interests of both groups; the Church had wealth, power, needs and privileges. The gangs had criminal savvy, brutality and few morals. The 'fur-collared clericus'[66] exercised all the power and secured the wealth; the lower orders often suffered because of this and since it was to the local churches that many felons would flee, priests were inevitably exposed to the life and temptations of opportunist criminals. In the instances that follow this exposure transitioned to full-time participation as 'illicit conventicles'[67] of quasi-professional criminal clerks.

The Coterels were a group of criminals who operated across much of the English Midlands and East Anglia. They first

---

[65] Stones, E.L.G. The Folevilles of Ashby-Foleville, Leicestershire, and Their Associates in Crime, 1326–1347, *Transactions of the Royal Society,* 5th Series, Vol. 7. (1957) pp. 117–136. p. 118 "It has been said that 'probably at no period in the fourteenth century were greater efforts made by the executive to improve the state of the peace than during the years 1327–1340"

[66] Hanwalt, Supra. introduces the term 'fur-collared' crime to articulate the nexus between the criminal acts of the nobility in the fourteenth century and the term employed by Sutherland ' white collar crime' to describe those in a position of authority and influence who commit crime. Hanwalt explains that in the fourteenth century only those of certain high social status were permitted by law to wear a fur collar. Bishops were of that high status and were permitted to wear ermine or maarten as a trim to the capitium hence 'fur-collared clericus'. E.g. 37. Edw. III. ch. 8–12. *Statutes of the Realm.* For greater discussion see: A History of British Dress, *The Saturday Review of Politics, Literature, Science and Art,* Vol. 76. No. 1,989 (9, Dec., 1893). pp. 654–655 and Baldwin, F.E., *Sumptuary Legislation and Personal Regulation in England,* Baltimore, Johns Hopkins University Press, 1923 (OCR Reprints 2010)

[67] Stones, Supra. p. 131

came to notice in 1327[68] when brothers James, John and Nicholas Coterel,[69] Roger le Sauvage and Robert Bernard, clerk of chancery, Oxford university teacher, registrar of Lichfield cathedral and parson to Edith Weston of Rutland, evicted vicar Walter Can from his parish church at Bakewell, Derbyshire. Robert Bernard sought the Church benefice for himself and got his friends to help him evict the incumbent. A number of local parishioners objected to Bernard's behavior and in a forceful display of anticlericalism they stripped him of his vestments and ejected him from the Church; alas, not before he had embezzled from the parishioners. Eventually he was removed from Bakewell Church; by papal mandate.[70] When Bernard appeared before the secular courts in answer to his attack upon vicar Walter Can, he claimed benefit of clergy. Throughout and beyond this episode Robert Bernard remained in post at Lichfield cathedral as chantry priest. As with many contemporary organized crime groups the Coterels were a loose collection of criminals who came together, with specialist help, as needed. The leaders, James, John and Nicholas, were of modest birth but not peasants. What is interesting about this group,[71] and the Folevilles, is that both had long-term, high ranking, gang members who were serving

---

[68] Bellamy., J.G., The Coterel Gang: An Anatomy of a Band of Fourteenth-Century Criminals, *English Historical Review*, Vol. 79. (Oct., 1964) pp. 698–717. p. 699. Some members had come to the attention of the authorities earlier in the year when they were suspected of rustling animals and poaching from an estate in Lancashire. Nicholas Coterel had received a pardon in 1322 for a number felonies. Ibid. p. 700

[69] Bellamy, Supra. Does not attribute James to this venture. Gregory-Abbot, Supra. p. 702 states that James, John and Nicholas were involved in the attack of August 2, 1328 at Bakewell

[70] Bellamy, *Coterel Gang*, Supra. p. 699. N. 1. The bishop of Lichfield was ordered by papal mandate to remove Bernard on 1 June 1328

[71] Bellamy, Supra. p.74 refers to them as a 'federation of criminal units' rather than a group of regular members within a' monolithic structure' and Bellamy, *Coterel Gang*, Supra. p. 709

priests and that those priests remained in ecclesiastic post throughout their years of criminality; with the full knowledge of their bishops.

Extortion, poaching and kidnapping by the Coterels continued throughout the remainder of the decade and into the first few years of the 1330s. In 1331 the Coterels were appealed for extortion from Robert Frauceys of Hardstoft, Nottinghamshire. The following year, 1332, the gang extorted money from the mayor of Nottingham. In 1331 a number of gang members appeared before the justices. James Coterel, appealed for two murders in Derby (one in 1329 and the second in 1330)[72] was tipped off about the arrival of the court. His informant was Geoffrey de Chintriaco,[73] the prior of Lenton.[74] On March 20, 1331 at the conclusion of the Trailbaston the Coterels were declared outlaws.[75] Ironically within three years James Coterel had re-gained the kings favor and was himself in lawful pursuit of a criminous clergyman from Leicestershire.[76]

On 14th January 1332 a puisne judge of the King's Bench, Sir Richard de Wylughby, (Willoughby)[77] was kidnapped as he travelled between hearings of the commission of oyer and terminer in the Midlands. The attackers comprised of members

---

[72] Stones, Supra. p. 123. Sir William Knyveton and John Matkynson at Bradley, Derbyshire. Bellamy, *Coterel Gang*, Supra. p. 701

[73] Geoffrey de Chintriaco, 1327–1331. (Resigned)

[74] Bellamy, Supra. p. 84

[75] Gregory-Abbot, Supra. p. 76. Bellamy, *Coterel Gang*, Supra. p. 702 citing *Nottinghamshire Assize Roll* 166. M. 21

[76] Bellamy, Supra. p.84

[77] Willoughby was no model citizen himself and was later in life accused of 'selling the laws like cattle'. Mortimer, I., *The Time Traveler's Guide to Medieval England*, London, Touchstone, 2008. pp 241–242 and Ormrod, *Boundaries of the Law*, Supra. p.12

of the Coterel gang and the Folevilles.[78] The kidnapping by this illicit enterprise became one of the better known events of that year's criminal calendar. It is very likely the incident was viewed with such contemptible magnitude that the direct response was the subsequent commission of trailbaston headed by the chief justice of England, Geoffrey le Scrope. The systemic involvement of the Lichfield canons was undeniable; the prior of Lenton was appealed but had died before his court date, none of the Coterels or the Lichfield canons were convicted. Subsequently Nicholas Coterel was appointed Queen Philippa's bailiff of the High Peak (her previous bailiff, Ralph de Spayne was also a Coterel gang member). James Coterel was given the wardship of Elizabeth Maverel by Queen Philippa (he was still a declared outlaw at the time). Robert Bernard remained in both his clerical and university posts and Gilbert de la Breune went on to become dean of St. Paul's, London.

Over the course of the career of this criminal organization six canons, one dean of chapter, and one cathedral registrar, were indicted for felonies: Richard de Havering, clerk of chancery, constable of Bordeaux, canon of Lincoln, York and bishop elect of Dublin,[79] Richard de Kynardseye, canon of Lichfield and holder of the prebend of Flixton, William de Leycaster, parson of Chinnor, canon of Lichfield 1325 and guardian of the bishop of Warwick and; canons John Clarel, who received

---

[78] An additional motive for the crime beyond ransom could have been that Wylughby had been appointed to hear the indictments into the murder of Roger Bellers, Infra. Bellamy, Supra. p. 7 and. Harding, Supra. p. 91

[79] He was also archdeacon of Chester which he lost in 1322 but it was reinstated to him in 1330. He also held the prebendary of Chichester and was precentor of St. Ethelberts, Hereford. Bellamy, *Coterel Gang*, Supra. p. 703. N. 4

a pardon for murder, Nicholas Teynturel and Philip Turvil, Gilbert de la Breuse, dean of chapter and the most active member of the clerical felons; Robert Bernard.[80] The Coterels relied upon the clergy to provide safe haven, to receive and distribute stolen goods, to assist in identifying criminal targets, to inform them of pending investigations, and to aid, abet, counsel and procure their criminal enterprises and; to supply a willing and able criminal workforce.[81]

On January 19, 1326 Roger Bellers, baron of the exchequer, was murdered as he travelled between Melton Mowbray and Leicester.[82] Ralph la Zouche of Lubbersthorpe drove a knife into Beller's collar and pierced the heart. The baron died at the scene. Also present were La Zouche's accomplices; Roger and Ivo la Zouche, brothers Eustace, Robert, Richard and Walter de Folville, and Robert Helewell and Robert Lovet, both priests. By 1331 the Folville brothers were employed by Alan of Baston, canon of Sempringham, and a second cleric, the cellarer of the Cistercian house of Haverholm, to destroy a rival's mill. Alan Baston already knew the Folville brothers because he had previously harbored them at the Sempringham priory and at Lestonholm grange.[83] The Folvilles obliged the canon for £20 and destroyed his neighbor's water mill.[84] In January 1332 the Folvilles joined forces with the Coterels to plan

---

[80] Robert Bernard and another cleric were once found guilty of receiving stolen goods before Bakewell justices. Both pled their clergy and subsequently purged themselves. Bellamy, *Coterel Gang*, Supra. p. 710

[81] Bellamy, *Coterel Gang*, Supra. p. 716 states "A group of men on whom Coterel continuously relied foe assistance were the nine Derbyshire chaplains and vicars named as his receivers'

[82] For possible motive beyond robbery see: Bellamy, *Coterel Gang*, Supra. p. 708

[83] Bellamy, *Coterel Gang*, p. 712. N. 4 and citing Stones E.L.G., *Assize Roll* 1411b. m. 1

[84] K.B. 27/285 m. 15d. Stones, Supra. pp. 121–122

and execute the kidnapping of justice Richard de Wylughby (Willoughby). On January 14, 1332, the two gangs, along with other accomplices, kidnapped the judge and held him for ransom as he travelled between courts. Willoughby paid 1,300 marks as ransom and had £100 of his personal property stolen whilst in the gang's custody. Robert Lovett, parson of Ashwell and a known associate of Richard Folville,[85] also assisted in this kidnapping. Only one principal ever appeared in court connected with the Willoughby kidnapping, Robert Lovet, parson of Ashwell. He successfully claimed his clergy. The other culprits failed to appear and in August 1326 the Folvilles were declared outlaws.[86] Later the same year the Folville (Foleville) brothers were appealed at Lincoln for robberies across the county. Just two weeks later in January 1327 they received pardons.[87] Over the course of the next two years Eustace Folville was suspected of committing three murders, one rape and three robberies. However, by 1329 the three brothers had all received pardons, a second time.

Over the course of his lifetime Eustace Folville committed five murders, brothers Robert, Richard and Walter were accessories to murder, principals in kidnapping and extortion and committed dozens of felonies involving theft and robbery. Throughout the entire duration of this criminal fraternity Richard de Folville was an ordained priest. He had been presented to the benefice of Teigh, Rutland in 1321 by his brother John[88] and he remained the benefice holder and parson

---

[85] Lovett had been presented to the bishop of Lincoln for the benefice by Sir Robert Touchet, another known associate of the Folvilles. Stones, Supra. p. 123

[86] Stones, Supra. p. 120 *Coram Rege Rolls* (KB 27) 272. M. 108d

[87] Stones, Supra. p. 120. N. 6. *Calendar of Patent Rolls* 1327–1330. p. 30

[88] Stones, Supra. p. 118. N. 5 *Lincoln Episcopal Registers*. No. 4. F. 162

throughout his entire life. It was inside this parish church he died a bloody death in 1341.

After a spectacular criminal career that involved murder, rape, kidnapping, robbery extortion and intimidation; being declared an outlaw and being pardoned; in February 1340 Richard de Folville, priest of Teigh, Rutland was again appealed. He apparently had little intention of putting himself on the country or claiming his clergy. Richard fled to the sanctuary of his own parish church; whether he intended on swearing before the coroner on arrival is not known. As Richard fled he was pursued by Sir Robert de Colville and a posse. Richard killed one and injured two others in what became a chase across the countryside. The criminal parson made it to his sanctuary and from inside continued a salvo of attacks upon the crown agents. Sir Robert and his men succeeded in storming the Church, removed Richard and beheaded him.[89]

Church and secular courts have much in common; special language, special costumes, separation of the laity from the professionals, a sense of solemnity, the administration of oaths[90] and much ritual.[91] The ritual of law; sacred and temporal. So far the blurred interface between secular and spiritual

---

[89] Following Pope Clement VI authorized the bishop of Lincoln to absolve Sir Robert Colville for his sacrilegious killing of a priest inside a church. Stones, Supra. p. 129. N.7. *Calendar of Papal Registers.* Letters iii. 142 and Arnold, J.H., *What is Medieval History,* Cambridge, Polity Press, 2008. p.21

[90] E.g. The coroners (abjuration), Sheriffs after the writ of exigent, the oath of excommunication, the oaths of office Ecclesiastic and secular judiciary, oaths of loyalty and fealty, the royal coronation oath

[91] Musson, A., (ed) Boundaries of the Law: Geography, Gender and Jurisdiction in Medieval and early Modern Europe, Aldershot, Ashgate, 2005. pp. 13–15, 20, 24, 217, 221–222

practices[92] has been explored through the examples of the analogous practices of benefit of clergy, sanctuary, abjuration and outlawry;[93] as it applied to all castes of society including the lower and higher orders of the clergy. Whatever the canon law stated it is clear that priests did take sanctuary,[94] did swear the secular oath of guilt and abjuration, and they did exile the realm. It is also the case that clerics were judicially outlawed or self-imposed outlawry.

The clergy of medieval England confidently demonstrated they could serve the law, they could defeat the law and they could abuse the law. Priests could embrace the law transparently and symbolize the value of leading a model life; spiritual and secular, or they could debase and vitiate the principles of legality and behave like the common villains some of them were. Given the examples shown in this book; the willingness of the clergy to use every possible mitigatory option available to avoid meaningful punishment for crime, it is perhaps inevitable that benefit of clergy and its associated privileges would eventually be removed. The clergy could not be trusted to behave in a manner fitting their exalted social status.

---

[92] The raising of the Hue and Cry was achieved by the ringing of the parish church bells. The religious calendar too closely mirrored the festival life temporal; Whitsun, Trinity, Corpus Christi and court calendars also, such as: when the courts Leet and Hundreds were held. See; Musson, *Medieval Law*, Supra. p. 244 and Arnold, Supra. p. 107

[93] Thornley, I.D., The Destruction of Sanctuary, Tudor Studies , Presented by the Board of Studies in History in the University of London to Albert Frederick Pollard, being the work of twelve of his colleagues and pupils. 1924. p. 305. Kesselring, K., Mercy and Authority in the Tudor State, Cambridge, Cambridge University Press, 2003. p. 356. For those who self-imposed outlawry for exclusively crimes spiritual, Logan, F.D., Runaway Religious in Medieval England c. 1250–1540, Cambridge, Cambridge University Press, 1996

[94] Shoemaker, K., *Sanctuary and Crime in the Middle Ages, 1400–1500,* New York, Fordham University Press, 2011. p.125 re clerics rarely claiming sanctuary and Thornley, I., Sanctuary in Medieval London, *Journal of the British Archaeological Association,* Vol. 38. (1932) pp. 293–315. p.305

In the increasingly secular world of fourteenth century criminal law the distinguishability between laws spiritual and secular would inevitably erode. The reliance that each system had upon each other was diminishing;[95] the ability of the Church to maintain absolute authority over all matters pertaining to its clerics could not be sustained in the climate of abuse that had been so ably demonstrated by clerics of the period. Punishment for murder, arson and robbery was no longer satisfied by penance, prayers and ecclesiastic ridicule when those who were unfortunate enough not to be able to claim privilege were being mutilated and hanged. The emblems of justice borrowed from the Church; the bar, penance, public spectacle, ritual, wearing of a uniform to denote criminal status, and juridical superiority, had been laicized. For Englishmen the distinguishing features of the laws spiritual and temporal were eroding. When social revolt came no distinction was made between prisoners sacred and profane. Angry peasants took both nobility and bishops as hostages and executed both.[96]

The damage that the actions of criminals like the Coterels and Folevilles caused the Church added much weight to moves towards the secularization of clerical privilege. But not all clergymen were stereotypically evil. Most were just

---

[95] It had been the case since the time of William I that the Church could call upon the secular law to assist in punishing those who failed to adhere to spiritual punishments and failure to subsequently adhere to the secular laws requirement that the miscreant answer to the courts secular within forty days they would be proclaimed an outlaw albeit the crime was originally spiritual. Logan, Excommunication, Supra. pp. 20–21

[96] E.g. the beheading of Walter Stapleton, bishop of Exeter, with a number of Knights, 15 October 1326 http://www.britannia.com/bios/wstapledon.html and Owen, D.M., *The Medieval Canon Law: Teaching, Literature and Transmission,* Cambridge, Cambridge University Press, 1990. p. 31

men; men of this world not another.[97] In the end though it would not be self-inflicted injury and the inability of the clergy to behave fittingly but a combination of the slow, subtle forces of social change that would secularize an 'evil' church anachronism.[98]

---

[97] Swanson, R.N., *Religion and Devotion in Europe, c.1215-c.1515*, Cambridge, Cambridge University Press, 1995

[98] 'That blasphemous farce'. (Benefit of Clergy) Cross, A.L., The English Criminal Law and Benefit of Clergy during the Eighteenth and early Nineteenth Century, *The American Historical Review*. Vol. 22 No. 3 (Apr., 1917) pp. 544–565. p. 553

# 8

# From Tonsure to Reading, From Demands to Requests

By the end of Edward I's (1272–1307) reign England was a broken nation. The country's barons had been alienated by the king as he strengthened the role of royal government. The nation was at war with Wales, Scotland and France[1] and the king had depleted the country of money to support his military campaigns. The rift between church and state had widened as Edward sought to increase taxation against the clergy and Boniface VIII responded with *Clericis laicos* in 1296.[2] Eventually this was to be a victory for the ageing monarch as England's recalcitrant clergy, including those holding the highest office, succumbed to the pressure of change.[3] Edward II (1307–1327) young, and ultimately ineffective, inherited a nation that was deeply unsettled. Young Edward's difficult personal life further weakened the monarchy and gave the English Church a last chance at retaining the unique protections of benefit of clergy. It failed and by the end of Edward III's reign the privilege had become laicized; tonsure and

---

1 King, E., *Medieval England from Hastings to Bosworth*, Stroud, The History Press, 2009

2 Denton, J.H., *Robert Winchelsey and the Crown 1294–1313: A Study in the Defence of Ecclesiastical Liberty*, Cambridge, Cambridge University Press, 1980

3 For example, Archbishop Robert Winchelsey (1245–1313) was threatened with outlawry or suspension from office

clerical garb had finally given way to a reading test, available in principle to all.

In this chapter I will discuss the final transition of benefit of clergy from the protected status of *privilegium fori* as a uniquely ecclesiastic benefit to one which was secularized and available to all Englishmen. In doing so I will argue that this period marks the completion of a two-hundred-year battle for supremacy over the ownership of the clerical privilege which commenced with the Becket debacle and concluded with the substitution of habit and tonsure for the Reading Test. Ultimately I do not wholly subscribe to the view held by many authors that clergy was a singular evil or a mere legal farce. I suggest that the use (and abuse) of clericus was a natural and organic growth of the developing justice system that was framed by the social and political environment of the thirteenth and fourteenth centuries. Benefit of clergy was not a singular legal oddity but one of a suite of four opportunities to avoid the gallows in Medieval England.

During the fourteenth century the English Church experienced the dilution of much of its power as the dominance it held over the life and death of everyday citizens slowly shifted and England transitioned towards a more prosperous, secular society and the beginnings of what would become a middle class. The involvement, and therefore influence, of the clergy in secular administration decreased throughout the century and the lower orders became less involved in 'the enveloping quicksand of parliament',[4] the courts and secular decision making.[5] Papal intervention in the legal administration of

---

[4] Heath, P. *Church and Realm 1272–1461*, London, Fontana, 1988.p. 88

[5] From 1341 onwards bishops proctors were no longer required to attend parliament. Heath, Supra. p. 89

England was to subside too and the control that Rome (and Avignon) held over the appointments of benefices diminished as new merchant classes could afford to create and finance chapels and benefices locally. The (growing) English parliament[6] was forceful in rejecting the continuation of granting lucrative benefices to aliens[7] such that by 1351 Edward III (1327–1377) gave his approval to the *Statute of Provisors* which authorized him to intervene in any disputed appointment to a benefice. The Church was also accommodating internal change as importance of regular clergy decreased and societal expectations of the clergy came under greater scrutiny across Christendom.

It had always been the case that monks engaged in crime.[8] What now changed was evidence of a move away from living the monastic life as the regular clergy left the enclosed world and married and lived as laymen or joined the lay (secular) clergy. Whether deliberate religious apostates or disaffected monastics that simply wandered away never to return the desire to live closer to the laity and embrace secular society was a strong motivation during the fourteenth century; one which added to the ease with which benefit of clergy transitioned into a temporal plea.

The high point of those living the religious life had peaked in the thirteenth century and the massive growth in monastic

---

[6] The 14th century was particularly important as many parliamentary institutions were established in this century. C.f. Lyon, B., *A Constitutional and Legal History of Medieval England* (2nd edition) New York, Norton & Co., 1980. Esp. Chapter XXXI 'The Sources and History of the Fourteenth Century'

[7] For the distinction between benefices and *sinecures* Heath, P. *Church and Realm 1272–1461*, London, Fontana, 1988. p. 24

[8] Per the case of Dr. Peter Dene. Infra

orders and religious houses started a path towards decline with a concomitant increase in lay clerics over regular. The rise in the number of recorded instances of abandonment of the monastic life, apostasy, is evidence of this. The largest increase occurred between 1331 and 1371 and whereas part of this growth may be explained by the Black Death it does not account for the particularly strong rise in recorded instances in the period between 1331 and 1350.[9] In particular that of the total number of apostates between 1271 and 1530 a full 23% (representing more than double for any other decade over the four centuries of data) occurred between 1341 and 1370.[10] What motivated a devoted monk to leave the protections (and mundanity) of the enclosed life will perhaps always be speculative and subjective. Crime was certainly a factor at times though; either committing crime to facilitate a departure from the monastic life or committing crime as a monk and then having to flee as a result of now being a felon.

In 1299 William de York stole a gold chalice and silver basins from St. Mary's Abbey, York.[11] In 1310 the *refectorius* of St. Mary's, Adam de Dalton stole the king's tenth (a tax paid by clergy to the crown) and fled to Wales,[12] this was closely followed by monk Peter de Wakefield who apostacized and took the huge amount of £60 from his abbey to set himself up for a life within the lay community. In 1304 Cistercian Henry Howden apostatized after stealing chalices and goods from Kirkstall Abbey.[13] In 1324 two Premonstratensian canons

---

[9] For thorough and engaging discussion see: Logan, F. D., *Runaway Religious in Medieval England c. 1240–1540,* Cambridge, Cambridge University Press, 2002. Esp. pp. 66–96

[10] Ibid. p. 71

[11] Logan, Supra. p. 76

[12] Ibid

[13] Logan, Supra. p. 76

stole books and goods valued at £20 from Halesowen Abbey.[14] Brother John de Coventry stole goods to the value of £10 from a lay visitor at Kenilworth priory. He was later pardoned for his felonious theft.[15] There are many further examples of departing monks stealing to provide for a new life in secular society throughout the fourteenth century.[16]

Theft was not the exclusive motivation for crime though as in some instances the monks were apparently so frustrated with their superiors they resorted to assaults upon them (and in some cases murder) and a quick departure from the monastic crime scene. Two such examples are: Cistercian Ralph de Byker who violently assaulted his abbot and then fled to London and Thomas de Tonge, also a Cistercian, who murdered his abbot.[17] Sexual misconduct was also a factor in leaving the monastic life. Although rarely criminal in nature the number of recorded instances of monks having sexual relationships with local villagers and townsfolk suggest that sins of the flesh were commonplace and a frequent precursor to abandonment of vows. Abduction of nuns (by monks, priests and the laity) was a problem in the thirteenth century. A particularly graphic example occurred in 1284 which resulted in the creation of *The Statute of Westminster II,* 1285.[18] The matter involved the abduction of two nuns of the Benedictine abbey at Wilton, Wiltshire by a local knight, Sir Osbert Giffard.

---

[14] Logan, Supra. p. 76

[15] *Calendar of Patent Rolls,* 1388–1392. p. 34 cited in Logan, Supra. p. 76. n. 19

[16] Ibid

[17] Ibid. p. 80

[18] 13 Edw I, c. 34 "He that carrieth a nun from her house, although she consent, [sic] shall be punished by three year's imprisonment and shall make convenient satisfaction to the house from whence she was taken, and nevertheless shall make fine at the king's will." Cited in Logan, Supra. p. 86

The outcome; Giffard was indicted by the secular courts and found guilty, demonstrates an interesting blend of secular and ecclesiastic penalties. The crown seized Giffard's lands and removed his title. The bishop's synod that heard the former knight's plea for absolution from his excommunication (the synod included his own cousin Godfrey Giffard, bishop of Worcester) was that Osbert Giffard 'appear barefoot and bareheaded, dressed in penitential dress, among the sinners in Salisbury Cathedral and, with them, to be ejected, not to be readmitted until Holy Thursday. On three holydays he was to be flogged around Salisbury Cathedral and on three Tuesdays through the marketplace at Salisbury'.[19] Giffard was furthermore to be flogged in Wilton (the scene of the crime), Amesbury and he was required to spend three years in the Holy Land. Instances of the abduction of nuns by monks and priests (as well as the laity) appear throughout the remainder of the thirteenth and the first three quarters of the fourteenth century.[20]

In a number of cases criminous monks returned to their monasteries; most frequently by force rather than of their own volition. The capturing of apostates marks another example of blurring between the jurisdictions of canon and secular law. When a monk was declared apostate by the Church he then became subject to arrest by the temporal authorities. This secular power of arrest then required that the apostate be returned to the holy order for punishment and reintroduction (education) to the monastic life. From 1298 onwards all apostates were *de facto* excommunicated,

---

[19] Logan, Supra. pp. 87–88

[20] Logan, Supra. pp. 89–90

they were ecclesiastic outlaws. Between 1250 and 1435 the English Church notified the Chancery of more than sixteen thousand excommunicates. Archbishops Pecham and Winchelsey even sought the crowns assistance in recovering excommunicate clergy who were delinquent in their payment of clerical taxes.[21]

The way in which the temporal law was involved in the arrest of religious apostates was unique to England (and further supports the view that the distance between the English interpretation of canon law and the Common Law was consistently narrowing). One of the first royal writs directing the sheriffs of a county to arrest an apostate occurred in 1240 when sheriffs of Yorkshire, Cumberland, Westmorland, Northumberland and Lancaster were informed of their authority to arrest and deliver Brother Siward back to his Dominican friars. From this point forward there are numerous recorded instances of the issuance of a royal writ to secure the arrest and return of religious apostates eventually resulting in the formalization of the procedure under writs *de apostate capiendo*.

One example of the context of writs temporal is of interest due to the criminal nature of the activities of all of the parties concerned. In 1317 the Cluniac priory of Lewes requested a writ for the arrest of two apostate monks from the Lewes dependency Prittlewell in Essex. This was followed by further writ applications for other members of the Prittlewell community who allegedly were frequently engaged in outings for sex with women in London. Of this group some were apostate but a number of others continued to live as monks in the

[21] Heath, Supra. p. 30

Prittlewell dependency. The escalation of misconduct resulted in the prior of Lewes sending a team of monks from Lewes to Prittlewell where during mass they dragged a monk from the altar, bound him at his hands and feet and attached him to a cart (this would appear to be a sacrilegious kidnapping) to deliver him to Lewes priory. Monk William de Avernaz died upon arrival in Lewes, most probably as a result of the injuries sustained on route.[22]

The ascendancy of the crown over the Church in the late Middle Ages was also apparent in a number of other ways: the increase in ecclesiastical patronage by secular society, the noticeable reduction in appointment of higher clergy, especially the monastic orders, to influential secular posts. Growing disaffection with the Church was even present in the move towards less grandiose and luxurious church architecture. In the two universities of England cleric scholars began to explore the natural sciences and letters as institutions of higher education started to gradually incorporate sciences and secular law into the curriculum.[23] As such the basis for universities to become colleges of learning had commenced. The trades and industry of England also flourished as the old manorial system started to move away from (unfree) labor services and rent being paid in kind to short-term leases and (free) wage labor. Class strife was virulent and the lower orders of the clergy were often caught between the competing demands of Church hierarchy and local life. Some authors have speculated that these factors

[22] Logan, Supra. pp. 119–120

[23] This was a gradual process though for in 1379 seventy per cent of scholars at Oxford read law; canon and then also civil. Heath, Supra. Chap 5. 'Learning and Literacy'. pp. 157–187

may have stimulated clergy to behave more criminally than they might have.[24]

Prosperity and wealth also had a negative effect on life as an extravagant and excessive lifestyle became available to more and more of the population. The crown responded by enacting limiting legislation aimed at curbing excesses in the consumption of food, drink and apparel. In October 1336 Edward III promulgated *Statutum de Cibariis*[25] in an attempt to halt idle extravagance, further sumptuary laws were passed later.[26] During the first twenty five years of Edward III's (1327–1377) reign the number or royal benefices created rose from 1,400 to 3,000[27] as he promoted the concept of a national Church, *Ecclesia Anglicana*.[28] Securement of confraternities increased substantially also. The largest growth occurred immediately after the Black Death but the

---

[24] Pike, L.O., *A History of Crime in England, Vol. 1.*, London, Elder & Co, 1873. pp. 296–297 gives the example of a parishioner who in 1348 alleged that her husband had died. With accomplices a body was found and buried. It was not her husband. The ruse was believed to have been perpetrated to secure the husband from a court appearance. The point Pike makes is that the contempt held for the clergy is apparent; either they local priest was complicit or distain for the clergy was so height at the time that even burial was not respected or conducted according to established Church rules. Example cited Gregory-Abbott, C., Sacred Outlaws: Outlawry and the Medieval Church in Appleby, J.C. and Dalton, P., (eds) *Outlaws in Medieval and Early Modern England: Crime, Government and Society, c. 1066-c.1600*, Farnham, Surrey, Ashgate, 2009. pp. 75–89. p. 84

[25] 10. Edw III s.3. (1336) Statute Concerning Foods to be Used

[26] Hammond, W.A., Sumptuary Laws and Their Social Influence, *Popular Science Monthly*, Vol. 37. (May-Oct) 1890. pp. 33–40. Riddel, W.R., The Food and Drink of an Englishman-By Statute, *Journal of Criminal Law and Criminology*, Vol.18. No.4 (Feb) 1928. pp. 527–532

[27] Saul, N., (ed) *The Oxford Illustrated History of Medieval England*, Oxford, Oxford University Press, 1997. p. 14

[28] By 1366 William Wykeham, bishop of Winchester and Edward III's chancellor was the most beneficed pluralist in Christendom. Davis, V., *William Wykeham: A Life*, London, Hambledon Continuum, 2007 and see Heath, Supra. p. 28 re: Ralph Hengham multiple pluralist, royal judge and member of the king's council

upward trend was a feature of the entire fourteenth century.[29] The bestowment of confraternity rose most among the lesser nobility, lower classes and the rising merchant classes (particularly London merchants).[30] The range of bequests and lifetime benefaction also diversified, for example London goldsmith Stephen de Munden bequeathed an annual rent to his Carmelite brother Peter.[31] Given the vows of poverty it is unclear as to how the brother could personally profit from this endowment but it was repeated some years later by Brother Peter's sister, Alice.[32] Confraternities gained in popularity due to a number of factors: being attached to a religious entity had kudos and social standing, it provided insurance (prayers and masses were said to ensure a place in heaven) and it allowed the laity some voice in the future of religious houses. The old order of business, including some elements of religious isolation, gave way to social inclusion during the thirteenth (with the meteoric rise of the friars) and fourteenth centuries as the monastic world actively sought contact with the temporal.[33] These factors were all important to the laity as the secularization of the English Church continued and increasingly, amongst the regular and lay clerics, appointments at the lower and higher orders were being made to Englishmen. Parishioners wanted and achieved a say in ecclesiastic appointments.

---

[29] Clark, J.G., 'Monastic Confraternity in Medieval England: The Evidence from the St. Albans Abbey *Liber Benefactorum*' in Jamroziak, E., and Burton, J., *Religious and Laity in Western Europe 1000–1400: Interaction, Negotiation, and Power, Vol. 2,* Turnhout, Brepols, 2006. pp. 315–332

[30] Ibid p. 325

[31] Clark, Supra. p. 352

[32] Ibid. p. 353

[33] Some confraternity societies moved towards holding meetings in secular churches. Ibid. p. 352

Royal patronage and a national church was harnessed further in 1353 when Edward promulgated legislation that prohibited appeal outside of the realm in cases decided before the king's courts. Failure to comply resulted in outlawry.[34] Further localization of the Church was brought about by the increase in the number of named saints; what this did was to make the domestic Church more appealing to the citizens of England whilst at the same time distancing the clergy from Rome. The increase in English saints was also attractive to the crown as pilgrimages within the realm produced significant levels of income for the Church which in turn created a tax revenue stream for the crown.

Alongside these ecclesiastical changes another major force was about to transform society; literature. An English language had steadily gained ground in becoming the accepted language of the nobility and gentry and use of the vernacular gained force in written verse, most notably the work of William Langland's *Vision of Piers the Ploughman,*[35] perhaps the pinnacle of a genre of protest writing that included: the 1305 contribution, *Outlaw's Song of Trailbaston*[36] followed later by *Poem on the Evil Times of Edward II* and then *Song of the Husbandman*, written about 1340, and of the same year *Song Against the King's Taxe'.*[37] Collectively these works satirized the power of the

---

[34] *Statute of Praemunire 1353*

[35] An allegoric poem in twenty-two chapters that lambasts the abusive gentry and the general excesses of the period. It is believed to have been written 1360–1387. Pearsall, D. (ed) *Piers Plowman The C-Text, Corrected Edition,* Exeter, Exeter University Press, 2010

[36] A 'baston' was a heavy club used to inflict serious assaults. The 'trailbaston' court developed into hearing a broad range of felonies

[37] For a discussion of the importance of protest poems and songs. Maddicott, J.R. 'Poems of Social Protest in Early Fourteenth Century England' in *England in the Fourteenth Century: Proceedings of the 1985 Harlaxton Symposium,* Woodbridge, Suffolk, Boydell Press, 1986. pp. 130–144

manors and estates (spiritual and secular) over the lives of the common man; corruption was rife at every level from the pope down to the local parson, the abbot to the monk and the king down through the judiciary to local sheriffs and wardens. These works portray a world where all strata of society are cheats and liars. It is the poor who are the victims. It is Maddicott's view that the authors of this 'crude satire' are most likely to be clerks, perhaps friars, university masters or educated parish priests.[38] There is every reason to believe he is correct. If so this too adds to my suggestion that the lower orders of the clergy had developed a new level of empathy for the poor of England and were complicit, in a variety of ways, in facilitating the secularization of clerical privileges within the broader context of social justice.[39] Also noteworthy of this time was the dissent and fervent anti-clericism articulated by the English theologian Wyclif and the Lollard movement.[40]

Throughout the fourteenth century levels of literacy across the English nation increased considerably and transition to the use of a reading test to establish clerical status had the effect of making a *clericus* claim available to most of the male population. On the international front the general decline in the papal monarchy further supported the social

---

[38] Maddicott, Supra. p. 144

[39] For an alternative view to Langland see: Bennett, N., 'Pastors and Masters: The Beneficed Clergy of North-East Lincolnshire, 1290–1340' in Hoskin, P., Brooke, C., Dobson, B., (eds) *The Foundations of Medieval English Ecclesiastical History: Studies Presented to David Smith*, Woodbridge, Boydell Press, 2005. pp. 40–62

[40] Of John Wyclif (1331–1384) and his followers: Scase, W., 'Lollardy' in Bagchi, D., and Steinmetz, D. C., (eds) *The Cambridge Companion to Reformation Theology*, Cambridge, Cambridge University Press, 2004. pp. 22–27, Engen, J.V., 'Anticlericalism Among the Lollards' in Dykema, P.A., and Oberman, H.A., (eds) *Anticlericalism in Late Medieval and Early Modern Europe*, Leiden, Brill, 1994

and political changes occurring in England that resulted in a better educated, informed and wealthier lay citizenry who were willing (and wanting) to become involved in greater secularization of public and private life. An inevitable concomitant of this domination of the Church by an English state was the erosion of the unique status of benefit of clergy. And whereas *privilegium fori* would limp along as a legal fiction for a further four hundred years the move towards applying a reading test, rather than papers of clerical appointment, haircut and attire, as proof of eligibility to secure escape from the gallows was such a fundamental transition the reign of Edward III effectively marks the end of *clericus* as a benefit available exclusively to England's clergymen.

The English people may well have hoped that the expansion of land use and greater commercialization across society would yield a period of prosperity and national stability. However, this was not to happen soon. Unprecedented wet summers in 1315, 1316 and 1317, caused the failure of many crops and famine followed. Edward I was soon to die and his dithering and unstable son, Edward II, was about to cause a period of intense social unrest before his deposition and subsequent murder. Perhaps inevitably a crime-wave emerged. Perhaps predictably some members of the Church took no time in applying themselves to the crime opportunities.

During the fourteenth century the lower orders of the English clergy served a community in transition. Life was short, dangerous, noisy and dirty. The world was a chaotic place. Opportunities for joy and relaxation were few. The Church was a central part of life and it provided an array of social services for this life and the next; hospitals, charity, food, housing, education, prayers. It also promoted the establishment of saints and their power to heal the sick. The Church also promised (for a price) a better life in the next world. For the rich travel was commonplace but for the peasantry mobility was restricted, for many the travel of a lifetime was pilgrimage. Villages were close knit and not only did the inhabitants know each other well they also knew strangers. The local priest was not only there to guide you to heaven he was also counsel, surrogate parent and a village elder who held wisdom and customary knowledge. If anyone knew the lives and gossip of a village it was the priest. Of course what this amounted to was a huge sphere of influence. The burgeoning towns, a rising merchant class and the establishment of guilds would all be highly influential in altering this well-established relationship.

The ignorance of medieval man was changing too, he had access to books and a society that was capable of producing wealth for a greater number of citizens; consumerism and purchasing luxury goods would no longer be the exclusive purview of the rich. Also, the childlike belief that miracles were a product of the daily intervention of God in the life of the faithful would be challenged as the century progressed and society crept further towards greater secularism. Divine intervention in the legal system, trials by ordeal, were no longer the foundation for establishing guilt, it was man not God who decided on the innocence or guilt of a defendant. As a result of these influences the role of the cleric was in transition and his exulted social position was to be redefined; one thousand years of elite status that protected clergymen from secular criminal accountability was to shift. The abhorrence that many people felt towards a system that permitted men who could prove, no matter how loosely, they were clericus, would now change beyond all recognition over the course of the first seventy-five years of the fourteenth century. One might think that the clergy would strongly object, they certainly had in the past. However, by the middle of the fourteenth century the changes in society were so great that neither Rome nor the local English clergy could prevent the absorption of benefit of clergy into mainstream English legal practice. Clericus was about to become an integral part of the Common Law. Henceforth both clerics and laymen would have equal opportunity to utilize the protections of benefit of clergy. Any defendant capable of reading from the bible would be legally entitled to claim ecclesiastic immunity.

The high levels of contempt that many citizens held for the clergy had grown throughout the Middle Ages. Much of this dislike was based upon the special privileges that clerics possessed. It was also framed, in part, upon the fact that local priests were the source of national news. They were required to transmit information[41] about matters spiritual[42] and secular: wars, the king, laws, call to

---

[41] Or in some cases not transmit per the papal bull *clericis laicos* when thirty-four priests and clerks in Cornwall were imprisoned for reading out the order from Rome contrary to orders from Edward I. Denton, Supra. p. 117

[42] Timmins, T.C., (ed) *The Register of William Melton, Archbishop of York, 1317–1340, Vol. V.* The Canterbury and York Society, Woodbridge, Boydell Press, 2002. p. 139. A mandate from Archbishop Melton to warn parishioners breaching assizes of ale and bread and to those committing murder, they must desist

military service.[43] Edward I had successfully used the Church as a 'ministry of information and propaganda'.[44] Not infrequently this was not good news for locals. The pulpit was also an opportunity for the priest to extol the virtues of a Christian life, regardless of whether or not they embodied it themselves.[45] Disdain was also founded upon the grotesque examples of criminal abuse identified in the previous chapters and the excessive wealth that the Church had accumulated over the centuries. By many the cleric's life was not viewed as one of abstinence and devotion but more of an opportunity for the second son of a nobleman to ensure a good life comparable to one had they been ineligible to inherit. The lower orders were perceived little better as monks and priests blatantly abused the rules against marriage and concubinage, gluttony and crime, simony and profligacy. The fact that those fortunate enough to secure a place at one of England's universities could escape any form of accountability to local townsfolk only compounded the contempt that much of society held towards its clerics. Combined with this sense of loathing

[43] It was the case that bishops engaged in warfare. Archbishop Melton performed active military service against the Scots in 1319 and subsequently pled poverty to the monarch as he had lost much plate and even his own armor. Hill, R., An English Archbishop and the Scottish War of Independence, *The Innes Review*, Vol. 22, Issue 2 (1971) pp. 59–71 and Raine, J., (ed) *Historical Papers and Letters from the Northern Registers*, London, Longman, 1873. p. 295. I am grateful to Dr. Craig Nakashian for bringing this to my attention. For commentary about 'warrior bishops', fictional and factual: Keen, M., *Chivalry*, New Haven, Yale University Press, 1984 esp. Chapter 3. Chivalry, the Church and the Crusade

[44] Heath, Supra. p. 106

[45] Apparently a number of clerics concerned themselves greatly over the content of sermons so much so that they lost sleep over them on a Saturday night. This spurned an industry in per-written sermons known as 'Sleepwells' as they literally afforded the priest the opportunity for a good night's sleep before his ritual Sunday sermon. Davis, H.W.C., (Ed) *Medieval England*, London, Studio Editions, 1993. p. 423

was also respect. Respect and fear for the office clergymen performed in helping citizens to navigate the numerous chances to ensure damnation and eternity in hell. The dilemma for many Englishmen was whether or not they should accept a priesthood that would frequently succumb to the temptations of the secular world or should the priesthood always be an example of holiness, righteousness and virtue? And, there were simply far too many of them; in 1291 the city of Winchester had a cathedral, forty-seven parish churches and three chapels. By the sixteenth century this had been reduced to fifteen in total.

Although many layman felt it necessary *Articuli Cleri*[46] did little to limit the actions of errant clerics. It was more a level of concession by the crown to complaints started during the previous century. Complaints compounded by developments in science and ideas which offended the Church and presented a growing challenge to its absolute authority over society and an increase in the reach of the English crown over *Ecclesia Anglicana* (in particular over ecclesiastical income, advowsons and appointments). The final two clauses of *Articuli* deal with benefit of clergy. Clause fifteen deals with fugitive clerics being forced to abjure the realm by lay justices which *de facto* meant priests could be killed with impunity if they returned to England without a royal pardon. This clause clarified the law and exempted clergy from compelled secular abjuration. Clause sixteen was also a minor victory for the clergy. It had become established practice that felonious clerks were treated the same as the laity in matters of sanctuarial confessions made to

[46] 1316 Cal. Pat. Rolls 1313–1317. PRO C 74/1 m. 34d

the coroner. There were two issues: clerics swore and then requested to abjure[47] or faced compelled abjuration,[48] or in instances where a cleric was prepared to accuse other felons (and be treated as an approver) they were regarded the same as lay approvers[49] and not handed over to the bishop. The fact that secular authorities permitted clerics to abjure and turn approver is, of itself, clear indication of the influence of the secular law in the everyday lives of lay and spiritual society and evidence of the forum shopping that criminous clerks employed to ensure the best possible outcome for their felonious behavior. Clause sixteen changed this situation and permitted cleric approvers to claim benefit of clergy and be claimed by their bishops. It also had the effect of improving further the options for recidivist criminal clerics.

If *Articuli* represented a win for the Church it was short lived in large part because the multifarious role of bishops as landowners and pastors, and as judges secular and spiritual continued to divide their loyalties.[50] Furthermore *Articuli* did not stem the practice of the crown retaining

[47] For example, Richard of Fulebroc in Cheney, C.R. The Punishment of Felonious Clerks, *The English Historical Review*, Vol. 51. No. 202 (Apr., 1936) pp. 215–236. p. 225 and n. 2

[48] Cheney, Supra

[49] The opportunity to become a King's approver was based upon the idea that a felon rarely operated in isolation and therefore he may well be capable of identifying and giving evidence against other felons and thereby assist the crown in bringing forth successful prosecutions and a reduction in crime. Contemporary use of this is seen in cases where a defendant gives evidence against an accomplice and today, as was the case during the Middle Ages, is potentially unreliable as thieves and felons tend to lie to save themselves and will often provide unreliable testimony. For a discussion of the role of approver: Hamil, F.C., The King's Approvers: A Chapter in the History of English Criminal Law, *Speculum*, Vol. 11 (1936) pp. 238–258

[50] Denton, J.H., The Making of the 'Articuli Cleri' of 1316, *The English Historical Review*, Vol. 101. No. 400 (Jul., 1986), pp. 564–595

the goods and chattels of a successful clergy claimant; his body went to the bishop but his wealth stayed with the king.[51] Eventually the combination of diminishing episcopal power[52] and increasing criminality by the lower orders of the clergy would combine to assist in legitimizing royal, and societal, pressure to laicize clericus. Perhaps the ultimate confirmation of this transition came when on the feast of St. Thomas, (29 December 1340) John Stratford, archbishop of Canterbury (1333–1348) used the Canterbury pulpit to defend himself against accusations levelled at him by Edward III. Subsequently the prelate of England insisted on adjudication by his equals, 'That he might be openly held for such as he was', a peer.[53] Stratford sought not the ecclesiastical courts of his bishops of England and the protections of benefit of clergy, he demanded to stand trial before the secular lords of the realm.[54]

Although I do not argue that the availability of the benefit of clergy to all members of secular society was planned by the clerics of England it is persuasive. By the process of laicization, the heat was taken out of the fire of societal contempt for clerics and those who held the key to literacy could

---

[51] Cheney, Supra. p. 231 and Denton, Supra

[52] Haines, R. M., The Episcopate during the Reign of Edward II and the Regency of Mortimer and Isabella, *The Journal of Ecclesiastical History*, Vol. 56. No. 4 (Oct 2005) pp. 657–707. Kynell, K von S., *Saxon and Medieval Antecedents of The English Common Law: Studies in British History Vol. 59*. Lampeter, Edwin Mellen Press, 2000

[53] Lapsley, G., Archbishop Stratford and the Parliamentary Crisis of 1341. Part II. *The English Historical Review*, Vol. 30. No. 118 (Apr., 1915) pp. 193–215. Two bishops and four earls were appointed but the matter was resolved before trial and Stratford returned to good favor with Edward III

[54] Jones, W.R., Bishops, Politics, and the Two Laws: The Gravamina of the English Clergy, 1237–1399, *Speculum*, Vol. 41. No. 2 (Apr., 1966) pp. 209–245 and King, E., *Medieval England from Hastings to Bosworth*, Stroud, The History Press, 2009. pp. 201–202

actually be complicit in schooling defendants in learning how to read and thus successfully claim immunity from the reach of a number of sanguinary laws. This would, if deliberate, actually raise the status of the local priest in the eyes of his community and it would deflect criticisms against the Church generally. In effect the priest was not only custodian of access to the afterlife, now he was also providing a valuable social service to village unfortunates in the mortal world. Evidence for this position is scant however and recorded instances of priests deliberately schooling secular defendants in the bible occur but are rare.

The first recorded instance of use of a reading test occurred in 1277[55] when cleric, Thomas le Blake, having been sent to the bishop's prison charged with theft, escaped from custody. He was recaptured and appeared before the secular tribunal for his escape felony. Apparently his status as a clerk was in doubt as the court noted that Thomas was not literate. Quite why the court required proof beyond *habitu clericali* is unclear other than the appropriate assumption that a man who could read was a cleric. This appears to be an isolated incidence until twenty years later when the Newgate Gaol Delivery 28 Edward I records that William Asshendene failed to prove his clergy by habit or literacy.[56] Five years later another defendant appeared before the Newgate justices in civilian clothing. He convinced the

[55] This example is given in Gabel, L. *Benefit of Clergy in England in the Later Middle Ages,* New York, Octagon Books, 1969. p. 65. As recent as 1274 Boniface VIII had confined benefit of clergy to those who wore correct clerical attire. Cheney, C.R. The Punishment of Felonious Clerks, *The English Historical Review,* Vol. 51. No. 202 (Apr., 1936) pp. 215–236. p. 217

[56] G.D. 38. m. 7d. Newgate. Also cited in Gabel, Supra. p 66

tribunal that he was a cleric as he could read.[57] Two further cases[58] of disputed clergy occurred before the end of the century indicting that a trend towards reading as a substitute for habit and tonsure was entering courts temporal practice.

The cases discussed below are indicative of the laicization of *privilegium fori* as a representation of the larger movements taking place across fourteenth century English society. The cases range in scope from murder, arson, extortion, kidnapping and maiming; they follow the same degrees of clerical criminality seen in previous chapters. What changes is the amelioration of the clericus plea into mainstream secular trials, the acceptance of the clerical status on the basis of a reading test (even by those who are abjectly not members of the Church). In a broader sense what these cases confirm is that England's polity and its Church had transitioned; the established Three Orders;[59] those who worked, those who prayed and those who fought, was moving over for a literate consumer as urban and mercantile classes started to assert a louder voice in the nature and form of English society. As the 'calamitous century'[60] progressed the laws temporal subsumed benefit of clergy and shaped it into a privilege available to any class of male citizen that could stumble through an agreed text.

---

[57] G.D. 39. m. 18. Newgate. 33 Edw. I

[58] G.D. 39. m. 19. Newgate. 33. Edw. I and G.D. 39. m.26. Westminster. 33 Edw. I. Also given in Gabel, Supra. p.67

[59] Holmes, G., *The Oxford History of Medieval Europe*, Oxford, Oxford University Press, 2001. pp. 127–128 and Summerson, H., The Criminal Underworld of Medieval England, *The Journal of Legal History*, Vol. 17. No. 3 (1996) pp. 197–224

[60] Tuchman, B., *A Distant Mirror: The Calamitous 14th Century*, New York, Balantine, 1978

The secularization of benefit of clergy and the associated privileges discussed previously; sanctuary, abjuration and outlawry are significant markers in the transition of the clergy from an exalted status *apart from society* to an integral *part of society*. The criminal cases discussed below reflect that move as the division between a criminal cleric and a criminal who becomes a cleric merge. As *Ecclesia Anglicana* became evermore absorbed by the state so too did *privilegium fori* become a part of the Common Law.

An interesting example of discerning clericus appears in the register of Roger Martival, bishop of Salisbury (1315–1330)[61] when Peter de Periton and John de Hakeneye, canons of Salisbury, were authorized to claim George de Birthmanstone (who was being held in secular prison). De Birthmanstone had pled his clergy before lay justices in response to a number of unspecified crimes. The commission report states that the applicant was not known to be a cleric. He was, therefore, to be examined to this effect by the ordinaries. Bishop Martival proceeded to give his envoys specific directions as follows: First ask if George is a cleric, if he claims he is then when and by whom was he ordained? The legates are then told to establish if the cleric remains married, the assumption being that since he is not known to be an ordained priest the defendant is a man from the lower orders and likely to be married. At this point it is crucial that the ordinaries investigate the legality of the marriage, that is; he is married to one woman only and when did that union take place? At canon law bigamous clerics had never been permitted to claim benefit of clergy. However, during

[61] Elrington, C.R., (ed) *The Registers of Roger Martival, Bishop of Salisbury, 1315–1330, Vol. 2 (The Register of Divers Letters, First Half)*, Oxford, Oxford University Press, 1963 available at www.fordham.edu/Halsall/source/1330martival.asp

the first forty years of the fourteenth century inquest of bigamy was secularized;[62] it returned to the Church under 18 Edward III, '...and if any man for us, or for the same party, will suggest, that he hath married two wives, or one widow, that upon the same the Justices shall not have the cognizance or power to try the bigamy by inquest, or in other manner, but it shall be sent to the Spiritual Court...'.[63] Martival's commissioners were then directed to ask if cleric de Birthmanstone was wearing holy orders at the time of his capture? How did he conduct himself? What were the circumstances of the alleged crimes and how was he viewed by the community from which he was taken? Once satisfied in all of the areas specified the legates should proceed to claim the criminal clerk and deliver him into the custody of their bishop. Why it should be that de Birthmanstone was not claimed after his secular conviction is not recorded. Presumably he was unsuccessful in convincing the bishop's envoys of his clerical status while he awaited trial. Or this may be another example of a case where the secular court proceeded with trial in the absence of the ordinary. If this is the case the court appears to have accepted the benefit of clergy claim at trial but not beforehand when he was in custody. How this was eventually established to the satisfaction of the lay court, *tonsuratus* or *literatus,* is not known.

Another example of written directions for collection of criminal clergy is given by Ralph of Shrewsbury, the bishop of Bath and

---

[62] Year Book V, Selden Society, Eyre of Kent I, 140–141 "If a clerk that be arraigned for felony shall plead his clergy, inquest shall be straightway made as to whether he is a bigamist, and if it be found that he be a bigamist, he shall be tried as though he were a layman'. 6 and 7 Edw. II. Given in Gabel, Supra. p. 90. n. 109

[63] 18. Edw. III, stat. 3, c.2. (1344) For case discussion see Gabel, Supra. p. 42. n.44. John Foljambe

Wells (1329–1363) in 1351. In this case the reading test is specifically mentioned as proof of clerical status. In this case the bishop directed that the ordinary was to conduct the literacy test and it was his task to establish that the claimant was not a bigamist.[64] What these examples (and others)[65] show is that during the fourteenth century authority to conduct enquiry into a clericus claim was no longer vested exclusively with the ordinary, it was fluid. During the reign of Edward II there followed a period of little development in the use of the reading test. The single example is that of a clerk who was required to read two verses from the bible to establish his clerical legitimacy.[66] Neither Gabel nor Bellamy[67] provide an explanation for this lacuna. I am persuaded to agree with Gabel that in fact the first true appearance of the reading test does not commence until Edward III.

Inclusion of the reading test in secular proceedings amounted to an 'examination'. This took place as soon as the defendant entered his claim of clericus. It would seem this might happen at the beginning of the trial or at its conclusion. Once entered the ordinary administered the reading examination[68] and declared 'he reads' or 'he does not read'. If successful, the defendant was then formally handed to the bishop's representative for appearance before the courts spiritual. If a defendant failed to read with the

---

[64] *Register of Ralph of Shrewsbury, Bishop of Bath and Wells, 1329–1363*, f. 288 (Somerset Record Society). pp. 756–757. Given in Gabel, Supra. p. 54. n. 83

[65] Further examples include Newgate Gaol Delivery , G.D. 109. m. 2 (2. Edw. II), G.D. 40. m. 10, G.D. 40. m. 24 (6. Edw. II), G.D. 41. m. 28, (13 Edw. II)

[66] Y.B. V. Selden Society, Eyre of Kent I. 151. 6 & 7 Edw II. Gabel, Supra. p. 67

[67] Bellamy, J. *Crime and Public Order in England in the Later Middle Ages*, London, Routledge, 1973

[68] It appears that with usage the preference became that the ordinary handed the defendant a psalter rather than bible. I have not been able to establish an exact date for the establishment of this trend

degree of fluidity expected of a cleric the secular judge was entitled to demand further reading or to deny the ordinary his cleric. This would seem to be a curios scenario, where the ordinary administered the test but the secular judge had authority to question the authenticity of the ordinary's decision. One celebrated instance of this nature took place in 1366 when John, son of Thomas Dennyson Trotter, appeared in answer to a number of charges including murder.[69] The vicar of St. Lawrence's, Appleby handed John the Psalter. Apparently John could neither read nor even pronounce words correctly. The presiding judge handed John *salternum reversum* to which he responded with the same level of ability unaware of the altered circumstances. As a result the ordinary refused to claim John Trotter. It transpired that Trotter had been permitted to receive visitors while on remand and he had been schooled (ineffectively) in reading whilst in gaol. The transition towards the secularization of claiming benefit of clergy marked an important point in the courts temporal asserting dominance over the criminal law. A small but important example of this took place in 1339 when in the absence of an ordinary the secular judge administered the reading test and proclaimed the defendant *legit ut clericus*.[70] The following year at Guildford another defendant was claimed *nec legit nec sillibicat* by the court rather than the ordinary.[71] What seems to be happening during this period of evolution of testing the validity of benefit of clergy claimants is that once a defendant enters his claim the ordinary (or periodically the temporal judge)

---

[69] G.D. 145. m. 56d. 39 Edw. III. Also given in Gabel, Supra. p. 73 and Bellamy, Supra. p. 153

[70] G.D. 129. m. 3. 12 Edw. III

[71] G.D. 129. m. 61. 13 Edw. III

administers a reading test. Initially this test may have been used to supplement clerical garb in cases of some doubt.

With time when an ordinary was not present the court proceeded to administer a reading test and decide upon the legitimacy of the claim. Importantly failure to read, not clerical attire, invalidated the claim and the defendant was tried, sentenced and punished by the courts temporal. It increasingly became the case that when a defendant failed to prove his status through reading the ordinary was less inclined to support the false claim by his brother; Edward III, 13, 18 and 19 are such examples.[72] In conjunction with this development the secular court appears less inclined to automatically accept the ordinary's statement of proof when he is present in court. In more than one instance the court returned the defendant to gaol and then conducted further investigation into the authenticity of the benefit claim.[73] In 1344 robber William Pernill failed to read at his first attempt and the ordinary refused to claim him. Pernill was sentenced to death. Whilst in Colchester gaol he was apparently schooled in reading and the ordinary made a subsequent claim upon him before execution.[74] Examples such as this help explain the adoption of the term 'neck verse' as slang for Psalm 51 (the misère) as the preferred reading sample utilized by the courts. Notwithstanding Pernill's case by the middle of the fourteenth century the ordinary was no longer the ultimate arbiter of the reading test it was the judge and jury of the courts temporal.

---

[72] G.D. 129. m. 61, m. 8 and m. 13d are all examples of where the Ordinary refused to accept the reading provided as a legitimate claim to clergy. Gabel, Supra. pp.68–69

[73] Gabel, Supra. p. 69. n. 33

[74] G.D. 129. m. 8. 18 Edw. III. Gabel, Supra. pp.72–73. Bellamy, Supra, pp.152–153

The use of the reading test is also testament to the surge in literacy that was taking place.[75] This is manifest in the court reports which now started to record the livelihood or occupation of the claimant alongside *legit* or not.[76] What this suggests is that the criminal law was moving from tacit to total acceptance that men who were manifestly not clerics may claim the protections of a clergy plea and avoid the gallows. Gabel describes this occurrence as a significant coincidence.[77] In my view she is correct. To officially record a defendant as a cleric and also ascribe to that defendant an occupation is a clear delineation between genuine clerics who are claiming their clergy and lay persons who are doing likewise.[78] By the middle of the century benefit of clergy had become a secular plea available to all.[79] What started as an opportunity, a defendant 'may read', had become a case of a defendant 'must read'.

The incentive to secure immunity from the harsh and increasingly sanguinary nature of English criminal law was great. The advantage of being literate was considerable and whereas it had increased for the laity it had not diminished for the clergy. What the law needed now was a means of gatekeeping and preventing abuse for if the secular law could not devise a mechanism to differentiate between habitual recidivist criminals and singular offenders it would be no better than the Church law it had

---

[75] For examples see: The books of Depositions of the Consistory Courts of London given by Gabel, Supra. pp. 82–85

[76] Gabel, Supra, provides excellent examples pp. 82–83

[77] Gabel, Supra. p. 77

[78] Bellamy, Supra. pp. 154–155

[79] Subsequently acknowledged in parliament in 1489, 4. Hen VII. C. 13 and Baker, J.H., *The Reports of John Spelman, Vol. 2*. Selden Society. Vol. 94. 1978. pp. 327–332 and Baker, J.H., *The Law's Two Bodies: Some Evidential Problems in English Legal History*, Oxford, Oxford University Press, 2001. pp. 127–133

subsumed. This happened.[80] Laymen successfully reciting the 'neck verse' were branded and clerics were not.[81] This distinction between claimants was not immediate though, if it had been then much criticism of the priesthood in the fourteenth century might have abated sooner. It did not, in large part because genuine clerics were still prone towards committing felonies of the gravest order; Thomas Porter being a case in point.

On February 17, 1362, chaplain Porter arrived at the house of William Webster. He proceeded to steal from Webster and then rape Agnes Webster. Two months later the cleric returned to Webster's house and when Agnes refused to have sex with him the cleric attacked and wounded her and set fire to the Webster's two-year-old son burning him so badly that the child lost his left foot. [82] As further grotesque examples of clerical criminality continued the dilution of the English sacerdotal escalated such that in 1377 the king ordered that bishops may no longer permit the purgation of notorious felons.[83]

---

[80] Baker, J.H., 'Benefit of Clergy in England and its Secularization 1450–1550' in Ascheri, M.,Ebel, F.,Heckel, M., Padoa-Schioppa,A., Pöggeler,W., Raneiri, F und Rütten, W., *Ins Wasser Geworfen und Ozeane Durchquet*, Köln, Böhlau Verlag, 2003. pp. 27–37

[81] But it took until 1489 to effectively achieve this. Lay claimants were branded on the brawn of the left thumb at the rear of the court. Second time claimants were refused and suffered the death penalty. Johnstone, P. *Benefit of Clergy in Colonial Virginia and Massachusetts*, Dubuque, Kendall Hunt, 2014. Esp. Chap.4. 4 Hen. VII. C.13, Baker, N.F., Benefit of Clergy-A Legal Anomaly, *Kentucky Law Journal*, Vol. 15. No. 2 (Jan., 1927) pp. 85–115. p. 106. Henry VIII even went as far as having clergy branded (28 Hen. VIII, c.I, c.3) but this move was abolished by his son, Edward VI (1. Edw. VI, c. 10)

[82] Aberth, J., *Criminal Churchmen in the Age of Edward III. The Case of Bishop Thomas de Lisle*, University Park, PA, Pennsylvania State University Press, 1993.p. 62

[83] Rot. Parl. iii. 23. McHardy, A.K., 'Church Courts and Criminous Clerks in the Later Middle Ages' in *Medieval Ecclesiastical Studies in Honour of Dorothy M. Owen*, Woodbridge, Boydell, 1995. p. 166 and Pugh, R., *Imprisonment in Medieval England*, Cambridge, Cambridge University Press, 1968. Treason against the body of the king and his family had become unclergyable in 1350. 25 Edw.III. St. 3. C.4

The registers of William Melton, archbishop of York (1317–1340) span the use of benefit of clergy throughout the troubled reign of Edward II and the first fifteen years of Edward III's monarchy. They are representative of many examples of the clergy plea. Like Gabel I feel it is not necessary to rehearse all the cases.[84] A range of these provide convincing evidence of the sustained criminality of the clergy throughout the first seventy-five years of the century and the national trend towards adoption of the literacy test and secularization. From the forty instances recorded in Melton's register at Beverley (1320) he ordered further inquiry into the charge of murder against a clerk,[85] and signed the certificate holding this clerk to ecclesiastic prison 'in strict confinement'.[86] Melton also approved that cleric, Andrew le Botier (he had appeared before Justice Henry le Scrop and been convicted of murder and other felonies) having claimed his clergy in the courts temporal be taken by the ordinary. Later (in November 1320) Melton summonsed the appearance of objectors to the purgation of le Botier. Apparently any objections that may have been earlier expressed were withdrawn and the cleric's purgation request was accepted on December 6, 1320.[87] Melton was in no hurry to have the purgation heard though as le Botier was not absolved of his crimes until January 22, 1323.[88] Many similar examples of criminous clerks appear for the archdeanery of Richmond,[89]

---

[84] She does not examine the three hundred identified

[85] Brocklesby, R., (ed) *The Register of William Melton, Archbishop of York 1317–1340*, Vol. IV. The Canterbury and York Society, Boydell Press, 1997. p. 35

[86] Melton. Vol. IV. Supra. p. 46

[87] Supra. pp. 42–43

[88] Supra. p. 64

[89] Hill, R. (ed) *The Register of William Melton, Archbishop of York, 1317–1340, Vol. I*, The Canterbury and York Society, The Devonshire Press, 1977. pp. 2, 26, 27, 119, 130

the archdeanery of Cleveland,[90] the cathedral chapter,[91] and the archdeanery of East Riding.[92] The outcomes are predictable; successful purgations for burglary,[93] adultery by the prior of Kirkham,[94] sodomy by the rector of Lowthorpe,[95] the imposition of penance on a cleric who killed a priest (the assailant was subsequently held in perpetual sanctuary at Beverley),[96] purgation for the secular conviction of a recidivist horse thief,[97] purgation for adultery and incest,[98] the purgation of William de Middleton for homicide[99] and John le Quaynte cleared himself of theft, burglary and robbery.[100]

In 1321 one of the most celebrated and recorded benefit of clergy issues occurred. Not in York but London. Only five cases of clergy are recorded in the Eyre Roll for London 1321 of these few the case of Isabel of Bury had ramifications far beyond the confines of the capital. Isabel of Bury and Henry

---

[90] Robinson, D., (ed) *The Register of William Melton, Archbishop of York 1317–1340, Vol. II* The Canterbury and York Society, The Devonshire Press, 2011. pp. 67, 86, 102, 110, 113

[91] Timmins, T.C., (ed) *The Register of William Melton, Archbishop of York, 1317–1340, Vol. V,* The Canterbury and York Society, Woodbridge, Boydell Press, 2002, pp. 3, 54, 139

[92] Robinson, D., (ed) *The Register of William Melton, Archbishop of York, 1317–1340, Vol. VI,* The Canterbury and York Society, Woodbridge, Boydell Press, 2011, pp. 4, 24, 197, 329, 105, 124, 144, 145, 181, 184, 202. There are no entries recorded for the diocese (not the metropolitan) of York per Hill, R., (ed) *The Register of William Melton, Archbishop of York, 1317–1340, Vol. III,* The Canterbury and York Society, York, Maxiprint, 1988. Also Smith, D.M., *Supplement to the Guide to Bishop's Registers of England and Wales: A Survey of the Middle Ages to the Abolition of the Episcopacy in 1646,* The Canterbury and York Society, 2004

[93] Melton, Vol. VI. p. 144, John de Rotse and Melton, Vol. II. p. 110 Richard Belle of Barton

[94] Melton, Vol. VI. p. 184

[95] Melton, Vol. VI. p. 58

[96] Melton, Vol. V. p. 54

[97] Melton, Vol. V. p. 139 Thomas de Oddesthorp

[98] Melton, Vol. II. p. 86 Sir Peter de Maulay

[99] Melton, Vol. II. p. 102

[100] Melton, Vol. I. p. 2

of Braundeston were both separately charged with committing sacrilegious homicide in a church. Henry was a nobleman with estates at Lapworth and Warwickshire as well as Braunstone in Leicestershire (from where he took his name). Isabel murdered a priest inside his church and then sought sanctuary at the crime scene, she was disowned by the Church and unable to claim benefit of clergy. Henry was more fortunate and avoided the gallows.

The first offence took place nine years before trial when Henry Braundeston and Edmund Wolmer attacked and killed Robert de Brome inside the church of St. Mary at Hill in the City of London. On November 10th 1312 the bishop of London issued letters of excommunication for Braundeston and Wolmer (to be read in every parish church in London). Bruandeston was arrested and committed to Newgate from where he paid 40s. for his freedom.[101] Soon after his release Bruandeston managed to bribe the mayor of London and was admitted, *ex post facto*, to the freedom of the city. His admission was fraudulently recorded as being effective from October 1312, before the murder took place. Accordingly, at the time of committing the felony he was entitled to the ancient privilege to be replevied until the next Eyre. It was not until 1321 that the next Eyre was commissioned. In November of 1321 the jury acquitted Bruandeston of his sacrilegious, unclergyable, crime of murder within a church. It would appear the defendant was comfortable in advance of the likely outcome as he elected to put himself upon the country rather than claim clerical privilege.

---

[101] Cam, H.,(ed) *The Eyre of London 14 Edward II. A.D. 1321. Vol. I*, London, Selden Society, 1968. p.113. n. 5

Isabel of Bury's future was determined within a few days of her crime. Lacking wealth and the ability to bribe and to sway a jury her proceedings were not protracted but swift and predictable. On February 19$^{th}$ 1321 Isabel and her maid had been in loud conversation inside All Hallows on the Wall Church, Billingsgate when the Church clerk, Gilbert Lyter, remonstrated with the pair about the volume of noise. Isabel responded by knifing him. He died from the injuries. The maid, Joan la Clerkes, was arrested. Isabel claimed sanctuary within All Hallows. After two days the ecclesiastical authorities ordered Isabel to be forcibly removed on the basis that the Church did not protect those who committed crimes within consecrated grounds. At her trial Isabel claimed self-defense. This was not accepted by the jury and she hanged.[102]

The Braundeston and Bury cases stimulated much commentary within canon and common law circles. At trial the issue of whether or not Bury could claim sanctuary was discussed at length and the justices requested written advice from the archbishop of Canterbury and the bishop of London. As we know denial of sanctuarial privilege was unequivocal. In fact at the time of Bury's forcible removal from All Hallows it was a combination of clerics and laymen that removed her.[103] Following the ruling from the church Justice Sir Edmund de Passeley related to his fellow judges an incident in Kent when two felons fled to a local church after escaping from temporal custody. De Passeley requested release of the men from the Church which fell within the see of Canterbury. Archbishop of Canterbury

[102] *Rex v Bury*, Cam, Supra, pp. 73–76

[103] Cam, Supra. p. 73

Winchelsey[104] (1293–1313) responded that because the crimes committed were thefts from church he did not 'acknowledge them as sons of the Church'. The felons were removed and hanged.[105] Unfortunately for Bury she was deemed not to be a sister of the Church and suffered the same fate.

The outcome of Bury and Bruandeston was predictable. A rich nobleman capable of bribing his way to freedom and a woman disowned by the Church to face certain death. If a jury could be purchased at a reasonable rate then what incentive was there for the nobility and higher clerical orders to risk the bishop's prison while awaiting purgation? As for reading tests, this group could read anyway. The incentive for secularization of clericus was not that it would better serve society's elite, it made little difference to them. The incentive was that it might spare the likes of illiterate, confused and frightened commoners such as Isabel Bury.

Returning to the register of William Melton in September 1323 he commissioned John de Trowell, rector of a mediety at Trowel and Matthew de Halifax, keeper of the hospital of St. John the Baptist, Nottingham to 'claim, receive and securely hold clerks' charged before the gaol delivery at Nottingham.[106] The following year he ordered the dean of Nottingham make enquiry into the case of John de Melton, a cleric who had been accused of burglary and was now

---

[104] Winchelsey experienced a difficult episcopate. He was greatly concerned over the declining authority and financial independence of the Church as expressed in the *gravamina*. Divisions within the episcopate and malaise in leadership did little to help his cause. See: Jones, W.R., Bishops, Politics, and the Two Laws: The Gravamina of the English Clergy, 1237–1399, *Speculum*, Vol. 41. No. 2 (Apr., 1966) pp. 209–245

[105] Cam, Supra. p. 76

[106] Melton, Vol. IV, Supra. p. 77

awaiting purgation hearing.[107] There are no further entries before Edward II reluctantly relinquished his crown in January 1327.[108]

During the transitional period of regency (between 1327 and 1330) ten cases of clergy appear in William Melton's register for the archdeaconry of Nottingham[109] these include: claiming cleric William Tusard of Bathley (Burglary),[110] John Touk (Robbery),[111] a commission to Matthew de Halifax and John Cosyn to claim and receive an unspecified number of clerks,[112] a case of highway robbery (clergyable until 1512)[113] against Walter de Webbeley and Richard le Bakere and simple robbery against Robert le Serjeant and Richard de Wygemor.[114] Entry 575[115] is the testimonial that Stephen and Henry de Thorp had been canonically purged of homicide. This is followed by a receipt for a recognizance for three hundred pounds in respect of Thomas de Radeclif. De Radeclif was held in the bishop's prison for abducting a woman. He was also a known member of the Folville gang.[116] Perhaps unsurprisingly de Radeclif was found guiltless of the crime before his bishop. Entry 613

---

[107] Ibid. p. 79 and for discussion of purgation hearing venues: McHardy, A., 'Church Courts and Criminous Clerks in the Later Middle Ages' in *Medieval Ecclesiastical Studies in Honour of Dorothy M. Owen*, Woodbridge, Boydell press, 1995. pp. 165–183

[108] Valente, C., The Deposition and Abdication of Edward II, *The English Historical Review*, Vol. 113. No. 453 (Sept., 1988) pp. 852–881

[109] In total there are six volumes of Melton's registers covering all archdeaconries of the York metropolitan and the cathedral chapter

[110] Melton Vol. IV, Supra. p. 97

[111] Ibid. p. 77

[112] Ibid. p.102

[113] 4 Hen. 8. c.2 (1512)

[114] Melton Vol. IV, Supra. p. 103

[115] Ibid. p. 131

[116] Ibid. p. 132 and n. 58 and this work chapter 3

records the bishop's request that Edward III restore the lands of Thomas de Radeclif.[117] 615 are letters patent that testify the purgation of de Radeclif and 'his good name was restored' on 13 August 1330.[118] In the same year cleric Stephen Pavely of Ruddington purged himself of the murder of Thomas de Corbrigg.[119] Archbishop Melton again wastes little time in requesting that Edward III restore the goods and chattels of Pavely.[120] Entry 610 directs the purgation of Thomas de Beltoft. The cleric had been charged before the secular justices with harboring an outlaw. In theory both unclergyable and attracting outlawry for the cleric. He was successful in purging himself before thirteen fellow clerks.[121] The felon that de Beltoft did 'not' harbor according to canon law was his father. Thomas de Beltoft senior had been outlawed for the murder of John de Bekyngham (and a number of other felonies). It is beyond belief that de Beltoft junior did not give his fleeing father safe harbor but according to the benefit of clergy he was innocent. Stephen de Misterton was equally innocent of his crimes according to his clerical peers at York Minster. He had been judged differently by the courts temporal who had found him guilty of numerous cases of theft and declared he was a 'common thief'.[122]

Once a purgation date was set the bishop made notice to receive objectors. It was extremely rare that any objectors ever came forward. There are two reasons for this; the laity

[117] Ibid. p. 139
[118] Ibid. p. 140
[119] Melton Vol. IV, Supra. p. 135
[120] Ibid. p. 138
[121] Ibid. p. 139
[122] Melton. Vol. IV. Op.cit. p. 141

were resigned to the inevitable outcome; clerks were almost guaranteed to purge themselves. More dangerously objectors (as well as the original victims of the crime) were liable to be fined for defamation once the cleric had cleared his name. This no doubt resulted in cases where no objectors came forward in the first instance. This can be seen in entry 618, 'No objectors appeared, and Stephen purged himself by suitable honest persons. His good name is restored'.[123] At this time previous conviction before a secular court followed by purgation was not a bar to further purgation. This is demonstrated in the case of William Tusard. He was first remanded to the bishop's prison in 1327. The offence was burglary. He successfully purged himself. By 1330 he purged himself again. This time for multiple theft convictions.[124] The remaining entries in Melton's register[125] confirm the likelihood of a successful purgation regardless of the severity of the crime or the designation of convicted felon, outlaw or recidivist imposed by the secular court.[126] Examining diocesanal registers confirms the number of cases transferred from the secular courts to those spiritual and provides insight into the disposition of the cases against criminous clerics. They also confirm that in most instances the cleric is successful in his purgation; his good name is restored and he returns to the community.

---

[123] Ibid. p. 141. Further examples follow at 622

[124] Ibid. p.144. Thomas Harmere is another case in point. A recidivist clerk he claimed his clergy after many years of crime that included highway robbery across Sussex and London. He successfully claimed his clergy. Riley, H.T., (ed) *Memorials of London and London Life in the XIIIth, XIVth, and IVth Centuries,* Memphis, General Books, 2012 (Facsimile copy). p. 131

[125] Melton Vol IV. Supra. Entries: 641, 663, 667, 682, 696, 699, 704, 721, 723, 829. Total number of entries 36, years 1319–1336

[126] Purgation was not permitted at common law. See: *Searle v Williams* [288] 376 Tr. 16 Jac. Rot. 1782. Hill. 17. Jac. In Robertson, M.A., & Ellis, G., (eds) *The English Reports Vol. LXXX King's Bench Division IX,* Edinburgh, William Green & Sons, 1907. pp. 433–438

In 1329 Edward III (1327–1377) instituted the Northamptonshire Eyre.[127] His court sat from November 1329 until September 1330. During the period the justices received eighteen benefit of clergy claims.[128] Two crimes tried at the Eyre that involved the active participation of clergymen stand out in particular; one due to the severity of the criminal act, the other the sacrilegious nature of the crime. In the first instance Joan, wife of John of Grymescote planned to murder John fitz John. Her intention was to burn him alive in the oven of Stephen le Chaundeler. To achieve her criminal objective she solicited the help of four accomplices; Malcolm of Potcote, Simon of Potcote, John le Warde and Carmelite friar Brother Robert of Maydenford.

On the agreed day the victim John fitz John was engaged into conversation with Joan's four accomplices and led to the house of le Chaundeler (where Joan had prepared the oven). Once at the house the four men seized the victim and 'placed him alive in the oven and burned him to ashes'.[129] Joan was subsequently arrested and hanged. John le Warde, Malcolm and Simon of Potcote died before trial. There is no mention of Stephen le Chaundeler whose oven was used to kill John fitz John. Carmelite Brother Robert of Maydenford was not found; he was exacted and outlawed. He had no chattels and was not in a tithing because he was a cleric. There is no record of Maydenford ever standing trial and consequently his use

[127] Eyres were established at Northampton and Nottingham. Sutherland, D.W., (ed), *The Eyre of Northamptonsgire 3–4 Edward III, Vol. I.* London, Selden Society, 1983, Ormrod, W. M., 'England: Edward II and Edward III' in Jones, M., (ed) *The New Cambridge Medieval History, Vol. VI c. 1300–1415,* Cambridge, Cambridge University Press, 2000, Chap. 13 (a). p. 273

[128] Pp. 157, 158, 159, 162, 165, 174, 188, 190, 195, 205, 219, 233, 241, 286

[129] Selden Society, *Northamptonshire,* Supra. p. 159. JUST 1/635 m. 20

of the clergy plea was never tested. Presumably he remained a cleric outlaw for the remainder of his life. Later in the Eyre proceedings appeared John of Halewyk, William of Burgh, Roger of Nassington and John of Yerdele; a group of felons indicted for horse theft and murder. Roger of Nassington was a cleric. It was alleged that the group had knocked John le Greynesone of Swaton off his horse, dragged the victim into a cemetery, killed him and then sold the horse. John of Halewyk pleaded not guilty and was acquitted by the jury. He was found guilty of trespass in taking the horse. William Burgh was also acquitted. John of Yerdele was found guilty and hanged. Cleric Roger of Nassington pleaded his clergy and was received by the ordinary (despite the sacrilegious nature of the crime rendering it unclergyable at canon law).[130]

Legal dexterity was also applied in the case of Geoffrey of Wodhull who became an approver after confessing a number of thefts. He appealed Simon of Wendlynburgh as an accomplice to theft of twenty-two sheep and a horse. When Wodhull and Wendlynburgh appeared together in court Wodhull claimed he could not prosecute his aforesaid appeal as he was a cleric. At this point the master of the hospital of St. John of Northampton (representing the bishop of Lincoln) received the approver.[131] What is particularly interesting about this case is that at the same time clerk convict Wodhull also approved John fitz Philip le Longe of Rothwell, and Le Longe was himself a convict cleric approver. Wodhull and Le Longe had a history of crime together, Wodhull was the thief and Le Longe the receiver of stolen sheep and horses. The record shows

---

[130] Ibid. pp. 205–206 JUST 1/635 m. 74, 91

[131] Ibid. pp. 162, 165. JUST 1/635 m. 88

that on May 14, 1329 Thomas le Corour stole cattle from the earl of Lancaster and that Le Longe '...bought from them two cows and six steers for 30s, of which the same Geoffrey [of Wodhull] received 14s., well knowing that the animals were stolen...'.[132] Both Wodhull and Le Longe then turned approver against le Corour. The two clerics, having committed theft and receiving stolen goods, then gave evidence against their accomplice, knowing he would hang. The clerks claimed their privilege and were handed to the ordinary.[133]

The case against Thomas fitz Hammond is interesting in that the murderous cleric claimed that he had already answered to the murder indictment.[134] In 1322 Thomas had been acquitted of murdering John fitz William. In 1323 he appeared in answer to murdering William fitz John. After he failed to convince the court that this was the same person and not a second victim, he pled his clergy. Unfortunately for Thomas the ordinary was not present in court and he was taken by the sheriff to the county gaol. Further investigation proved that Thomas had indeed been acquitted for the murder of John fitz William and there was no second murder. He was released. Similarly, in the case against Thomas fitz Ralph Lambert of Multon, he was indicted for the murder of Roger Deyessone. In court the cleric claimed that he had already purged himself of the crime before his bishop, Henry of Lincoln. The court believed him and he was released.[135] The same court deliberated over the

---

[132] Selden Society, *Northamptonshire,* Supra. p. 165. JUST 1/635 m. 89

[133] This case is followed by another benefit of clergy claim when Richard le Clerk of Ocle, having slain a servant pleaded his clergy before the Eyre. Selden Society, *Northamptonshire,* Supra. p. 166. JUST 1/635 m. 89d and JUST 1/632 m. 91d

[134] Selden Soc, *Northamptonshire,* Supra. p. 174

[135] Ibid. pp. 218–219

issue of pardons in another homicide case involving a cleric. William was convicted of felony and claimed he had received a king's charter of pardon.[136] The court held that the cleric must chose as he could not have both benefit of pardon and benefit of clergy.[137] This followed the established position that temporal justices were responsible for imposing a sentence of outlawry upon all manner of felons, including clerics, regardless of whether or not the Church accepted that determination.[138]

By this time it was common practice that clerics stood trial before a jury and were either acquitted or convicted.[139] If convicted they then proceeded to claim their benefit of clergy. If acquitted by a lay jury claiming clericus was unnecessary and the clerk was released without recourse to his bishop. What this confirms is that typically criminous clerics were not seeking the protections of the Church at the earliest opportunity because they were clerics and believed they should only answer to their bishop, but rather more they used benefit of clergy as a last resort once all other lay options had been used up. This blatant abuse of clerical position would add further weight to the contempt that lay society already held for its clergymen.

To ameliorate secular disdain for clericus abuse whilst also appearing to appease ecclesiastic unrest an Ordinance for

---

[136] Ibid. p.188 See also the interesting use of a pardon by Sir Robert de Veer, Selden Soc, *Northamptonshire.* pp. 214–215 (after de Veer committed the sacrilege of theft from a parson)

[137] Likewise it was the temporal court that determined the charge and as seen above (Roger of Nassington) an assault could be heard as a trespass for which no clergyman could claim his privilege. By the sixteenth century an indictable trespass became known as a 'misdemeanor'. See also case of John of Naysworth, chaplain, convicted of trespass and fined. Selden Soc, *Northamptonshire,* Supra. pp. 194–195

[138] Ibid. p. 190

[139] E.g. Selden Soc, *Northamptonshire.* p. 286. Gabel, Supra. pp. 31–61 esp. 35–37

the Clergy, *Statutum Pro Clero,* was made at Westminster in 1352. It held that 'That all manner of Clerks as well secular as religious...shall from henceforth freely have and enjoy the privilege of Holy Church'.[140] Following on from the more famous treason statute of the same year[141] (in which Edward III defined the offence of treason against the body of his majesty) *Pro Clero,* intimated a collegial approach[142] towards the demands of the clergy. What the legislation actually achieved was to diminish the strength of clericus and make it openly available to all Englishmen.

Edward III's reign was long and ultimately it was a successful kingship, one that paved the way forward to a new level of harmony and consensus amongst England's prelates after decades of blatant clerical criminality,[143] mistrust and complaint. The case of Guy Mortimer is a good example. Guy, rector of Kingston-upon-Hull Church, held a grudge against parishioner William Joye. As a result of which he had Joye held down by two other clerics as he proceeded to cut off Joye's upper lip with a knife. Mortimer and one accomplice were captured and brought before the secular justices where

[140] 25 Edw. III Stat. 6. c. 4 (This statute has periodically been erroneously cited as 1350)

[141] 25 Edw. III Stat 5. c.1&2. Under this provision treason other than against his majesty was deemed to be a clergyable felony and see Ormrod, Supra. p. 289

[142] 25 Edw. III Stat. 4. *The Statute of Provisors of Benefices* had spoken to a number of the clergy's grievances, *gravamina, Pro Clero* followed this up with a further conciliatory tone. Hamilton, J.S., (ed) *Fourteenth Century England, Vol VIII,* Woodbridge, Boydell Press, 2014. pp. 445–446

[143] E.g. Folevilles and Cotterals. Chap. 3. Also Gabel, Supra, cites 1500 benefit of clergy cases recorded between Edward I and 25 Edw. III p. 39. Of which 500 occur during Edward II. (p.67). For numerous further examples *Coram Rege* Roll No. 342. 19 Edw. III, Mich. Rex. M. 60 given by Richardson, H.G., Year Books and Plea Rolls as Sources of Historical Information, *Transactions of the Royal Historical Society, Fourth Series,* Vol. 5 (1922) pp. 28–70

both defendants repeatedly attempted to claim their clergy. The court did not refute the claim but instead treated the case of one of trespass against the injured parishioner. Trespass was not a clergyable crime. The offenders were then convicted, fined one hundred pounds in damages and imprisoned in the local secular prison. It is almost inconceivable to think that this would have occurred in the time of Edward I and if it had then their bishop would have protested strongly and demanded redress.[144] Times had changed and whereas England's bishops had once made demands they were now making requests.

---

[144] Pike, L.O., *A History of Crime in England, Vol. 1.*, London, Elder & Co, 1873. p. 212 Example given in Gregory-Abbott, C., Sacred Outlaws: Outlawry and the Medieval Church in Appleby, J.C. and Dalton, P., (eds) *Outlaws in Medieval and Early Modern England: Crime, Government and Society, c. 1066-c.1600*, Farnham, Surrey, Ashgate, 2009. pp. 75–89. p. 82

# 9

# Untenable Legal Dilemmas: The Bishop and The Monk

Examining cases of benefit of clergy, sanctuary, abjuration and outlawry committed by clergymen exposes the extent of their involvement in crime. It also provides a window into the life of England's clerics and the society around them. The previously cited examples of the Folville and Coteral gangs vividly demonstrated the close proximity of clerics to all ranks of medieval society, licit and illicit. Edward III was challenged by the criminal behavior of clerics and he responded with creative legislation.[1] Perhaps the most acrimonious and memorable personal challenge to his regal authority was the matter against bishop Thomas De Lisle. This case demonstrated that a frustrated king would himself usurp the law when sufficiently exasperated by an errant prelate.[2] The lack of commentary written about De Lisle is perhaps itself evidence of his contamination of the

[1] Musson, A., 'Second English Justinian or Pragmatic Opportunist? A Re-Examination of the Legal Legislation of Edward III's Reign' in Bothwell, J., (ed) *The Age of Edward III*, York, York Medieval Press, 2001. pp. 69–88

[2] Of royal flounting of laws see: Ormrod, Supra. p. 293

English clergy.[3] His crimes stand alone in the catalogue of benefit of clergy abuse.

Thomas De Lisle (1297–1361) was elevated to the see of Ely in 1345. He was not the expected candidate for the position but had managed to secure the support of Pope Clement VI (1342–1352)[4] and in this instance Edward acquiesced and did not obstruct the appointment. De Lisle was a Dominican; ordained priest in December 1322 aged twenty- five. He took possession of the Ely temporalities on September 10, 1345. Unlike many of his fellow bishops De Lisle had little experience in budget management and the running of estates. During Edward III's reign in the region of thirty per cent of his bishops served for the crown,[5] De Lisle never did. His appointment was one of few that derived exclusively from papal patronage and he was the sole Dominican to hold an English bishopric at that time. These factors may help explain

---

[3] The most comprehensive is Aberth, J., *Criminal Churchmen in the Age of Edward III: The Case of Bishop Thomas De Lisle*, University Park, PA, Pennsylvania State University Press, 1996. There is reference to De Lisle in Ormrod, W.M., *Edward III*, New Haven, Yale University Press, 2011. p. 381, Mortimer, I., *The Perfect King: The Life of Edward III Father of the English Nation*, London, Vintage Books, 2008. p. 318, Haines, R., *Lisle, Thomas 1298–1361*, Oxford Dictionary of National Biography, Oxford, Oxford University Press, 2004 at http://www.oxfordnb.com/view/article/16758, Gregory, S., *The Devil's Disciples*, London, Sphere, 2008. pp. 485–487

[4] Clement was himself a very poor example of papal humility. He famously stated that he had 'lived as a sinner among sinners'. He was renowned for his lavish lifestyle and lived more like a wealthy prince of Europe than leader of a Christian faith. Clement was an Avignon pope and he inherited a brothel in the city when he took up residence. Ciobanu, E.A., *The Spectacle of the Body in Late Medieval England*, Lumen, Romania, 2012. P. 193. n. 180 and www.womenpriests.org/historic/13giovanna.asp

[5] Keeper of the Privy Seal, Thomas Hatfield (Bishop of Durham), John Thoresby, archbishop of York, (later Chancellor of England) Simon Islip, archbishop of Canterbury, Michael Northburgh, bishop of London, William Eddington, keeper of the wardrobe (bishop of Winchester) given in Aberth, Supra. p. 11

his apparent inability to manage his prelatory finances and his social exclusion from the other prelates of England. If De Lisle was close to the pope he was certainly not close to the king or the episcopate of England.[6] Additionally De Lisle had been elevated to the third richest bishopric in England, a position that held a bishop's palace, forty one manors spread across seven counties and a townhouse in Holborn, London which together produced between £2000 and £2500 revenue per annum. The Dominican friar immediately attracted few friends and plenty of jealous enemies. Within the first year of his bishopric De Lisle became embroiled in litigation and rumors of criminal activities. In keeping with established practice newly promoted bishops received a loan from the pope; John Offord, archbishop of Canterbury had borrowed 16,000 florins, the prior of Westminster abbey borrowed 1000 florins as had prelates Simon Islip, William Eddington, John Thoresby (twice) and many other contemporaries of De Lisle.[7] Disguised as a 'charitable subsidy' (*servitia*) this was effectively a tax imposed by the pope for the bishopric. De Lisle was in debt before he returned from receipt of the pallium. Once in Ely he assumed an extravagant and expensive lifestyle. He maintained a number of knights, a large household of servants and spared little expense in what became a reckless lifestyle that even the wealth of Ely could not support. As for his role as bishop it would seem that he was unimpressive but adequate. As a criminal he was spectacular.

As bishop De Lisle soon embarked upon visitations; much like many diocese Ely held a number of priories, religious houses

---

[6] Aberth, Supra. p. 93

[7] For full list see Aberth, Supra. p. 15

and monasteries. It would seem that De Lisle irritated his clerics, secular and ordinary, from the outset as he pressed for taxes and accountability. In one instance the monks of Thorney opposed the intervention of the bishop in an alleged pornography scandal that involved the prior, cellarer and steward. De Lisle was forced to take the matter before the Court of Arches in London to obtain redress.[8] Further disputes followed at Thorney, Ickleton, Ramsey and his own Ely Cathedral Priory as De Lisle attempted to assert his authority across the diocese to the resentment of local clergy. External events were also contributory in De Lisle's downfall. The Black Death of 1348–50 devastated the economy of the diocese and his income dropped considerably as a result. In some areas the rental income was reduced by fifty per cent and corn sales reduced by two–thirds.[9] As the local population struggled to survive and the opportunity to bribe and corrupt local officials into withholding payments to the bishop increased, De Lisle found himself in need of an army of enforcers; he turned to his brother, John, and a band of loyal and trusted men who would act upon the orders of the bishop without question.

De Lisle's first major civil dispute started in August 1346 when brothers Richard and William Spynk complained that they had been the victims of sustained and violent physical intimidation orchestrated by De Lisle. The Spynk brothers were wealthy merchants who lived in Norwich, a city within

---

[8] Ibid. p. 27. The Court of Arches, originally held in the Church of St. Mary le Bow, London was the main consistory court of the Archbishop of Canterbury. Before the Reformation all appeals from this court lay to the pope. Under Henry VIII it was transferred to the King in Chancery. C.f. Blackstone, W. *Commentaries on The Laws of England in Four Books. Vol. III.* New York, Harper & Brothers, 1852. Chap. V. 'Of Courts Ecclesiastical, Military, and Maritime'. pp. 61–67

[9] E.g. Wisbech. Aberth, Supra. p.43

the diocese of Ely. They alleged that De Lisle's men had stolen sheep, cattle and other goods from them to the value of several hundreds of pounds. When they complained the bishop's men responded with physical violence and threats to the effect that the Spynks would be murdered. The brothers specifically reported that on one occasion John De Lisle and the bishop's nephew, William Michael, along with others ambushed the Spynks for many days such that for 'fear of death, mutilations of their members and capture and incarceration of their bodies they fled thence, wholly abandoning their dwelling places, and have not dared return'.[10] According to Richard Spynk he became a virtual prisoner having to remain within the safety of the walls of the city of Norwich. The dispute eventually reached the attention of the king who on August 29, 1347 ordered a review of the case.[11] The litigants appeared before the king's council in 1348.

The basis for the dispute was the status of the Spynk brothers. De Lisle viewed them as serfs and his villeins. The Spynks, on the basis of charitable works and donations to the city of Norwich, were granted the freedom of the city of Norwich and accordingly considered themselves freemen exempt from all taxes and civic duties. The king's court ruled in De Lisle's favor, in part due to the poor quality of representation the Spynks received from their lawyers.[12] For some reason De Lisle did not seize upon the opportunity to submit the suit

---

[10] PRO. C 66/217 mm. Id–4d. CPR, 1345–1348. 186–188 cited in Aberth, Supra. p. 99

[11] Only a few months previously the dire financial straits of De Lisle had become public when on 11 May the bishop wrote to his king to explain that he could not loan the monarch wool as the prelates own debts were such that he was 'exhausted of money'. Cambridge University Library, Ely Diocesan Records. G/I/I, Reg. De Lisle, fol. 72v. cited in Aberth, Supra. p. 114. N. 81

[12] Aberth, Supra. p. 107

to arbitration and in doing so bring closure to the matter; he waited until 1353 and when he did it was De Lisle who agreed to give up all claims and actions against Richard and William Spynk. The authority on De Lisle, John Aberth, is of the view that the reason De Lisle did not capitalize on the arbitration hearing is because his attack on the Spynk brothers was a 'case of barely lawful extortion rather than law abiding indignation'.[13] De Lisle did require Richard Spynk to pay monetary compensation though in the form of a manumission, a release from servitude,[14] which to some extent would confirm that De Lisle's ultimate motivation for pursuing the Spynks over seven years was financial, not manorial justice or legal redress. Furthermore, by 1352 De Lisle had many other issues of gravitas to occupy his concerns, not least was that his own bailiff, Henry de Burton, had been summoned before the justices for armed robbery, theft and criminal damage. At trial de Burton stated he was the bishop's villein and acting on his lord bishop's orders.[15] De Burton was again indicted in 1354 when despite royal orders to the contrary he failed to release Richard Bythwall from custody. Blythwall was being held, illegally, in bishop De Lisle's prison. It was also in 1354 that the most egregious of De Lisle's crimes took place; arson that resulted in murder.

Blanche of Lancaster, Lady Wake, was the wealthy widow of Thomas, second Baron Wake of Liddell. She was also a cousin of Edward III.[16] The dispute between Wake and De Lisle started at Colne, Huntingdonshire in July 1354 when a

---

[13] Aberth, Supra. p. 112

[14] British Library. Add. Ms. 41612, fol. 114r. Cited in Aberth, Supra. p. 113

[15] Ibid. p. 112

[16] A blood-tie that was impossible for De Lisle or the king to avoid

number of De Lisle's men (including his brother) burned down four houses, a sack of sedge and a horse that was trapped by the fire. The value of the property was set at £200. All the goods destroyed belonged to Lady Wake.[17] Within two months the arson was brought before the Court of Common Pleas. The defendants were; John De Lisle, chief steward of the bishop's estate, William de Pecham, friar and vicars-general, Robert de Godington, parson, Thomas Durant, parson, Henry de Shankton, parson, the bishop's auditor; Stephen de Brokesbourn, Robert Hale, De Lisle's baliff of Somersham, Thomas de Baa, De Lisle's constable of Wisbech Castle, John Balhorn of Colne and Ralph Carles. It was never suggested that De Lisle was himself present at the attack but he was charged with having ordered and consented to the arson and harboring the felons (at his Somersham manor) after the attack. At the center of the dispute was Lady Wake's valet, William Holm. The main antagonist from De Lisle's camp was the bishop's chamberlain, Ralph Carles. The servants were in dispute over lands that De Lisle had given to Carles in Colne. Holm was strongly of the view that the lands were owned by Lady Wake and therefore his. The servant's patrons, Wake and De Lisle, were therefore drawn into the dispute as original ownership was contested.

In October 1354 at Huntingdon, De Lisle and his men were indicted for the arson. The bishop's men were bailed to appear again before Chief Justice Shareshull on May 15, 1355. Bishop De Lisle was dealt with separately. On 19th November 1354 De Lisle was named as principal instigator of the arson. The

---

[17] It was customary practice that lords often became involved in disputes between disagreeing servants, Wake and De Lisle were unavoidably drawn into this disagreement. Aberth, Supra. p. 124

jury at Yaxley (Huntingdonshire) initially found De Lisle an accessory to the arson. The presiding justices ordered the jury to retire and reconsider. They duly returned with the 'correct verdict' guilty as principal. De Lisle was ordered to pay Lady Wake £900 compensation; equivalent to half De Lisle's yearly income from Ely. What followed were a series of attempts by De Lisle to have his conviction (and massive fine) overturned. In each instance the original conviction and compensation amount was upheld. At some point De Lisle decided to appeal personally to Edward III. At Common Law peers were permitted personal appeal before the king, a practice that Edward III (in the spirit of chivalry and knightly loyalty)[18] embraced. It was an ill-thought out move by De Lisle as the king would be forced to take the side of his cousin. Reluctantly De Lisle agreed to pay the £900.

In May 1355 the arson defendants returned to court and were again bailed pending future hearings. In August 1355 Ralph Carles murdered William Holm. He then failed to appear with his co-accused at the following arson hearing presumably because he was now a murder suspect and unlikely to be bailed. Carles was outlawed.[19] The murder took place in Gunnokjlyle, Somersham when Holm was attacked by Carles and an accomplice, Walter Ripton of Little Whyke. It was alleged that Carles took the life of Holm as revenge for the arson suit against De Lisle.[20] Whether this is true and it was a

---

[18] Edward was notorious for his love of the concept of chivalry. He was responsible for the establishment of The Most Noble Order of the Garter. www.britannica.com/topic/The-Most-Noble-Order-Of-The-Garter

[19] PRO, KB 27/382, rex. M. 17 cited in Aberth, Supra. p. 126. N. 50. When the others were finally apprehended they were refused bail and remained in custody until after De Lisle's death in Avignon 1361

[20] Aberth, Supra. p. 131

contract killing ordered by the bishop or it was a continuation of the local dispute between Carles and Holm is not known. De Lisle denied any involvement in the murder. The coroner's inquest named Carles and Ripton as principal felons and De Lisle of consent to murder. De Lisle was also accused of receiving Carles and Ripton to his manor at Somersham after the crime (the second time in which De Lisle had been indicted for harboring felons). De Lisle soon realized that he would be lucky to avoid being implicated in the Holm's murder and he instructed his administrators to commence the sale of all livestock and moveable goods. The bishop then placed the sale proceeds into safe keeping (suggesting that he knew at some point cash and mobility would become necessary). Edward III had been kept abreast of the De Lisle developments and was also probably aware of the likelihood De Lisle would abscond the realm.

On November 23, 1355 Edward issued a writ summoning De Lisle to appear before parliament. De Lisle was warned that failing to attend would result in the seizure of his temporalities.[21] De Lisle appeared before his king in response to a long list of grievances alleged by Lady Wake; arson, murder, terrorizing Lady Wake and her servants and breach of the king's peace. Blanche Wake asked that the king personally intervene and bring closure to the matter. Technically Edward III should not have taken part, the *Ordinance for the Justices*, 1346[22] specifically forbade the monarch from involvement in personal quarrels. Edward was not moved to follow this law and dramatically informed De Lisle 'I take the quarrel into my

---

[21] An option under the Statute of *Praemunire* 1353

[22] 20 Edw. 3. C.4. (1346) in which I Edw. 3. S.2. c.14 and 4. Edw. 3. C.11 (1330) are referenced. Also cited in Aberth, supra. p. 134. N. 83. SR 1:304

own hand'.[23] Edward was clearly much angered by De Lisle and at one point called him a liar in front of parliament.[24] The archbishop of Canterbury, Simon Islip (1349–1366) attempted to placate Edward. He and other bishops knelt before the king and pleaded for mercy on behalf of De Lisle. To the amazement of the assembled audience De Lisle remained defiant and neither bowed nor knelt before his king. De Lisle then withdrew from the court. He never saw his king again. Edward III proceeded to attempt the seizure of De Lisle's temporalities, despite the illegality of the action.[25]

Pursuant to the Holm's murder charges Carles, Ripton and De Lisle were summoned to appear in Huntingdonshire on July 8, 1356. De Lisle appeared. Carles and Ripton did not. De Lisle requested he be permitted trial before his peers, the knights of the realm. The court refused this request and he then submitted a plea of benefit of clergy. De Lisle was then convicted of receiving the murderers Carles and Ripton and was handed to the ordinary. King Edward was now within the law to seize the bishop's temporalities which he attempted to do immediately. De Lisle had alternative plans; having pled his clergy he now requested a date for his purgation hearing from archbishop Islip. If De Lisle successfully purged himself then he would, by right, demand the king restore his goods and chattels and De Lisle would return to his former position at Ely. Islip was acutely aware of the implications of De Lisle purging himself

---

[23] *Rotuli Parliamentorum*, 6 Vols. London, 1810–1822. 2: 267. Cited in Aberth, Supra. p. 134. n. 84 and his Appendix B, p. 245

[24] Aberth. Supra. p. 134

[25] To take possession of De lisle's temporalities it was necessary that he had been convicted. De Lisle had not accepted the accusations before the king and the dispute between them was not resolved. Aberth. Supra. p. 137

and pleaded with the prelate to seek a royal pardon. 'My most beloved brother, lord bishop, take my advice, I beg you...'.[26] De Lisle refused. Archbishop Islip then reluctantly agreed to the purgation but reminded De Lisle that ultimately the matter could only be ended with the king's consent. De Lisle rejected his archbishop's interpretation and left England to appeal the pope. The remaining five years of De Lisle's life were spent in Avignon seeking audience with the pope.[27]

Thomas De Lisle was bishop for eleven years. He was known to be criminally active for at least seven of those years and most probably throughout his entire bishopric. In total sixteen indictments were recorded against De Lisle and his men, the first in 1349 the last in 1356. There is no evidence of De Lisle himself actively participating in all the arsons, murders and thefts. He was indicted for arson in 1354. He was most definitely an organizer, receiver and the provider of a safe haven to which his gang of criminals could find housing and immunity. In 1356 a group of forty of De Lisle's men murdered the servant of John de Grey, in the same year Robert at Berne sued De Lisle and three of his men for stealing from him and in the same term Adam of Honyter was assaulted and wounded by Thomas Bacon, another of De Lisle's gang members.[28] In 1357 another of De Lisle's men, Thomas Wyliot, was indicted for a murder committed in 1354 at Shipdham, Norfolk.

---

[26] Aberth, Supra. p. 142

[27] In 1357 justice Sir Willaim Shareshull (1289–1370) and others were indicted to appear before the papal court at Avignon in the pending hearing relating to bishop Thomas De Lisle. Shareshull ignored the citation and he was excommunicated. The papal hearing never took place. *Oxford Dictionary of National Biography*. www.odnb2.pubfactory.com/view/article/25204

[28] Aberth, Supra. p. 155

To apply the term gang leader to De Lisle is not an exaggeration. De Lisle knew the company he kept, they were thieves, robbers and murderers; his brother, his nephews (William and Richard Michel) and a group of men who he supported throughout his time at Ely (even when those men were indicted and convicted of serious felonies). With few exceptions all his criminal associates were clerics, many with previous convictions; Richard de Middleton, had already killed a man in a deadly brawl when he came into the bishop's service, John Botner had already been absolved by De Lisle for assault on another cleric, and John Poucher had allegedly served a prison term.[29] 'Guilty by association' is a value- laden term with severe negative connotations, but it is hard not to apply this label to De Lisle. This bishop of Ely surrounded himself with gang of criminals who throughout his tenure caused havoc across the diocese. He was personally indicted for arson, extortion, complicity to murder, kidnapping and harboring escaping felons. Also, by association, De Lisle was responsible for arsons, murder, extortion, kidnapping, theft, robbery and fraud. It is no surprise that he was loyal to his own gang members. He kept them in his ecclesiastical employment; on his farms, manors and estates. He paid much of their expenses when they were summoned to court and he defended their names despite felony convictions before the courts temporal.

Because De Lisle wore the bishop's mitre he was able to navigate his way through the loopholes that existed between Common and canon law. He was able to exploit benefit of clergy for himself and his criminal followers so that cases were delayed, goods and chattels were never seized, disputes were

---

[29] Aberth, Supra. p. 157

elongated (and appealed to the pope in Avignon), and he was able to manipulate the exceptional jurisdictional immunities enjoyed by the bishop of Ely so that matters remained within his purview to his own and his gangs advantage.[30] Thomas De Lisle was an organized criminal. He was a mafia bishop who exploited his position to achieve criminal gain. Whether Thomas De Lisle was criminal before he took possession of the Ely temporalities is not known. He was certainly in financial straits very soon after his appointment and a criminal career seemed to come easily to him. Bishop De Lisle was reckless, extravagant, pompous and deeply foolish. His criminality as a bishop vitiated all clergymen and provided further ammunition for those seeking to eradicate the protections that surrounded England's clerics.

The case of Thomas De Lisle is exceptional. It is included because it is such an important example of the heights to which abuse of clericus was attempted. Previous examples of the activities of the Folvilles and Cotterels are an exception too. These groups were a medieval mafia. But even these groups were not headed by a prelate. Thomas De Lisle differs even from these rabble. Whether De Lisle would have eventually been pardoned and returned to favor we shall never know. What his case does show is that if pushed enough even the monarch could be biased and arbitrary, especially when demonstrating protections to a female relative. It also makes clear that De Lisle had every intention of manipulating all the available laws and seek purgation for a crime he was convicted of before his king. De Lisle's archbishop, Simon Islip, was apparently sensitive to the questionable validity of Benefit

[30] For examples see Aberth, Supra. p. 205

of Clergy and he attempted (in vain) to get De Lisle to seek a royal pardon rather than force his fellow prelates to find a bishop purged of a crime that had been prosecuted personally by the monarch. The extraordinary career of bishop De Lisle ended as inconsequentially as his life before elevation to Ely. He died in exile. Comments on his life are few and church records of De Lisle are (unsurprisingly) meagre.

By the end of Edward III's reign the era of the dissident cleric answering exclusively to a higher authority was over, even for a bishop. Thomas De Lisle, ended life as a political refugee without a diocese or benefices and (most importantly of all) without the ear of his pontiff. The distinction between a clerk and a layman had eroded so far that by the end of the third quarter of the century a differentiation was to all purposes unidentifiable. Clerics, pseudo-clerics, artisans, serfs and merchants would all be permitted to apply the reading test and avoid the full might of many sanguinary laws. Henceforth the issue was not abuse of the privilege by the clergy it was abuse of the privilege by all criminal defendants.

The final example used in this chapter is also unusual. It is relevant because it demonstrates the dilemma that the Church had constructed for itself over the issue of criminally errant clerics; if a cleric was bent upon total disregard for ecclesiastic rules, regular or secular, then it was possible to move around the world spiritual with relative freedom and capitalize on the variety of options available when needed. In the case of Peter Dene, this meant freedom and wealth as a secular pluralist and absolute protection from harm by the monastic world when in flight. It is unlikely that Thomas De Lisle was conversant with the exploits of Peter Dene as Dene was an active criminal during the 1320s and 1330s. He would have provided the bishop with an interesting case study though.

Dene started his career as a secular priest of the diocese of Chichester. He was also a doctor of canon and civil laws.[31] For many years he maintained a relationship with the Benedictines at St. Augustine's Abbey, Canterbury; he held an annual retainer to represent their interests in legal matters (A relationship he would later exploit). At some point in his life Dene swore an oath of faithfulness to the prior of Canterbury Cathedral Priory. Dene was a pluralist, he held canonries at York, Wells, London, Southwell and Wimbourne. In addition to his fruitful and complex ecclesiastic life Dene (much like many of his religious contemporaries) took an active role in politics. To his cost Dene sided with Thomas, Earl of Lancaster, in the failed attempt to overthrow King Edward II. Lancaster was defeated at Boroughbridge on 16th March 1322 and executed at Pontefract one week later. Dene, conscious of his exposure and risk of arrest for complicity and treason, took flight and found sanctuary with his friends the Benedictines at St. Augustine's Abbey. In a surprisingly accommodating turn of events Dene was not required to spend twelve months on probation nor was there a formal profession.[32] His habit was blessed just one week after he entered the abbey. Dr. Peter Dene, priest and

[31] For a detailed discussion of the life of Peter Dene; Logan, F.D., *Runaway Religious in Medieval England, c. 1240–1540*, Cambridge, Cambridge University Press, 2002. 'The Case of the Questionable Monk of Canterbury' pp. 34–41

[32] Professing vows of obedience, poverty and chastity, either explicitly or implicitly bound a person to the religious life with no real chance of dispensation. Any friar, monk or nun abandoning the religious life was declared apostate, *apostasia a religion*, and subject to excommunication and capture (in much the same way as felonious laity were declared outlaws). See Logan, Supra. Chap I. 'A Question of Terms', pp. 9–41

lawyer was now also Brother Dene. This strange scenario took a number of further twists and turns as it soon became clear that Dene had no intention of living a life of poverty and abstinence. And he had no intention of handing over his considerable wealth to the abbey. What Dene had achieved was a safe (and luxurious) haven for himself for the period of time he viewed as necessary before he could rejoin civilian society. In December 1331, eight years after fleeing from the temporal world, Dene scaled the walls of St. Augustine's, donned civilian clothing and headed for the nearby village of Bishopsbourne. When he escaped he took with him silver that he had given to the abbey (A crime of sacrilegious larceny, and not clergyable). His escape was soon discovered and the Prior notified the civilian authorities. A writ of apostate was issued.

At this point there was a turn of further events. Dene was first captured by a steward of the archbishop of Canterbury and was in his custody on route to a royal (not religious) jail. Along the way the custodial entourage was intercepted by monks from St. Augustine's who kidnapped Dene and took him back to the monastery. (The kidnapping of a cleric by other clerics was also a sacrilegious crime and would not have provided the brothers with the option of claiming their clergy either). Upon arrival at St. Augustine's Dene was presented to the Benedictine community. Recognizing he was likely to face immuration Dene immediately took the only course available to him; he proclaimed that he had had genuinely professed and was a monk. Not surprisingly within the year Dene rescinded this claim and appealed to Pope John XXII (1316–1334) to be declared priest but not monk.

The pope appointed three commissioners to establish whether or not Dene had professed. If he had he would remain with the monks, if not he would be released. Despite physical and verbal objections to the commission (the monks barred entrance doors into the abbey and formed a cordon around Dene when the papal delegation attempted to speak with him) it appears that Dene, as usual, attempted to play the regular and secular religious world against each other. He would make one claim aloud for his brothers to hear and another (as a whisper) to the papal commissioners.[33] Quite why Dene decided that ultimately he would publically proclaim that he had professed (thus ensuring he would spend the rest of his life at St. Augustine's) is not known. However, the papal commission, having completed its charge, accepted he had become a monk in full and left Dene to spend the remainder of his life with the brothers.

Peter Dene lived a complex life. He acquired considerable wealth which he was loathed to relinquish. He chose the wrong side politically and therefore needed to take advantage of his relationship with the monks of St. Augustine's to acquire a quick and suspect blessing of the habit. He then turned on his protectors and became apostate after stealing from those who had protected him. Over his lifetime Dene committed a range of ecclesiastic offenses and at least one secular felony. Unlike Thomas De Lisle he was never brought before justices temporal to answer for his crime. The monks of St. Augustine were never prosecuted for the sacrilegious felony of kidnapping of Dene from the archbishop of Canterbury's escort and the diocese of Chichester never

---

[33] Logan, Supra. pp. 40–41

sought to claim priest Dene at the time when he alleged he was being held against his will by the monks. Peter Dene was a consummate liar and much like bishop Thomas De Lisle he was the epitome of the criminal clergyman that the laity of England had learned to despise. Dene abused the priesthood and then habit to provide him with sanctuary until such a time as he thought it was safe to escape and rejoin the civilian world. In some respect it is unfortunate that Dene was kidnapped by his Order as had he been put before the courts temporal Dene would have placed himself into an untenable scenario. If he successfully claimed benefit of clergy he would be returned, as a convicted felon, to the Order that he had committed the crime against. The brothers would then have had to either allow his purgation, which as the victims of the crime they would have known was a lie, or failed him his purgation and then sentenced him to solitary confinement for life. Either way the Church faced an untenable legal dilemma; denial of benefit of clergy to a legitimate claimant or the satisfactory purgation of sacrilegious crimes before his religious victims.

Dene was not in the same criminal league as De Lisle but he does represent an example of the complex relationship that existed between canon laws regular and secular and how both interacted with the laws temporal. Dene usurped all of the laws of England at the time. He was a pluralist, a sacrilegious thief and an apostate. He never claimed his benefit of clergy because the theft he committed was dealt with by the religious order he stole from, but this was after he had been kidnapped by his Brothers. Whether Dene would have relied upon the clerical privilege if he had been presented before a secular judge we shall never know. Given Dene's legal virtuosity it is likely he would have as this would have been his most advantageous option. He certainly provided lay society with convincing evidence of one clergyman's absolute contempt for any laws and the further erosion of the moral standards of (some of) England's clerics.

The medieval English Church had monopolized benefit of clergy through the separate legal system of canon law for two hundred years. The primary focus of the Church was spiritual welfare and the regulation (and prosecution) of lay Christians, churchmen and the institutions of the Church. Church courts had traditionally prosecuted sinners and provided a safe haven to criminals. In time this control gave way to royal justice so that before the end of the fourteenth century clear demarcations existed at canon and temporal law. Benefit of clergy was a conduit for these changes to occur.[34] Gabel (and the few other commentators) have not depicted clericus in this way. They viewed it as a farce, a legal fiction, a queer old anomaly or simply an evil.

In the final chapter I will challenge the established view of *privilegium fori* within the context of the clergy as integrated members of medieval society; as a body of men who would no longer obstruct the laicization of the clerics plea but instead accept it as a tool. A tool that could bring them closer to the parishioners they served in an effort to unite in the cause of social improvement. Ecclesiastic seclusion was no longer a viable option for *Ecclesia Anglicana* in the late Middle Ages. The secularization

[34] For a discussion of the impact of the common law upon canon law in matters civil, Milon, D., Medieval and Early Modern Law: The Birth of Modern Jurisprudence: Ecclesiastical Jurisdiction in Medieval England, *University of Illinois Law Review*. No. 7. (1984). pp. 621–639

of immunities was a significant step towards the integration of a contemporary church into English society.

The clergy plea can be viewed as a progression of secular legal development. It can also be seen as a diminution of the role (and gravitas) of canon law. It is also a vehicle through which the role of the (mostly) lower orders of the clergy can be observed as they transitioned from unquestionable spiritual authority to a partner in local society; working alongside the laity to achieve justice, equity and a quality of life, temporal and spiritual. Helping to make sense of the untidy and challenging business of life in the fourteenth century became a shared goal. Opening up benefit of clergy to all men was in part a response to this. The first three-quarters of the fourteenth century was a time of societal, political, administrative and religious change. The involvement of all of England's communities in authorizing these changes was paramount to future success. It was also a time when the chance for opportunistic criminals (of every hue) to achieve the same levels of protections previously afforded to the few became a reality. Then filling the lacuna secularization created would take another five hundred years.

Ultimately it is only possible to speculate upon why the English Church did not continue to defend clericus exclusivity more vigorously. But how that position has been portrayed so far in history can be revisited and adjusted according to our understanding of the events as new evidence, cases and interpretations are posited. So far the overwhelming majority of commentators have viewed benefit of clergy as an unjustifiable anachronism. In the final chapter I will argue that I am even more convinced that this this not the case.

# 10

# Immunity for All

Few years of the late Middle Ages are without graphic and offensive examples of clerics that manipulated the laws to profit from a $4^{th}$ century immunity initiated to provide the means for clerics to focus exclusively on matters spiritual. The assumption that the Christian Church would evolve into groups of men and women apart from society proved to be incorrect though as regular clergy gave way to secular. What transpired was the reduction of rules that applied to one class in exchange for laws that had wider application for society as a whole. Classes merged, new ones developed and the nation state evolved to subsume a range of penal measures contained previously within canon law. In some measure the English Church's desire to retain a position of social supremacy for its clergy had the reverse effect and led to the demise of its vicars in the eyes of parishioners. Internal struggles to retain sovereignty over the lives of the lower orders and class divisions between noble bishops and peasant priests (both of whom were periodically far short of exemplary behavior towards each other or parishioners) made it easy to view the Church as a system in conflict that no longer warranted being at the core of English life. Ecclesiastical justice was exposed as ineffective and nepotistic and the secular law stepped in to act on behalf of England's new literate laity. The English Church was ultimately impotent to prevent secularization and therefore it acquiesced. In doing so this had the effect of bringing the (secular) clergy closer to the lay population than it had ever been. Along the way the immunity benefit of clergy was held to be 'evil', a 'legal farce', or simply 'bad', dismissed by commentators as a 'curiosity'. Far from a mere curiosity the environment that stimulated the movement of clericus into mainstream secular law was complex, relevant and progressive. It may only represent one manifestation of the numerous changes taking place across society in the later Middle Ages but it is an important one and one that managed to traverse the Atlantic to Colonial America and the Caribbean as well as remain active under English statutes until the nineteenth century.

The pace of change in late medieval England was rapid. Transitioning from an ostensibly feudal system based on deference to a wealth economy with increased opportunity for upward social mobility created a dynamic, complex world. One in which opportunists would flourish and those who could not adapt faced even greater deprivation. In 1189 there were just twelve Earls throughout the realm. In the fourteenth century twenty-four new earldoms were created and the first dukedom.[1] The absorption of penal canon law into English law was equally swift. As this society grew in wealth, education and freedom so language would grow to include terms such as fashion and consumerism. One of the most obvious signs of social rank was clothing and England's bishops were renowned for their luxurious attire and extravagant lifestyles.

[1] Edward, The Black Prince was created Duke of Cornwall. Coss, P. 'An Age of Deference' in Horrox, R., & Ormrod, W.M.,(eds) *A Social History of England 1200–1500,* Cambridge, Cambridge University Press, 2006. p.40

Even the purportedly modest monastics were famous for feasting between periods of fasting. The monks at Westminster Abbey ate dinner every day and on a Saint's day extra meals and extra dishes were on the menu. The prohibition on eating flesh on a fast day was circumvented by re-defining fowl, pre-cooked and chopped meat so that it was consumable.[2]

Change was also apparent in a trend towards elevating more secular (rather than regular) prelates to joint religious and civilian appointments. The potential challenge this caused was to increase the possibility of decisions being made on the basis of preference rather than good law as secular prelates had a vested interest in retaining the favor of the crown in the lucrative joint roles they held whilst at the same time being seen to be treating their clergy with respect and support. Homicidal archdeacon Osbert of Richmond provides an interesting example as he committed sacrilegious murder (of his archbishop) and yet still managed to claim privilegium.[3] Sacrilegious homicide of another archbishop was the basis for the great drama of the twelfth century as England's former chancellor took holy orders one Saturday and the bishop's mitre a few days later. In response to one instance of clerical abuse we see archbishop Becket devising his own sentence. A cleric who had seduced a girl and then murdered the girl's father was degraded and then branded. The branding was administered as 'an appeasement to the king'. Failing purgation was nevertheless a very rare event; so rare that when bishop Jocelin failed an applicant he wrote to Becket for advice. Becket responded by ordering the cleric be kept in

---

[2] Kowaleski, M., 'A Consumer Economy' in Horrox, R., & Ormrod, W.M.,(eds) *A Social History of England 1200–1500*, Cambridge, Cambridge University Press, 2006. p. 246

[3] Chap. 3

solitary confinement for life; a sentence far harsher than the secular law may have imposed.[4] What these cases demonstrate are early examples of the process of the amelioration of laws and a softening of the English Church's absolute ownership of criminal clerics. On both sides the laws were viewed as malleable with bishops and monarchs applying local interpretation that reflected their own views of the limits of their power. Meanwhile the legal excuse itself was spiraling out of control with an increasing number of felons manipulating all available mitigatory pleas. For benefit of clergy this meant that as it moved slowly towards secular ownership Holy Orders would end up including the literate, blind men, bastards and medieval mafia.

The Common Law had developed into a basic structure by 1200 yet it managed to exclude much of the rural population from justice due to inaccessibility. Eyres, courts of Oyer and Terminer and Commissions of the Peace would follow but for now the lacuna was filled by parish priests. Clergymen who helped locals navigate through tenancy issues, ownership disagreements, and villeinage disputes with their local lords. Often poor and with few chances of upward mobility this partnership in destitution between priest and villager was necessary and advantageous to both. If the local priest assisted in hiding the spoils of crime or harboring a fleeing local felon they were not perceived as criminal, quite the reverse, they were serving the parish. But being the principal in crime was viewed as going too far. That was crime for personal gain not protection of the flock. Social order had been a local affair in medieval England, as this changed *Ecclesia*

[4] Chap. 3

*Anglicana* was forced to change also. Softening of its position on ecclesiastic privilege was one piece of this dialog. Making the clergy more accessible and approachable to its parishioners was another.

Not everyone gained from the prosperity of the fourteenth century. Not everyone flocked to the new industries that were growing in the towns and provinces. The growth in consumerism was not positively distributed across the country[5] and the village priest was still fully employed working more closely than ever with his impoverished parishioners. Little wonder he too strayed from the law periodically and he if shared the spoils with locals it could be legitimized as just another form of charity alongside charitable donations.[6] These were times of war, famine and violent crime. England experienced political upheaval, abdication and the murder of a king. The population expanded to overpopulation, 1.1 million in 1086 had swelled to 3.7 million in 1346. Crime followed hunger throughout towns and villages and discontent became violent protest. In 1326 the bishop of Exeter was dragged from St. Paul's cathedral, London and beheaded by an angry mob. His naked body was left to rot nearby in a shallow grave.[7] Despite the severity of the times the crown needed revenue to pay for wars and the burden of purveyance[8] combined with poor harvests hit the lower classes most acutely. Clerics and parishioners must no doubt have consoled each other with tales of hardship and woe during these

---

[5] Kowaleski, Op. cit. p. 257

[6] Ibid

[7] Walter Stapleton (1261–1326) The murder occurred 15th October 1326. www.britannia.com/bios/wstapledon.html

[8] Supplying victuals to the royal household. It was by now an established form of taxation

challenging years. They must also have provided practical support and when necessary collusion, at times criminal.

Laicization was not about to end the abuse of the clergy plea by clerics of every rank. In fact repeat offender clerks continued to be such a problem that bishops were told should they permit a recidivist cleric a second purgation then the prelate himself would be fined £100. Another attempt at similar legislation in 1455 held that a second conviction for recidivism was to be considered high treason and unclergyable.[9] The leniency towards recidivist criminal clerics shown by William Bothe, bishop of Coventry and Lichfield (1447–1452) cannot have helped pacify the public. During his brief tenure Bothe permitted Edward Leche (a laborer who pled his clergy through literacy) purgation twice. A further eight literate clerics purged themselves over the course of the next five years. Bishop Bothe also released nine men held awaiting purgation.[10] The court records for Leche and the others confirm that all of the nine were bogus clerics, they had specific recorded occupations and all proved their clergy by literacy.[11]

The adoption of a literacy test did not happen by chance. It was the culmination of slow but deliberate adoption by the civilian legal system for and on behalf of the law abiding laity in response to a steady stream of abuse by clergymen. The Church had attempted its own reforms many times over, on balance it failed. Bishops had attempted to reign-in errant

---

[9] 1449 and 1455 respectively. Bates, J.C., Edward Leche; a Recidivist Criminous Clerk, *Nottingham Medieval Studies*. Vol. 30. Issue 1. (1986) pp. 97–100

[10] Bates, Supra. p. 98

[11] Bates, Supra. p. 98

clerics; punishments increased, bishop's prisons were built, sanctuary and abjuration were (officially) denied to clerks. But in practice Church law was applied inequitably and with much local interpretation. There is no reason to think that the Church was not attempting genuine reforms throughout the period but the scale of the task defeated these efforts and the nature of the reform was of itself one that had to be driven by the laws temporal. Murder, kidnapping, corruption, bribery, the entire spectrum of felonious behavior that clergymen engaged in was too great a task for the Church to control. It was at times too great a task for civilian society to control also.[12]

To what level lawlessness increased significantly throughout the Middle Ages is an ongoing discussion. Our view of history is always susceptible to revision as new evidence is uncovered and fresh commentary stimulates further considered speculation. The crown was sufficiently concerned that it implemented specific legislation to deal with gangs of criminals operating across the realm. Court records confirm that much of this involved clerics; during the period 1241 to 1261 7.4 per cent of all accused killers were defined as clerics.[13] Priests, friars and monks were prosecuted as gang members and are known to have perpetrated criminal offences in groups with civilians or as gangs that comprised exclusively of clerics. The temporal law responded by starting to limit the classifications of 'clergyable' crimes and increase the range of offences deemed to be 'unclergyable'. Perhaps in response to this pressure there is evidence of an increase in forum shopping by

[12] Hence the establishment of the Northamptonshire Eyre

[13] Given, J.B., *Society and Homicide in Thirteenth-Century England*, Stanford, Stanford University Press, 1977. p.85

defendant clerics between the courts secular and spiritual (to ensure the best legal arena for disposition of their crimes). Clerics claiming sanctuary and abjuring the realm continued (largely unabated). Secular courts across the country passed sentences of outlawry and coroners heard sworn testimony of priests admitting guilt in exchange for secure passage to Dover and exile. The courts Christian rarely intervened as intermingling of the two laws progressed; to the blatant advantage of the criminal clerk. No doubt in some cases bishops were keen not to get involved as the spurious immunity claimant was known to all to be a bogus cleric. If the secular law was content to permit exile why should the bishop prevent this? If the courts secular were comfortable determining an outlawry why would a bishop want to upset this if he knew the alleged cleric was a hardened recidivist felon with no association to the Church? Clerics Walter le Norreys and Nicholas de Nodariis are such examples; one guilty of robbery and rape, the other guilty of theft and murder, neither of whom held a benefice. Both were declared outlaws and no bishop came forward to object.[14] Yet on other occasions some bishops seemed to go out of their way to step in and claim a cleric, even to the point of ordaining a priest after he had been indicted for murder.[15] Becket's concerns over double jeopardy were also ignored as time distanced itself further from the martyr. Clerics Ralph and William of Nettleham were accused of murder. One was degraded, the other brother degraded and then outlawed. There is no record of the Church stepping in and requesting an explanation for the different sentences or the outlawing of a cleric. In the same vein when six clerics were condemned to death for murder and rescued on route to the gallows by

[14] Chap. 4

[15] Chap. 4

other clerics and given safe haven in a church (from which they abjured the realm)[16] neither the secular nor spiritual laws articulated concerns over the confusing duality of legal abuses the case presented.

The fourteenth century also stimulated a revision of much theological thought with influences from the canonized Dominican friar, Thomas Aquinas (1323) and the living Franciscans; Duns Scotus, Peter Auriol and François de Meyronnes. Later in the century William of Ockham pushed the social aspects of religious thinking even further. Across Europe universities responded to new thinking with the creation of theology faculties that challenged traditional responses to questions of morality and the pastoral role of the clergy.[17] As universities turned their attention towards matters of theology the number of clerics attending institutions such as Oxford and Cambridge rose significantly. These newly educated lower orders then transmitted their knowledge through the pulpit to enlighten local villagers and townsfolk.[18] As this was happening changes also took place in the nature and form of worship. Local saints and domestic centers of devotion transplanted a number of traditional European pilgrimage sites[19] and physical acts of devotion fused with civic events culminating (in the fifteenth century) with the creation of full scale Passion Plays. Civic involvement was also apparent in the increasing number of hospitals being established by confraternities and lay guilds

---

[16] Chap. 4

[17] Catto, J., 'Currents of Religious Thought and Expression' in Jones, M., (ed) *The New Cambridge Medieval History Vol. VI, c. 1300–1415*, Cambridge, Cambridge University Press, 2000. pp. 42–65

[18] Evidence of the work of clerics to make sense of theology for the laity is clear in many of the extant sermons from this period. Catto, Supra.pp. 44–45

[19] E.g. St. James the Greater of Compostela

that were run in association with regular Orders. Informal religious associations flourished too in an environment of increasing tolerance towards alternative modes of religiosity. John Wycliff's 'Poor Preachers' appear to be such an association; formed from a corpus of university trained preachers the group expanded to include lay members from a number of social levels that met on a random basis and supported individual rather than traditional collective displays of worship.[20] From what has been described as the 'bewildering variety'[21] of religious ideas present in the fourteenth century it is understandable that the role of the theologian would fluctuate. This was a time of confusion and questioning one in which the very fallibility of religion was questioned and the need for plausible explanations for crises such as early century famine and mid-century Black Death were sought.

Throughout England a new class of 'freeman' was emerging as towns sought to recruit (entice) a population; freedom was given to any serf who served the community and lived within its walls for one year and a day.[22] Monasticism had changed also with fewer monks joining the traditional orders[23] and many that had joined turned apostate. Church

---

[20] Catto, J., 'The King's Government and the Fall of Pecock 1457–1458' in Archer, R.E., and Walker, S., (eds) *Rulers and Ruled in Late Medieval England: Essays Presented to Gerald Hariss*, London, Hambledon Press, 1995

[21] Catto (1995) Supra. p. 50

[22] Bishop, M. *The Middle Ages*, Boston, Mariner Books, 2001. pp.178–179

[23] Lepine, D., 'Church and Clergy' in Rigby S.H., (ed) *A Companion to Britain in the Middle Ages*, Chichester, Wiley-Blackwell, 2009 estimates there were in the order of 18,000 regular clergy in England circa 1320. Numbers for Benedictines peaked in the mid-twelfth century and for Cistercians and Augustinians early thirteenth. Numbers for friars peaked in the early fourteenth century. p. 369. Lepine's commentary is located within England. The period also saw the establishment of new orders connected to Modern Devotion, the Beguines. See; Blockmans W., and Hoppenbrouwers, P.C.M., *Introduction to Medieval Europe 300–1500, Second Edition*, London, Routledge, 2014. Chap. 12

donors, patrons and worshippers of every social hue started to invest more heavily in the secular church than regular. Private chapels, oratories[24] and elaborate crypts,[25] became fashionable manifestations of wealth and importance. This was in sharp contrast with the early Middle Ages when only a saint was permitted an elaborate decorated tomb.[26] The perpetual fear of Purgatory was also influential in supporting the expansion of secular chantries and obits, the better endowed resulted in permanent colleges of secular priests.[27] Religion had changed. In one respect it was less a private business and more a public affair that was shared between the spiritual expertise of the ordained clergy and an increasingly engaged laity with specific religious aspirations for themselves. In another respect it was more private as in the late Middle Ages religion became a more personal and individual manifestation. And the issue of the 'two nations'[28] of beneficed and unbeneficed clergy was unresolved.[29] A few fortunate rectors, vicars and chantry priests held a minor benefice. The vast majority was without sufficient income

---

[24] Lepine, D. 'England: Church and Clergy', in Rigby, S.H. (ed) *A Companion to Britain in the Later Middle Ages*, Chichester, Wiley-Blackwell, 2009. pp. 359–380. p. 361

[25] Such as Edward II's at Gloucester and Pope John XXII's at Avignon. Crossley, P. 'Architecture' in Jones, M., (ed) *The New Cambridge Medieval History Vol. VI, c. 1300–1415*, Cambridge, Cambridge University Press, 2000. p. 242

[26] Bishop, Supra. p. 279

[27] Lepine, Supra. p. 361. A chantry was a formal arrangement that paid a priest a stipend to celebrate mass (often daily) at a specific altar, normally one within an existing parish church. An obit was less expensive than a chantry as the mass was celebrated less frequently. Monasticism was still well supported though. By 1320 there were more than one thousand monastic houses in England after which the decline is more noticeable. On monasticism see: Lepine, Supra. pp. 363–368

[28] Lepine, Supra. p. 370

[29] William Langland is perhaps the most famous unbeneficed cleric of the fourteenth century. Langland, William (c.1325–c.1390) Kane, G., *Oxford Dictionary of National Biography*, Oxford University Press, 2004 http://www.oxforddnb.com/view/article/1602

or held no benefice at all. The temptation to commit crime simply to make ends meet must have been great.[30] To many laymen the Church appeared unable address its own internal disorder. Regular and secular clergy were visible rivals. Dissention was not uncommon. Medieval life had become increasingly ambiguous and the high point of influence the Church held in the lives of the faithful was declining. What ensued was the 'Great Schism' (1378–1417), the prolonged papal habitation of Avignon by one pope and the concurrent habitation of Rome by a second.[31]

The language of the fourteenth century Church was also expressed in the physical manifestation of its architecture. It had been the case that the most impressive buildings across Europe were its cathedrals. This too would undergo revision as civic buildings, castle-palaces and fortresses assumed an important role in articulating power and authority. Even in those instances where new buildings were religious the growth in personal chapels made them a venue for making visible statements about temporal authority.[32] Fortified-palaces such as Windsor (1348) 'the Versailles of its age'[33] and Edinburgh (1356), were dramatic statements about power, wealth and authority that were soon followed across

---

[30] 'The success of the late medieval Church in broadly satisfying the needs of the laity owes a good deal to them; they bore the brunt of pastoral work in the parishes' Kane. Supra. p. 372

[31] Blockmans, W., & Hoppenbrouwers, P., Introduction to Medieval Europe, 300–1500 (2nd edition), London, Routledge, 2014. Chap. 12. 'Crises in the Church and the Reorientation of the Faithful'

[32] St. Stephen's Chapel, Westminster is an example. Crossley, P. 'Architecture' in Jones, M., (ed) *The New Cambridge Medieval History Vol. VI, c. 1300–1415*, Cambridge, Cambridge University Press, 2000. pp. 234–256

[33] Ormrod, W.M., *Edward III*, New Haven, Yale University Press, 2011. p.274

Europe. Windsor cost £51,000 and was the most expensive building ever constructed.[34] Edward III's Queenborough castle (1361–5) was considered the most futuristic building of its kind.[35] In many respects these castle-palaces were now taking the place of traditional (Church) representations of authority.

The vulgarity of brandishing personal wealth had arrived. New domestic architecture, personal fashion, the purchase of art for pleasure; there was even growing interest in establishing art markets for the sale of investment artworks. The design and building of new towns and cities also reflected the growing status of artisans and merchant classes (bourgeois) who were in a position to display their new wealth through the commission of civic and personal construction. Extravagance and pretentious architecture was no longer the exclusive preserve of the Church. Guildhalls and municipal buildings competed with chapels and palaces for recognition[36] as the 'commercial revolution' and urbanization gathered momentum.[37] In England it was new building work commissioned by the crown that stimulated the development of the English 'Decorated style' 1290–1350. This was followed by creation of unique 'Fan Vaulting' and the 'Perpendicular style' introduced through Edward III's

---

[34] Ibid. p. 235

[35] Ibid. p. 238 and http://www.gatehouse-gazetteer.info/English%20sites/1646.html Edward financed his monarchy through a number of questionable methods including borrowing 1,400,000 pounds from the Florentine Bardi and Peruzzi houses. He then defaulted and claimed himself bankrupt. Bishop. Supra. p. 198

[36] For example, the town halls in Bruges completed in 1377–1387 and the later Cloth Halls 1482–86. Coventry Guildhall 1394. Crossley, Supra

[37] Cantoni, D., & Yuchtman, N, Legal Institutions, Medieval Universities, and the Commercial Revolution. *NBER Working Paper, No. 17979* (Apr. 20102) www.nber.org/paper/w17979

remodeling of Gloucester cathedral (1331–1367).[38] Religious works commissioned by monarchs also made important statements about ownership of the Church.[39]

Occurring alongside these events was the growth of a literate population and adoption of the English language. Society now possessed the tools to criticize[40] through the printed word. Literary guilds were formed and booksellers employed lay copyists. The image of a solitary monk working on a handwritten volume illuminating pages for years was descending into obscurity. Writers were no longer anonymous clerics and authors claimed ownership of their work. Widening literacy produced a more cultivated, conscious and critical population. Gradually preaching was conducted in English, first by the monastics and then the secular orders. As the behavior of clerics came under greater scrutiny satire entered the language. Monks and priests were ridiculed for their irreligious participation in the Feast of Fools and Maundy Thursday parades that mocked established ceremonies. Contempt for the Church resulted in the ransacking of churches, abbeys and chapels.[41]

---

[38] Crossley, P. 'Architecture' in Jones, M., (ed) *The New Cambridge Medieval History Vol. VI, c. 1300–1415*, Cambridge, Cambridge University Press, 2000

[39] Also (increasingly) manifest in *ecclesia propria, Eigenkirche*, the system of building churches, abbeys and cloisters on private land owned by feudal lords which at English law under the provisions of advowson created a method for the lord to nominate the clerical personnel of the clerical premises. For further commentary, Wood, S., *The Proprietary Church in the Medieval West*, Oxford, Oxford University Press, 2006. Part IV, Ideas, Opinions, Change

[40] Matthews, W., 'Inherited Impediments in Medieval Literary History' and Nichols, S. G., 'Ethical Criticism and Medieval Literature' in Matthews, W., (ed) *Medieval Secular Literature*, Los Angeles, Center for Medieval and Renaissance Studies, 1967. Havely, N., 'Literature in Italian, French and English: Uses and Muses of the Vernacular' in Jones, M., (ed) *The New Cambridge Medieval History Vol. VI, c. 1300–1415*, Cambridge, Cambridge University Press, 2000. pp. 257–270 Clanchy, M.T., *From Memory to Written Record England 1066-1307*, (3rd Edition) Chichester, West sussex, Wiley-Blackwell, 2013

[41] Bishop, M., *The Middle Ages*, Boston, Martiner, 2001. pp. 174–175

Sacred chalices and vestments were stolen and religious gowns and artifacts were made into everyday wear and household goods.[42] Inevitably papal omnipotence was brought into question and found to be hollow; the Church could never return to the stature it once held. Any justification for special treatment there might have been in previous times was over.

But *privilegium fori* should not be dismissed as a relic of Emperor Constantine or simply 'bad'.[43] Clericus had always been organic; it had shifted and grown to finally retract as the moods, swings and needs of society changed across the time it lived. Clear lines of legal demarcation were not applicable to clericus since its formation. The privilege much like the associated provisions for sanctuary and abjuration never protected the clergy exclusively. What benefit of clergy did achieve was a means of protection from the secular law for all felons and in particular those in that lived on the margins; the margins of poverty, famine, abuse, survival. Not that clergy was always impartial as it certainly was. The privilege was never available (in principle) to bastards or blind men, and sacrilegious crimes were not clergyable either (this too was not rigidly applied). Women were excluded the privilege until the seventeenth century. This would appear to have always included nuns as there is no evidence of a nun having ever claimed her clergy during the late Middle Ages. Bigamists were excluded from the plea (at canon and secular law) and clerics committing forgery of papal documents were excommunicated and then handed to the secular authorities.

---

[42] Ibid. p. 175

[43] Gabel. L. *Benefit of Clergy in England in the Later Middle Ages*, New York, Octagon Press, 1969 (reprinted). p. 126

Defeating the objectives of English criminal law was never only achieved through benefit of clergy. Sanctuary and self-chosen exile were well established practices long before the hiatus of *clericus*. Attention has been given to each excuse individually but there is little commentary on them collectively despite the volume of evidence that criminal clergymen pleaded all. Prior to 1261 the bishop's court was authorized to impose outlawry and abjuration. The nexus was formal in London throughout the thirteenth century where proclamation of outlawry was made inside St. Paul's cathedral.[44] Regardless of what England's bishops may have wanted outlawry was a sentence and it was imposed on the clergy after degradation, double jeopardy or not. Under Edward II's *Articuli Cleri*, clerical abjuration was given statutory legitimacy. The Church did not express objection to this measure even though it offended canon law.[45]

Defiantly ignoring the law was practiced by all ranks of clergy; Abbots and bishops snubbed the law as well as the lower orders when it suited their purposes. At times prelates actively encouraged abuse. In extreme cases even the prohibition against sanctuary and benefit of clergy for sacrilegious murder were totally disregarded. The abbot of Bordesley dressed Nicholas the Bigot in a habit and secured his escape from a church; the same church at which Nicholas had taken sanctuary after committing a murder in the grounds. Incredibly after being granted perpetual sanctuary by abbot Bordesley Nicholas was later permitted to stand trial, claim his clergy

---

[44] Chap. 7

[45] In part this may be due to the fact that Edward still treated the clergy as a special case; laymen who returned from exile without having secured a pardon 'bore the wolves head' and were subject to summary beheading, the clergy were not eligible for such brutal treatment

and then purge himself to walk free again in secular society. Henry the Summoner was equally offensive in his abuse of all laws. He murdered a man in front of a number of witnesses and then fled the scene and was declared an outlaw. Summoner later presented himself to the justices at Eyre and pled his clergy. He was found guilty of murder and then having been released to his lord bishop purged himself (despite the number of eye witnesses to the homicide). Adding insult to injury the bishop then promptly demanded that the goods of chattels of cleric Summoner be hastily returned to him as he was an 'innocent man'.[46]

Abuse of sanctuary was perpetrated by monks, secular clerics, bishops and the crown. In the significant struggle for control over England in the absence of king Richard (1189–1199) Geoffrey, archbishop of York (1189–1212) was forcibly removed from asylum within St. Martin's Church, Dover, by bishop William Longchamp.[47] Fugitive William de Lay was dragged away from the churchyard of St. Philip and St. James' and beheaded by a priest and some locals. The bishop ordered the offenders to exhume the deceased and then be flogged by priests (presumably not to the point of drawing blood as this would offend the papal ban on clerical participation in sanguinary punishment). An interesting case because the bishop saw fit to apply a secular punishment on a cleric. This was technically possible due to their duality of roles as justices spiritual

---

[46] Chap. 4

[47] Geoffrey was the illegitimate son of Henry II and Richard's half-brother. Richard probably feared that in his absence Geoffrey would attempt to seize the crown and he appointed Longchamp, bishop of Ely, 1190–1197, and Lord Chancellor as his regent (Chief Justiciar) whilst overseas. Palgrave, K.H., *The Collected Works of Sir Francis Palgrave, K.H. Reviews, Essays and Other Writings in Two Volumes. Vol. 1.* Cambridge, Cambridge University Press, 1922. Esp. pp. 30–34

and secular at the same time.[48] (Presumably on this occasion the bishop wore a wig not mitre).[49] The students of Oxford University supply plenty of examples of their complicity in prison escapes followed by sanctuary or outlaw status too. Student Simon de Wanetynge was taken by his fellow clerics on route to the scaffold. Contrary to common law he was then provided with sanctuary and the coroner accepted his oath.[50] This case is not exceptional as Oxford students developed a penchant for fighting, drunkenness, murder and prison breaking throughout the thirteenth and fourteenth centuries. Until formalized many medieval judges appeared reticent in dealing with the dilemma created by clergymen claiming asylum and exile.[51] There are a few isolated cases of bishops stepping in.

Sacrilegious sanctuarial crimes were also treated with an array of confusing double standards. Murderer Isabel Bury was ordered to be forcibly removed from her church asylum by the bishop. She was executed for her crime. When a

---

[48] Prior to 1836 the Bishop of Durham was also a prince-bishop and held the title Earl Palatine. For a discussion of the history of clerical judges sitting in secular courts Raffield, P. *Images and Cultures of Law in Early Modern England: Justice and Political Power 1558–1660*, Cambridge, Cambridge University Press, 2004. Chap. 1, Dodd, G., Reason, Conscience and Equity: Bishops as the King's Judges in Later Medieval England, *History*. Vol.99. Issue 335 (Apr. 2014) pp. 213–240, Turner R.V. *Judges, Administrators and the Common Law in Angevin England*, London, Hambledon Press, 1994, 'Clerical Judges in English Secular Courts; The Ideal versus the Reality'. pp. 159–180

[49] One of the most respected judge/clerics of the thirteenth century was Martin de Pattishull (Wiiliam of Pattishall) (died 1229) who served as archdeacon, dean of St. Paul's, London, justice of the Tower of London, justice of Westminster, itinerant justice for Yorkshire and Northumberland and eventually as Chief Justice of the Common Pleas from 1217 until his death in 1229, Hunt, W., *Dictionary of National Biography 1885–1900*, Vol. 44. https://en.wikisource.org/wiki/Dictionary_of_National_Biography,_1885-1900/Vol_44_Paston_-_Percy A list of bishop judges is provided by Turner, supra. pp. 150–156

[50] Chap. 6

[51] Chap. 6

sanctuarian was forcibly removed bishops often employed the services of clergymen and civilians to evict the felon. In one instance the archbishop of Canterbury took personal involvement in obtaining the king's pardon of a gang of criminal clerics (mostly canons). The canons had rescued two of their former gang members whilst they were on route to the gallows. All then took sanctuary inside Lincoln cathedral.[52] On occasions it was not crown agents that abrogated sanctuary and forced out a fleeing felon but the reverse, the monarch enforced sanctuary. Cleric William de Chesterton was in perpetual sanctuary at Westminster abbey as a result of a dispute with the bishop of Ely. The bishop sought the assistance of parliament to evict Chesterton from asylum. Richard II stepped in and proclaimed that the sanctity of Westminster could not be violated, even by a prelate.[53]

Locations for sanctuary varied greatly as well. Some were perpetual, some curtilage specific, some itinerant that travelled with the king or a bishop and some joint secular and spiritual, the 'bastard sanctuaries'. Viewed by some as an 'irrational gift'[54] from the state sanctuary has been subject to much singular commentary but little as part of a broader brush of discussions about the suite of clerical immunities available in England. Sanctuary was a custom of the secular law. Its origin lay with the Church. Much like clericus, abjuration and outlawry, sanctuary existed conterminously at the intersection of the laws sacred and temporal, not at their disjuncture.

[52] Chap. 6

[53] Chap. 6

[54] Hyams, P.R. *Rancor and Reconciliation in Medieval England,* Ithaca, N.Y., Cornell University Press, 2003, Chap. 3. pp. 71–110. p. 95

When a clerk purged himself it was legal proof that he was innocent of the crime, regardless of whether or not that clerk had been convicted before the courts temporal. If the same clerk was to swear his guilt before the coroner it too was proof of guilt and he abjured. We know this commonly occurred. The third option was outlawry; for a number of clerics this was a deliberate decision because they neither wanted to run the risk of a spiritual sentence of perpetual solitary confinement[55] or be accosted on route to the port of departure by aggrieved relatives of the crime victim. Another twist on options occurred in 1238 when the bishop of Exeter took the most extraordinary steps of providing sanctuary to an outlawed subdeacon who had abjured the realm and then returned without a pardon. Bishop William then proceeded to hear the cleric's purgation and absolve him, contrary to all established canon and common law protocols. Geoffrey the chaplain's case was also unusual but indicative of the fluid interpretation of established laws that both spiritual and secular society applied. Geoffrey said mass whilst in the bishop's gaol awaiting trial for conspiracy. The issue was that at the time he had been excommunicated (and therefore ineligible to say mass) and he was not being held as the bishop's prisoner awaiting purgation but as a secular prisoner. The king ordered that Geoffrey be released for trial. His bishop refused on the basis that the spiritual crime of saying mass while excommunicated trumped the common law offence of conspiracy. Canon law pervaded and Geoffrey's status changed. He was now held as an ecclesiastic prisoner of the bishop to stand trial spiritual. The king's wishes did pervade in the heist of the crown jewels though. Tonsured cleric Thomas Pudlicott having pulled off the crime of the century

---

[55] Thomas Wayland. Chap. 4

was refused permission to claim benefit of clergy by the king. Given the severity and temerity of the crime the Church did not intercede and Pudlicott hanged as a commoner not cleric. By mid-century this was followed in audacity by the murder of a secular judge whilst he was in his home. The culprit was a chaplain and a paid contract killer.[56]

The relationship between secular criminals and the Church is beyond question. Examples of thugs, contract killers, arsonists and kidnappers in the direct pay of the Church are plentiful. The likes of Sir John Molyns, the Coterels and the Folvilles are exceptional but there is no shortage of examples of individual or transient groups of monks and priests prepared to take up criminal arms at the behest of bishops and abbots seeking to assert ownership of lands and property. Intermingling of secular and spiritual criminals within these groups is commonplace. Priests were often gang members working with lay felons, they also formed small illicit groups comprised exclusively of churchmen. Providing safe haven to fleeing felons was frequent too with bishops and priests hiding criminals in their manors, houses, chapels and churches. As with contemporary crime groups diversity has always been the hallmark of criminal success and the thirteenth and fourteenth centuries produced a large number of enterprising and resourceful crime groups. The fact that membership of these groups comprised of varying numbers of practicing clergymen attests to the interconnectivity that the English clergy had amongst the life of their parishioners, it does not single them out as unique. In theory clerics were men of God and warranted special treatment because they

[56] Chap. 7

were above the temptations of crude and base criminality. In reality clerics did commit crime and with relish in many instances. These same men would then return to the parish and deliver sermons, some of which sought to guide parishioners towards the path of righteousness. This may well be hypocrisy but hypocrisy is not a crime. Living double standards was commonplace among the higher orders of the Church and nobility, mimicry of this should not be so surprising when replicated by the lower orders.

To view English clerics as members of an intellectual avant-garde who carefully orchestrated an abuse of secular law through benefit of clergy would be misleading. This accolade belonged to the few not the many. By the end of the fourteenth century perhaps fourteen per cent of clerics held a baccalaureate degree; even reciting the Lord's Prayer was a noted challenge for some.[57] Most secular clerics were poorly educated working class men who needed *tonsurati* as a means of proving clericus because once literacy became the standard many clerics were found to be as illiterate[58] as their fellow peasant felons. (Lewis de Beaumont, bishop of Durham (1316-1333) was incapable of using Latin at his own consecration ceremony, fortunately he was never in need of the language in a secular courtroom).[59] Clericus was abused because it could be rarely because it was planned to be.

---

[57] Chap. 5

[58] Chap. 5. It seems the situation did not improve for some time. Reginald Pecock, bishop of Chichester, 1450–1461, commented, '...the clergy do not always understand the Latin Bible, but they are doubtless edified by what they read'. Green, V.H.H., *Bishop Reginald Pecock: A Study in Ecclesiastical History and Thought*, Cambridge, Cambridge University Press, 2014. p. 45

[59] Mills, J.T., *The Great days of Northumbria; Three Lectures*, London, Longmans, 1911. pp. 188–189. N. I

The differences between the laws canon and secular in criminal matters were never as divergent as history has periodically portrayed. The English Church and the English criminal justice system worked closely over many matters; issuance of writs, the role of ordinaries, claiming priests and apostates, sharing venues for hearings, sharing resources to evict sacrilegious felons and sharing the immunities within the 'Excusory Quartet'. The laws were applied in a liberal fashion until civic society gained the upper hand and the power of clergymen to dominate the lives of the faithful lessened. If England's clergy had ever deserved the right to be spared the indignity of answering to a criminal charge before laymen, that privilege had gone. What was good for clerks was good for all. In time even the (hotly) contested issue of clerics facing double jeopardy would reverse. Priests were required to appear before the secular courts and *after* conviction claim their clergy. The lay felon did not need to purge himself as his literacy was sufficient to prove (bogus) clericus. After conviction he was released. Eventually criminal churchmen would be treated even more like lay criminals;[60] recidivist clerics were prohibited from purgation, treasonists were prohibited from claiming their clergy and gradually even more crimes became unclergyable. By the last quarter of the fourteenth century men who were known to have no association with the Church now lied in court, read and justice was achieved.

Previous commentary on the topic of benefit of clergy has focused upon the egregious nature of the provision and the apparent ease with which clerics were allowed to avoid

---

[60] In one recorded case a priest was branded in the face with the keys of the Church from which he stole. In practice though branding became a distinguishing feature as the laity were branded but not the clergy. Chap. 6

meaningful punishment for felonies. In this book I have suggested that many more factors are relevant than have been previously introduced into the discussion. These factors do include criminal clerics who abused the law and an increasingly impotent Church protecting its own regardless of the depravity of the cleric's crimes. But these are only a partial explanation for the perpetuation of the plea. The broader discussion brought to the topic is the social setting for the privilege: a new priesthood, less special, earthier, more worldly. Spectacular developments in literacy, architecture, urbanization. The merging of laws, the demise of monasticism and the growth in probing questions about the role of the Church; all these are contributory factors. Laicization of the offensive protection extended to members of the English Church was a natural, organic, development of the two hundred years in which this was achieved.

Final judgment about benefit of clergy must be to some extent subjective. Examples of outrageous criminality by members of the Church that 'never took place' according to canon law are despicable to any society. But simple condemnation is not enough. It does not explain why the plea was allowed to be used so freely and how it was, piecemeal, reigned in, not by the Church but by secular law. The journey was complex, numerous factors came to bear. As confidence in the secular world increased so admiration for the spiritual declined. Everyday clergymen were caught in the middle of this and they manipulated whatever opportunities they had within the new world that was happening around them. They were men, nothing more. Some were chaste, religious, obedient, humble servants of God. Others were vile creatures of greed who hid behind the status of cleric to facilitate a life of crime. As the Middle

Ages progressed demanding a level of responsibility from the clergy different from the laymen they served was unrealistic. It was a time for the laity to reap the benefits of *privilegium fori* also.

In July 1356 bishop Thomas De Lisle demanded his right to purgation from archbishop Islip. Islip knew the lie that successful purgation would reveal. De Lisle had been found guilty of felony before the king. How could the archbishop now endorse a process that would confirm the prelate's innocence and proclaim him to be in 'good standing'? De Lisle had already shown that he would have preferred trial before secular peers over his fellow bishops, once that had failed he was turning to clerical purgation as a last resort. In many respects this last effort by a notorious criminal exemplified all that benefit of clergy had come to represent, a legal excuse. The justification for benefit of clergy being exclusively for the clergy was finished. Its life as a lay plea to compensate for excessive use of the death sentence was about to begin. Justice Holmes once noted that for the law to be consistent it would have to stop growing.[61] Benefit of clergy would grow for another five hundred years; not as a farce, a fiction, nor as an excuse for 'evil' clerics but as a tool for allowing the law to develop and accommodate justice for all citizens, lay and spiritual.

In 1623 women were permitted their clergy in cases of theft of goods valued at less than ten shillings. In 1691 women were granted clergy on the same basis as men. In 1706 the Reading Test was abolished in England and benefit of clergy

[61] Dalzell, G.W., *Benefit of Clergy in America,* Winston-Salem, Blair, 1955. p. 270

became automatic for all felonies[62] other than those deemed 'non-clergyable'. In 1718 the *Transportation Act* was promulgated. This law permitted the transportation of benefit of clergy claimants to the American colonies.[63] Branding of benefit of clergy claimants (to prevent using the plea twice or more) ended in 1779. Benefit of clergy was abolished in England in 1827.

[62] In effect by 6. Anne, c.9 (1707) (Also cited as 5. Anne. c.6 1706) commonly known as the Benefit of Clergy Abolition of Reading Test Statute, all crimes that carried the death penalty in England were now 'clergyable' (unless specifically designated otherwise) to all men and women. The legal implications of this legislation may not have been appreciated to the full at the time but in many respects being able to mitigate a death penalty felony on the basis of simply claiming an immunity without proof and making it available to men and women was ostensibly both a pre-cursor to plea bargaining and the substitution of capital punishment for alternative correctional measures

[63] Johnstone, P. *Benefit of Clergy in Colonial Virginia and Massachusetts*, Kendall Hunt, Dubuque, IA, 2015

# Bibliography

## Primary Sources

Adams, N., and Donahue, C., *Select Cases from the Ecclesiastical Courts of the Province of Canterbury, c. 1200–1301*, London, Selden Society, 1981. Vol. 95

Baker, J.H., *The Reports of John Spelman, Vol. 2*. London, Selden Society, Vol. 94. 1978

Bain, J.,(ed) *Calendar of Documents Relating to Scotland 1108–1276*, Edinburgh, HMSO, 1881

Blackstone, W., *Commentaries on The Laws of England in Four Books*, New York, Harper & Brothers, 1852. Vol. III. Chapter V. 'Of Courts Ecclesiastical, Military, and Maritime'

Blackstone, W., *Commentaries on the Laws of England A Facsimile of the First Edition of 1765–1769 Volume IV of Public Wrongs (1789)*, Chicago, The University of Chicago Press, 1979. Chapter 28

Blackstone, W. *Commentaries on the Laws of England in Four Books. Vol III*, New York, Harper Brothers, 1852. Chapter V

British Library. Add. Ms. 41612, fol. 114r

Brocklesby, R., (ed) *The Register of William Melton, Archbishop of York 1317–1340*, Vol. IV. The Canterbury and York Society, Boydell Press, 1997

Brown, W., (ed), *Register of William Wickwane Lord Archbishopof York 1279–1285*, London, Surtees Society. 1907. Vol. 114. pp. 37–38

Bund, J.W., (ed) *Episcopal Registers for the Diocese of Worcester, Bishop Godfrey Giffard, September 23, 1268 to August 15, 1301*, Volume I, Worcestershire Historical Society, 1902

*Calendar of Patent Rolls* (1216–1452) digitization by Boynton, G.R. of Iowa University http://www.uiowa.edu/~acadtech/patentrolls/

*Calendar of Patent Rolls Edward II. 1317–1321* Vol. III. m. 6. p.69

*Calendar of Patent Rolls under Edward III, 1364–1367.* Dec. 6. Vol. 13. m. 7

*Cal. Pat. Rolls 1313–1317. PRO C 74/1 m. 34d*

*Cal. Close Rolls*, 1279–1288

*Calendar of Patent Rolls 1281–1292*

*Calendar of Patent Rolls under Edward III, 1364–1367.* Dec. 6. Vol. 13. m. 7

*Close Rolls of the Reign of Henry III 1261–64*

CP 40/149, m. 389 Michaelmas Term, 1304

Cam, H.,(ed) *The Eyre of London 14 Edward II. A.D. 1321. Vol. I*, London, Selden Society, 1968

*Chapter 12 of the 3rd Lateran Council* http://www.oxforddnb.com/templates/article.jsp?articleid=20245&back

Chew, H.M. and Weinbaum, M., (eds) *The London Eyre of 1244*, London, London Record Society, 1970

Clanchy, M.T. (ed) *The Roll and Writ File of the Berkshire Eyre of 1248*, London, Selden Society, 1973. Vol. 90. No. 872 and No. 868

*Common Pleas 40/131, m. 21d (1300)*

Crown Pleas: 1 Edward I - 4 Edward I (nos 238–294), *The London Eyre of 1276* (1976), pp. 66–83. URL: http://www.british-history.ac.uk/report.aspx?compid=35999

*Decretum Magistri Gratiani.* Edited by Emil Friedberg. In *Corpus Iuris Canonici*, volume 1. Leipzig: Bernhard Tauchnitz, 1879. Reprint Graz: Akademische Druck- u. Verlagsanstalt, 1959. Hosted by Columbia University Libraries Digital Collections. https://colbycanonlaw.wordpress.com/decretists/

De Lepinois, E and Merlet, L., (eds) *Cartulaire de Notre Dame de Chartres*, Chartres, Garnier, 1865. 3 vols. Translated by Richard Barton at www.fordham.edu/source/1224chartres.asp

Elrington, C.R., (ed) *The Registers of Roger Martival, Bishop of Salisbury, 1315–1330, Vol. 2 (The Register of Divers Letters, First Half)*, Oxford, Oxford University Press, 1963 www.fordham.edu/Halsall/source/1330martival.asp

*Eyre of Kent 6 and 7 Edw II, Vol. 5. 140–141*

*Fine Rolls Henry III. 39. Hen. III* (28 Oct 1254–27 Oct 1255) Membrane 13. 74. 13th January 1254 at Westminster http://www.finerollshenry3.org.uk/content/calendar/roll_052.html#it074_013

Fowler, G.H., *Rolls of the Justices in Eyre at Bedford 1227*, Bedford Historical Record Society, 1916. Vol. 3. No. 361

Fowler, G.H., *Calendar of the Rolls of the Justices in Eyre at Bedford 1247*. Bedford Historical Record Society, 1939, Vol. 21

Furber, E.C. (ed) *Essex Sessions of the Peace, 1351, 1377–1379*, Essex Archeological Society Occasional Publications 3, Colchester, 1953

Gross, C., (ed) *Select Cases from the Coroners' Rolls A.D. 1265–1413: With a brief account of the history of the office of coroner*, London, Selden Society, 1896.Volume IX

Harding, A., (ed) *Roll of the Shropshire Eyre 1256*, London, Selden Society, 1981

Hill, R., (ed) *The Register of William Melton, Archbishop of York, 1317–1340, Vol. I*, The Canterbury and York Society, The Devonshire Press, 1977

Hill, R., (ed) *The Register of William Melton, Archbishop of York, 1317–1340, Vol. III*, The Canterbury and York Society, York, Maxiprint, 1988

Horwood, A.J (ed) *Year Books in the Reign of King Edward the First 30–31*, London, 1863–79

Hoskin, P. *De vi laica amovenda: Testing the bounds of secular and ecclesiastical jurisdiction in the reign of Henry III*. Fine Rolls Project Henry III, 1.1. C 60/48 Fine Roll 35 Henry III (28 October 1250–27 October 1251), membrane 7 http://www.finerollshenry3.org.uk/content/month/fm-01-2011.html

House of York, *Chronicles of the White Rose: A ser. Of Hist. Fragments Relating to the reign of Edward the Fourth,* London, Stevens (2012 Reprint. Ulan Press)

Hunt, W., *Dictionary of National Biography 1885–1900,* Vol. 44. https://en.wikisource.org/wiki/Dictionary_of_National_Biography,_1885–1900/Vol_44_Paston_-_Percy

*Laws of Richard I.* (Coeur de lion) *Concerning Crusaders Who Were To Go To Sea. 1189 A.D. Roger of Hoveden. III. p. 36 Rolls Series*

Maitland, F.W. Harcourt, V. and Bolland, W.C. (eds) *6 and 7 Edw. II. Eyre of Kent, Year Book Series,* Vol. V. London, Selden Society, 1909

Maitland, F.W.; Leveson, W.V.H.; Craddock Bolland, W. (eds). The *Eyre of Kent 6 and 7 Edw. II. 1313–1314,* London, Selden Society, 1910

Maitland, F.W. and Turner, G.J. (eds) *1–4 Edw II. Eyre of Kent, Year Books of 3 and 4 Edward II (1310), Vol. IV.* London, Selden Society, 1907

Millon, D., (ed) *Select Ecclesiastical Cases From The King's Court 1272–1307,* London, Selden Society, 2009. Vol. 126. 2009. p. xv

Newgate Gaol Delivery, G.D. 109. m. 2 (2. Edw. II), G.D. 40. m. 10, G.D. 40. m. 24 (6 Edw. II), G.D. 41. m. 28, (13 Edw. II), G.D. 129. m. 3. (12 Edw. III),G.D. 129. m. 61. (13 Edw. III), G.D. 145. m. 56d. (39 Edw. III)

*Northamptonshire Coroners Rolls, August 9, 1323*

Pearce, E.H., *The Monks of Westminster: Being a Register of the Brethren of the Convent from the Time of the Confessor to the Dissolution, with the List of the Obendientaries and an Introduction,* Cambridge, Cambridge University Press, 1916, (2010 Reprint Ulan Press)

Public Records Office, *List of Plea Rolls of Various Courts Preserved in the Public Record Office, Lists and Indexes, No. IV,* London, HMSO, 1894

PRO. C 66/217 mm. 1d-4d. CPR, 1345–1348. 186–188

PRO, KB 27/382, rex. M

Raine, J., (ed) *Historical Papers and Letters from the Northern Registers*, London, Longman, 1873

*Register of Ralph of Shrewsbury, Bishop of Bath and Wells, 1329–1363,* f. 288 (Somerset Record Society)

Rex Roll of Civil, King's and Crown Pleas, Goal Deliveries and Plaints. 30 Edw. I. Cornwall Eyre 130220 Nov 1301–19 Nov 1302 National Archives. JUST 1/117A M. 68

Richardson, H.G., and Sayles, G.O., (eds) FLETA. Vol. III. Books 3 and 4. Vol. 72, 1952 and Vol. 89, 1972

Riley, H.T. (trans) *Memorials of London and London Life in the XIIIth, XIVth, and XVth Centuries: Being a Series of Extracts, Local, Social, and Political, from the Early Archives of the City of London,* A.D. 1276–1419, London, Longmans, 1868

Robertson, M.A., & Ellis, G., (eds) *The English Reports Vol. LXXX King's Bench Division IX*, Edinburgh, William Green & Sons, 1907

Robinson, D., (ed) *The Register of William Melton, Archbishop of York 1317–1340, Vol. IV,* The Canterbury and York Society, Woodbridge, Boydell Press, 2011

*Roll and Writ File of the Berkshire Eyre of 1248*

Rolls of the Justices in Eyre for Lincolnshire (1218–1219) *and Worcestershire (1221)* (Selden Society Publications) pp. 558–9. No. 1141

*Rotuli Parliamentorum*, 6 Vols. London, 1810–1822. 2: 267

Rule, M. (ed) Rolls Series 81: London, Longman, 1884

Sayles, G.O. (ed) *Select Cases in the Court of the King's Bench Under Edward I,* London, Selden Society 1936. Vol. 1

Sayles, G.O., (ed) *Select Cases in the Court of the King's Bench Under Edward II,* London, Selden Society, 1955. Vol. 74

*Select Cases in the Court of the King's Bench Under Edward I. 1272–1307.* Selden Soc. Vol. III. m. 63

*Select Cases from the Ecclesiastical Courts of the Province of Canterbury, c. 1200–1301*

Stenton, D., (ed) *The Earliest Northampton Assize Roll A.D. 1202 and 1203,* Northampton, Northants. Rec. Soc. 1930 Vol. 5

Stenton, D., (ed) *Lincolnshire Assize Rolls A.D. 1202–1209,* Lincolnshire Rec. Soc. 1926 Vol. 22

Stewart, S., (ed) *The 1263 Surrey Eyre,* Guildford, Surrey Record Society, 2006. no. 53

Storey, R.L. (ed) *The Register of John Kirkby, Bishop of Carlisle, 1332–1352* and *The Register of John Ross, Bishop of Carlisle, 1325–1332,* Canterbury and York Society, 2 Vols. 1993–1995

Sutherland, D.W., (ed), *The Eyre of Northamptonshire 3–4 Edward III, Vol. I.* London, Selden Society, 1983

The Assize of Clarendon http://avalon.law.yale.edu/medieval/assizecl.asp

*The Earliest Northampton Assize Roll A.D. 1202 and 1203 and Gaol Delivery Rolls*

*The Rolls and Register of Bishop Oliver de Sutton , 1280–1289.* 6 Vols. Hereford, Lincoln Record Society, 1948–49

*The Register of William Wickwane: Lord Archbishop of York, 1279–1285.* 1907. Reprint. London: Forgotten Books, 2013

Thorold Rogers, J. E., (ed). *Proceedings of the Eyre of Oxfordshire 1285, Oxford City Documents, Financial and Judicial, 1268–1665,* Oxford Historical Society, vol.18 (1891), 194–236

*Three Rolls of the Kings Court in the Reign of Richard the First A.D. 1194–1195,* xxii-xxiii

*Three Rolls of the Kings Court* (Pipe Roll Soc., xiv) p.2. http://archive.org/stream/piperollsociety33pipeuoft/piperollsociety33pipeuoftdjvu.txt

Timmins, T.C., (ed) *The Register of William Melton, Archbishop of York, 1317–1340, Vol. V.* The Canterbury and York Society, Woodbridge, Boydell Press, 2002

Weinbaum, M (ed) *The Eyre of London 1276,* London, London Record Society, 1976. p. xviii

Willis, J.W., (ed) *Register of Godfrey Giffard. Bishop of Worcester 1268–1302. Worcester Historical Society. 2 Vols.* Oxford, 1902. p.97. n.77

*Yorkshire Eyre of 1231. Roll of Civil and Crown Pleas. 20 Oct 1230–27 Oct 1231 Rots 24. M. 20*

*17. Edw. III Patent Rolls. Part I. M. 23*

*21 Edw. I. Staffordshire Eyre of 1293 Berwick's Roll of Crown Pleas, Gaol Deliveries and Jury Calendar. 12 Nov 1292 – 19 Nov 1293. National Archives. JUST I/806 m. 18 and 21 Edw. I. Gaol Delivery Roll 36, m.39, m. 44*

## Books

Aberth, J., *Criminal Churchmen in the Age of Edward III. The Case of Bishop Thomas de Lisle*, University Park, PA, Pennsylvania State University Press, 1993

Andrews, W. *Old Church Life*, London, Andrews & Co, 1909

Appleby, J.C. and Dalton, P., (eds) *Outlaws in Medieval and Early Modern England: Crime, Government and Society, c. 1066–c.1600*, Farnham, Surrey, Ashgate, 2009

Archer, R.E., and Walker, S., (eds) *Rulers and Ruled in Late Medieval England: Essays Presented to Gerald Hariss*, London, Hambledon Press, 1995

Arnold, J.H., *What is Medieval History*, Cambridge, Polity Press, 2008

Bagchi, D., and Steinmetz, D. C., (eds) *The Cambridge Companion to Reformation Theology*, Cambridge, Cambridge University Press, 2004

Baker, D., (ed) *Studies in Church History, Vol. 11, The Materials, Sources and Methods of Ecclesiastical History*, Oxford, Oxford University Press, 1975

Baker, J.H., *Benefit of Clergy in England and its Secularization 1450–1550*, in Ins Wasser geworfen und Ozeane durchquert: Festschrift fűr Knut Wolfgang Nőin, Kőln, Bőhlau, 2003

Baker, J.H., *The Law's Two Bodies: Some Evidential Problems in English Legal History*, Oxford, Oxford University Press, 2001

Baldwin, F.E., *Sumptuary Legislation and Personal Regulation in England*, Baltimore, Johns Hopkins University Press, 1923 (OCR Reprints 2010)

Baldwin, J.W. *The Government of Philip Augustus: Foundations of French Royal Power in the Middle Ages*, Berkeley, CA, University of California Press, 1986

Bartlett, R., *England Under the Norman and Angevin Kings*, Oxford, Oxford University Press, 2000

Barlow, F., *Thomas Becket*, Berkeley, University of California Press, 1990

Barnes, T., *Constantine: Dynasty, Religion and Power in the Later Roman Empire*, Chichester, Wiley-Blackwell, 2014

Bellamy, J.G., *Crime and Public Order in England in the Later Middle Ages*, London, Routledge, 1973

Bellamy, J.G., *Criminal Law and Society in Late Medieval and Tudor England*, New York, St. Martin's Press, 1984

Bennett, N., 'Pastors and Masters: The Beneficed Clergy of North-East Lincolnshire, 1290–1340' in Hoskin, P., Brooke, C., Dobson, B., (eds) *The Foundations of Medieval English Ecclesiastical History: Studies Presented to David Smith*, Woodbridge, Boydell Press, 2005. pp. 40–62

Berman, H.J., *Law and Revolution: The Formation of the Western Legal Tradition*, Cambridge, Mass, Harvard University Press, 1983

Bishop, M. *The Middle Ages*, Boston, Mariner Books, 2001

Bizzell, P. (ed) *Rhetorical Agendas: Political, Ethical, Spiritual*, New Jersey, Lawrence Erlbaum, 2006

Blair, J., and Golding, B., *The Cloister and the World: Essays in Medieval history in Honour of Barbara Harvey*, Oxford, Clarendon Press, 1996

Blockmans, W., & Hoppenbrouwers, P., *Introduction to Medieval Europe, 300–1500* (2nd edition), London, Routledge, 2014

Bothwell, J., (ed) *The Age of Edward III*, York, York Medieval Press, 2001

Boureau, A., 'Privilege in Medieval Societies from the Twelfth to the Fourteenth Century, or: How the exception proves the rule' in Linehan, P., and Nelson, J.L., (eds) *The Medieval World*, London, Routledge, 2001

Boyd, W.K. *The Ecclesiastical Edicts of the Theodosian Code*, New York, AMS Press, 1969

Brandon, D., & Brooke, A., *Bankside: London's Original District of Sin*, Stroud, Amberley, 2011

Britnell, R., 'Town Life' in Horrox, R., & Ormrod, W.M.,(eds) *A Social History of England 1200–1500*, Cambridge, Cambridge University Press, 2006

Brooke, C., Highfield, R. and Swan, W., *Oxford and Cambridge*, Cambridge, Cambridge University Press, 1988

Brooke, Z.N., *The English Church and the Papacy: From the Conquest to the Reign of John*, Cambridge, Cambridge University Press, 1989

Brundage, J.A., *Medieval Canon Law*, London, Longman, 1997

Brundage, J.A., *The Medieval Origins of the Legal Profession*, Chicago, University of Chicago Press, 2008

Brundage, J.A., *Law, Sex, and Christian Society in Medieval Europe*, Illinois, Chicago University Press, 1987

Brundage, J. A., 'Sin, Crime and Pleasures of the Flesh' in Linehan, P. and Nelson, J.L., (eds) *The Medieval World*, London, Routledge, 2001. Chapter 17

Burt, C., *Edward I and the Governance of England 1272–1307*, Cambridge, Cambridge University Press, 2013

Bury, J.B., *Cambridge Medieval History: The Contest of Empire and Papacy*. Vol. 5 (Dalen, P. ed), Cambridge, Cambridge University Press 1911

Burger, M., *Bishops, Clerks and Diocesan Governance in Thirteenth-Century England: Reward and Punishment*, Cambridge, Cambridge University Press, 2012

Burns, J., 'Fullness of Power? Popes, Bishops and the Polity of the Church 1215–1517' in Linehan, P. and Nelson, J.L., (eds) *The Medieval World*, London, Routledge, 2001

Cantoni, D., & Yuchtman, N, *Legal Institutions, Medieval Universities, and the Commercial Revolution*. NBER Working Paper, No. 17979 (Apr. 20102) www.nber.org/paper/w17979

Catto, J., 'Currents of Religious Thought and Expression' in Jones, M., (ed) *The New Cambridge Medieval History Vol. VI, c. 1300–1415*, Cambridge, Cambridge University Press, 2000

Catto, J., 'The King's Government and the Fall of Pecock 1457–1458' in Archer, R.E., and Walker, S., (eds) *Rulers and Ruled in Late Medieval England: Essays Presented to Gerald Hariss*, London, Hambledon Press, 1995, Chap. 12

Cheney, C.R., *The English Church and its Laws 12th–14th Centuries*, London, Variorum Reprints, 1982

Cheney, C.R., *The Papacy and England 12th–14th Centuries*, London, Variorum Reprints, 1982

Cheney, C. 'England and France' in Powell, J. (ed) *Innocent III Vicar of Christ or Lord of the World*, Washington, DC, Catholic University of America Press, 1994 (2nd edition)

Ciobanu, E.A., *The Spectacle of the Body in Late Medieval England*, Lumen, Romania, 2012. P. 193. N. 180

Clark, J.G., 'Monastic Confraternity in Medieval England: The Evidence from the St. Albans Abbey *Liber Benefactorum*' in Jamroziak, E., and Burton, J., *Religious and Laity in Western Europe 1000–1400: Interaction, Negotiation, and Power, Vol. 2*, Turnhout, Brepols, 2006

Clanchy, M.T., From Memory to Written Record England 1066-1307 (3rd Edition) Chichester, West Sussex, Wiley-Blackwell, 2013

Committee of the Association of American Law Schools, Select Essays in Anglo-American Legal History, by various authors, compiled and edited by a committee of the Association of American Law Schools, in three volumes (Boston: Little, Brown, and Company, 1908). Vol. 2. Chapter: PART III.: PROCEDURE Accessed from http://oll.libertyfund.org/title/2082/158495

Constable, G., 'Religious Communities 1024–1215' in Luscombe, D. and Riley-Smith, J., (eds) *The New Cambridge Medieval History, Volume IV, c. 1024–1198, Part I.* Cambridge, Cambridge University Press, 2004

Coss. P., 'An Age of Deference' in Horrox, R. and Ormrod, W.M., (eds) *A Social History of England 1200–1500*, Cambridge, Cambridge University press, 2006

Cox, J.C., *The Sanctuaries and the Sanctuary Seekers of Mediaeval London*, G. Allen & Sons, 1911

Crossley, P. 'Architecture' in Jones, M., (ed) *The New Cambridge Medieval History Vol. VI, c. 1300–1415,* Cambridge, Cambridge University Press, 2000

Dalzell, R., *Benefit of Clergy in America*, Winston-Salem, NC, Blair Publishing, 1955

Davis, H.W.C., *England Under the Normans and Angevins* 1066–1272, New York, Putnam, 1905

Davis, H.W.C., (Ed) *Medieval England*, 1928. London, Studio Editions, 1993 (Facsimile reprint)

Davies, J.S., (ed) 'The Abjuration of Reginald Pecock, Bishop of Chichester, 1457', in, Myers, A.R. (ed) Punishment for Violation of Sanctuary, *English Historical Documents*, Vol. IV c. 1327–1485 Part III. Sec. 7. Doc. 516

Davis, V., *William Wykeham: A Life*, London, Hambledon Continuum, 2007

Dean, T., *Crime in Medieval Europe 1200–1500*, London, Pearson, 2001

Deansley, M., (7th Edition) *A History of the Medieval Church 590–1500* London, Methuen, 1951

Denton, J.H., *Robert Winchelsey and the Crown 1294–1313: A Study in the Defence of Ecclesiastical Liberty*, Cambridge, Cambridge University Press, 1980

Doherty, P., *The Great Crown Jewels Robbery of 1303: The Extraordinary Story of the First Big Bank Raid in History*, London, Constable, 2005

Donahue, C., 'A New Synthesis' of the History of the Canon Law in the Classical Period 1140–1243, Zeitschrift der Savigny-Stiftung für Rechtsgeschichte. Kanonistische Abteilung, Vol. 127, No. 96 (2010), pp. 609–615

Douie, D.L. and Farmer, D.H. (Eds) *Magna Vita Sancti Hugonis: Volume II The Life of St. Hugh of Lincoln* (Oxford Medieval Texts) Oxford, Oxford University Press, 1962

Downer, L.J., *Leges Henrici Primi*, Oxford, Oxford University Press, 1972

Duclaux de Martin, P. T., *Le droit d'asile*, Paris: Librairie du Recueil Sirey (société anonyme), 1939

Duffy, E. 'Religious Belief' in Horrox, R. and Ormrod, W.M., (eds) *A Social History of England 1200–1500*, Cambridge, Cambridge University Press, 2006

Duggan, C., The Reception of Canon Law in England in the Later Twelfth Century, *Proceedings of the Second International Congress of Medieval Canon Law, Boston College, 12–16 August, 1963*

Duggan, C., Richard of Ilchester, Royal Servant and Bishop, *Transactions of the Royal Historical Society*, Vol. 16 (Dec., 1966) pp. 1–21

Duggan, C., *Canon Law in Medieval England*, London, Variorum, 1982

Dykema, P.A., and Oberman, H.A., (eds) *Anticlericalism in Late Medieval and Early Modern Europe*, Leiden, Brill, 1994

Elrington, C.R., (ed) *The Registers of Roger Martival, Bishop of Salisbury, 1315–1330, Vol. 2 (The Register of Divers Letters, First Half)*, Oxford, Oxford University Press, 1963 available at www.fordham.edu/Halsall/source/1330martival.asp

Edwards, J.G., Galbraith, V.H., and Jacob, E.F., (eds) *Historical Essays in Honour of James Tait*, Manchester, Manchester University Press, 1933

Engen, J.V., 'Anticlericalism Among the Lollards' in Dykema, P.A., and Oberman, H.A., (eds) *Anticlericalism in Late Medieval and Early Modern Europe*, Leiden, Brill, 1994. pp. 53–62

Evans, G.R. *The Church in the Early Middle Ages*, London, Tauris, 2007

Franklin, M.J. and Harper-Bill, C., (eds) *Medieval Ecclesiastical Studies in Honour of Dorothy M. Owen*, Woodbridge, Suffolk, Boydell Press, 1995

Fleming, R., *Domesday Book and the Law*, Cambridge, Cambridge University Press, 1998

Fletcher, J.S., *The Cistercians in Yorkshire*, London, Forgotten Books, 2013 (Original work published in 1919)

Frank, T. and Plucknett, T., *A Concise History of the Common Law* Chapter Three: Misdemeanors, Trespass and Tort , [1956] Edition used: Indianapolis: Liberty Fund, 2010 http://oll.libertyfund.org/?option=com_staticxt&staticfile=show.php%3Ftitle=2458&chapter=243120&layout=html&Itemid=27

Fryde, N. A Medieval Robber Baron: Sir John Molyns of Stoke Pages in Hunnisett, R., and Post, J. (eds) *Medieval Legal Records Edited in Memory of C.A.F. Meekings*, London, HMSO, 1978

Gabel. L. *Benefit of Clergy in England in the Later Middle Ages*, New York, Octagon Press, 1969 (reprinted)

Genestal, R., *Le Privilegium Fori en France du Décret de Gratien à la Fin du XIVe Siècle*, Paris, Le Roux 1921 and 1924 (2 Vols)

Geremek, B., *The Margins of Society in Late Medieval Paris*, Paris, Editions de la Maison des Sciences de l'Homme, 1987 (Reprinted 2006)

Given, J.B., *Society and Homicide in Thirteenth-Century England*, Stanford, Stanford University Press, 1977

Goodman, A., *John of Gaunt: The Exercise of Princely Power in Fourteenth-Century Europe*, London, Longman, 1992

Gorski, R., 'Justices and Injustice? England's Local Officials in the Later Middle Ages' in Appleby, J.C. and Dalton, P., (eds) *Outlaws in Medieval and Early Modern England: Crime, Government and Society, c. 1066–c.1600*, Farnham, Surrey, Ashgate, 2009

Grant, M. *Constantine the great: the man and his time*, New York, Scribner, 1994

Greatex, J., Monks and Mendicant in English Cathedral Cities: Signs of a Mutual Benefit Society? *The Friars in Medieval Britain: Proceedings of the 2007 Harlaxton Symposium.* (2010)

Green, J., *Henry I, King of England and Duke of Normandy*, Oxford, Oxford University Press, 2006

Green, V.H.H. *Reginald Pecock; A Study in Ecclesiastical History and Thought*, Cambridge, Cambridge University Press, 2014

Gregory, S., *The Devil's Disciples*, London, Sphere, 2008

Gregory-Abbot, C., 'Sacred Outlaws: Outlawry and the Medieval Church' in Appleby, J.C. and Dalton, P., (eds) *Outlaws in Medieval and Early Modern England: Crime, Government and Society, c. 1066–c.1600*, Farnham, Surrey, Ashgate, 2009

Gross, C., (ed) *Select Cases from the Coroners' Rolls A.D. 1265–1413: With a brief account of the history of the office of coroner*, London, Selden Society, 1896.Volume IX

Haines, R.M. *Oxford Dictionary of National Biography*, Oxford, Oxford University Press, 2004

Hall, J., *Theft, Law and Society*, Indianapolis, Bobbs-Merill, 1935

Hamilton, B., *Religion in the Medieval West*, London, Arnold Press, 1986

Hamilton, S., 'The Unique Favour of Penance: the Church and the people c.800–c.1100' in Linehan, P. and Nelson, J.L., (eds) *The Medieval World*, London, Routledge, 2001. Chap 13. pp. 240–242

Hamilton, J.S., (ed) *Fourteenth Century England, Vol VIII*, Woodbridge, Boydell Press, 2014. pp. 445–446

Haines, R., *Lisle, Thomas 1298–1361*, Oxford Dictionary of National Biography, Oxford, Oxford University Press, 2004 at http://www.oxfordnb.com/view/article/16758

Hanwalt, B., *The Ties that Bound, Peasant Families in Medieval England*, Oxford, Oxford University Press, 1989

Harding, A., *The Law Courts of Medieval England*, London, Allen and Unwin, 1973

Harding, A., 'Early trailbaston proceedings from the Lincoln roll of 1305', in R. F. Hunnisett & J. B. Post (eds.), *Medieval Legal Records Edited in Memory of C. A. F. Meekings* ,London, H. M. S. O., 1978

Harmer, F.E. (Trans and Ed) 'Cnut's Confirmation of the Liberties of Christ Church, Canterbury (1017–1020)' in Harding, A., *The Law Courts of Medieval England*, London, Allen and Unwin, 1973. pp.130–131

Hastings, R., *Universities of Europe in the Middle Ages*, Oxford, Clarendon Press, 1895. Vol. II, Part I

Havely, N., 'Literature in Italian, French and English: Uses and Muses of the Vernacular' in Jones, M., (ed) *The New Cambridge Medieval History Vol. VI, c. 1300–1415*, Cambridge, Cambridge University Press, 2000

Heath, P., *Church and Realm 1272–1461 Conflict and Collaboration in an Age of Crisis*, London, Fontana, 1988

Helmholz, R.H. *Canon Law and the Law of England*, London, Hambledon Press, 1987

Helmholz, R., *The ius commune in England: Four Studies*, Oxford, Oxford University Press, 2001

Helmholz, R.H., *The Oxford History of the Laws of England: Volume I The Canon Law and Ecclesiastical Jurisdiction form 597 to the 1640's*, Oxford, Oxford University Press, 2004

Henderson, E. F., *Select Historical Documents of the Middle Ages*, London, George Bell & Sons, 1896

Holdsworth, W. S. *The Ecclesiastical Courts and Their Jurisdiction-Select Essays in Anglo-American Legal History*, Vol. 2 [1907] Boston, Little Brown, 1908

Holmes, G., *The Oxford History of Medieval Europe*, Oxford, Oxford University Press, 2001

Horrox, R., & Ormrod, W.M.,(eds) *A Social History of England 1200–1500*, Cambridge, Cambridge University Press, 2006

Hoskin, P., Brooke, C., Dobson, B., (eds) *The Foundations of Medieval English Ecclesiastical History: Studies Presented to David Smith*, Woodbridge, Boydell Press, 2005

Hovvland, A. C., (ed) *Ordeals, Compurgation, Excommunication and Interdict*, Philadelphia, University of Pennsylvania Press http://archive.org/stream/ordealscompurgat0404howl/ordealscompurgat0404howl_djvu.txt

Hudson, J., 'Constitutions of Clarendon, Clause 3, And Henry II's Reforms of Law and Administration' in Jenks, S., Rose, J., and Whittick, C, *Laws, Lawyers and Texts: Studies in Medieval Legal History in Honour of Paul Brand*, Leiden, Brill, 2012

Hunisett, R.F., *The Medieval Coroner*, Cambridge, Cambridge University Press, 1961

Hyams, P.R. *Rancor and Reconciliation in Medieval England*, Ithaca, N.Y., Cornell University Press, 2003

Jamroziak, E., and Burton, J., *Religious and Laity in Western Europe 1000–1400: Interaction, Negotiation, and Power*, Vol. 2, Turnhout, Brepols, 2006

Johnstone, P. *Benefit of Clergy in Colonial Virginia and Massachusetts*, Dubuque, IA, Kendall Hunt, 2015

Jones, M., and Johnstone, P., *History of Criminal Justice* ($5^{th}$ Edition) Waltham, Mass, Elsevier, 2012

Jones, T. and Ereira, A., *Medieval Lives*, London, BBC Books, 2004. pp. 78–80

Jones, W. Ecclesiastical History in a Course of Lectures (vol. II), London, Wightman, 1838

Jordan, W.C. *From England to France: Felony and Exile in the High Middle Ages*, Princeton, Princeton University Press, 2015

Jordan, W. C. A., ' Fresh Look at Medieval Sanctuary' in Karras, R.M., Kaye, J., and Matter, E. A., (eds) *Law and the Illicit in Medieval Europe*, Philadelphia, University of Pennsylvania Press, 2008

Kane, G., Langland, William (c.1325–c.1390), Oxford Dictionary of National Biography, Oxford University Press, 2004 http://www.oxforddnb.com/view/article/1602

Karras, R.M., Kaye, J., and Matter, E. A., (eds) *Law and the Illicit in Medieval Europe*, Philadelphia, University of Pennsylvania Press, 2008

Keen, M., *The Outlaws of Medieval England*, London, Routledge, 1961 (Revised Edition 2000)

Keen, M., Chivalry, *New Haven*, Yale University Press, 1984

Kendall, C., "Nooses and Neck Verses: The Life and Death Consequences of Literacy Testing" in Bizzell, P. (ed) *Rhetorical Agendas: Political, Ethical, Spiritual, New Jersey, Lawrence Erlbaum, 2006*

Kerr, J., *Life in the Medieval Cloister*, London, Continuum, 2009

Kesselring, K., *Mercy and Authority in the Tudor State*, Cambridge, Cambridge University Press, 2003

King, E., *Medieval England from Hastings to Bosworth*, Stroud, The History Press, 2009

Knight, B., *The Medieval English Coroner System, Part* 4, Brittania.com 2007 www.Brittania.com/history/coroner4.html

Knowles, D., *The Episcopal Colleagues of Archbishop Thomas Becket*, New York, Cambridge University Press, 1951

Kowaleski, M., 'A Consumer Economy' in Horrox, R., & Ormrod, W.M.,(eds) *A Social History of England 1200–1500*, Cambridge, Cambridge University Press, 2006

Kynell, K von S., *Saxon and Medieval Antecedents of The English Common Law: Studies in British History Vol. 59*. Lampeter, Edwin Mellen Press, 2000

Lander, J.R., *Government and Community: England, 1450–1509*, Cambridge, Mass, Harvard University Press, 1980

Lawrence, C.H., 'The English Parish and its Clergy in the Thirteenth Century' in Linehan, P. and Nelson, J.L., (eds) *The Medieval World*, London, Routledge, 2001

Lea, H.C., *Studies in Church History*, London, Sampson Low & Marston, 1869

Lebow, R.N., *A Cultural Theory of International Relations*, Cambridge, Cambridge University Press, 2008

Lepine, D., 'Church and Clergy' in Rigby S.H., (ed) *A Companion to Britain in the Middle Ages*, Chichester, Wiley-Blackwell, 2009

Linehan, P., and Nelson, J.L., (eds) *The Medieval World*, London, Routledge, 2001

Lobel, M., (ed) *A History of the County of Oxford: Dorchester and Thame Hundreds. Vol. 7*. Oxford University Press, London, 1962

Logan, F.D., *A History of the Church in the Middle Ages*, London, Routledge, 2002

Logan, D.F., (ed) *The Medieval Court of Arches*, The Canterbury and York Society, Woodbridge, Suffolk, Boydell Press, 2005

Logan, F.D. *Excommunication and the Secular Arm in Medieval England*, Toronto, Pontifical Institute of Medieval Studies, 1968

Logan, F.D., *Runaway Religious in Medieval England c. 1250–1540*, Cambridge, Cambridge University Press, 2002

Luscombe, D., and Riley-Smith, J., (eds) *The New Cambridge Medieval History Vol. 4. C. 1024–1198 Part I and 2*, Cambridge, Cambridge University Press, 2004

Lyon, B., *A Constitutional and Legal History of Medieval England* (2nd edition) New York, Norton & Co., 1980

Maddern, P.C., 'Social Mobility' in Horrox, R. and Ormrod, W.M., (eds) *A Social History of England 1200–1500*, Cambridge, Cambridge University Press, 2006

Maddicott, J.R. 'Poems of Social Protest in Early Fourteenth Century England' in *England in the Fourteenth Century: Proceedings of the 1985 Harlaxton Symposium*, Woodbridge, Suffolk, Boydell Press, 1986

Maitland, F. W., The Deacon and the Jewess; or; Apostacy at Common Law, *The Collected Papers of Frederic William Maitland*, Ed by H.A.L. Fisher, Cambridge, Cambridge University Press, 1911. Vol. 1

Maitland, F.W., *The Collected Papers of Frederic William Maitland*, Vol. 2, (Ed. H.A.L. Fisher) Cambridge, Cambridge University Press, 1911

McHardy, A.K., 'Church Courts and Criminous Clerks in the Later Middle Ages' in *Medieval Ecclesiastical Studies in Honour of Dorothy M. Owen*, Woodbridge, Suffolk, Boydell Press, 1995. pp. 165–183

Mansfield, M.C., *The Humiliation of Sinners: Public Penance in Thirteenth-Century France*, Ithaca, Cornel University Press, 1995

Matthews, W., 'Inherited Impediments in Medieval Literary History' and Nichols, S. G., 'Ethical Criticism and Medieval Literature' in Matthews, W., (ed) *Medieval Secular Literature*, Los Angeles, Center for Medieval and Renaissance Studies, 1967

Mills, J.T., *The Great days of Northumbria; Three Lectures*, London, Longmans, 1911

Mortimer, I., *The Time Traveler's Guide to Medieval England*, London, Touchstone, 2008

Mortimer, I., *The Perfect King: The Life of Edward III Father of the English Nation*, London, Vintage Books, 2008

Murray, K.M.E., Faversham and the Cinque Ports, *Transactions of the Royal Historical Society (Fourth Series)* Vol. 18 (Dec., 1935) pp. 53–84

Musson, A., 'Crossing Boundaries: Attitudes to Rape in Late Medieval England' in Musson, A., (ed) *Boundaries of the Law: Geography, Gender and Jurisdiction in Medieval and early Modern Europe*, Aldershot, Ashgate, 2005

Musson, A., 'Second English Justinian or Pragmatic Opportunist? A Re-Examination of the Legal Legislation of Edward III's Reign' in Bothwell, J., (ed) *The Age of Edward III*, York, York Medieval Press, 2001

Musson, A. *Medieval Law in Context: The Growth of Legal Consciousness from Magna Carta to the Peasant's Revolt*, Manchester, Manchester University Press, 2001

Myers, A.R. (ed) *Punishment for Violation of Sanctuary, English Historical Documents*, Vol. IV c. 1327–1485 Part III. Sec. 7.London, Eyre and Spottiswoode, 1969 (Reissued 1996, Routledge)

Norland, E., *From Four Royal Persian Stars to Jesus and the Sun*, Bloomington, IN, iUniverse LLC, 2013

Ogle, A., *The Canon Law in Medieval England: An Examination of William Lyndwood's "Provinciale" in reply to the late Professor F.W. Maitland*, London, John Murray, 1912

Olson, T., 'Sanctuary and Penitential Rebirth in the Central Middle Ages' in Musson, A., (ed), *Boundaries of the Law: Geography, Gender and Jurisdiction in Medieval and Early Modern Europe*, Aldershot, Ashgate, 2005

Ormrod, W.M., 'Law in the Landscape: Criminality, Outlawry and Regional Identity in Late Medieval England' in Musson, A., (ed) *Boundaries of the Law*, Aldershot, Ashgate, 2005

Ormrod, W. M., 'England: Edward II and Edward III' in Jones, M., (ed) *The New Cambridge Medieval History, Vol. VI c. 1300–1415*, Cambridge, Cambridge University Press, 2000

Ormrod, W.M., *Edward III*, New Haven, Yale University Press, 2011

Oulton, J.E. (tran) and Lawlor, H.J., (ed) *Eusebius: The Ecclesiastical History*, Cambridge, Mass, Harvard University Press 1973

Owen, D.M., *The Medieval Canon Law: Teaching, Literature and Transmission*, Cambridge, Cambridge University Press, 1990

Owen, D.M., 'Ecclesiastical Jurisdiction 1300–1500: The Records and Their Interpretation' in Baker, D., (ed) *Studies in Church History*,

*Vol. 11, The Materials, Sources and Methods of Ecclesiastical History*, Oxford, Oxford University Press, 1975. pp. 199–221

Palgrave, K.H., *The Collected Works of Sir Francis Palgrave, K.H. Reviews, Essays and Other Writings in Two Volumes. Vol. 1.* Cambridge, Cambridge University Press, 1922

Pearsall, D. (ed) *Piers Plowman The C-Text, Corrected Edition*, Exeter, Exeter University Press, 2010

Pennington, K. 'Innocent III and Canon Law' in Powell, J. (ed) *Innocent III Vicar of Christ or Lord of the World*, Washington, DC, Catholic University of America Press, 1994 (2nd edition)

Pike, L.O. *A History of Crime in England* illustrating the changes of the laws in the progress of civilization, London, A history of crime in England *Luke Owen Pike* Smith Elder, 1873 Vol. I. pp. 199–203 https://openlibrary.org/books/OL23378300M/A_history_of_crime_in_England

Pollock, F., and Maitland, F.W., *The History of English Law Before the Time of Edward I, (2nd Edition)* Volume I. Cambridge, Cambridge University Press 1968

Poole, A.L. 'Outlawry as a Punishment of Criminous Clerks' in Edwards, J.G., Galbraith, V.H., and Jacob, E.F., (eds) *Historical Essays in Honour of James Tait*, Manchester, Manchester University Press, 1933

Powell, J. (ed) *Innocent III Vicar of Christ or Lord of the World*, Washington, DC, Catholic University of America Press, 1994 (2nd edition)

Powicke, M., *The Thirteenth Century* 1216–1307, Oxford, Clarendon Press 1953

Pryce, H., *Native Law and the Church in Medieval Wales*, Oxford, Clarendon Press, 1993

Pugh, R.B., *Imprisonment in Medieval England*, Cambridge, Cambridge University Press, 1968

Pugh, R.B., The King's Prisons before 1250, *Transactions of the Royal Historical Society, Fifth Series*, Vol. 5 (1955), pp. 1–22

Purvis, J.S., *An Introduction to Ecclesiastical Records*, London, St. Anthony's Press, 1953

Raffield, P. *Images and Cultures of Law in Early Modern England: Justice and Political Power 1558–1660*, Cambridge, Cambridge University Press, 2004. Chap. 1

Rashdall, H., *Universities of Europe in the Middle Ages*, Oxford, Clarendon Press, 1895 (2 Vols)

Richardson, H.G. *Year Book Plea Rolls as Sources of Historical Information*, Transactions of the Royal Historical Society, Fourth Series, Vol. 5 (1922)

Rigby, S.H., (ed) *A Companion to Britain in the Later Middle Ages*, Chichester, Wiley-Blackwell, 2009

Rodes, R.E., *Lay Authority and Reformation in the English Church: Edward I to the Civil War*, London, The University of Notre Dame Press, 1982

Rosser, G., 'Sanctuary and Social Negotiation in Medieval England' in Blair, J., and Golding, B., *The Cloister and the World; Essays in Medieval History in Honour of Barbara Harvey*, Oxford, Clarendon Press, 1996

Rothwell, H., (ed) Sanctuary and Abjuration of the Realm, and Outlawry, *English Historical Documents*, c. 1189–1379,Part III. Vol. III. Doc. 110 at www.englishhistoricaldocuments.com/document/view.htm?id=723

Rowland, A.C., (ed) 'Ordeals, Compurgation, Excommunication and Interdict' in *Original Sources of European History*, Philadelphia, Pennsylvania University Press, Vol. IV. No. 4. C. 9. Abolition. p. 9 Corp. Jut. Can., c. 9, Extra III, 50 (Can. 18. Ann. 1215) https://archive.org/details/translationsrepro1univiala

Rubin, M. and Simons, W., *The Cambridge History of Christianity Volume 4 Christianity in Western Europe c. 1100–c.1500*, Cambridge, Cambridge University Press, 2009

Saul, N., (ed) *The Oxford Illustrated History of Medieval England*, Oxford, Oxford University Press, 1997

Scase, W., 'Lollardy' in Bagchi, D., and Steinmetz, D. C., (eds) *The Cambridge Companion to Reformation Theology*, Cambridge, Cambridge University Press, 2004. pp. 22–27

Schaff, P. & Wace, H. (eds) *Eusebius: Church History*, Trans in Nicene and Post-Nicene Fathers, 2nd series. Grand Rapids, MI, Eerdines, 1955

Shepherd, R. *Westminster: A Biography From the Earliest Times to the Present*, London, The National Archives, 2012

Shoemaker, K., *Sanctuary and Crime in the Middle Ages, 400–1500*, New York, Fordham University Press, 2011

Smith, D.M., *Supplement to the Guide to Bishop's Registers of England and Wales: A Survey of the Middle Ages to the Abolition of the Episcopacy in 1646*, The Canterbury and York Society, 2004

Sparrow Simpson, W., *Chapters in the History of Old S. Paul's*, London, Elliot Stock, 1831

Spencer, A., *Nobility and Kingship in Medieval England: The Earls and Edward I, 1272–1307*, Cambridge, Cambridge University Press, 2013, Part II "The Earls in Local Society'

Staunton, M., *Thomas Beckett and His Biographers*, Woodbridge, Suffolk, Boydell and Brewer, 2006

Stewart, S., 'Outlawry as an Instrument of Justice in the Thirteenth Century' in Appleby, J.C. and Dalton, P., (eds) *Outlaws in Medieval and Early Modern England: Crime, Government and Society, c. 1066–c.1600*, Farnham, Surrey, Ashgate, 2009

Stephenson, P., *Constantine: Unconquered Emperor, Christian Victor*, London, Quercus, 2011

Stones, E.L.G. The Folevilles of Ashby-Foleville, Leicestershire, and Their Associates in Crime, 1326–1347, *Transactions of the Royal Society*, 5th Series, Vol. 7. (1957) pp. 117–136

Strohm, P. 'Writing and Reading' in Horrox, R. and Ormrod, W.M., (eds) *A Social History of England 1200–1500*, Cambridge, Cambridge University Press, 2006

Swanson, R.N., *Church and Society in Late Medieval England*, Oxford, Oxford University Press, 1989

Swanson, R.N., *Religion and Devotion in Europe, c.1215–c.1515*, Cambridge, Cambridge University Press, 1995

Tierney, B., *The Crisis of Church and State in 1050–1300*, Englewood Cliffs, N.J., Prentice-Hall, 1964

Thompson, H., *The English Clergy and Their Organization in The Later Middle Ages*, Oxford, Oxford University Press, 1947

Thornley, I.D., The Destruction of Sanctuary, *Tudor Studies , Presented by the Board of Studies in History in the University of London to Albert Frederick Pollard, being the work of twelve of his colleagues and pupils.* 1924

Tout, T.F., The Human Side of Medieval Records, *Transcripts of the Royal Historical Society* Fourth Series, Vol. II (1928)

Trenholme, N.M., *The Right of Sanctuary in England*, Columbia, University of Missouri, 1903

Tuchman, B., *A Distant Mirror: The Calamitous 14th Century*, New York, Balantine, 1978

Turner R.V. Judges, *Administrators and the Common Law in Angevin England*, London, Hambledon Press, 1994, 'Clerical Judges in English Secular Courts; The Ideal versus the Reality'. pp. 159–180

Van Caenegem, R.C.(ed) *English Lawsuits from William 1 to Richard 1*, Vol. 107 (I and II), London, Selden Society, 1991 Case 520 pp. 571–578

Van de Weil, C., *History of Canon Law*, Louvain, Peeters Press, 1991

Visser, S., and Williams, T., Anselm: *Great Medieval Thinkers*, Oxford, Oxford University Press, 1965

Von Bar, L. *A History of Continental Criminal Law*, Boston, Little Brown, 1916

Wallach, L., *Alcuin and Charlemagne: Studies in Carolingian History and Literature*, New York, London-Johnson Reprint, 1968

Watkiss, L., and Chibnall, M., (Eds and Trans) *The Waltham Chronicle*, Oxford, Oxford University Press, 1994

Williams, G.A., *Medieval London: From Commune to Capital*, London, University Press, 1970. (2nd Edition)

Whitman, J.Q., *The Origins of Reasonable Doubt: Theological Roots of the Criminal Trial*, New Haven, Yale University Press, 2008

Wood, S., *The Proprietary Church in the Medieval West*, Oxford, Oxford University Press, 2006

Woodbine, G.E. (ed) Thorne, S.E. (trans) *Bracton on the Laws and Customs of England*, Cambridge, MA, Harvard University Press, 1968–1977. 4 Vols. Vol. 2

Wormald, P., *The Making of the English Law: King Alfred to the Twelfth Century. Vol. 1. Legislation and Its Limits*, Oxford, Blackwell, 1999 (2001 reprint)

## Articles

Alexander, J.W., The Beckett Controversy in Recent Historiography, *Journal of British Studies*, Vol. 9, No. 2 (May. 1970), pp. 1–26

Baker, J.H., The English Law of Sanctuary, *Ecclesiastical Law Journal*, Vol. 2. No. 6 (Jan. 1990) pp. 8–13

Baker, N. F., Benefit of Clergy-A Legal Anomaly, *Kentucky Law Journal* Vol. XV. No. 2 (Jan. 1927) pp. 85–115

Bates, J.C., Edward Leche-A Recidivist Criminous Clerk, *Nottingham Mediaeval Studies*, Vol. 30. (1986) pp. 97–100

Bellamy., J.G., The Coterel Gang: An Anatomy of a Band of Fourteenth-Century Criminals, *English Historical Review*, Vol. 79. (Oct., 1964) pp. 698–717

Bethel, D. L., English Black Monks and Episcopal Elections in the 1120's, *The English Historical Review*, Vol. 84. No. 333 (Oct. 1969) pp. 673–698

Bullen, W.R., The Right of Sanctuary in England, *The Tablet*, 19 May, 1923. p. 6

Carpenter, D.A., Magna Carta 1253: The Ambitions of the Church and the Divisions of the Realm, *Historical Research*, Vol. 86, No. 232 (May, 2013), pp. 179–190

Cheney, C.R. The Punishment of Felonous Clerks, *The English Historical Review*, Vol. 51. No. 202, (Apr. 1936), pp. 215–236

Cheney, C.R. The so-called Statutes of John Pecham and Robert Winchelsey for the Province of Canterbury, *The Journal of Ecclesiastical History*, Vol. 12, Issue 1 (March/April, 1961), pp. 14–34

Comments, The Regression of Ecclesiastical Jurisdiction, *The Yale Law Journal*, Vol. 32, No. 6 (Apr. 1923), pp. 594–602. p. 595

Cross, A.L. The English Criminal Law and Benefit of Clergy during the Eighteenth and Nineteenth Centuries, *American Historical Review*, Vol. 22. No. 3. (Apr. 1917), pp. 544–565

Denton, J.H., The Making of the 'Articuli Cleri' of 1316, *The English Historical Review*, Vol. 101. No. 400 (Jul. 1986), pp. 564–595

Dodd, G., Reason, Conscience and Equity: Bishops as the King's Judges in Later Medieval England, *History*. Vol. 99. Issue 335 (Apr. 2014) pp. 213–240

Duggan, C., The Beckett Dispute and the Criminous Clerks, *Bulletin of the Institute of Historical Research*, Vol. 65 (1962) pp. 1–28

Firth, C.B., Benefit of Clergy in the Time of Edward IV, *The English Historical Review*, Vol. 32, No. 126 (Apr. 1917), pp. 175–191

Galbraith, V.H., A Visitation of Westminster in 1444, *English Historical Review*, Vol. 37. (1922) pp. 83–88

Geltner, G., Medieval Prisons: Between Myth and Reality, Hell and Purgatory, *History Compass*, Vol. 4, Issue 2, (March, 2006), pp. 261–274

Geltner, G., Detrusio, Penal Cloistering in the Middle Ages, *Revue Bénédictine*, Vol. 118, No. 1 (2008), pp. 89–108

Haines, R. M., The Episcopate during the Reign of Edward II and the Regency of Mortimer and Isabella, *The Journal of Ecclesiastical History,* Vol. 56. No. 4 (Oct 2005) pp. 657–707

Hammond, W.A., Sumptuary Laws and Their Social Influence, *Popular Science Monthly*, Vol. 37. (May-Oct) 1890. pp. 33–40

Hamil, F.C., The King's Approvers: A Chapter in the History of English Criminal Law, *Speculum*, Vol. 11 (1936) pp. 238–258

Hanwalt, B., Fur-Collar Crime: The Pattern of Crime Among the Fourteenth-Century Nobility, *Journal of Social History*, Vol. 8. No. 10 (1975) pp. 1–17

Helmholz, R.H., The Early History of the Grand Jury and the Canon Law, *The University of Chicago Law Review*, Vol. 50, No. 2, Fiftieth Anniversary Issue (Spring, 1993) pp. 613–627

Helmholz, R.H., Conflicts Between Religious and Secular Law: Common Themes In The English Experience, 1250–1640, *Cardozo Law Review*, Vol. 12, (1990–1991), pp. 707–728

Helmholz, R.H., Scandulum in the Medieval Canon Law in the English Ecclesiastical Courts, *Zeitschrift der Savigny-Stiftung für Abteil;ung, Rechtsgeschichte. Kanonisteische* Vol. 96, No. 127 (2010), pp. 258–274

Hertzler, J.R., The Abuse and Outlawing of Sanctuary for Debt in Seventeenth-Century England, *The Historical Journal.* Vol. 14. No. 3 (Sep. 1971) pp. 467–477

Hill, R., An English Archbishop and the Scottish War of Independence, *The Innes Review*, Vol. 22, Issue 2 (1971) pp. 59–71

Hume, D. *The History of England from the Invasion of Julius Caesar to the Revolution in 1688* at www.olllibertyfund.org

Hunnisett, R.F., The Origins of the Office of Coroner: The Alexander Prize Essay, *Transactions of the Royal Historical Society,* Fifth Series, Vol. 8 (1958), pp. 85–104

Hyams, P., Feud and the State in Late Anglo-Saxon England, *Journal of British Studies,* Vol. 40 (2001), pp. 1–43

Jeffrey, C.R., The Development of Crime in Early English Society, *Journal of Criminal Law and Criminology*, Vol. 47, Issue 6, 1957 pp. 647–666

Jones, W.R. Bishops, Politics, and the Two Laws: The Gravamina of the English Clergy, 1237–1399, *Speculum: A Journal of Mediaeval Studies*, Vol. 151. N. 2 (Apr., 1966) pp. 209–245

Jones, W.R., The Two Laws in England: The Later Middle Ages, *The Journal of Church and State*, Vol. 1. Issue. 1. (1969) pp. 111–131

Lapsley, G., Archbishop Stratford and the Parliamentary Crisis of 1341. Part II. *The English Historical Review*, Vol. 30. No. 118 (Apr. 1915) pp. 193–215

Lee, F.N. *King Alfred the Great and Our Common Law*, http://www.dr-fnlee.org/docs6/alfred/alfred.pdf

Logan, W., Criminal Law Sanctuaries, *Harvard Civil Rights-Civil Liberties Law Review*, Vol. 38 (Summer, 2003) pp. 321–391

Maitland, F.W. Henry II and the Criminous Clerks, *The English Historical Review*, Vol. 7. No. 26 (Apr. 1892), pp. 224–234

Maxfield, D. K., St. Mary Rouncivale, Charing Cross : The Hospital of Chaucer's Pardoner, *The Chaucer Review*, Vol. 28, No. 2 (1993) pp. 148–63

McEwan, J., William FitzOsbert and the Crisis of 1196 in London, *Florilegium,* Vol. 21 (2004) pp. 18–42

Milon, D., Medieval and Early Modern Law: The Birth of Modern Jurisprudence: Ecclesiastical Jurisdiction in Medieval England, *University of Illinois Law Review*. No. 7. (1984). pp. 621–639

Morris, C., William I and the Church Courts, *The English Historical Review*, Vol. 82. No. 324 (Jul.,1967) pp. 449–463. p. 449–450

Murray, A. Immunity, Nobility and the *Edict of Paris*, *Speculum,* Vol.69, No. 1 (Jan., 1994), pp. 18–39

Murray, K.M.E., Faversham and the Cinque Ports, *Transactions of the Royal Historical Society (Fourth Series)* Vol. 18 (Dec., 1935) pp. 53–84

Myers, A.R. (ed) Punishment for Violation of Sanctuary, *English Historical Documents*, Vol. IV c. 1327–1485 Part III. Sec. 4

Neville, C.J. "The Bishops Ministers": The Office of Coroner in Late Medieval Durham, *Florilegium*, Vol. 18. Issue 2 (2001) pp. 47–60

Ockler, C., Augustine, Episcopal Interests, and the Papacy in Late Roman Africa, *The Journal of Ecclesiastical History*, Vol.42. No.2 (Apr., 1991) pp. 179–201

Pattenden, M., The Exclusion of the Clergy from Criminal Trial Juries: An Historical Perspective, *Ecclesiastical Law Journal*, Vol. 5. No. 24 (Jan. 1999) pp. 151–163

Pope, S., Sanctuary: The Legal Institution in England, *University of Puget Sound Law Review*, Vol. 10. (1986–1987) pp. 677–697. p. 680

Postman, N., On the Origin of Childhood and Why it is Disappearing, *Childhood Education* March/April 1985 pp. 286–293

Reynolds, S., What Do We Mean By "Anglo-Saxon" and "Anglo-Saxons"? *Journal of British Studies*, Vol. 24, No. 4 (Oct., 1985), pp. 395–414

Riddel, W.R., The Food and Drink of an Englishman-By Statute, *Journal of Criminal Law and Criminology*, Vol.18. No.4 (Feb) 1928. pp. 527–532

Riddell, W.R. Erring Judges of the Thirteenth Century, *Michigan Law Review*, Vol. 24, No. 4, (Feb., 1926), pp. 329–343

Riddel, W.R., The Food and Drink of an Englishman-By Statute, *Journal of Criminal Law and Criminology*, Vol.18. No.4 (Feb) 1928. pp. 527–532

Riggs, C. H., 'Criminal Asylum in Anglo-Saxon Law', *University of Florida Monogrpahs*, Social Sciences, Vol. 6. No. 18 1963

Ross, M.C., Concubinage in Anglo-Saxon England, *Past and Present*, No. 108 (Aug., 1985) pp. 3–34

Sherman, C.P., A Brief History of Medieval Roman Canon Law in England, *University of Pennsylvania Law Review and American Law Register*, Vol. 68, No. 3 (Mar. 1920), pp. 233–258

Smith C.E., Clerical Violence in the Pontificate of Innocent III, *Journal of Religion*, Vol. 24. No. 1. (Jan, 1944), pp. 37–41

Smith, C.E., Innocent III, Defender of the Faith, *The Catholic Historical Review*, Vol. 32, No. 4 (Jan. 1947), pp. 415–429

Spitzer, A.L. The Legal Careers of Thomas of Weyland and Gilbert of Thornton, *The Journal of Legal History*, Vol. 6, Issue 1, (1985) pp. 62–83

Summerson, H., The Enforcement of the Statute of Winchester, 1285–1327, *The Journal of Legal History,* Vol. 13, No. 3 (1992), pp. 232–250

Summerson, H., The Criminal Underworld of Medieval England, *The Journal of Legal History*, Vol. 17. No. 3. (1996) pp. 197–224

A History of British Dress, *The Saturday Review of Politics, Literature, Science and Art*, Vol. 76. No. 1,989 (9, Dec., 1893) pp. 654–655

Thorne, S.E. The Assize "Utrum" and Canon Law in England, *Columbia Law Review*, Vol. 33. No. 3 (Mar. 1933) pp. 428–436

Thornley, I., Sanctuary in Medieval London, *Journal of the British Archaeological Association*, Vol. 38, (1932–33), pp. 293–315

Turner, R.V., The Origins of Common Pleas and King's Bench, *The American Journal of Legal History*, Vol. 21. No. 3, (Jul. 1977), pp. 238–254

Turner, R. V., The *Miles Literatus* in Twelfth-and Thirteenth Century England: How Rare a Phenomenon? *The American Historical Review*, Vol. 83. No. 4 (Oct. 1978), pp. 928–945

Turner, R.V., Richard the Lionheart and the Episcopate in His French Domains, *French Historical Studies*, Vol. 21. No. 4 (Autumn, 1998), pp. 517–542

Valente, C., The Deposition and Abdication of Edward II, *The English Historical Review*, Vol. 113. No. 453 (Sept. 1988) pp. 852–881

Walker, C.H., The Date of the Conqueror's Ordinance Separating the Ecclesiastical and Lay Courts, *The English Historical Review*, Vol. 39, No. 155 (Jul., 1924) pp. 399–400

White, E.J., Benefit of Clergy, *The American Law Review*, Vol. 46, (1912), pp. 78–94. p. 82

Zutshi, P., The Dispersal of Scholars from Oxford and the Beginnings of a University at Cambridge: A Study of the Sources, *English Historical Review*, Vol. 127. N. 528 (2012) pp. 1041–1062

## On-Line Sources

www.avalon.law.yale.edu/medieval/ordwill.asp

www.britannica.com/topic/wergild

www.britannica.com/history/coroner3.html

www.heinonline.org/HeinDocs/Selden_Society.pdf

www.piperollsociety.co.uk/page5.htm

www.nationalarchives.gov.uk/search/search_results.aspx?Page=1&QueryText=KB+27&SelectedDatabases

www.churchofengland.org/media/40668/chpter2.pdf

www.fordham.edu

www.hist.com.ac.uk/research

www.fordham.edu/halsall/basis/lateran4.asp

www.britannica.com

www.britannica.com/topic/The-Most-Noble-Order-Of-The-Garter

www.clerus.org

www.newadvent.org

www.British-History.ac.uk

www.british-history.ac.uk/report.aspx?compid=57718.

www.scientificamerican.com/article.cfm?id=forensic-exam-of-king-richard-the-lionheart-reveals-embalming-practices

www.news.bbc.co.uk/local/oxford/low/people_and_places/history/newsid_8405000/8405640.stm

www.papalencyclicals.net/Councils/ecum14.htm#16.

www.stedmundsburychronicle.co.uk/Chronicle/1216-1539.htm

www.nationalarchives.gov.uk/records/research-guides/outlawry

www.theoriginalrecord.com/database/search/search/annesley

www.gatehouse-gazetteer.info/English%20sites/1646.html

www.womenpriests.org/historic/13giovanna.asp

www.odnb2.pubfactory.com/view/article/25204

## Statutes

Statutes of the Realm I.3 Exeter version Domini M.C. XXXVI

Constitutions of Clarendon 1164

Second Council of Lyon 1274 16. Article 22

Gratian's Decretum, Pars I., Dist. XXXII., c. vi. http://www.fordham.edu/halsall/basis/trullo.asp

1235 19 Hen. III. c.I

1267 52 Hen. III

1276 4 Edw. 1, St. 3. c. 5

1283 4 12 Edw. I

1284 13 Edw. I. St. c. 2

1295 23 Edw. I. St 1. c. 113

1346 20 Edw. 3. c.4

1350 25 Edw. III. St. 3. c. 4

1350 25 Edw. III St. 4

1496 12 Hen. VII, c.7

1512 4 Hen. VIII, c. 2

1531 23 Hen. VIII, c. 15, sec. 13

1576 18 Eliz. c.7. sec. 2, 3

1547 1 Edw. VI. c. 12. sec. 14

1623 21 Jac. 1 c.6

1692 3 W. & M. c.9. sec. 5, 6

1707 6 Anne. c. 9 (1705 5 Anne. c.6, sec. 6)

1833 3 Will IV. c. 42, sec.13

## Unpublished

Clark, J.K., 'Of Kings and Popes and Law: An Examination of the Church and State Relationship in England During the High Middle Ages and the Influence of that Relationship on the Structure and Processes of English law' MA Thesis, University of Victoria, 2012 (Unpublished)

# Index

**Note:** Page numbers followed by "n" refer to footnotes


A

abduction, of nuns, 211, 212

abjuration, 1, 90, 133–134, 136, 147–148, 284

- benefit of clergy, 27
- defined, 133n2
- and ecclesiastical sanctuary, 178
- and exile, 35
- legal options and jurisdictional cooperation, 134
- oath of, 141, 157, 158, 163, 167
- role of hearing, 137
- sanctuary and, 275, 283
- secular provisions, 35

*absque purgatione,* 80, 124

abuse

- of benefit of clergy, 2, 12
- *of privilegium fori,* 14
- of sanctuary, 35

Aethelbert, Kent, 39

Alan, Baston (canon of Sempringham), 194

Alexander II (Pope), 43

Alexander III (Pope), 61–63

Alfred (King of England), 40–41, 40n27

'The Anarchy,' 55

Anglo-Saxon, 9, 37, 50n56, 54

- laws, 38, 39

Anselm, 47–48

Aquinas, Thomas, 277

archdeacons, 18, 25

*Articuli Cleri,* 23, 151n71, 284
  clauses of, 223–224
  Edward II (King of England), 284
Arundel, Thomas (Bishop of Ely), 172–173, 173n139
Asshendene, William, 94
Assize of Clarendon, 60n6, 73–74, 178n161
Auriol, Peter, 277

B
Balliol, John (King of Scotland), 101
bastard feudalism, 195
bastard sanctuaries, 145, 287
Baston, Alan, 200
Becket, Thomas (Archbishop of Canterbury), 31–32, 59–60, 62, 64n13, 65, 69–70, 71n39, 72, 78, 86, 149, 271–272
  Case 409 and, 66–67
  Henry II (King of England) and, 73–74
  murder of, 63–64, 72, 156
  violent protestations of, 5
Bellers, Roger, 200
benefit of clergy, 1, 4, 291–294
  abuse of, 2, 12, 32
  abuse of secular law through, 290
  claims, 228, 229, 231, 237, 243, 246
  clauses of *Articuli,* 223–224
  in England
    development of, 31
    seventh century, 32–3
  and English criminal law, 73, 285
  expansion of, 6
  in the Eyre Roll for London 1321, 236–237
  felonious clerics, 134
  laicization of, 35
  mitigatory plea, 13
  opportunity for criminal clerics, 136

protections, 7, 221, 225, 283
in reign of Edward II, 235
secularization of, 73, 228, 231, 233
secular trial, 41
and secure law, 283
transition, 209
Benefit of Clergy Abolition of Reading Test Statute, 294n62
Berkshire justices, for murder, 188
Bernard, Robert, 197, 200n80
Beverley sanctuary, 144
bishopric, 25, 251
Black Death, 27, 210, 252, 278
Blanche of Lancaster (Lady Wake), 254, 257
blind obedience, 41
Boniface VIII (King of England), 207
Bourchier, Thomas (dean of St. Martin's, London), 173
Boyet, Nicholas, 194
Bronescombe, Walter (Bishop of Exeter), 21
Burdon, Philip, 190
Bythwall, Richard, 254

C

canonical compurgation, 58
canon law, 5, 8–10, 86, 96, 103, 108n102, 113, 260, 266–268, 267n34, 269, 284, 288, 292
absorption into English law, 270
classical period of, 13
denial of outlawry, 135
features, 73
sanctuary, 133–134, 149, 155
and secular law, 16, 291
thirteenth century, 15
Carles, Ralph, 255–258
*cause célèbre,* Clarendon Constitution, 32
Celestine (Pope), 94

chantries, growth of, 19
Chlothar II (King of the Franks), 8
Christian jurisdiction legal system, 75
Ciprian, Henry (canon of Waltham), 173
Cistercians, 20
Clarendon debacle, implications of, 65
Clement VI (Pope), 250
clergy plea, 36n11
    changing status of, 2
*clerici/capellini,* 85
*clerici convicti,* 100
*clericis laicos,* 78, 221n41
cleric plea, 28
clericus, 221
    claim, 218
    incentive for secularization of, 239
*clericus convictus,* 80
*clericus quietus,* 110
Clerk, Roger, 116–117
Cnut (King of England), 144
Common Law, 3, 31, 42, 79, 105, 118
    basic structure, 272
    benefit of clergy, 3
    canon law and, 104, 213, 238, 288
    development by Henry II, 31
    issue for, 130
    local laity, 169n128
    by William I, 42
compurgation, 38n19, 79
    canonical, 58
Constantine (Roman Emperor), 138
Constitution of Clarendon, 32, 60n6, 73–74
    article 8 of the, 60
Cornwall, Hugh, 119
Coroners, roles and responsibilities, 154–155, 154n87

*Corpus iuris canonici,* 54
Coterel, James, 199
Coterels gang, 193, 196–199
Council of Lerida, 39
Council of Lillebonne, 45
Council of Lyon, 120
Council of Rheims, 45
Council of Valence, 39
counterfeiting, 190
Crepyn, Ralph, 106, 107
crime gangs, range of crime, 135
crime, theft, 210–211
criminal clergymen
    secular pardons, 135
    secular/spiritual gaols, 136
criminal gangs, 180
criminal justice system, English Church and, 291
criminous clerks
    bands of, 193
    crimes of, 194
    status of, 45
curfew, 144
*curia a cruore,* 92
*curia regis,* 65, 83, 93

D
Dalderby, Peter de (canon of Lincoln), 169
Dalton, John, 192
*de apostate capiendo,* 213
de Asshenden, William, 123
de Baskerville, William, 103
de Beaumont, Louis (Bishop Lewis of Durham), 290
de Bracy, William, 99
de Broi, Philip (canon of Bedford), prosecution for murder, 67–68, 67n26

de Burton, Henry, 254
Decretals, 37–38
de Erkalewe, Edward, 87
*de facto,* 8, 37, 62, 96, 129–130, 133, 140, 212, 223
    appeals, 62
defendant, 38
de-frocking, 41
de Grey, John, 259
de Hakeneye, John (canon of Salisbury), 228
de Hauekenese, Thomas, 87–88
de la Beche, Margery, abduction of, 147
de Lay, William, 285
de Leffrement, William, 107
De Lisle, John, 253–255
De Lisle, Thomas (Bishop of Ely), 249–253, 259–266, 293
de Meyronnes, François, 277
de Mortimer, Geoffrey (archdeacon of London), 113
Dene, Peter, 262–266
de Nodariis, Nicholas, 88–89, 188, 276
Deodand, 154n86
de Pavely, William, 122
de Periton, Peter (canon of Salisbury), 228
De Pont L'Eveque, Roger, 21
de Roches, Peter (Bishop of Winchester), 157–158
de Shope, Hugh, 87
de Stauren, Walter (canon of Lincoln), 169
de Sutton, Oliver (Bishop of Lincoln), 118
de Swinfield, Richard (Bishop of Hereford), 166
de Trempedhwy, David, 86
de Uilers, Nicholas, 87
de Wanetynge, Simon, 286
de Wylughby, Richard, 198, 201
discords, 59, 61
    between Rome and England, 64
dissensions, 59, 61

double jeopardy, 5, 41, 55, 59, 62
Droxford, John, 120–121
dual legal system, canon and secular law, 74

E
*Ecclesia Anglicana,* 17, 27, 215, 223, 228, 267, 272–273
ecclesiastical changes, 214
ecclesiastical jurisdiction, 49
ecclesiastical justice, 269
ecclesiastical law, 54. *See also* benefit of clergy
ecclesiastical patronage, 214
ecclesiastical process, 1
ecclesiastic privilege, 273
Ecclesiastic seclusion, 267
Eddington, William (Bishop of Winchester), 250n5, 251
Edmunds, Bury St., 193
Edward (Black Prince), 270n1
Edward I (King of England), 23, 78, 93n52, 96, 96n60, 106n100, 109, 111, 121, 176, 179n1, 207, 219, 222, 226, 248
Edward II (King of England), 96, 96n63, 123, 168, 178, 195, 207, 219, 225n52, 230, 235, 240, 247, 247n143, 279n25
  *Articuli Cleri,* 284
Edward III (King of England), 2, 80, 93, 97, 147, 169, 169n127, 171n135, 195, 207, 209, 215, 215n28, 219, 225, 225n52, 229, 230, 232, 235, 241, 243, 247, 247n143, 249, 250, 254, 256–258, 262, 280n33, 281–282
  Queenborough castle, 281
Edward VI (King of England), 95n58, 97, 97n66
endorsement of Christianity, 6
English Church
  Anglo-Saxons, 54–55
  control, 23

criminals in, 136
and English criminal justice system, 291
fourteenth century, 208–209
impotent, 135–136
Middle Ages, 12, 267
organizational structure, 17
period between Becket and Black Death, 27
perpetual exile, 150
secularization of, 216
social supremacy for its clergy, 269
English Lawsuits from William I to Richard I, 32
Ethelbert (King of Kent), 139
*Evil Times of Edward II,* 217
excommunications, 63, 145n45, 212–213
Excusory Quartet, 134, 291
*ex post facto,* 237

F
felonies, 180, 199. *See also* benefit of clergy
behavior, 32
cleric gang, 189
felonious clerics, 134
feudalism, 195
in England, 74
Fitwalter, John, 184
Fitzherbert, William, 57
Foleville gang, 193, 194, 197–199, 201
Foliot, Gilbert (Bishop of Hereford and London), 68–69, 71, 71n39
Folville, Eustace, 201
Folville, Richard, 201
Fourth Council of Toledo, 39–40
Fourth Lateran Council of 1215, 1, 13, 17, 39
fugitive status, 186
'fur-collared clericus,' 196

G

gang members
    Coterel and Foleville, 193, 194
    of criminal clerics or illicit groups, 190, 193–194
    Hertfordshire, 181
    Rutland, 181
Geoffrey (Archbishop of York), 156, 285, 285n47, 288
Giffard, Geoffrey (Bishop of Worcester), 97–98, 97n67, 106, 108n102, 160–161, 160n104, 170
Giffard, William (Archbishop of York), 97–98, 108n102, 113n13
Gloucester cathedral, remodeling of, 282
*gravamina,* 98
Great Schism, 280
Gregory IX (Pope), 148
Grey, Willam (Bishop of Ely), 174
Grossesteste, Robert (Bishop of Lincoln), 22
Guy Mortimer, case of, 247

H

*habitu clericali,* 226
*habitum et tonsuram clericalem,* 94
Hallum, Robert, 25
Harold II (King of England), 83
Hatfield, Thomas (Bishop of Durham), 250n5
Helewell, Robert, 194
Henry (Bishop of Winchester), 56
Henry, Blois, (Bishop of Winchester), 55, 55n77
Henry I (King of England), 31, 47
Henry II (King of Engaland), 31–32, 64, 72n44, 143
    centralized secular judicial system, 75
    and outright abolition of *privilegium fori,* 65
    in the reign of, 57
        Case 360, 61
        Case 371, 66–67
        Case 409, 66

Case 410, 67
Case 411, 67–68
Case 413, 68–69
Case 415, 69
Case 416, 69–70
Case 419, 70
Case 432, 70–71
Case 449, 71
Case 503, 64n13
role of, 32
secular concessions, 73
Henry III (King of England), 23, 84–85, 84n19, 98, 101, 104n92, 105n98, 107, 154n88, 155
Henry VI (King of England), 173
Henry VIII (King of England), 152, 152n75
Hertfordshire gang, murder of, 181
Holm, William, 255–258
Homicidal archdeacon Osbert of Richmond, 271
homicide, 52–53
Hugh (Bishop of Lincoln), 145
*hujusmodi occasions statute,* 92

I
immuration, 162n109
Ine (King of Wessex), 139
Innocent III (Pope), 74, 77–79, 83, 91, 91n38, 92, 94, 95n57, 107, 148
Inquisitorial model, with bishops, 33
*ipso facto,* 5n6
irrational gift, 287
Islip, Simon (Archbishop of Canterbury), 250n5, 251, 258, 259, 261
*Isodore Mercator,* 37

J
Jocelin (Bishop of Salisbury), 69–70, 75, 271–272
John (King of England), 82

John, Bratford (monk), 102
John, Edward, 118–119
John, Frome, 124, 126, 159, 167
John XXII (Pope), 23, 264, 265
Joye, William, 112
Judgments of Blood, 92
Justinian (Roman Emperor), 7

K
Kirkham, Walter (Bishop of Durham), 101

L
laicization, 93, 274, 292
    of benefit of clergy, 35
    of clergy plea, 13, 267
    of *privilegium fori,* 227
Lanfranc, (Archbishop of Canterbury), 44, 46–47
Langton, Stephen (Archbishopric of Canterbury), 83
Laws of King Wihtraed, 39
legal dexterity, 244
legal discord, 137
*Leges Henrici Primi,* 31, 48, 52
*legit ut clericus,* 231
le Noreys, John, 87
le Norreys, Walter, 276
Leo IX (Pope), 43
*lese majeste,* 8
le Waleys, Henry (Mayor of London), 161
Lichfield cathedral, 197
    canons of, 193, 199
literacy
    in England, 130, 218, 282
    test, 230, 235, 274
Longchamp, William (Bishop of Ely), 156, 285, 285n47
Lovett, Robert, 201
Lucius III (Pope), 94

M
*Magna Carta,* 91, 91n42, 105n97
Martival, Roger (Bishop of Salisbury), 228
Masca, Pandulf (Bishop of Norwich), 98
*mater et magistra,* 91
Melton, William (Archbishop of York), 221n42, 222n43, 235, 239–240
Michael, William, 253
Midnygh, Thomas, 191
miscreant cleric, 36, 54–55
misdemeanor, 246n137
mitigatory plea, 13
Molyns, John, of Stoke Poges, 191–192, 289

N
*Nec enim Deus iudicat bis in idipsum,* 60
Neck Verse, 93
*nec legit nec sillibicat,* 231
Nicholas (abbot of Bordesley), 284
*noli episcopari,* 59
*non convictus,* 80

O
Odo, (Bishop of Bayeux), 44
Offord, John (Archbishop of Canterbury), 251
Oliver, Lincoln (Bishop of Lincoln), 164, 176
Ordained clergy, 36n13, 53
Ordeal process, 38–39
*ordinance,* 31
Ordinance and Oxford Charter (William and Stephen), 65–66
*Ordinance for the Justices,* 257
ordination process, 22
Orleton, Adam (Bishop of Hereford), 22
*ornamentum clericale,* 36
Osbert, Bayeux (Archdeacon of York), 57
Osbert, William Fitz, 156–157

outlawry, 90
  denial of, 135
outlaws, 111n6, 179, 183n18
  ecclesiastic, 186
  exactions and proclamations of, 183, 183n19
*Outlaw's Song of Trailbaston,* 217
Oxford University, student violents and murder in, 165–166, 165n115

P

Palmer, Walter, 103
Palmer, William, 120
papal intervention, 208–209
papal mandate, refuse by England's bishops, 64
Papal reaction, 62
pardon, 184–185
Paschal II (Pope), 54
Pecham (Archbishop of Canterbury), 213
Pecock, Reginald (Bishop of Chichester), 174
perpetual exile, 141, 150
Philpot, John, 150
Pimley, William, 102
The Plague, 17
Poule, Roger, 190
Presentment of Englishry, 154n85
priesthood, privilege of, 16
priest oath, 50–51
*privilegium,* 37, 57
*privilegium canonis,* 5n6
*privilegium clericale,* 3, 3n1
*privilegium clericus,* 9, 95, 106
*privilegium fori,* 2, 3, 14, 22, 31–32, 82, 98, 208, 219, 283, 293
  laicization of, 227
  secularization of, 35
*privilegium immunitatis,* 5n7

proclaimed (by the courts)/self- selected outlawry, 90
*Pro Clero,* 23, 247
Professionalization, of secular bench, 181
Pseudo-Isodorian Decretals, 37
Pudlicott, Richard, 120, 121, 189
punishment, for murder, arson and robbery, 204
purgation
    of clerk, 81, 99
    hearing, 97
    successful, of cleric, 241–242

R
Ralph (Archdeacon of Cornwall), 186–187
Ralph, Shrewsbury (Bishop of Bath and Wells), 229–230
reading test
    abolition, 293
    for clerical status, 218, 227, 230
        first recorded instance of use, 226
        in the reign of Edward II, 219, 230
        secular proceedings, 230–231
*regnum,* 46, 72
regular clergy, 22, 24
    in Middle Ages, 20
'religious' clergy, 19n45, 45
Rex v Bury (1321), 147, 147n52
Richard (Bishop of Ilchester), 63, 71n39
Richard, Dover (Archbishop of Canterbury), 21
Richard I (King of England), 81, 81n7, 83n13, 156n91, 285, 285n47
    clerical abuse, 81
    compurgation, 79
Richard II (King of England), 154n88, 155, 173, 285, 285n47
Ripton, Walter, 256–258
Roger, (Bishop of Salisbury), 56, 56n81
royal justice, 180

Rufus (William II) (King of England), 46–47
Rushock, Robert, 82
Rutland gang, murder of, 181

S
*sacerdotium,* 46, 72
Sacred Ban, 152n75
sacred boundary, protection of, 152
sacrilegious crime, 134
sacrilegious homicide, 271
Sacrilegious sanctuarial crimes, 286
*salternum reversum,* 231
salvatio, 138
sanctuary, 1, 12, 34
  abolishion, 153n77, 153n78
  abuse of, 35, 285, 290
  benefit of, 176
  canon law, 133–134
  chartered, 143–144
  of churches, 196
  forms of, 139
  legal options and jurisdictional cooperation, 134
  locations for, 287
  physical parameters of, 138n11
  in pre-Christian society, 138
  privilege of, 141
  special status of, 175n150
  thirteenth century, 147
sanctuary watch, 149n64
Scotus, Duns, 277
secular clergy, 20, 24, 36
secular criminals, relationship between church and, 289
secularization, 2
  of benefit of clergy, 73, 228, 231, 233
  of *privilegium fori,* 35

secular law, 7, 16, 224, 276
    abuse of, 290
    Benefit of Clergy and, 283
    canon and, 27, 74, 155, 212
    provisions of, 164
    sanctuary as a custom of, 155, 287
sexual misconduct, 211
Shareshull, Willaim, 259n27
Sleepwells, 222n45
*Song Against the King's Taxe,* 217
*Song of the Husbandman,* 217
Spynk, Richard, 252–254
Spynk, William, 252–254
Stapleton, Walter (Bishop of Exeter), 204n96
*Statute of Marlborough,* 84–85
Statute of Provisors, approval, 209
*The Statute of Westminster II,* creation of, 211–212
*Statute of Winchester,* 109
*Statutum de Cibariis,* 215
*Statutum Pro Clero,* 247
St. Augustine's Abbey, 263–265
St. Martins le Grand, London, 35, 143–144, 174
Stratford, John (Archbishop of Canterbury), 225
sumptuary laws, 215
Synod, Ravenna, 36

T
temporal jurisdiction, 71
    legal system, 75
Theobald, Bec (Archbishop of Canterbury), 57, 59
Theodosius (Roman Emperor), 138
Thomas (Earl of Lancaster), 263
Thomas (second Baron Wake of Liddell), 254
Thoresby, John (Archbishop of York), 250n5, 251
*Tonsurati,* 291

*tonsure clericus,* 36
tonsure, to reading, 207
trailbaston, 180, 198, 199
Transportation Act, 294
tribalism, in England, 74

U
unbeneficed clergy, 26, 279

V
*Vision of Piers the Ploughman* (Langland), 217

W
Wager of Law. *See* Anglo-Saxon laws
Wake, Baron, 254
Walter, Hubert (Archbishop of Canterbury), 156–157, 170
Waltham, John, 25
Wayland, Thomas, 115–116
Westminster Abbey, 21, 34, 120, 121, 125, 251, 287
    monks at, 271
    special status of, 143
    unusual clerical sanctuary cases, 172
Wickwane, William, 113
Wihtraed (King of England), 39
William (Bishop of Exeter), 98–99
William, Brettenwald (monk), 102
William, Brompton (monk), 102–103
William, Calais (Bishop of Durham), 47
William I (King of England), 31, 42, 44, 58, 74, 140
William II (King of England), 46–47
William Little, Notton (monk), 102
William, Ockham, 277
William the Conqueror, 41, 45, 46
Willoughby, Richard, 180
Winchelsey, Robert, 115

Winchelsey, Robert (Archbishop of Canterbury), 23, 111, 213, 239, 239n104
Wyclif and the Lollard movement, 218
Wycliff, John, 278
Wykeham, William (Bishop of Winchester), 215n28
Wyliot, Thomas, 258

www.ingramcontent.com/pod-product-compliance
Lightning Source LLC
LaVergne TN
LVHW052225200926
848481LV00001B/220
* 9 7 8 1 4 6 5 2 9 1 6 8 4 *